# New Jersey Elder Law

## A RESOURCE AND PLANNING GUIDE

**2015**

**BY JOHN W. CALLINAN**

New Jersey Law Journal

For further information about New Jersey Law Journal Books contact:
New Jersey Law Journal
P.O. Box 20081
238 Mulberry St.
Newark, NJ 07101-6081
(973) 642-0075
www.njlj.com
www.alm.com
www.lawcatalog.com

This book is not intended to offer advice or counsel. Nor is it intended to serve as a substitute for professional representation. Since the information in this book may not be sufficient in dealing with a client's particular problem, and because this area of law constantly changes, lawyers and others using this publication should not rely on it as a substitute for independent research.

International Standard Book Number
978-1-57625-875-0 [print]
978-1-57625-876-7 [eBook]

Printed in the United States of America

Desktop composition by HOV Services.

**New Jersey Law Journal Books**
Other publications:

# Acknowledgment

To my parents, Richard Ryan Callinan, Sr., and Eileen Rita Callinan, who provided me with a loving foundation.

To my wife, Cathleen, whom I love and who, surprisingly, loves me.

To my children, John Christopher Callinan, Catherine Elizabeth Callinan, and Maeve Eileen Callinan, who are the focus of my life.

And to the Honorable Patricia Del Bueno Cleary, P.J.Ch., who gave me my start in the practice of law and whose integrity and dedication to the law has always been an inspiration to me.

# Preface

There is no one single definition of "elder law." In general, the practice of elder law includes general estate planning (Wills and Trusts), guardianship law, estate administration, and Medicaid planning.

As people age, they will inevitably need some or all of the services that an elder law attorney provides. The elderly individual's children will come to your office confused and, oftentimes, scared by the fact that their parent—the individual who, until this point, cared for them their entire lives—is now the person in need of care.

Being able to provide answers to the client and his family will provide a true service and a tremendous amount of comfort. But the practice of elder law is complex, partly because it spans so many subfields and partly because of the density of the law governing those subfields.

With regards to understanding the governing laws, I have always found elder law attorneys to be very willing to provide advice and guidance to their fellow attorneys. Because the practice of elder law spans so many subfields, no one elder law attorney has all the answers to all the questions, but my colleagues in the practice of elder law have always made themselves available to provide answers and suggested solutions to me and to others.

In that vein, this book is designed to provide guidance to both the general practitioner and the more advanced practitioner. The book addresses issues the practitioner will encounter almost every day in the fields of estate planning, estate administration, guardianship law, and Medicaid planning in an easy-to-read, practical manner that I hope you will enjoy.

# About the Author

**John William Callinan** is a Certified Elder Law Attorney, certified by the National Elder Law Foundation as accredited by the American Bar Association. John was graduated from Rutgers University in 1990 with a B.A. in psychology. In 1993, John was graduated from Rutgers School of Law-Camden from which he received his Juris Doctor with Honors.

John is admitted to practice law in New Jersey and Pennsylvania. He is also admitted to practice before the New Jersey federal district courts and the United States Court of Appeal for the Third Circuit.

John clerked for the Honorable Patricia Del Bueno Cleary, J.S.C. He has concentrated his practice in elder law since 2000.

John has been made a member of the Council of Advanced Practitioners (CAP) of the National Academy of Elder Law Attorneys (NAELA). CAP membership is limited to those NAELA members who have been members of NAELA for 10 years or more, who have a Martindale-Hubbell rating of AV, and who are Certified Elder Law Attorneys. Membership in CAP is by invitation only and is designed to recognize those members of NAELA who are perceived to be innovators in the field of elder law and instrumental to the future of elder law. John is also a member of the Litigation Committee of the National Academy of Elder Law Attorneys, the committee responsible for deciding whether or not NAELA will participate in particular litigation throughout the United States.

John is the immediate-past Chair of the New Jersey State Bar's Elder and Disability Law Section.

In 2014, in addition to receiving a Super Law Award in the practice of Elder Law, John was named a Top 100 Law in the State of New Jersey by Super Lawyers. To date, John has received a Super Lawyer Award in the practice of Elder Law in 2011, 2012,

2013, and 2014. In 2010, John's peers voted him to be the Most Outstanding Member of the National Academy of Elder Law Attorneys, New Jersey Chapter. In 2011 and 2013, John received a Five Star Wealth Manager Award. The wealth manager award is awarded to the top 7% of wealth managers in the state of New Jersey as chosen by their clients. John has received a Martindale-Hubbell rating AV, which is the preeminent peer rating.

John is a recipient of the New Jersey State Bar Association, Elder and Disability Law Section's, Distinguished Service Award. The Distinguished Service Award is made in recognition and appreciation for outstanding advocacy and service to New Jersey's seniors, those with disabilities, and the legal profession. There are only a handful of elder law attorneys who have ever received this award.

He frequently lecturers on topics of elder law to the general public and professionals.

# Summary of Contents

# Table of Contents

# Chapter 1

# The General Durable Power of Attorney

## 1-1 THE GENERAL DURABLE POWER OF ATTORNEY

A general durable power of attorney[1] is one of the three, fundamental estate planning documents, along with a last will and testament (Will) and an advance health care directive (living will). Of the three, it could probably be said that a general durable power of attorney is the most important document.

When you hear the phrase "power of attorney," clients are most often referring to a general durable power of attorney for financial decisions. Sometimes, a client is referring to a living will, which is discussed in Chapter Two, but more often than not they are referring to a general durable power of attorney. Accordingly, when used in this book, the phrase "power of attorney" means a general durable power of attorney for financial decisions.

A power of attorney is probably the most important estate planning document because it can be the most helpful document for the client. A Will is a document that is not even effective until after the client dies; therefore, a Will is really a document for other people, since the person making the Will must be dead before his Will has any effect at all.

While a living will can be very helpful and is very important, many health care providers will abide by the decision of close

[1] N.J.S.A. 46:2B-8.1. et seq. (the "Revised Durable Power of Attorney Act").

family members when it comes to health care decisions for a patient. Assuming all family members agree as to the proper course of treatment for the patient, the family may get by without having a living will signed by the patient.

But, without a power of attorney, no family member—not a spouse, not a child, not a sibling—is going to be permitted to make financial decisions for a now-incapacitated person. There is no bank or brokerage house that is going to honor the financial decisions of a family member who cannot present a power of attorney document duly executed by the client, not even if that family member is a spouse or a child.

As discussed more thoroughly below, without a power of attorney, family or friends may have to have the client adjudicated as being incapacitated through an expensive and time-consuming guardianship action[2] before they can make financial decisions for the client. Ensuring that the client has a well-drafted power of attorney is extremely important.

When a client signs a power of attorney, the client is the "principal" of the power of attorney. The person the client nominates to make financial decisions for him is called his "attorney-in-fact" or "agent."

The term "attorney-in-fact" is a bit of a poorly worded phrase. When the layperson hears the phrase "attorney-in-fact," they immediately think "attorney at law" and are confused. For this reason, the phrase "agent" will be used when referring to the person nominated to make financial decisions for the principal, instead of the phrase "attorney-in-fact."

### 1-1:1 The Revised Durable Power of Attorney Act

There are actually two acts that govern powers of attorney: the Revised Durable Power of Attorney Act,[3] which was effective in the year 2000, and an unnamed act commonly known as the banking power of attorney act,[4] which was effective in the year 1991. These two acts will be collectively referred to as the "Act" in this book.

---

2. N.J.S.A. 12-1 et seq. (guardianship statutes).
3. N.J.S.A. 46:2B-8.1. et seq.
4. N.J.S.A. 46:2B-10 et seq.

The Revised Durable Power of Attorney Act repealed and replaced a prior power of attorney act in the year 2000. The act was amended in 2004 to add a provision specifically addressing an agent's ability to gratuitously transfer the assets of the principal.[5]

### 1-1:2 The Banking Power of Attorney Act

The banking power of attorney act specifically addresses the interaction of financial institutions with respect to a power of attorney document.[6] The banking power of attorney act grants greater deference to banks than the Revised Durable Power of Attorney Act. For instance, a bank can refuse to rely upon a power of attorney if the bank "believes in good faith" that the power of attorney is not genuine, that the principal is dead, that the power of attorney has been revoked or that the principal was disabled when he executed the power of attorney.[7]

## 1-2 THE PRINCIPAL

The principal of a financial power of attorney is the person who executes the power of attorney document, nominating another person, called the "agent" or "attorney-in-fact," to act for him with regard to his financial affairs.[8]

## 1-3 THE ATTORNEY-IN-FACT OR AGENT

The attorney-in-fact is the person whom the principal nominates to make those financial decisions for him that are specified in the power of attorney document.[9] In this book, for purposes of convenience, the attorney-in-fact is referred to as the "agent." Most laypersons are confused by the phrase attorney-in-fact, equating "attorney-in-fact" with "attorney at law."

The statutes governing powers of attorney in the state of New Jersey can be divided into two separate set of statutes: those

---

5. N.J.S.A. 46:2B-8.13a.

6. N.J.S.A. 46:2B-10 to -19.

7. N.J.S.A. 46:2B-13.b.

8. N.J.S.A. 46:2B-8.2.a. (defining "principal" and "attorney-in-fact" for purposes of the Revised Durable Power of Attorney Act); N.J.S.A. 46:2B-10 (defining "agent" and "principal" under the banking power of attorney act).

9. N.J.S.A. 46:2B-8.2.a.

governing banking transactions and the Revised Durable Power of Attorney Act. The Revised Durable Power of Attorney Act refers to the agent as an "attorney-in-fact."[10] The banking power of attorney act refers to the agent as an "agent," but indicates that the agent may also be known as an "attorney-in-fact."[11]

A principal can nominate one agent, successor individual agents or co-agents.[12]

### 1-3:1 Sole Agent

A principal can nominate a single individual to make financial decisions for him. If the principal nominates a sole agent, then the sole agent does not have to seek the permission of any other person in order to make financial decisions for his principal.

Naming a sole agent permits the power of attorney to be used efficiently and easily. The principal, when he was handling his own affairs, did not have to obtain other people's consent to make financial decisions for himself. Permitting the agent to do the same allows decisions to be made with ease.

### 1-3:2 Successor Agents

If a principal nominates a sole agent, he should also nominate successor agents.[13] A principal who has nominated co-agents can nominate successor agents, as well, but when the principal only has one agent serving, that is, a sole agent, he should ensure that he has a successor agent if his sole agent refuses to serve or is unwilling to serve.

If a power of attorney document only names a sole agent without naming successor agents and the sole agent is unable or unwilling to serve as the agent, then the power of attorney document will fail, because no named agent exists. By naming successor agents, the principal can better ensure that other individuals will be available to make financial decisions for him in the event that he cannot make those decisions for himself.

---

10. N.J.S.A. 46:2B-8.2.a.
11. N.J.S.A. 46:2B-10.
12. N.J.S.A. 46:2B-8.7.
13. N.J.S.A. 46:2B-8.7.c.

A power of attorney should nominate at least one successor agent but can nominate an unlimited number of successor agents. A primary agent and two successor agents (first alternate agent and second alternate agent) are probably sufficient in most cases.

Sometimes clients wish to nominate every one of their children in the power of attorney document as either a primary agent or a successor agent. Typically, the reason the client wishes to do this is because the client doesn't want to exclude any child from his document. For a client who has more than three children, this desire can be burdensome from a drafting standpoint and probably wholly unnecessary, but the client is the boss.

### 1-3:3 Multiple Agents

A principal can nominate multiple or co-agents.[14] Having more than one agent serving at any point in time can be quite unwieldy. However, the Act permits a principal to name multiple agents, so the Act contemplates two or more agents serving at the same time. This can be compared with the New Jersey Advance Directives for Health Care Act, which does not permit multiple agents.[15]

Thankfully, the vast majority of clients who want to name multiple agents do not want to name more than two agents to serve at any point in time; accordingly, in this book, multiple agents will also be referred to as "co-agents."

There is not a one-size-fits-all estate plan. For some people, having multiple agents can be quite helpful or quite appropriate for one reason or the other. For most people, having multiple agents is unnecessary and cumbersome.

The number one reason a client wishes to name co-agents has to do with the client's desire not to hurt the feelings of one child. The client doesn't wish to be perceived as choosing one child over the other to make financial decisions for him. This reason is far more psychological than legal.

Legally, the Act permits the nomination of multiple agents. Practically, having co-agents can be quite cumbersome. Clients will sometimes return to their attorney after nominating co-agents

---

14. N.J.S.A. 46:2B-8.7.

15. N.J.S.A. 26:2H-53 et seq.

asking the attorney to modify the document because the client failed to understand the implications of nominating two (or more) people to serve as his agent at the same time.

The Act permits the principal to nominate agents who must serve either severally or jointly.[16]

### 1-3:3.1 Multiple Agents Who May Act Severally

The Act permits a principal to nominate multiple agents who may act severally.[17] Severally means that either agent can engage in whatever financial transactions are outlined in the power of attorney document without obtaining the permission of the other agent(s).

Severally means separately, so although there is more than one agent, either agent is permitted to act for the principal without the other agent being involved in the action.

Co-agents who can act severally can be beneficial because the principal has nominated two agents either one of which can act for the principal. If one agent cannot sign a document because he lives in another state, for instance, the other agent can sign the document and bind the principal without the other co-agent signing.

Some financial institutions will claim that they only permit co-agents to serve in a several capacity. The financial institution may believe it is too difficult to administer a power of attorney that requires co-agents to act jointly (for instance, a bank teller may not realize that both agents signatures are required and cash a check that is only signed by one of the co-agents who must act jointly according to the power of attorney document).

Co-agents who can act severally can also be very dangerous if the co-agents do not agree on an issue and make opposing decisions that are opposing on the same issue. For instance, assume that the principal is residing in a nursing home and one of his co-agents who can act severally wants to sell his house and the other co-agent does not want to sell the principal's house. If the one co-agent signs the contract of sale, the other co-agent may institute

---

16. N.J.S.A. 46:2B-8.7.b. and c.

17. N.J.S.A. 46:2B-8.7.b.

an action in court to void the sale or, at the very least, in-fighting and bad feelings will ensue.

Ironically, it was hurting the feelings of the co-agents/children that the principal was trying to avoid when he nominated co-agents. Without question, nominating a sole agent can lead to hurt feelings as well. The sole agent might make decisions with which the principal's other children do not agree; however, nominating a sole agent has a far smaller chance of causing litigation than nominating co-agents.

When a principal-parent is failing and requires the assistance of his children, a tremendous amount of anxiety arises for the entire family. This anxiety can cause tension even in those families that get along well. A client-parent who says "my children all get along" has never seen his children have to provide or arrange for his care and those circumstances can change the family dynamic in unforeseen ways.

Having co-agents can increase the likelihood that the co-agents, each of whom has the legal right to make decisions, will make opposing decisions on the same issue.

### 1-3:3.2 Multiple Agents Who Must Act Jointly

A principal can nominate multiple agents who must act jointly.[18] Multiple agents who must act jointly must agree as to all decisions that are made. So, for instance, if the agents sell the principal's house, all of the agents must sign the contract of sale. If the agents pay a bill of the principal, then all of the agents should sign the check paying the bill.

Nominating co-agents can be quite a hassle from a practical perspective. While it sounds nice to the principal-parent that his children must agree before a financial decision can be made for him, from a practical standpoint, having all of the agents agree to every decision can be very burdensome.

Some financial institutions will tell the client that they do not accept power of attorney documents that nominate multiple agents who must act jointly. While the law does compel financial institutions to recognize co-joint agents, it can be disconcerting for

18. N.J.S.A. 46:2B-8.7.c.

the client to be told that the power of attorney they signed with their attorney is, in the words of the bank's employee, "no good."

### 1-3:4 Qualified Bank as Agent

A principal can name one individual as his agent, multiple agents or a qualified bank within the meaning of N.J.S.A. 17:9A-28.[19] Few clients wish to appoint a bank as their power of attorney agent, but the act does permit an individual to name a bank as his agent.

Because very few clients name a bank as their agent, throughout this book, agents will be discussed as being persons, not financial institutions.

### 1-3:5 Qualities of the Good Agent

A power of attorney agent handles the financial affairs of the principal. A good agent will be a person with good financial skills and good organizational skills. In many instances, the agent may find himself managing his own life and the life of the principal. For instance, if the principal is mentally incapacitated and residing in a nursing facility, the agent will have to handle all of the principal's financial affairs—paying medical bills, selling the principal's home, etc.

The principal should ensure that the person he is choosing as his agent has the time to take on the responsibility of serving as his agent and the willingness to serve.

Being an agent is often a thankless job. Most power of attorney documents fail to address compensation of the agent, so the agent cannot take compensation.[20] Furthermore, the agent's actions are often questioned by others (for instance, other family members) who are not named as the agent.

Making decisions for a parent who is now a resident of a nursing home can make the agent the lightning rod for other family members' discontent with their failing parent's circumstances. Family members who are not named as the agent may blame the agent for the parent's/principal's circumstances.

---

19. N.J.S.A. 46:2B:8.2.a.

20. N.J.S.A. 46:2B-8.12

### 1-3:6 Death of the Agent

Upon the death of an agent, the successor agent assumes the role of the primary agent.[21] Upon the death of a co-agent, the remaining co-agent serves as the sole agent.[22]

### 1-3:7 Disability of the Agent

The act provides that an agent is under a disability "if the attorney-in-fact is unable to exercise the authority conferred by the power of attorney effectively."[23] If the agent is under a disability, by definition, the agent cannot serve as the agent in which case the successor agent or remaining co-agent will serve.

### 1-3:8 Failure of Agent to Serve

For a multitude of reasons, an agent may not wish to serve. Most agents do not receive compensation for their services.[24] Many agents are the targets of frustration or anger from family members or friends who fail to accept or fail to see the fact that the principal requires assistance managing his affairs.

An agent is a fiduciary. If an agent does accept his role, he can be held liable for failing to act appropriately. For this assumption of liability—unlike an executor, unlike a trustee—a power of attorney agent, typically, receives no compensation.

A nominated agent is not required to act and, for the reasons stated, may be well-advised not to act. Despite this, most people who are nominated as agents do accept their role: If the agent fails to act, then the successor agent can assume the role of primary agent or the remaining co-agent can assume the role of sole agent.

## 1-4 WHO SHOULD HAVE A POWER OF ATTORNEY?

Without a power of attorney, no person can make financial decisions for the principal, not the principal's spouse, not the principal's children, not any other family member of the principal.

---

21. N.J.S.A. 46:2B-8.7.e.
22. N.J.S.A. 46:2B-8.7.a.
23. N.J.S.A. 46:2B-8.2.c.
24. N.J.S.A. 46:2B-8.12.

If a person has attained the age of majority, age 18,[25] no other person can make financial decisions for that person who is now an adult in the eyes of the law. Accordingly, every person who has attained the age of 18 should have a power of attorney.

Many people think of a power of attorney document as something that cedes control over their life to another person, as financial independence is frequently associated with independence in general; however, the fear of losing control is far from the reality when it comes to having executed a power of attorney.

The fact of the matter is that a principal must have a sufficient level of mental capacity to sign a power of attorney and the principal retains the right to revoke the power of attorney at any time.[26] A power of attorney agent cannot impose his will upon the principal of the power of attorney. The principal is always free to disagree with, contradict or override the decision of his agent, though, as discussed below, third-parties are entitled to rely on the decisions that the agent makes in most instances.

## 1-5 MENTAL CAPACITY TO EXECUTE A POWER OF ATTORNEY

In order to execute a power of attorney, the principal must have a certain level of mental capacity. A principal must have the level of mental capacity necessary to enter into a contract in order to sign a power of attorney.

Contractual mental capacity is defined as follows:

> The test of mental capacity to contract is whether the person in question possesses sufficient mind to understand, in a reasonable manner, the nature, extent, character, and *effect of the act* or transaction in which he is engaged; the law does not *gauge contractual capacity* by the standard of *mental capacity possessed* by *reasonably prudent* men. It is not necessary to show that a person was *incompetent* to *transact* any *kind of business*, but

25. N.J.S.A. (9:17B-1.a.).

26. N.J.S.A. 46:2B-8.10.

> to *invalidate* his contract it is sufficient to show that he was *mentally incompetent* to deal with the *particular contract* in issue.[27]

A client who lacks contractual mental capacity cannot sign a power of attorney document.

## 1-6 WHAT IF THERE IS NO POWER OF ATTORNEY?

In the absence of a power of attorney, no person can make financial decisions for the client. A bank or brokerage house isn't going to permit a wife to make financial decisions for her husband simply because she is married to her husband, not even if that marriage is 50 years in duration.

From a practical standpoint, the wife who does not have a power of attorney for her husband may find herself unable to access bank accounts that are in her husband's name alone or to access his IRA or 401(k) or to access his life insurance or sell or mortgage their home. Without a power of attorney, the wife may find herself able to do very little for her incapacitated husband from a financial perspective.

A great many clients fail to realize this fact. Many clients believe that their spouse or their children can simply step in and handle their financial affairs if they are unable to handle their finances. This is simply untrue.

Assuming that the husband now lacks the mental capacity to execute a power of attorney, the wife may find that her only option is to file for guardianship of her incapacitated husband. As discussed elsewhere in this book, a guardianship action is somewhat involved, requiring two doctors to declare the person as being unable to make decisions for himself and involving the appointment of court-appointed counsel for the alleged incapacitated person.[28] Even if the guardianship action goes smoothly, it can cost thousands of dollars and take months to finalize.

---

27. *In the Matter of William Schiller*, 148 N.J. Super. 168, 180 (Ch. Div. 1977), citing 17 C.J.S., Contracts § 133(1).

28. N.J. CT.R. 4:86-1 et seq.

### 1-6:1 Effectiveness of Guardianship versus Power of Attorney

In addition to being substantially less costly than a guardianship action, a power of attorney can be far more effective than a guardianship action in many cases. For instance, the guardian of a ward frequently has to return to court when the guardian wants to sell the ward's real property[29] or make gifts of the ward's assets for purposes of Medicaid planning.[30]

For instance, if the guardian wants to sell the ward's house, the guardian must file an action requesting the court's permission to accomplish that sale. A power of attorney document can be drafted to permit the agent to sell the principal's real estate without the need to obtain court approval.

A guardian may wish to engage in Medicaid planning or tax planning with his ward's estate. This type of planning often involves gifting of the ward's assets to family members. A power of attorney document can be drafted in such a way as to permit the agent to gift the principal's assets in appropriate circumstances, such as for Medicaid planning or estate tax planning.

When a court has adjudicated a person as being incapacitated in the context of a guardianship, the guardian cannot gift the assets of the ward for Medicaid or tax planning purposes without the permission of the court.[31] To obtain this permission, as with obtaining permission to sell the real property of the ward, the guardian must return to court and ask the court's permission to engage in these forms of planning.

While courts frequently do grant the guardian permission to sell the ward's real property and even to gift the ward's assets, when appropriate, having to return to court to obtain the court's permission for these expanded powers costs money and takes time. It also raises the possibility that the court may not grant

---

29. N.J. CT.R. 4:94-1

30. *In the Matter of Mildred Keri, a mentally incompetent person*, 181 N.J. 50 (2004) (holding that the guardian for a mentally incapacitated individual can gift the assets of the ward in order to engage in Medicaid planning if the guardian proves to the court the existence of certain criteria).

31. 3B:12-58; *In the Matter of Mildred Keri, a mentally incompetent person*, 181 N.J. 50 (2004) (holding that the guardian for a mentally incapacitated individual can gift the assets of the ward in order to engage in Medicaid planning if the guardian proves to the court the existence of certain criteria).

the guardian the authority to engage in these transactions, notwithstanding the fact that the ward, if competent, may have wanted the guardian to do these things for him.

With a guardianship, people whom the client would not want involved in his life—the court, family members, friends—could have a big impact on what his guardian can and cannot do. A fundamental principal of estate planning is that the client is planning for his future and putting in place a comprehensive plan that permits the people whom he has chosen to make whatever decisions need to be made. Contrariwise, a good estate plan prevents people whom the client would not want involved in his life from being involved.

While a guardianship can be very helpful in those instances in which a client has failed to plan properly, a guardianship is not the best possible solution for surrogate decision-making, that is, a means of permitting one person to make decisions for another person. The best solution, as far as financial decisions are concerned, is the well-drafted power of attorney document that permits the power of attorney agent to make any financial decision that the agent may need to make for the power of attorney principal.

There are instances in which a guardianship can be more effective than a power of attorney. These instances are far rarer than those instances in which a power of attorney is more effective than a guardianship, but they do exist. A power of attorney is a voluntary document. Unless a court has adjudicated the principal of the power of attorney as mentally incapacitated, the principal retains the right to make his own decisions, including the revocation of the power of attorney document.[32]

A power of attorney agent cannot force the principal to do anything. For instance, if the principal is living in his home and continuously engaging in unsafe behavior (leaving the gas stove on, wandering out of the house and getting lost, falling down the stairs), the agent cannot tell the principal that he must leave his house and live in an assisted living residence or nursing facility. Even if it were clear to every person who met the principal that the principal lacks mental capacity and is making extremely poor

---

32. N.J.S.A. 46:2B-8.10.

decisions, the principal retains the right to disregard the decisions of the agent and to revoke the power of attorney document.

In these circumstances, it can be very helpful to have the person adjudicated as being incapacitated and have a guardian of his person and property appointed over him. The guardian then has the legal right to compel the ward to do what is in his best interest, such as reside in an assisted living residence. (From a practical standpoint, it may be quite difficult to force a person to live in an assisted living residence—most facilities would not want a person as a resident who clearly does not want to be there—but a guardian does have the legal right to override the decisions of his ward in most instances.)

### 1-6:2 The Poor Man's Power of Attorney

Many people are hesitant to contact an attorney for one reason or the other, so they engage in self-help measures. One method of self-help involves the "poor man's power of attorney."

A poor man's power of attorney involves adding one or more family members to the financial accounts of the person. For instance, a mother might add the names of one or more of her daughters to her bank account. She now believes that her daughters can access the money in her bank account to pay her bills if she cannot handle her affairs for herself.

In this example, the mother's beliefs are accurate, her daughters can access the money in her bank account to pay her bills. The daughters could also access the money in the account to pay their own bills. The creditors of the daughters could also access the accounts to pay any debts the daughters may owe. If a daughter dies, the bank account will be included in her estate for inheritance tax and estate tax purposes. If a daughter files for divorce her soon-to-be ex-spouse might claim the property is subject to equitable distribution just to gain advantage in the divorce or might claim that the assets in the account offset the daughter's need for alimony.

Furthermore, adding a child's name to a bank account only grants the child access to that account. If mom goes to live in a nursing home and her home needs to be sold, her child will not be able to sell her house without a power of attorney, even if mom added the children's name to her deed as co-owners. All owners of the real estate would have to sign the deed and closing papers in order to transfer title.

A "poor man's power of attorney" is a very dangerous form of planning. It has only limited effectiveness and exposes the client to a tremendous amount of danger, yet people engage in this type of "planning" quite frequently.

## 1-7 EFFECTIVE DATE OF POWER OF ATTORNEY

Most clients fail to realize when the power of attorney document is effective. Most people believe that a power of attorney document is only effective when they can no longer make decisions for themselves. As discussed below, this is a misconception.

### 1-7:1 Springing Power of Attorney

A principal can have his power of attorney drafted in such a way that it is only effective upon his disability.[33] This type of power of attorney is called a "springing power of attorney," because the power of attorney springs into effectiveness upon the disability of the client.

Most people, if asked and when provided with little or no information on the pros and cons of a springing power of attorney, would prefer that their power of attorney be effective only upon their disability. Most people want to be "in charge" of their lives, and most people do not want to think of a day when they are incapable of being in charge of their lives.

But having a springing power of attorney as opposed to a power of attorney that is immediately effective can have numerous cons, which will be discussed below. Most power of attorney documents that you will see, simply because of the manner in which they are drafted, are immediately effective.

#### 1-7:1.1 When Is the Principal Disabled?

The banking power of attorney act provides that if a bank is presented with a springing power of attorney, the institution is not obligated to honor the power of attorney unless the agent provides the bank "with proof to italicize satisfaction that the principal is

33. N.J.S.A. 46:2B-8.2.b., N.J.S.A. 46:2B-8.13.c.

then under a disability as provided in the power of attorney."[34] Obviously, this provision places an amount of discretion in the hands of the bank to honor or not honor the directions of the power of attorney agent.

Also, be aware that the agent must prove that the principal is disabled at the time the agent seeks to use the power of attorney. Assume that the agent presents the bank with a doctor's letter stating that the principal is unable to handle his affairs, but the letter is six months old. Should the bank rely upon the opinion stated in the letter? Probably not. Is the bank obligated to honor the power of attorney? No.

So now the agent must have a doctor examine the principal again and write another letter stating that the principal continues to labor under a disability.

If the power of attorney is a springing power of attorney, it is good practice to define in the power of attorney document what it means for the principal to be disabled. Many springing powers of attorney simply say "This power of attorney is only effective upon the disability of the principal."

When the agent takes that power of attorney down to the local branch of the bank at which the principal does his banking and hands that power of attorney to the bank teller there is little to no chance that the bank teller will know the legal definition of "disability" as contained in the New Jersey power of attorney Act. There is even less chance that a bank teller in another state will know the definition of "disability" as contained in the New Jersey power of attorney Act.

The Act defines a principal as being under a disability "if the principal is unable to manage his property and affairs effectively."[35] How does an agent prove that the principal is disabled since the act fails to provide a methodology for proving disability and provides only a broad definition of disability? Good question.

Most agents would probably obtain a letter from the principal's physician stating that the principal is unable to manage his property and affairs. Most financial institutions would probably accept the

---

34. N.J.S.A. 46:2B-13.c.

35. N.J.S.A. 46:2B-8.2.c.

letter from the physician as sufficient evidence, but it is important to note that the power of attorney Act fails to provide a definitive methodology for proving disability.

An experienced elder law practitioner drafts a springing power of attorney so that the document defines disability and defines the methodology for proving disability. For instance, the power of attorney document might define disability to mean that two licensed physicians have determined the principal to be unable to handle his affairs.

Having a definition of disability in the document can eliminate the concerns of people to whom the power of attorney document is presented, so they know, simply from reading the document, that the agent has proven the disability of the principal. The agent can present reports from two physicians stating that the principal cannot handle his affairs in the opinion of those doctors, and the bank employee can match the wording from those two doctors' reports to the wording in the power of attorney document.

### 1-7:2 Immediately Effective

Most powers of attorney are effective immediately because of the manner in which the power of attorney is drafted. Unless the power of attorney document specifically states that it is only effective upon the disability of the principal, the power of attorney document is effective immediately.

Most people who have thought about the issue would probably tell you that they believe a power of attorney document is only effective upon the disability of the principal. If you ask without giving the person further information, most people would tell you that they do not want their power of attorney document to be effective immediately, but those initial thoughts may be inappropriate.

There are benefits to having a power of attorney document be effective immediately. An immediately-effective power of attorney imposes no barriers to use. The agent can use the power of attorney for his principal's benefit without having to prove that the principal labors under a disability.

More importantly, because the agent does not have to prove disability, the probability that a financial institution will recognize and honor the authority of the agent is much higher. In fact, except in limited circumstances, a financial institution must recognize and honor a duly executed power of attorney.[36]

## 1-8 RELIANCE ON THE POWER OF ATTORNEY

Under the Revised Durable Power of Attorney Act, any third party may rely upon an agent's authority until the third party receives actual notice of the revocation of the power of attorney, the termination or suspension of the agent's authority or the death of the principal.[37] A third party may request an agent to execute an affidavit stating that the agent did not have actual knowledge of the termination of the power of attorney, the suspension of his authority or the death of the principal.[38]

Under the banking power of attorney act, a financial institution shall accept—which is to be compared with third parties who "may rely upon" a power of attorney—a power of attorney unless certain circumstances exist, but those circumstances are rather broad.[39]

A bank can refuse to rely upon a power of attorney if the signature of the principal is not genuine.[40] A bank can also refuse to rely upon a power of attorney if the bank has actual notice of the death of the principal, the revocation of the power of attorney or the disability of the principal at the time the principal signed the power of attorney.[41]

Another exception to a bank honoring a power of attorney is an exception that provides banks with broad discretion to refuse to rely upon the power of attorney. A bank can refuse to honor a power of attorney if the bank "believes in good faith" that the power of attorney is not genuine, that the principal is dead, that the power of attorney has been revoked or that the principal was disabled at the time he signed the power of attorney.[42]

A bank may refuse to honor a power of attorney "first presented to it more than 10 years after its date or on which it has not acted for a 10-year period unless the agent is either the spouse,

36. N.J.S.A. 46:2B-13.
37. N.J.S.A. 46:2B-8.6.a.
38. N.J.S.A. 46:2B-8.6.b.
39. N.J.S.A. 46:2B-13.
40. N.J.S.A. 46:2B-13.a.(1).
41. N.J.S.A. 46:2B-13.a.(2).
42. N.J.S.A. 46:2B-13.b.

parent or a descendant of a parent of the principal."[43] Both the Revised Durable Power of Attorney Act and the banking power of attorney act provide that a power of attorney remains effective until the principal dies or revokes the power or until the power of attorney terminates by its own terms.[44] The ten-year exception found in the banking power of attorney is an exception to the no-lapse provision of both acts.

Though poorly worded, most attorneys believe that the agent who is a spouse, parent or a descendent of a parent of the principal caveat applies to both the "first presented" and "failed to act" provisions of this exception.[45] Since most principals name a spouse, parent or child (who would be a descendent of a parent of the principal), most powers of attorney are unaffected by the ten-year exception. Nevertheless, because of this wording in the banking power of attorney act, it is probably good practice to revise a power of attorney every 10 years.

A bank may also refuse to rely upon a power of attorney if the power of attorney states that it is only effective upon the disability of the principal—that is, a springing power of attorney—and the agent has failed to provide to the bank proof to the satisfaction of the bank that the principal is currently laboring under the disability as that disability is defined in the power of attorney document.[46]

### 1-8:1 Photocopies versus Original

Both the Revised Durable Power of Attorney Act and the banking power of attorney act require the agent to present the original power of attorney document.[47] While both acts permit a third party or bank to rely upon a copy of the power of attorney once the third party/bank has been presented with the original power of attorney, with one limited exception,[48] both acts require the agent first to present the original document.

---

43. N.J.S.A. 46:2B-13.b.

44. N.J.S.A. 46:2B-8.3., N.J.S.A. 46:2B-13.

45. N.J.S.A. 46:2B-8.13.b.

46. N.J.S.A. 46:2B-8.13.c.

47. N.J.S.A. 46:2B-8.11 ("Any third party to whom the power of attorney is presented may retain and rely upon a photocopy of the original signed document"); N.J.S.A. 46:2B-13.f.; N.J.S.A. 46:2B-18.

48. N.J.S.A. 46:2B-13.f. (permitting a banking institution to accept an affidavit from the agent and a photocopy of the power of attorney certified to be a true copy by either another

The one exception to the agent's obligation to present the original power of attorney exists in the banking power of attorney act, but this exception is extremely limited. A financial institution can rely upon a photocopy of the power of attorney document if the agent signs an affidavit that the original of the power of attorney is unavailable and the photocopy of the power of attorney is certified to be a true copy of the original of the power of attorney by either another bank or the county recording office of the county in which the original was recorded.[49]

Since most power of attorney documents are never recorded, unless the power of attorney document is being used to conduct a transaction involving the real property of the principal, this exception to the requirement to present an original power of attorney document leaves only another banking institution to sign such a certification. Getting another bank to sign such a certification is a task that is probably far easier said than done.

The obligation of the agent to present an original power of attorney document to a third party or a bank is an excellent check on an agent using a power of attorney at a time when the principal does not want the agent using it. For instance, even if the power of attorney is effective immediately, assuming the principal holds onto all the originals of the power of attorney document, none of his nominated agents could use his power of attorney.

The principal could tell his agent where he keeps the original power of attorney in the event the principal needs his agent to act on his behalf. By doing this, the principal is preventing his agent from acting on his behalf without the requirement of and hassle associated with a springing power of attorney.

## 1-9 DULY SIGNED

A power of attorney must be in writing;[50] accordingly, no agent can claim that he has power of attorney for the principal because

---

bank institution or the county recording office of the county in which the original was recorded).

49. N.J.S.A. 46:2B-13.f. (permitting a banking institution to accept an affidavit from the agent and a photocopy of the power of attorney certified to be a true copy by either another bank institution or the county recording office of the county in which the original was recorded).

50. N.J.S.A. 46:2B-8.2.a.; N.J.S.A. 46:2B-8.9.

the principal verbally told him that the purported agent was the principal's agent.

A power of attorney must also be "duly signed and acknowledged in the manner set forth in" N.J.S.A. 46:14-2.1. The referenced statute requires the principal to appear before a notary or attorney at law and acknowledge that he signed the power of attorney as his own act. So, if a principal signs the power of attorney and the principal's signature is "notarized" by a notary public or attorney at law, then the power of attorney document is "duly signed."

Some attorneys have the principal's signature notarized and witnessed and the signature of the witness notarized as well. This is good practice because the referenced statute requires that in order to prove that a power of attorney contains the genuine signature of the principal, a witness must swear that he or she witnessed the principal sign the power of attorney. The signature of the witness, like that of the witness's must be notarized.

So, if someone challenges the genuineness of the principal's signature on a power of attorney, only if the power of attorney contains the signature of a witness whose signature was also notarized is the agent going to be able to prove the principal's signature in accordance with the provisions of N.J.S.A. 46:14-2.1. While the agent may be able to prove the genuineness of the principal's signature in other ways, he will not be able to prove it in accordance with the statute unless there is a witness to the principal's signature and that principal's signature is also notarized.

Stated otherwise, not having the notarized signature of a witness on the power of attorney is not fatal to a power of attorney being "duly signed," but not having the notarized signature of a witness on the power of attorney makes it more difficult for the agent to prove that the power of attorney was duly signed if someone challenges the genuineness of the principal's signature. A power of attorney that is signed by the principal and a witness with both of their signatures notarized is a self-contained document that is both duly signed and self-proving.

## 1-10 DELEGATION OF POWERS BY THE AGENT

The Revised Durable Power of Attorney Act permits the agent to delegate some or all of the powers conferred upon the agent in the power of attorney document if the power of attorney document specifically authorizes the agent to delegate those powers.[51] In delegating the powers, the agent must exercise reasonable care, skill and caution. In short, if the agent delegates his powers to another person and that person does not do a good job, the agent can be on the hook for failing to exercise reasonable care in delegating his authority.

## 1-11 FOR HOW LONG IS A POWER OF ATTORNEY EFFECTIVE?

A power of attorney is effective until such time as the principal revokes or suspends the power of attorney or until the death of the principal or until such time as the power of attorney document expires by its own terms.[52] The passage of time does not, in and of itself, cause a power of attorney document to lapse.

The banking power of attorney act permits a bank to refuse to honor a power of attorney that is more than ten years old in certain circumstances,[53] discussed more thoroughly above, but as a general rule, the passage of time does not cause a power of attorney to lapse. While good practice may require that a power of attorney be revised every ten years, in most cases this is not absolutely necessary.

### 1-11:1 Durable

Most power of attorney documents are durable. A durable power of attorney is a power of attorney that contains words to the effect that "this power of attorney shall not be affected by the subsequent disability or incapacity of the principal, or lapse of time" or that contains words to the affect that "this power of attorney shall become effective upon the disability or incapacity of the principal."[54]

If a power of attorney were not durable, then the power of attorney would be ineffective if the principal ever became incapacitated. Since most people sign a power of attorney so their

---

51. N.J.S.A. 46:2B-8.8.
52. N.J.S.A. 46:2B-8.3.
53. N.J.S.A. 46:2B-13.b.
54. N.J.S.A. 46:2B-8.2.b.

agent can act for them when they can no longer act for themselves, having a power of attorney that is durable is a fundamental part of any well-drafted power of attorney document.

The durability of a power of attorney is to be distinguished from the level of mental capacity that the principal must have in order to sign a power of attorney document, which is discussed above. A principal must have a contractual level of mental capacity in order to sign a power of attorney and cannot sign the power of attorney if he lacks that level of mental capacity. On the other hand, durability concerns the continued effectiveness of a duly signed power of attorney if the principal subsequently becomes disabled, lacking mental capacity.

## 1-12 GENERAL POWER OF ATTORNEY

A general power of attorney is a power of attorney that permits the agent to engage in multiple types of financial transactions for the principal. A general power of attorney might permit the agent to engage in transactions involving the real property of the principal, the bank accounts of the principal, the life insurance of the principal, the brokerage accounts, etc. A general power of attorney can be contrasted with a limited power of attorney, which might permit the agent to engage in only one type of financial transaction or one financial transaction.

### 1-12:1 The Power to Gift

In 2004, the Revised Durable Power of Attorney Act was amended to provide that an agent cannot gift the principal's assets either to himself or to others unless the power of attorney document specifically authorizes the agent to make such gifts.[55] Words in a power of attorney document to the effect that "the agent can do all acts that the principal could do" are insufficient to grant a power to gift the principal's assets to the agent.[56]

Gifting of the principal's assets can be one of the most important delegations of power that a principal can make in his power of attorney document. If asked, most people probably would not want their agent to be able to gift their assets, but if the reasoning

55. N.J.S.A. 46:2B-8.13a.

56. N.J.S.A. 46:2B-8.13a.

behind having such power were explained to them, most people change their minds on the issue.

Gifting is very important when engaging in Medicaid planning. Many Medicaid planning techniques require the gifting of the applicant's assets to others.

If a power of attorney fails to specifically address the gifting of the principal's assets, then the principal's ability to engage in Medicaid planning is greatly curtailed. In all likelihood, if the power of attorney document lacks the grant of a gifting authority, then someone will need to have the principal declared incapacitated in the context of a guardianship proceeding and to request permission from the court, in the guardianship proceeding, to engage in Medicaid planning.

While there is substantial case law on the concept of gifting by a guardian for a ward for purposes of Medicaid planning,[57] obtaining a guardianship can be very costly and is never guaranteed; moreover, for one reason or another, the court may deny the request to gift the ward's assets. Having a power of attorney document with broad gifting authority can eliminate all of the concerns and problems that could arise in a guardianship proceeding.

Sometimes a power of attorney document addresses gifting of the principal's assets but fails to give the agent broad enough authority to gift. For instance, the document might limit the agent's ability to gift to the amount that is exempt from federal gift tax under the annual exclusion provision of the Internal Revenue Code,[58] which is currently only $14,000 per year, per person. Or the power of attorney document might prevent the agent from gifting the principal's assets to himself, yet the agent is typically the spouse or a child and the agent is probably the person or one of the people whom the principal would most want to benefit from gifts.

By having a power of attorney document that permits the agent to make unlimited gifts of the principal's assets and that permits the agent to gift assets to himself, the principal makes it easier for his family to engage in Medicaid planning and save some or all of the principal's assets.

---

57. *In the matter of Mildred Keri, an incompetent person*, 181 N.J. 50 (2004); *In re Labis*, 314 N.J. Super. 140 (App. Div. 1998).

58. 26 U.S.C. § 2503(b)(1).

### 1-12:2 Bank Accounts

The banking power of attorney act, which is cited at N.J.S.A. 46:2B-10 et seq., permits the agent to engage in a multitude of transactions with banking institutions.[59] Those transactions are listed in the statute. Typically, a power of attorney will incorporate all of the powers specified in the banking power of attorney act simply by referencing the act by citation in the power of attorney document.

### 1-12:3 Retirement Accounts

Retirement accounts—such as individual retirement accounts, 401(k) and 403(b) plans—deserve special attention in the power of attorney document. The power of attorney should specifically authorize the agent to engage in all transactions involving retirement accounts: surrendering the account, contributing to the account, rolling-over the account, changing the beneficiaries of the account. There could be various reasons why an agent may need to effect changes to the principal's retirement account.

The agent may need to engage in Medicaid planning for the principal and may need to surrender the account or change the beneficiary. The agent may need to engage in tax planning for the principal or the beneficiaries of the account and may need to change the beneficiaries of the account.

If the document fails to address these issues, the financial institution at which the retirement account resides may refuse the agent's request to make changes to the account using a basic power of attorney document.

## 1-13 LIMITED POWER OF ATTORNEY

A limited power of attorney is a document that only permits the agent to engage in a limited type of transaction for the principal. For instance, a limited power of attorney might permit the agent to only engage only in transactions involving the principal's real estate or one specific parcel of real property that the principal owns. A limited power of attorney might permit the agent to engage in transactions that only relate only to the principal's bank accounts or one specific bank account.

---

59. N.J.S.A. 46:2B-11.

A client who is planning for his disability would not want to have a limited power of attorney or only a limited power of attorney. A good estate plan would include a durable general power of attorney with very broad authority in favor of the agent. The principal wants the agent to be able to engage in any type of financial transaction, so the agent has the authority to conduct all financial transactions for the principal.

A limited power of attorney is typically used for a specific, known purpose. For instance, a businessman might give his agent authority to purchase a specific parcel of real estate and to sign any documents necessary to consummate that sale. The businessman might not be in the area because of a commitment elsewhere, so he might sign a power of attorney in favor of another person so that person, his agent, can enter and finalize the purchase of a specific parcel of real estate.

## 1-14 COMPENSATION OF THE AGENT

Being a power of attorney agent can be a tremendous amount of work. In many cases, an agent must essentially take over the life of another individual. Since most people find it hard enough to find time in the day to complete their own affairs, juggling working and family, having to handle the affairs of another adult can be quite trying.

In addition, being an agent can result in the assumption of a tremendous amount of liability. An agent is a fiduciary,[60] charged with the utmost duty of care in handling the affairs of the principal. If the agent fails to uphold his obligation of care, he could be sued by the principal or interested parties, such as family members.

Executors, trustees, guardians—these are all examples of other fiduciaries, and all of these other fiduciaries are entitled to compensation as of right pursuant to various statutes.[61] Contrariwise, a power of attorney agent is not entitled to compensation unless the principal provides for his compensation in the power of attorney document or in a separate written document;[62] absent a written provision for compensation from the

60. N.J.S.A. 46:2B-19.

61. N.J.S.A. 3B:18-1 et seq.

62. N.J.S.A. 46:2B-8.12.

principal, an agent is not entitled to compensation unless a court awards compensation to the agent.[63]

Most power of attorney documents fail to provide for the compensation of the agent, and very few agents ever petition a court to award them compensation. The result is that very few power of attorney agents ever receive compensation. It is probably far more common for a power of attorney agent to pay for items from his own pocket for the principal than it is for an agent to receive compensation for his work and for his assumption of liability.

### 1-14:1 Rate of Compensation

A principal has to direct whether or not his agent will receive compensation with either a direction in the power of attorney document or in a separate writing. The principal can also direct the method by which compensation shall be calculated and when the compensation shall be paid.

As stated, unlike an executor, trustee or guardian, a power of attorney agent is not entitled to compensation as of right. The compensation of the agent is wholly up to the discretion of the principal. The principal determines whether or not the agent receives compensation, the amount of the compensation and when the compensation is paid.[64]

The vast majority of power of attorney documents fail to contain a clause that permits the agent to be compensated. The failure to compensate an agent can be a very bad decision.

First of all, being a power of attorney agent is a tremendous amount of work and the assumption of a tremendous amount of liability. When someone is doing work for the principal and assuming liability for his actions, he should be compensated. For these reasons an executor is compensated, a trustee is compensated and a guardian is compensated; all are compensated as a matter of law. Principals should take a lesson from the laws that permit these fiduciaries to be compensated and compensate their agent.

Secondly, compensating a power of attorney agent can be a good planning technique under certain circumstances. Many principals

---

63. N.J.S.A. 46:2B-8.12.

64. N.J.S.A. 46:2B-8.12.

nominate a child as their agent. The child-agent is working very hard for the parent-principal, typically because the principal is in failing health and can no longer handle his affairs.

The principal may eventually end up in a long-term care facility, such as an assisted living residence or a nursing facility. Care in these facilities can cost many thousands of dollars a month. The principal may wish to preserve a portion of his estate for his child's benefits and qualify for Medicaid benefit, which will pay for the assisted living residence or nursing facility.

Having a power of attorney that provides for a reasonable rate of compensation to the agent for the work that the agent performed on behalf of his principal can provide an excellent method for transferring a portion of the principal's wealth to the agent-child in a manner that does not disqualify the parent from Medicaid benefits. This and other techniques will be discussed more extensively elsewhere in this book.

The rate of compensation that a principal pays his agent is wholly up to the principal. If the principal is applying for certain benefits, such as Medicaid, third-parties may scrutinize the rate of compensation, but in the absence of third-party scrutiny, the principal is free to establish any rate of compensation that he desires, including no compensation at all. There are companies and professionals who make a living handling other people's financial affairs. Finding out what these companies/professionals charge may be a good way to establish a fair rate of compensation.

## 1-14:2 Court-Ordered Compensation

In the absence of a directive in the power of attorney document or a separate document that the principal drafts, an agent can petition a court of competent jurisdiction for an award of compensation, and the court may make an award of reasonable compensation.[65]

The reality is that very few agents ever file such a petition, so an agent acting under a power of attorney that fails to provide for compensation, which is the vast majority of powers of attorney, does his work and assumes the liability without being compensated.

---

65. N.J.S.A. 46:2B-8.12.

## 1-15 THE AGENT AND THE GUARDIAN

If a guardian of the estate, a conservator or another fiduciary charged with the management of the principal's property is appointed, then the agent must account to that fiduciary, as well as the principal.[66] The appointment of a guardian of the estate does not revoke a power of attorney. Only the principal can revoke a power of attorney, unless a court revokes a power of attorney for good cause.[67]

In the power of attorney document, the principal can nominate whom he would wish to serve as the guardian of his estate or person or as his conservator if proceedings to appoint a guardian or conservator are every initiated.[68]

## 1-16 THE DUTY TO ACCOUNT

An agent owes a fiduciary duty to the principal and to the guardian of the principal's property, if such a guardian has been appointed.[69] An agent may only engage in those transactions that are specifically delegated to him in the power of attorney document. For this reason, a power of attorney should be broadly drafted, so the agent has the full authority to perform any action which he may need to perform for his principal.

As a fiduciary, the agent must act solely for the benefit of the principal, within the confines of those powers that have been delegated to him in the power of attorney document.

A power of attorney agent must maintain accurate records of the actions that he takes as an agent for the principal under the authority granted to him in the power of attorney document.[70] The principal, guardian, conservator or personal representative of the principal's estate can require the agent to render an accounting of his actions.[71]

The Superior Court can compel an agent to account, if an heir of the principal or "other next friend" files an application with the

---

66. N.J.S.A. 46:2B-8.4.a.
67. N.J.S.A. 46:2B-8.4.c.
68. N.J.S.A. 46:2B-8.4.b.
69. N.J.S.A. 46:2B-8.4.a., N.J.S.A. 46:2B-19.
70. N.J.S.A. 46:2B-8.13.b.
71. N.J.S.A. 46:2B-8.13.b.

court requesting the agent to account.[72] To compel an accounting, the court must be satisfied that the principal is incapacitated and there must be doubt or concern that the agent is working within the confines of the authority granted to him or is acting solely for the benefit of the principal.

In most instances, a power of attorney document eliminates the need to have a guardian or conservator appointed for the principal, so very few principals will have a guardian or conservator. For this reason, most agents can only be compelled to account if someone files an action in court and the court finds that there is causes to believe that the principal is incapacitated and that the agent is not acting for the principal's sole benefit or within the scope of the authority delegated to him in the power of attorney document. From a practical standpoint, this isn't going to happen too frequently as most people would be turned off by the need to file an action in court.

For this reason, good practice would dictate drafting a power of attorney document with an obligation for the agent to account. The accounting provision in the power of attorney document should specify who can request an accounting, the frequency with which the named persons can request an accounting and the circumstances under which a request can be made.

By providing for the agent to account in the document, the principal eliminates the need for people to file an action in court, because everyone reading the document knows when the agent must account. At the very least, the principal is giving others the right to file an action in court to compel the agent to account and those filing the action know with certainty that they have the right to compel the agent to account because the power of attorney document says they have the right to an accounting.

## 1-17 DEATH OF PRINCIPAL

The death of the principal causes a power of attorney to lapse.[73] Many people believe that the effectiveness of a power of attorney continues after the death of the principal. The child of a principal may believe that the power of attorney document permits him to

---

72. N.J.S.A. 46:2B-8.13.b.

73. N.J.S.A. 46:2B-8.5.a.; *Smith v. Cynfax Corp.*, 261 N.J. Super. 378 (Law Div. 1992).

pay his father's, the principal's, bills after the father's death. This is not the case.

After the death of the principal, the executor nominated in the decedent's last will and testament or the administrator of his intestate estate is the only person who can access the decedent's assets.

## 1-18 REVOCATION OF POWER OF ATTORNEY

A power of attorney is terminated upon the death of the principal.[74] A non-durable power of attorney is revoked upon the disability of the principal.[75]

A power of attorney is revoked when the principal causes all originals of the power of attorney to be destroyed;[76] accordingly, if the principal signed two originals of the power of attorney document and the principal destroys both of those originals, then the power of attorney is revoked.

A power of attorney is also revoked when the principal signs and has his signature acknowledged in the matter set forth in N.J.S.A. 46:14-2.1.—which is the same statute concerning the manner in which the power of attorney must be signed—a written revocation of the power of attorney document.[77] So, if the principal signs a document revoking the power of attorney and the principal's signature is acknowledged before a notary, then the power of attorney is revoked.

A power of attorney is also revoked when the principal signs a revocation of the power of attorney and delivers the revocation to the agent.[78] In this instance, because the principal is delivering the revocation to the agent, the signature of the principal on the revocation does not have to be acknowledged in the manner set forth in N.J.S.A. 46:14-2.1. If the principal is handing the revocation to the agent, there is no reason for a notary to acknowledge the signature of the principal.

---

74. N.J.S.A. 46:2B-8.5.a.
75. N.J.S.A. 46:2B-8.5.b.
76. N.J.S.A. 46:2B-8.10.
77. N.J.S.A. 46:2B-8.10.
78. N.J.S.A. 46:2B-8.10.

## 1-18:1 Notice of Revocation

While the death of the principal terminates a power of attorney, an agent who acts under the authority granted to him by the power of attorney lacking actual notice of the principal's death and who acts in good faith continues to have authority to bind the principal.[79] Similarly, an agent acting under a non-durable power of attorney who lacks actual notice of the principal's disability and who acts in good faith continues to have authority to bind the principal.[80]

79. N.J.S.A. 46:2B-8.5.a.
80. N.J.S.A. 46:2B-8.5.b.

# Chapter 2

# The Advance Health Care Directive

## 2-1 THE ADVANCE HEALTH CARE DIRECTIVE

The state of New Jersey has a long history with surrogate health care decision-making. Starting with the Karen Ann Quinlan case in 1976,[1] and its progeny,[2] this state has been at the forefront of surrogate health care decision-making.

In 1992, New Jersey enacted the New Jersey Advance Directives for Health Care Act (the "Act").[3] An advance health care directive is one of the three, fundamental estate planning documents, along with a last will and testament and a financial power of attorney. In my opinion, every person over the age of 18[4] should have an advance health care directive.[5]

An advance health care directive could be one of two different directives—an instructive directive[6] and a proxy directive.[7] However,

---

1. *In the Matter of Karen Quinlan*, 70 N.J. 10 (1976).

2. *In re Conroy*, 98 N.J. 321 (1985).

3. N.J.S.A. 26:2H-53 "This act shall be known and may be cited as the 'New Jersey Advance Directives for Health Care Act.'"

4. N.J.S.A. 26:2H-55 "'Adult' means an individual 18 years of age or older."

5. N.J.S.A. 26:2H-55 "Advance directive for health care or (advance directive) means a writing executed in accordance with the requirements of this act. An (advance directive) may include a proxy directive or an instruction directive, or both."

6. N.J.S.A. 26:2H-55 "Instruction directive means a writing which provides instructions and direction regarding the declarant's wishes for health care in the event that the declarant subsequently lacks decision making capacity."

7. "Proxy directive means a writing which designates a health care representative in the event the declarant subsequently lacks decision making capacity."

typically these documents are combined into one document,[8] so the client is unaware of the fact that his document actually contains two discrete directives.

A proxy directive is a document that nominates one person—called the health care representative,[9] health care proxy, or representative—to make decisions for another person, called the declarant.[10] A proxy directive, in and of itself, does not state the declarant's health care directives. For instance, "I appoint my spouse to make health care decisions for me" is a proxy directive. A proxy directive is sometimes called a health care power of attorney.

An instructive directive is more commonly known as a living will. A true living will does not nominate a representative to make decisions for the declarant. A true living will only states how the declarant would or would not want to be treated in a given health care situation. For instance, "If I am permanently unconscious, I do not want to be resuscitated" or "Even if I am permanently unconscious, I want to be resuscitated."

Many people think of a living will as a "pull-the-plug" document, but that is not necessarily the case. While most people do not wish to have extraordinary medical procedures performed upon them if they were, say, permanently unconscious, some people do. So, their living will could state that they want all possible medical procedures performed upon them no matter how dire their medical condition. In other words, a living will could be a "keep-the-plug-in" document, if that is what the client wants.

Most clients who already have estate planning documents will not have true living wills. If the client's living will is from the early 1990s or earlier,[11] then it may be a true living will. But for the past 20 years or so, most attorneys have been drafting advance health care directives that are a combination living will/health care

---

8. See, infra, N.J.S.A. 26:2H-55 "Advance Directive for health care"

9. N.J.S.A. 26:2H-55 "Health care representative means the individual designated by a declarant pursuant to the proxy directive part of an advance directive for the purpose of making health care decisions on the declarant's behalf, and includes an individual designated as an alternate health care representative who is acting as the declarant's health care representative in accordance with the terms and order of priority stated in an advance directive."

10. N.J.S.A. 26:2H-55 "Declarant' means a competent adult who executes an advance directive."

11. The New Jersey Advance Directive for Health Care Act became effective January 7, 1992. N.J.S.A. 26:2H-53.

power of attorney. The law permits this type of document to be drafted.[12]

Because there are so many colloquial phrases for advance health care directives (living will, health care power of attorney, power of attorney, health care proxy, advance health care directive), pracatitioners typically refer to an advance health care directive as a living will when speaking with clients, even though the document to be drafted is a combination living will/health care power of attorney. The phrase "living will" is known to most people, and most people understand what the lawyer means when he uses that phrase; accordingly, throughout this book, the phrase "living will" will be used, meaning an advance heath care directive or a living will/health care power of attorney.

As discussed below, a living will is only effective when the declarant cannot make decisions for himself.[13] If the declarant is capable of making decisions for himself, then he makes those decisions and his living will isn't effective. The Act is very much written in favor of preserving the personal autonomy of the individual.[14]

When effective, a living will is an important surrogate decision-making tool. A living will permits the representative to make health care decisions for the declarant and, if drafted properly, to access the personal and private health care information of the individual for whom the representative is making decisions.[15]

Perhaps more importantly, a living will gives a representative, who is frequently a close family member of the declarant, peace of mind. Many clients are thankful to have a living will drafted for

---

12. "A declarant may execute an instruction directive, pursuant to the requirements of section 4 of this act, stating the declarant's general treatment philosophy and objectives; or the declarant's specific wishes regarding the provision, withholding or withdrawal of any form of health care, including life-sustaining treatment; or both. An instruction directive may, but need not, be executed contemporaneously with, or be attached to, a proxy directive." N.J.S.A. 26:2H-58(b).

13. "An advance directive becomes operative when (1) it is transmitted to the attending physician or to the health care institution, and (2) it is determined pursuant to section 8 of this act that the patient lacks capacity to make a particular health care decision." N.J.S.A. 26:2H-59(a).

14. "Competent adults have the fundamental right, in collaboration with their health care providers, to control decisions about their own health care. This State recognizes, in its law and public policy, the personal right of the individual patient to make voluntary, informed choices to accept, to reject, or to choose among alternative courses of medical and surgical treatment." N.J.S.A. 26:2H-54(a).

15. See, Chapter 2 section 2-9, discussing the Health Insurance Portability and Accountability Act.

their parent, because it permitts the representative-child to make an end-of-life health care decision for his declarant-parent knowing that he was simply doing what "dad told me to do in writing."

In the consultation process, some older clients will say, "I'll let my child decide when the time comes," but that is somewhat cruel to the client's family member. It isn't easy making end-of-life decisions, particularly when that decision involves someone you love. The fact that, in many cases, the person is older makes it somewhat easier, but still far from easy.

When a client-declarant takes the time to put his feelings and directives in writing, that document can give a child-representative a tremendous amount of solace. So, to a large extent, a living will isn't for the client but for his family.

### 2-1:1 The Living Will

A living will is an instructive directive.[16] In the narrow sense, a living will, in and of itself, does not appoint a representative to make decisions for the declarant. A living willing simply states how the declarant would or would not want to be treated if he could not make decisions for himself.

There are two primary issues that clients will raise with you when you discuss a living will (in the narrow sense and in the broad sense, that is, a living will/health care power of attorney) with them. Some clients are concerned that if they have a living will they will not get necessary, life-sustaining treatment.[17] The client fears that the hospital/doctor/nurse will simply let them die because they have a living will. (This feeling is often heightened when you discuss organ donation with the client. Some clients are of the opinion that if they are organ donors, their health care providers[18] will let them die so that their organs can be harvested.)

---

16. "'Instruction directive' means a writing which provides instructions and direction regarding the declarant's wishes for health care in the event that the declarant subsequently lacks decision making capacity." N.J.S.A. 26:2H-55

17. The Act defines "life-sustaining treatment" as follows: "Life-sustaining treatment' means the use of any medical device or procedure, artificially provided fluids and nutrition, drugs, surgery or therapy that uses mechanical or other artificial means to sustain, restore or supplant a vital bodily function, and thereby increase the expected life span of a patient." N.J.S.A. 26:2H-55.

18. As used in this book, for purposes of simplicity, the term "health care providers" is meant to encompass three terms used in the Act—health care institution, health care professional, and other health care professionals. "Health care institution' means all

The other issue is that some clients believe that their health care providers will not adhere to their health care directives as stated in their living will. "I had an aunt who had a living will, and the doctors just ignored it and hooked her up to the machines anyway." I will discuss this issue in Chapter 2, section 2-14.

As for the first issue—the client's concern that health care providers will simply leave them to die if they have a living will—this belief could not be further from what the law mandates or from the reality of health care.

As for reality, I have been a guardian—either temporary,[19] plenary,[20] or special medical guardian[21]—for probably a hundred or more people. I have made numerous end-of-life decisions for my wards, probably more than any one person should have to make. I have never seen an instance where a health care provider wanted to stop treating an individual who could be helped by the current state of medicine. In fact, I find the opposite to be true, that our health care system is designed to continue medical procedures for individuals who, in all likelihood, will find no improvement from the procedure.

There is a distinction between quality of care and the care that is provided. Some doctors, some nurses, some hospitals are better than others. Some plumbers are better than other plumbers and so on. That is just a fact of life. While not every patient receives the best possible care that he could receive, I have never witnessed a situation where a health care provider willfully stopped providing or failed to provide care to a patient because the patient had a living will (nor had a guardian appointed for him). In fact, as stated, what I have experienced is health care providers who provide every

---

institutions, facilities, and agencies licensed, certified, or otherwise authorized by State law to administer health care in the ordinary course of business, including hospitals, nursing homes, residential health care facilities, home health care agencies, hospice programs operating in this State, mental health institutions, facilities or agencies, or institutions, facilities and agencies for the developmentally disabled. The term health care institution shall not be construed to include health care professionals as defined in this act." N.J.S.A. 26:2H-55. "'Health care professional' means an individual licensed by this State to administer health care in the ordinary course of business or practice of a profession." N.J.S.A. 26:2H-55. "Other health care professionals' means health care professionals other than physicians and nurses." N.J.S.A. 26:2H-55.

19. N.J.S.A. 3B:12-24.1(c)

20. N.J.S.A. 3B:12-24.1(a)

21. N.J. Ct. R. 4:86-12

possible procedure and test to individuals notwithstanding their dire medical condition.

For those clients who do not want a living will because they fear their health care providers will fail to provide care to them if they have a living will, there is no easy answer because the answer is anecdotal. I tell the client what I have just told you, but the fact of the matter is, like you, the client hasn't experienced what I have experienced, just as I have not experienced what they have.

The good news is a living will can be drafted to say whatever the client wants the document to say. A living will could state "pull the plug if I am permanently unconscious," which is what most living wills state, but it doesn't have to be drafted that way. A living will could state that the declarant wants to be kept alive no matter what, a "keep-the-plug-in" document. The choice is the client's to make.

#### 2-1:1.1 The "Treat-Aggressively" Living Will

Every once in awhile, I have a client who wants what I call a "treat-aggressively" living will. A treat-aggressively living will essentially says that the client wants to be kept alive no matter what the circumstances may be. For instance, "I want all possible medical procedures to be provided even if I am permanently unconscious" would be a treat-aggressively living will.

I always ask clients if they want to be kept alive no matter what their medical condition may be or if they would want to stop treatment if they were "a vegetable," as the saying goes. While most clients do not wish to be kept alive, some do. You should never assume how a client wants to be treated—ask the client.

Most of my clients who do want to be kept alive no matter what their circumstances tell me that they have heard of situations where individuals were in a coma for years and eventually came out of it. I have never had a client who told me such a story who actually knew the person who benefitted from this miracle recovery or, for that matter, know who the person was who came out of the seven-year coma, but a living will is a personal document. Few decisions could be more personal than how a person wishes to be treated with regard to their health care, so if a client wants to be kept alive no matter what, then that is what their living will should state.

### 2-1:1.2 The "Do-Not-Treat" Living Will

Most clients with whom you will meet will not want to be kept alive if they are "a vegetable." For these clients, the "do-not-treat" living will is appropriate.

This type of living will is what most people think of when they think of a living will. "If I am ever permanently unconscious,[22] then I do not wish to be kept alive." This is what a do-not-treat living will states.

As with the treat-aggressively living will, how the client wants a living will drafted is up to them. There are few decisions that are as personal as a health care decision. The purpose of a living will is for the client to state in advance how he would like to be treated in those circumstances where he can no longer make decisions for himself.[23]

### 2-1:1.3 How Specific Is Too Specific?

Whether the client wants a treat-aggressively living will or a do-not-treat living will, the client will have to decide how specific he wants to get in his living will. Some clients wish to get very specific as to which medical procedures they do or do not wish performed upon them. For instance, "I do not wish to be placed on a ventilator."

I believe a living will should not be too specific and should be treated merely as a general statement as to how the client would or would not want to be treated if he were unable to make decisions for himself. While most people would say they would never want to be placed on a ventilator, being placed on a ventilator is not a permanent situation in most cases.

---

22. "Permanently unconscious" is a defined phrase. "Permanently unconscious" means a medical condition that has been diagnosed in accordance with currently accepted medical standards and with reasonable medical certainty as total and irreversible loss of consciousness and capacity for interaction with the environment. The term 'permanently unconscious' includes without limitation a persistent vegetative state or irreversible coma." N.J.S.A. 26:2H-55.

23. In part, the legislative findings section of the Act states the following: "In order that the right to control decisions about one's own health care should not be lost in the event a patient loses decision making capacity and is no longer able to participate actively in making his own health care decisions, this State recognizes the right of competent adults to plan ahead for health care decisions through the execution of advance directives, such as living wills and durable powers of attorney, and to have the wishes expressed therein respected, subject to certain limitations." N.J.S.A. 26:2h-54(c).

Many people are placed on ventilators and are weaned off the ventilator in time. Placing a patient on a ventilator is sometimes necessary so that other, necessary procedures can be performed on the patient. If a client says that they do not wish to be placed on a ventilator under any circumstance, then he may die because necessary medical procedures cannot be performed on him.

When a client comes to you to have a living will drafted, in most instances, the client is in good health. Neither the client nor you knows what medical issues the client may have someday or what medical procedures may or may not be performed to help the client overcome their medical issues. Moreover, given the advancements in medical technologies and medications, how can someone today state in detail what they would and would not want when they need medical attention, say, ten years from now.

Even if the client were currently ill, for instance, had cancer, the client still doesn't know every medication or procedure that could help him with his battle against his cancer. No medical professional knows everything about all fields of medicine.

In short, it is best to leave options open and to think of the living will as a general statement as to how the client would or would not want to be treated in certain circumstances.

## 2-1:2 The Health Care Power of Attorney

I call an advance health care directive a living will, but in most instances, an advance health care directive is really an instructive directive and a proxy directive. The instructive directive is a living will. The proxy directive is a health care power of attorney or health care proxy.

Unlike an instructive directive, which merely states how the client would or would not want to be treated in given circumstances,[24] the health care power of attorney appoints one person, called the representative, to make decisions for the declarant if the declarant lacks decision-making capacity.[25] "If I am permanently unconscious, then I want my spouse to make medical decisions for me."

---

24. "Instruction directive' means a writing which provides instructions and direction regarding the declarant's wishes for health care in the event that the declarant subsequently lacks decision making capacity." N.J.S.A. 26:2h-55.

25. "Proxy directive' means a writing which designates a health care representative in the event the declarant subsequently lacks decision making capacity." N.J.S.A. 26:2H-55.

When used in combination with an instructive directive, a health care power of attorney can be a very effective and important tool. The document appoints a representative to make decisions for the client if the client is unable to make those decisions for himself and the document gives some guidance to the representative as to how the client wants to be treated.

## 2-2 THE DECLARANT

The "declarant" is the person who executes the living will.[26] The declarant is typically your client, the person for whom you are drafting the living will.

## 2-3 THE REPRESENTATIVE

The "health care representative" is the person whom the declarant has nominated in the proxy directive section of his living will to make health care decisions for him.[27]

### 2-3:1 Who May Serve as Representative?

Typically, when a client-declarant comes to you to draft a living will for him, the client is naming a family member as his representative. Few decisions are as important and as personal as health care decisions, particularly end-of-life decisions. In most cases, it is appropriate that the declarant name a close family member to make decisions for him.

In some circumstances, the client may not have a family member to make decisions for him or he may simply wish to name someone other than a family member for one reason or another. With limited exceptions, a client can name most any person of his choosing to make decisions for him.[28]

---

26. N.J.S.A. 26:2H-55.

27. N.J.S.A. 26:2H-55.

28. "A declarant may execute a proxy directive, pursuant to the requirements of section 4 of this act, designating a competent adult to act as his health care representative. (1) A competent adult, including, but not limited to, a declarant's spouse, domestic partner as defined in Section 3 of P.L.2003, c. 246 (C.26:8A-3), adult child, parent or other family member, friend, religious or spiritual advisor, or other person of the declarant's choosing, may be designated as a health care representative. (2) An operator, administrator or employee of a health care institution in which the declarant is a patient or resident shall not serve as the declarant's health care representative unless the operator, administrator or employee is related to the declarant by blood, marriage, domestic partnership or adoption. This restriction does not apply to a physician, if the physician does not serve as the patient's

It is easier to list those individuals who cannot serve as a declarant's representative. A representative must be both competent and an adult, so a declarant cannot name a minor or mentally incapacitated individual as his representative.

A declarant's attending physician cannot serve as the declarant's representative for obvious reasons. You cannot have the doctor who is treating the patient making the decision as to whether or not to treat the patient. A doctor can serve as an individual's representative if the doctor is not serving as the patient's attending physician.

The operator, administrator, or employee of a health care institution in which the declarant is a patient cannot serve as the declarant's representative unless the operator, administrator, or employee is related to the declarant by blood, adoption, marriage, or domestic partnership.

## 2-3:2 Sole Representative vs. Co-Representatives

The New Jersey Advance Directive for Health Care Act does not permit a declarant to name co-representatives.[29] Unlike with a financial power of attorney, which does specifically permit co-agents to make financial decisions for the principal,[30] the law does not permit co-representatives for health care.

Personally, I think this is a good thing. If you have co-representatives, you have the potential of a conflict between the co-representatives. For instance, assume that the declarant chooses his two children to make his health care decisions. Suppose the co-representatives disagree as to whether or not to remove the declarant from a ventilator? What is the attending physician to do?

---

attending physician and the patient's health care representative at the same time." N.J.S.A. 26:2H-58(a)(1), (2).

29. The Act never specifically prohibits the designation of co-representatives, but throughout the Act, there are references to a "health care representative," using the singular tense, and to the designation of alternate representatives listed in order of priority. "Health care representative' means the individual designated by a declarant pursuant to the proxy directive part of an advance directive for the purpose of making health care decisions on the declarant's behalf, and includes an individual designated as an alternate health care representative who is acting as the declarant's health care representative in accordance with the terms and order of priority stated in an advance directive." N.J.S.A. 26:2H-55. "(3) A declarant may designate one or more alternate health care representatives, listed in order of priority." N.J.S.A. 26:2H-58(a)(3). Unlike the Revised Durable Power of Attorney Act (the act addressing financial powers of attorney), which does permit co-agents for financial decisions, in no place does the Advance Directive for Health Care Act permit co-agents.

30. N.J.S.A. 46:2B-8.7.

When you have one representative imbued with the authority to make health care decisions for the declarant, health care providers know whom they can listen to with regard to health care decisions affecting the declarant. Moreover, the health care providers are relieved of liability when they listen to the one named representative.[31]

As an attorney, you will frequently come across clients who want to name co-representatives. Perhaps the client has two children and doesn't want one child to feel excluded from the health care decision-making process. Or perhaps, for one reason or another, the client simply wants to name two family members as his representative.

I have explained to numerous clients that they can only name one person at a time as their representative, and how this is a good thing. I have also seen numerous living wills that are drafted by attorneys and that name co-representatives. At times, when clients insist, I've named co-representatives, but it is not right, and with good reason.

When it comes to life-or-death decisions, there should only be one person in charge. This is a clear situation where too many cooks can spoil the broth. As discussed below, the declarant can advise the representative to consult with other people before making his decision for the declarant, and those other people can include the other children of the declarant.[32]

## 2-3:3 Successor Representatives

A declarant cannot name co-representatives, but the law permits a declarant to name successor representatives and the attorney should encourage his client to do so.[33] Making important health

---

31. A health care professional shall not be subject to criminal or civil liability or to discipline by the health care institution or the respective State licensing board for professional misconduct for any actions performed in good faith and in accordance with the provisions of this act, any rules and regulations established by the Department of Health pursuant to this act, and accepted professional standards to carry out the terms of an advance directive. A health care institution shall not be subject to criminal or civil liability for any actions performed in good faith and in accordance with the provisions of this act to carry out the terms of an advance directive." N.J.S.A. 26:2H-73(b), (c).

32. "(4) A declarant may direct the health care representative to consult with specified individuals, including alternate designees, family members and friends, in the course of the decision making process." N.J.S.A. 26:2H-58(a)(4).

33. "(3) A declarant may designate one or more alternate health care representatives, listed in order of priority. In the event the primary designee is unavailable, unable or unwilling to serve as health care representative, or is disqualified from such service pursuant

care decisions is not easy, and the fact of the matter is, some people who are named as representative may find themselves unable for one reason or another to make the necessary decision for the declarant.

Successor representatives serve in the order of priority in which they are named. So, if the declarant names his son as his representative then his daughter as his successor representative, that is the order in which the children will serve as their declarant-father's representative.

### 2-3:4 Failure of Representative To Serve

A representative is not financially compensated for his decisions.[34] In most cases, no one praises the representative for the decisions he makes for the declarant. If anything, people may criticize the representative's decision. So, being a representative and making decisions for the declarant is not an easy job at all.

A representative who has been nominated in a living will to serve does not have to accept their role as representative. The representative may be unwilling to serve. If the representative is unwilling to serve, for whatever reason, it is good practice for the declarant to have a back-up or successor representative. In fact, having two successor representatives isn't a bad idea.

## 2-4 WHEN IS AN ADVANCE HEALTHCARE DIRECTIVE EFFECTIVE?

The Act has a very heavy focus on maintaining the personal autonomy of the declarant over his health care decisions.[35] Unlike a financial power of attorney, which is typically effective upon

---

to this section or any other law, the next designated alternate shall serve as health care representative. In the event the primary designee subsequently becomes available and able to serve as health care representative, the primary designee may, insofar as then practicable, serve as health care representative." N.J.S.A. 26:2H-58(a)(3).

34. Unlike the Revised Durable Power of Attorney Act, N.J.S.A. 46:2B-8.1 et seq., which does permit a financial power of attorney to provide for the compensation of an attorney-in-fact. (N.J.S.A. 46:2B-8.13) at no place does the New Jersey Advance Directives for Health Care Act permit a representative to be compensated for his services.

35. "Competent adults have the fundamental right, in collaboration with their health care providers, to control decisions about their own health care." N.J.S.A. 26:2H-54(a).

execution, a living will is only effective when the declarant lacks the capacity to make his own health care decisions.[36]

In addition, in order to be effective, the living will must be transmitted to the declarant's attending physician or the health care institution in which the declarant is residing. Finally, a living will is only effective to permit the withholding or the withdrawing of life-sustaining treatment when the declarant is in one (or more) of the following states: terminally ill, permanently unconscious, when the life-sustaining treatment is experimental, or when the cost of the life-sustaining treatment is expected to outweigh the benefit of the treatment.[37]

## 2-4:1 Inability To Make Decisions

The inability of the declarant to make his own decisions is of paramount concern throughout the Act. A living will is only effective if the declarant is unable to make his own decisions.

Many clients are fearful of relinquishing control of their health care to another individual, even if the named representative is the declarant's spouse or child. The Act recognizes that a person has a right to autonomy over his health care decisions and has a very strong interest in decisions made regarding his health.

In one way or the other, a client may express to you his concern that someone is going to "un-plug" him too quickly. I have always expressed to the client the fact that a living will is only effective if the client cannot make decisions for himself and life-sustaining treatment can only be withdrawn if the client is in one of the four statutory conditions, for instance, clinically permanently unconscious. Furthermore, a living will can be suspended at any time.

Here is a quote from the Act that I find quite informative with regard to how the Act favors the personal autonomy of the

---

36. "An advance directive becomes operative when (1) it is transmitted to the attending physician or to the health care institution, and (2) it is determined pursuant to section 8 of this act that the patient lacks capacity to make a particular health care decision." N.J.S.A. 26:2H-59(a). The Act defines "decision making capacity" as follows: "Decision making capacity means a patient's ability to understand and appreciate the nature and consequences of health care decisions, including the benefits and risks of each, and alternatives to any proposed health care, and to reach an informed decision. A patient's decision making capacity is evaluated relative to the demands of a particular health care decision." N.J.S.A. 26:2H-55.

37. N.J.S.A. 26:2H-67.

declarant over the opinion of all others: "An incompetent patient may suspend an advance directive, including a proxy directive, an instructive directive, or both, by any of the means stated [above]."[38] Think about this section of the Act. An "incompetent patient" may suspend a living will! That's a fairly strong statement to health care providers that the declarant maintains autonomy over his health care decisions if he is able to express those intentions in any manner whatsoever.

An incompetent person cannot make informed medical decisions. To accommodate this fact, our law provides for the appointment of a special medical guardian,[39] temporary,[40] or plenary guardian[41] for such an individual, but an incapacitated individual can suspend his living will. That is quite amazing and quite a statement about the extent to which health care providers must and should listen to the wishes of the declarant.

A declarant can revoke or suspend his living will verbally, in writing, or "by any other act evidencing an intent to revoke the document."[42]

To take it to an extreme, if a declarant were to make facial expressions that evidenced an intent to suspend his living will, even if he were incapacitated, then his health care provider should treat his living will as being suspended. That fact should assuage the concern of most clients with regard to someone pulling-the-plug on them prematurely.

The declarant's attending physician makes the determination that the declarant lacks decision-making capacity.[43] A second physician must confirm the determination of the attending physician, unless the declarant's lack of capacity is clear and both the attending physician and representative agree that the opinion of a confirming

---

38. N.J.S.A. 26:2H-57(d).

39. N.J. Ct. R. 4:86-12.

40. N.J.S.A. 3B:12-24.1(c).

41. N.J.S.A. 3B:12-24.1(a).

42. N.J.S.A. 26:2H-57(b), (d).

43. "The attending physician shall determine whether the patient lacks capacity to make a particular health care decision. The determination shall be stated in writing, shall include the attending physician's opinion concerning the nature, cause, extent, and probable duration of the patient's incapacity, and shall be made a part of the patient's medical records." N.J.S.A. 26:2H-60(a).

physician is unnecessary.[44] A determination of incapacity shall be entered into the declarant's medical records.[45]

## 2-4:2 Transmission to the Health Care Provider

In addition to the requirement that the declarant be incapable of making his own health care decisions in order for a living will to be effective, the living will must be transmitted (or given to) the declarant's attending physician or the health care institution in which he presently resides.[46] The representative for the declarant cannot simply go the hospital and say "I'm my dad's health care representative." The attending physician or health care institution must have the document.

What I tell clients is to, bring the original living will to your doctor or to the hospital and let them make a copy of the document. The doctor or hospital will then enter the copy of the document into the declarant's medical record.

Will the doctor or hospital insist upon seeing an original of the living will before they honor the document? I don't know. I think it depends upon the thoroughness of the doctor or hospital. As with a financial power of attorney, I think the person acting upon the document should insist upon seeing the original and making a copy for their file, but whether or not the health care provider will be thorough or not is a real-life question that cannot be answered in a textbook. All that I can say is that they should do so.

Having the doctor or hospital actually have the document is another requirement of the Act that protects the autonomy of the declarant over his health care decisions.

## 2-4:3 Statutory Conditions When Life-Sustaining Treatment Can Be Withheld or Withdrawn

In keeping with the Act's strong proclivity to maintaining a declarant's autonomy over his health care decisions and in keeping with the State's interest in preserving human life,[47] the Act only

---

44. N.J.S.A. 26:2H-60(b).

45. N.J.S.A. 26:2H-60(e).

46. N.J.S.A. 26:2H-59(a).

47. "The right of individuals to forego life-sustaining measures is not absolute and is subject to certain interests of society. The most significant of these societal interests is the preservation of life, understood to embrace both an interest in preserving the life of the

permits life-sustaining treatment to be withheld or withdrawn in certain, limited circumstances.

The Act defines the term "life-sustaining treatment" quite broadly:

> "Life-sustaining treatment" means the use of any medical device or procedure, artificially provided fluids and nutrition, drugs, surgery or therapy that uses mechanical or other artificial means to sustain, restore or supplant a vital bodily function, and thereby increase the expected life span of a patient.[48]

### 2-4:3.1 Experimental Treatment

Life-sustaining treatment can be withheld or withdrawn when the treatment is experimental in nature and not a proven form of treatment or when the treatment is unlikely to prove effective and merely prolongs the dying process. A person should not be forced to undergo experimental treatment with a small chance of preserving his life.[49]

### 2-4:3.2 Permanently Unconscious

Most people think of a living will as a document that permits someone to "pull-the-plug" on them when they are a "vegetable." The "vegetable" state is officially called "permanently unconscious." The declarant's attending physician and a second physician must determine that the declarant is in a state of permanent unconsciousness.[50]

### 2-4:3.3 Terminally Ill

Life-sustaining treatment can be withheld or withdrawn when the declarant is in a terminal condition, as determined by his attending

---

particular patient and a related but distinct interest in preserving the sanctity of all human life as an enduring social value. A second, closely related societal interest is the protection of individuals from direct and purposeful self-destruction, motivated by a specific intent to die. A third interest is the protection of innocent third parties who may be harmed by the patient's decision to forego therapy; this interest may be asserted to prevent the emotional and financial abandonment of the patient's minor children or to protect the paramount concerns of public health or safety." N.J.S.A. 26:2H-54(d).

48. N.J.S.A. 26:2H-55.

49. N.J.S.A. 26:2H-67(a)(1).

50. N.J.S.A. 26:2H-67(a)(2).

physician and confirmed by a second physician.[51] The Act defines "terminal condition" as follows:

> "Terminal condition" means the terminal stage of an irreversibly fatal illness, disease or condition. A determination of a specific life expectancy is not required as a precondition for a diagnosis of a "terminal condition," but a prognosis of a life expectancy of six months or less, with or without the provision of life-sustaining treatment, based upon reasonable medical certainty, shall be deemed to constitute a terminal condition.[52]

#### 2-4:3.4 Cost-Benefit Analysis

Finally, life-sustaining treatment can be withheld or withdrawn when the risks and burdens of the treatment are likely to outweigh the benefits of the treatment. The State isn't interested in forcing people to undergo painful procedures that have little benefit or chance of helping the person.[53]

### 2-4:4 The Living Will and Emergency Care

Some clients will say, "If I suffer a heart attack, I don't want this living will to prevent the first aid squad from coming and trying to help me." I have had several clients who serve as members of local first aid squads, and, without exception, each of those clients have told me that emergency responders do not adhere to the declarant's directives in a living will. If you don't want EMS to try and revive you after you have suffered a serious health event, such as a heart attack, then tell your family not to call the EMS. If your family calls the EMS to try to save your life, the EMS is going to try to save your life.

This fact is written into the law. The Act provides that emergency personnel are not required to withhold or withdraw emergency care in situations that do not afford an opportunity to evaluate

---

51. N.J.S.A. 26:2H-67(a)(3).
52. N.J.S.A. 26:2H-55.
53. N.J.S.A. 26:2H-67(a)(4).

the living will without endangering the life of the declarant.[54] From a practical standpoint, almost every "emergency" health care situation fails to afford an opportunity for a first-responder to evaluate a living will.

A paramedic, for instance, is in your house trying to revive and stabilize you after a heart attack. He isn't going to stop what he is doing so he can read your living will and interpret what the living will says. That paramedic is going to do his job and transmit the declarant to the hospital, where decisions about withholding future treatment or withdrawing treatments already implemented can be made in a more studied and stable environment.

As my clients have told me, if you don't want EMS to try to save your life, don't call EMS. Obviously, in the panic and fear of the situation that is easier said than done. However, most assuredly, a client does not have to be concerned about the local EMS failing to try to revive him because he has a living will.

## 2-5 EXECUTION OF THE LIVING WILL

Certain requirements must be satisfied in order for a living will to be effectively executed. A declarant must be an adult in order to sign a living will. An "adult" is defined as an individual who has attained the age of eighteen.[55] A declarant must be competent.[56]

It is of some note that a declarant must be competent to executed a living will, yet a declarant can suspend a living will even if he is incompetent.[57]

The living will must be signed and dated by the declarant, or signed and dated at the direction of the declarant. The signing must occur in the presence of two subscribing adult witnesses who must attest that the declarant was of sound mind and free from duress and undue influence. Neither of the witnesses can be designated

---

54. "The provisions of this act shall not be construed to require emergency personnel, including paid or volunteer fire fighters; paramedics; members of an ambulance team, rescue squad, or mobile intensive care unit; or emergency room personnel of a licensed health care institution, to withhold or withdraw emergency care in circumstances which do not afford reasonable opportunity for careful review and evaluation of an advance directive without endangering the life of the patient." N.J.S.A. 26:2H-70(b).

55. N.J.S.A. 26:2H-55, defining "Adult."

56. N.J.S.A. 26:2H-55, defining "Declarant."

57. N.J.S.A. 26:2H-57(d).

in the living will as a representative. In the alternative, a living will must be signed in the presence of a notary public, attorney at law, or other person authorized to administer oaths. [58]

The execution of the living will can be supplemented by a video or audio tape recording but must be executed in writing.[59]

## 2-6 WHAT ARE "HEALTH CARE DECISIONS"?

A "health care representative" is an individual whom the declarant has designated to make health care decisions for the declarant. The Act defines the term "health care decision" very broadly, essentially covering all forms of medical treatment, service, or procedure, and includes the selection of the declarant's health care professional and health care institution.[60]

Primarily, when a client thinks of a living will, they think of a document that permits another individual, called the health care representative or representative, to make end-of-life decisions for them if they cannot make such decisions for themselves. The Act defines "life-sustaining treatment" as follows:

> ... the use of any medical device or procedure, artificially provided fluids and nutrition, drugs, surgery or therapy that uses mechanical or other artificial means to sustain, restore or supplant a vital bodily function, and thereby increase the expected life span of a patient.[61]

When it comes to withholding or withdrawing life-sustaining treatment, the Act requires that the declarant be in one or more of four medical conditions, discussed Section 2-4:3.

---

58. "A declarant may execute an advance directive for health care at any time. The advance directive shall be signed and dated by, or at the direction of, the declarant in the presence of two subscribing adult witnesses, who shall attest that the declarant is of sound mind and free of duress and undue influence. A designated health care representative shall not act as a witness to the execution of an advance directive. Alternatively, the advance directive shall be signed and dated by, or at the direction of, the declarant and be acknowledged by the declarant before a notary public, attorney at law, or other person authorized to administer oaths." N.J.S.A. 26:2H-56.

59. N.J.S.A. 26:2H-56.

60. N.J.S.A. 26:2H-55.

61. N.J.S.A. 26:2H-55.

### 2-6:1 Fluids and Nutrition

Of all of the life-sustaining forms of treatment, fluids and nutrition are perhaps the most controversial. Many people recall the case of Terry Schiavo, a disabled woman from Florida who was in a persistent vegetative state, and the controversy that surrounded her husband's decision to withdraw fluids and nutrition from her.[62] In fact, I specifically ask clients if they would want their representative to have the authority to withhold or withdraw fluids and nutrition, and I frequently mention the Terry Schiavo case to give the client some context as to what I am talking about.

Some clients believe that their religion prevents them from having fluids and nutrition withheld or withdrawl. For instance, Roman Catholics tend to believe that withholding or withdrawing these forms of treatment is not permitted by their religion; however, as discussed below, this belief is unfounded. Some clients believe that withholding or withdrawing fluids and nutrition is painful for the patient or inhumane. "I don't want to starve to death," the client will say.

While almost everyone can agree that withdrawing a ventilator is appropriate if the person is, for example, permanently unconscious, there is disagreement about withholding or withdrawing fluids and nutrition. In the end, like all medical decisions, this one is highly personal.

The Act defines fluids and nutrition as a form of life sustaining treatment.[63] So, if the declarant is unable to make decisions for himself and if the declarant is in one or more of the four statutory conditions, for instance, permanently unconscious, then the declarant can give his representative the authority to demand that fluids and nutrition be withheld or withdrawn from the declarant.

### 2-6:2 Do Not Resuscitate Orders

Some clients equate a living will with a do not resuscitate order. Some clients want their living will to provide a do not resuscitate order. The fact of the matter is that a physician enters a do not resuscitated order, not the patient.

---

62. See, generally http://en.wikipedia.org/wiki/Terri_Schiavo_case

63. N.J.S.A. 26:2H-55.

The Act permits a declarant to grant to his representative the authority to request a do not resuscitate order, and the Act permits the attending physician to enter such an order.[64] In and of itself, however, a living will is not, and cannot be, a do not resuscitate order.

## 2-7 RELIGIOUS CONSIDERATIONS

I am an attorney, not a theologian, but every now and again, I have a client raise a religious issue when it comes to his health care decisions. For instance, some of my clients say, "I'm Roman Catholic. I don't know if my religion permits that."

I went to Catholic grammar school and high school, and quite frankly, I don't know what the Roman Catholic religion says about health care decisions with a high degree of certainty. I have read the Catholic living will several times, and essentially what it says is that the declarant is a Catholic and wants to be treated in accordance with the Catholic religion.[65]

Even the Catholic living will permits the representative to withhold or withdraw life-sustaining treatment, including fluids and nutrition, if there is no hope of a viable and meaningful life. So, quite frankly, I see very little difference between the Catholic living will and what the Act specifies. Nevertheless, if the client is particularly concerned about his Catholic beliefs, I might state the following in the living will: "*I am a Roman Catholic and wish to be treated in accordance with the teachings and practices of the Roman Catholic Church.*"

Some clients have told me that they are Jehovah's Witnesses and cannot have blood products of any kind or blood transfusions. As previously stated, a living will is, in part, an instructive directive. As an instructive directive, the living will can say whatever the client wants the document to say. In cases such as this, I might state the following in the living will: "*I do not want blood or blood products of any kind or blood transfusions.*"

Cases such as these give the attorney the opportunity to show the client that the attorney is sensitive to his individual concerns.

---

64. N.J.S.A. 26:2H-68

65. *See, e.g.*, http://diometuchen.org/assets/Uploads/Documents/RespectforLife-2/AdvDirHealthCare20111.pdf

Some religions do not favor donating organs. For instance, I have had a number of my Jewish clients tell me that their religion doesn't permit them to donate their organs. Whether or not this is true is unknown to me, but it is a religious consideration that I have heard on more than one occasion from clients.

## 2-8 WHO DECIDES: DOCUMENT FINAL OR REPRESENTATIVE'S WORD

The most common concern that you will hear from a client is the fear that their health care provider will simply abandon them because they have a living will. The client believes that if the hospital or their doctor knows that he signed a living will, the hospital or doctor will simply stop treating him.

This concern raises the inherent conflict between the instructive directive and proxy directive of the modern living will. As discussed above, a living will is typically both an instructive directive and a proxy directive. The document states how the declarant wishes to be treated (the instructive directive section) and appoints a representative to make decisions for the declarant (the proxy section). But which section takes priority?

For instance, if the living will says, "I do not wish to be placed on a ventilator," but the representative instructs the physician to place the declarant on a ventilator, what should the physician do?

In the living wills that I draft, I insert a conflict clause. This clause can either say that the instructions of the representative take precedence over the instructions in the document or that the instructions in the document take precedence over the directives of the representative. It is up to the declarant-client to choose, but I advise having the instructions of the representative take precedence over the instructions in the directive.

For one, having the directions of the representative, who is frequently a trusted family member, take precedence over what is in writing gives the client peace of mind. The declarant is appointing a family member to advocate for him if he is unable to advocate for himself. He typically trusts this individual. It is easier to appoint an advocate than it is to make a final decision about your health care. I want my spouse to advocate for me given my health situation at the time is easier to say than "pull the plug."

Having the directives of your representative take precedence over the directives that you placed in writing simply makes sense. Typically, when a client signs a living will, he is in good health. The client may not want to be kept alive if he were permanently unconscious, but as it stands today, the client is healthy and has no idea what medical condition he may or may not suffer from many years in the future.

Furthermore, in this age of technology, it is impossible to predict what the state of medicine might be five, ten, or twenty years from today. A health concern that may be deadly today could be easily and successfully treated in the future.

I tell clients that the instructions in their living wills are simply general statements to their representative, but it is the representative who will make the final decision after consulting with the client's health care providers and family. This fact typically makes the client feels better about the decision they are making. Essentially, they are appointing an advocate, not making an end-of-life decision there and then in your office.

## 2-9 HEALTH INSURANCE PORTABILITY AND ACCOUNTABILITY ACT

The Health Insurance Portability and Accountability Act of 1996[66] ("HIPAA") has brought significant changes to the manner in which a patient's health care information is handled. HIPAA prevents health care providers from sharing an individual's health care information with anyone other than the individual or his designated personal representative. While a nominated health care representative in a living will should be treated as a personal representative for purposes of HIPAA, it is questionable whether that is common knowledge.

For this reason, many living wills need to be updated. HIPAA became effective in 2003, so almost all living wills that pre-date 2003 need to be updated to address HIPAA. And, even though ten years have now passed since the enforcement of HIPAA began, most living wills still fail to address this law. It is ironic, because almost every doctor's office or hospital requests that the patient

[66] 42 U.S.C. section 1320d et seq.; 45 C.F.R. parts 160 to 164

sign a HIPAA release form before the doctor/hospital will share information with others.

Since a person's representative needs information in order to make informed decisions, it is important to specifically and conspicuously address HIPAA. The declarant should nominate their health care representative to be their personal representative for purposes of HIPAA. In that way, the representative is entitled to all of the declarant's health care information.

## 2-10 CONSULTATION WITH OTHERS

A declarant can only appoint one representative to serve at a time. While a declarant can appoint multiple, successor representatives, a declarant cannot appoint co-representatives.[67]

Many clients have more than one person whom they would like to make health care decisions for them. For instance, the client may have two children and doesn't want to exclude either child from the decision-making process.

While the declarant cannot name co-representatives, he can suggest that the representative consult with other people before making his decision.[68] For instance, the living will may instruct the representative to consult with the primary physician, spouse and children of the declarant before making a health care decision.

After consultation, the representative may decide to do something diametrically opposed to the suggestion of those individuals with whom he was directed to consult, but at least he had to consult with those individuals. In the majority of cases, important health care decisions are a family affair and are made by the family as a whole, but it gives the declarant peace of mind to know that he instructed his representative to consult with the other members of his family before making a health care decision.

## 2-11 FOR HOW LONG IS A LIVING WILL EFFECTIVE

In short, a living will is effective while the declarant is incapable of making health care decisions for himself and after the living will has been transmitted to his physician or health care institution

---

67. N.J.S.A. 26:2H-55, N.J.S.A. 26:2H-58(a)(3).

68. N.J.S.A. 26:2H-58(a)(4).

or until such time as the declarant modifies, revokes or suspends the living will.[69] Unlike with a financial power of attorney that a bank can refuse to honor if it was first presented to the bank more than ten years after its execution,[70] a living will doesn't get too old to be valid.

With that said, I recommend that clients renew their living wills every ten years. The law tends to change over time. The Health Insurance Portability and Accountability Act brought about a change to health care in the past ten years that I believe should be addressed in a client's living will. Furthermore, an old living will may not express the current wishes of the declarant.

For instance, assume that the declarant signed his living will fifteen years earlier at a time when he was in good health. Assume that the declarant currently suffers from cancer and is unable to make decisions for himself. It could be argued that the wishes of the declarant have changed since he last signed his living will and that the statements made in the old living will fail to reflect his current feelings on the care he would wish to receive.

## 2-12 ADVANCE HEALTH CARE DIRECTIVE FROM ANOTHER STATE OR COUNTRY

A living will executed in another state is valid in New Jersey if the living will meets the requirements specified in the New Jersey Advance Directives for Health Care Act[71]or if the living will is executed in accordance with the laws of the other state.[72] To be executed in accordance with the laws of New Jersey, the living will has to be signed by the declarant and witness by a notary or witnessed by two disinterested witnesses. A living will executed in another country is valid if executed in accordance with the laws of New Jersey or if executed in accordance with the laws of the other

---

69. N.J.S.A. 26:2H-57, N.J.S.A. 26:2H-59.

70. N.J.S.A. 46:2B-12(b).

71. "A declarant may execute an advance directive for health care at any time. The advance directive shall be signed and dated by, or at the direction of, the declarant in the presence of two subscribing adult witnesses, who shall attest that the declarant is of sound mind and free of duress and undue influence. A designated health care representative shall not act as a witness to the execution of an advance directive. Alternatively, the advance directive shall be signed and dated by, or at the direction of, the declarant and be acknowledged by the declarant before a notary public, attorney at law, or other person authorized to administer oaths." N.J.S.A. 26:2H-56.

72. N.J.S.A. 26:2H-76.

country and the laws of the other country are not contrary to the public policy of the state of New Jersey.

In addition, in order for the living will to be effective, the declarant must be incapable of making decisions for himself and the living will must be transmitted to the declarant's physician or the health care institution in which he resides.[73]

If a living will from, Florida for instance, meets the signing requirements of the Act, then the living will is valid in New Jersey irrespective of where the living will originates. Alternatively, if the living will was executed in accordance with the laws of Florida, then the living will is valid in this State. With that said, I recommend that clients have a "New Jersey living will."

One of the major benefits of a living will is that the New Jersey Advance Directives Act for Health Care provides immunity for health care providers and institutions that rely upon the living will/representative in implementing health care decisions for the declarant.[74] For instance, if a living will is valid and effective and if the physician relies upon the living will, then the physician cannot be sued for implementing the directives of the document or the representative.

I think health care providers and institutions would feel more comfortable relying upon a living will that discusses the laws of New Jersey and that is from this state. So, I frequently advise clients to have a "New Jersey living will" and to execute a living will in any other state in which the client may spend a substantial amount of time. For instance, many New Jersey residents have a vacation home in Florida. I think it is advisable for these clients to have a "New Jersey" living will and a "Florida living will."

Most lawyers do not know what the laws of another state or country provide, so I don't feel comfortable that a doctor, nurse, or hospital staff member will know whether a "Florida living will" was validly executed.

## 2-13 WHAT IF A DOCTOR OR HOSPITAL REFUSES TO HONOR THE LIVING WILL?

A common refrain that clients will voice is a concern that a doctor or a hospital will simply ignore the declarant's living will and do

73. N.J.S.A. 26:2H-59(a).

74. N.J.S.A. 26:2H-73.

whatever the doctor or hospital thinks is best, which could mean too little or too much care, depending on the situation. Invariably, a client will tell you about some family member or friend who had a living will and the "doctor simply ignored it."

I have no doubt that some health care providers have ignored living wills, but the law does not permit a living will to be disregarded.[75] While a health care provider or institution could refuse to honor a living will for various reasons, for instance, on religious or moral grounds, the health care provider or institution is obligated to transfer the declarant's care to another health care provider or institution that will honor the declarant's health care decisions.[76]

A provider or institution cannot simply ignore a living will and basically say, "We're going to do it my way." Health care decisions are one of the most personal decisions an individual can make. No one other than the person or his designated representative gets to make those decisions for the declarant, legally speaking. The instructive directives in the living will or directives of the proxy must be honored, as long as those directives are within the bounds of the Act.

Failure of a health care provider or institution to abide by the provisions of the Act can result in the punishment of the provider or institution.[77]

## 2-13:1 Resort to Courts

Because clients fear the reluctance of health care professionals and institutions to honor their health care directives, it is appropriate to draft a "resort to courts" provision in the living will. Essentially, such a provision authorizes the representative to file a suit against a professional or institution that fails to abide by the directives in the living will or those made by the representative and grants the representative access to the declarant's assets to the extent necessary to retain legal counsel in order to institute the suit.

Such a provision in a living will can serve both a psychological and practical purpose. A health care professional or institution

---

75. N.J.S.A. 26:2H-78.
76. N.J.S.A. 26:2H-62(b), (c); N.J.S.A. 26:2H-65(b).
77. N.J.S.A. 26:2H-78.

that is reluctant to abide by the terms of the Act may realize that the declarant has thought such a circumstance through and think twice about their decision to refuse to honor the living will. From a practical standpoint, such a provision gives the representative real authority to enforce the provisions of the living will, if necessary.

## 2-14 ORGAN DONATION

Frequently, a living will addresses organ donation, if the declarant is so inclined.[78] For those clients who believe that health care providers write-off patients who have signed living wills for dead, donating their organs tends to be the straw that breaks to donate their organs, then their health care providers will let them die so that their organs can be harvested.

Other clients believe that they are too old to donate their organs. I have spoken with several physicians, and apparently, some parts of the human body, such as bones, may be available for transplant to others even if those parts come from elderly individuals.

Sometimes, a medical condition may prevent donation. For instance, if the client suffers from cancer, his organs would probably be non-suitable for donation.

Whether or not an individual wishes to donate their organs after they die is a highly personal issue. The point here is that if the client wishes to donate his organs, this issue can be addressed in his living will. The declarant can specifically state that he wishes to donate his organs for transplant or even that he wishes to donate his body or organs for research.

## 2-15 REVOCATION OF THE LIVING WILL

A living will can be revoked in writing, orally, or by any other act evidencing an intent to revoke the document.[79] The oral or written revocation must be communicated to the representative, physician, nurse, other health care professional, or other reliable witness. An example of an "other act" would be the destruction of the living will by the declarant by tearing or burning the document. In addition,

---

78. 26:6-66 et seq., discussing the New Jersey Hero Act, which deals with the donation of organs and tissue.

79. N.J.S.A. 26:2H-57(b).

the execution of a subsequent living will revokes a prior living will. A revocation is effective upon communication to any person capable of transmitting the information about the revocation to the representative, attending physician, nurse, or other health care professional responsible for the declarant's care.

The designation of a spouse as a declarant's representative shall be revoked upon the divorce of the declarant and representative.[80]

## 2-16 PHYSICIAN ORDERS FOR LIFE-SUSTAINING TREATMENT ACT OR POLST

In 2012, the Physician Orders for Life-Sustaining Treatment Act, or POLST, was enacted.[81] POLST is designed to complement the New Jersey Advanced Health Care Act[82] by converting a person's medical wishes regarding life-sustaining treatment, such as those expressed in a living will, into medical orders.[83]

POLST establishes a standardized, brightly-colored form, called the POLST form, containing immediately-actionable medical orders that address a range of life-sustaining interventions and patient preferences as to intensity of treatment.[84] The POLST form is particularly appropriate for persons with a compromised medical condition or terminal illness.[85] A POLST form is signed by the patient's attending physician or advanced practice nurse and is more readily available to medical professionals than a living will, which, the Legislature held, are often locked in drawers and unavailable to medical professionals.[86]

A POLST form shall be deemed complete if it contains the following: (1) the patient's health care preferences,[87] (2) the voluntary signature of the patient who has decision-making capacity or the signature of the patient's representative, such as a

80. N.J.S.A. 26:2H-57(c).
81. N.J.S.A. 26:2H-129 et seq.
82. N.J.S.A. 26:2H-53 et seq.
83. N.J.S.A. 26:2H-130(b).
84. N.J.S.A. 26:2H-130(c).
85. N.J.S.A. 26:2H-130(d).
86. N.J.S.A. 26:2H-130(e), (f).
87. N.J.S.A. 26:2H-134(b)(1).

designated representative under a living will,[88] and (3) the signature of the patient's attending physician or the signature of an advanced practice nurse (APN).[89] Health care professionals[90] and emergency care providers[91] are required to honor the patient's preferences stated in a completed POLST form.[92]

The fact that emergency care providers, such as paramedics, must honor a completed POLST form is a key differentiating feature of a POLST form as compared to a living will. Emergency responders will not abide by the patient's preferences stated in a living will; if the family did not want emergency responders to provide medical treatment to the individual who signed a living will, the family should not have called the emergency responders in the first place. Once called, the emergency responders will respond and will attempt to stabilize the patient, even if the patient has a properly executed living will.

Contrariwise, emergency responders must abide by the patient's preferences stated in a POLST form, because a POLST form, unlike a living will, contains medical orders.

Under various circumstances specified in the POLST Act, the POLST form can be modified by the attending physician, APN, patient or patient's representative.[93] The overriding intent of the Act is to fulfill the patient's health care preferences in accordance with the terms of the Act.

Similar to the New Jersey Advanced Directives for Health Care Act, the POLST Act grants immunity to health care professionals,[94] health care institutions[95] and emergency care providers[96] who abide by the patient's preferences stated in a POLST form.[97] Similarly, as with the health care act, the POLST Act imposes

---

88. N.J.S.A. 26:2H-134(b)(2).
89. N.J.S.A. 26:2H-131 (defining "Advanced practice nurse"), N.J.S.A. 26:2H-134(b)(3).
90. N.J.S.A. 26:2H-131 (defining "Health care professional").
91. N.J.S.A. 26:2H-131 (defining "Emergency care provider").
92. N.J.S.A. 26:2H-134(a).
93. N.J.S.A. 26:2H-135.
94. N.J.S.A. 26:2H-131 (defining "Health care professional").
95. N.J.S.A. 26:2H-131 (defining "Health care institution").
96. N.J.S.A. 26:2H-131 (defining "Emergency care provider").
97. *Compare* N.J.S.A. 26:2H-138 *with* N.J.S.A. 26:2H-73.

liability on those health care professionals who fails to honor a POLST form.[98]

In short, the POLST form is appropriate for those individuals who have compromised health and who want a medical order regarding their treatment preferences. A POLST form is inappropriate for healthy individuals.

---

98. *Compare* N.J.S.A. 26:2H-139 *with* N.J.S.A. 26:2H-78.

# Chapter 3

# The Last Will and Testament

## 3-1 WHAT IS A WILL?

A last will and testament (Will) is a document the primary purpose of which is to distribute the estate of a deceased individual, typically to his family or friends.[1] But a Will can also be a document through which the decedent ensures that a beneficiary's inheritance is managed properly, through the use of a testamentary trust. A Will can be a document through which the decedent provides for the care and custody of his minor or disabled child, through the nomination of a guardian.

With a Will, a decedent can nominate whom he wants to handle his estate and to manage the money that he has left in trust for his beneficiaries. Through a Will, a decedent can allocate estate and inheritance tax among the various beneficiaries.

An individual might die with $20,000 or $20,000,000, and his Will could be the document that manages his assets after his death. For many people, no single document may be as important as a Will given its potential for sweeping control over the decedent's assets and affairs.

A Will is merely a contingent document until the testator dies; it is contingent upon the testator's death before becoming a legally binding document. Putting aside a testator who becomes mentally incapacitated after the execution of his Will, the testator can modify or revoke his Will any time he wants before his death.[2] For that reason, a Will has no effect whatsoever until the death of the testator.

---

1. N.J.S.A. 3B:1-2 (defining "Will").
2. *But see* N.J.S.A. 3B:1-4, *Contractual arrangements relating to death.*

## 3-2 TESTATOR/TESTATRIX

A testator or testatrix,[3] depending upon the person's gender, is the person who makes a last will and testament. While a person can draft his own Will, most have an attorney draft the Will for them.

## 3-3 REQUIREMENTS OF A WILL

A document must satisfy certain requirements in order to be a Will.[4] The document must be in writing in order to be a Will;[5] New Jersey does not recognize verbal Wills.

The testator must have signed the Will in his own hand; alternatively, the Will must have been signed in the testator's name by an individual other than the testator who signed the testator's name in the testator's conscious presence and at the testator's direction.[6] In other words, if a testator is unable to sign the document, perhaps because of paralysis suffered from a stroke, the testator can instruct another person to sign the document for him if the testator is present during the signing and if the testator is conscious and competent to make a Will.

The fact that the testator does not need to sign the Will himself is a bit disconcerting even to the experienced elder law practitioner. A Will can be a very important legal document that could control most, if not all, of the decedent's estate. The fact that the testator does not have to sign the Will with his own hand scares some practitioners when they are presented with a client who cannot sign because of some physical infirmity that prevents him from physically signing the document.

But the law does permit another individual to sign for the testator in the testator's presence and at the testator's direction. What is important is that the testator is having someone sign his name of his own free will and that the testator has the requisite mental capacity to execute a Will.

The Will must also be signed by two individuals who either witnessed the testator (or his designee) sign the Will or who

---

3. N.J.S.A. 3B:1-2 (defining "Testator" in a gender neutral manner).

4. N.J.S.A. 3B:3-1 et seq.

5. N.J.S.A. 3B:3-2(a)(1).

6. N.J.S.A. 3B:2-1(a)(2).

witnessed the testator acknowledge the fact that he signed the Will or acknowledged the document to be his Will.[7] The witnesses must sign the document "within a reasonable time" after witnessing the signature of the testator or the testator's acknowledgement of his signature on the Will.[8]

## 3-4 TYPES OF WILLS

### 3-4:1 Self-Proving Will

A Will that satisfies the requirements of N.J.S.A. 3B:3-2 can be made self-proving if the Will satisfies several other requirements.[9] If a Will is self-proving, the proponent of the Will after the death of the testator does not have to prove the genuineness of the signatures of the testator or the witnesses; the original Will can simply be admitted to probate before the appropriate surrogate without further proof as to its validity or genuineness; this is called submitting a Will to probate in "common form."[10]

In order to be self-proving, the testator must sign an acknowledgement of the Will and the witnesses must sign affidavits and all of the signatures must be acknowledged before an individual authorized to take oaths, such as a notary public or attorney-at-law.[11] The wording of the testator's acknowledgement and the affidavits of the witnesses is provided in the self-proving statute.

### 3-4:2 Holographic Will

A holographic Will is an exception to the general requirements of a Will that are discussed immediately above.[12] A holographic Will is a Will the material portions of which are in the testator's handwriting. In order to be valid, a holographic Will must also be signed by the testator.

---

7. N.J.S.A. 3B:3-2(a)(3).

8. N.J.S.A. 3B:3-2(a)(3).

9. N.J.S.A. 3B:3-4.

10. N.J. Ct. R. 4:80-1 et seq.

11. N.J.S.A. 41:2-1.

12. N.J.S.A. 3B:3-2(b), *In the Matter of the Probate of the Alleged Will and Codicil of Louise Macool, deceased*, 416 N.J. Super. 298, 308 (App. Div. 2010).

### 3-4:2.1 Material Portions

Note that the "material portions" of the Will must be in the testator's handwriting. If the administrative provisions of the Will were typed, for instance, but the material portions of the Will were in the testator's handwriting, then this requirement of the holographic Will statute would be satisfied.

Contrariwise, if the "Will" were a wholly typed document, which is probably the way more and more people would draft a document given the pervasiveness of computers, and signed by the testator, the "material portions" requirement would not be satisfied.

### 3-4:2.2 Signature of Testator

Unlike with a Will that satisfies the requirements of N.J.S.A. 3B:3-2, which permits a testator to merely direct another individual to sign the Will for him, the testator must sign a holographic Will himself; the testator of a holographic Will cannot direct another individual to sign for him.[13]

Since a holographic Will has no witnesses, the validity of the document can easily be questioned, so the testator must sign the document himself.

## 3-4:3 Writing Intended to Be a Will

A Will that does not satisfy the requirements of N.J.S.A. 3B:3-2 (either as a "standard will" or a holographic Will) may still be considered a "writing intended to be a Will."[14] In order to be considered a writing intended to be a Will, the proponent of the document must establish by clear and convincing evidence that the decedent intended the document to constitute his Will.

The case law interpreting the writing intended to be a Will statute is still evolving. A document that the testator failed to sign has been held to be a writing intended to be Will.[15] A photocopy of a

---

13. N.J.S.A. 3B:3-2(b).

14. N.J.S.A. 3B:3-3.

15. *In the Matter of the Estate of Richard D. Ehrlich, deceased*, 427 N.J. Super. 64 (App. Div. 2012), *In the Matter of the Probate of the Alleged Will and Codicil of Louise Macool, deceased*, 416 N.J. Super. 298, 311-312 (App. Div. 2010).

letter with notations in the margin may be admitted to probate as a writing intended to be a Will.[16]

## 3-5 WHO MAY WITNESS A WILL?

The basic requirements of a Will are that the signature of the testator or the testator's acknowledgement of his signature or his acknowledgement of the document as his Will be witnessed by two people.[17] But what are the requirements to be a witness?

The general rule is that any person competent to be a witness may act as a witness to a Will and testify regarding the execution of the Will.[18] Since young children have been held to be competent witnesses, the general requirements of a witness are not very high.

Furthermore, a statute specifically permits an individual who is interested in the Will to be a witness.[19] In other words, one of the beneficiaries of the Will could be a witness to the testator's signature or his acknowledgement.

Most practitioners would not permit a young child to act as a witness to a Will or someone under the age of eighteen for that matter, though the law does not prohibit using individuals under the age of eighteen. Moreover, experienced practitioners would not use an interested party to be a witness to the Will if there is some expectation that the Will may be challenged.

For instance, it would be perfectly acceptable to use an adult child of the testator as one of the witnesses to the Will if the Will devises everything equally to the all the children. On the other hand, using an interested party to a Will that disinherits one of the testator's children would not be advisable.

## 3-6 COMPETENCY TO MAKE A WILL

In order to make a Will, a testator must have a certain level of mental capacity. This level of mental capacity is typically referred to as testamentary mental capacity.[20]

---

16. *In the Matter of the Estate of Leigh Cameron Randall*, 2011 N.J. Super. Unpub. Lexis 808 (Ch. Div. 2011).

17. N.J.S.A. 3B:3-2(a)(3).

18. N.J.S.A. 3B:3-7.

19. N.J.S.A. 3B:3-8.

20. *In the Matter of Will of Liebl*, 260 N.J. Super. 519, 524 (App. Div. 1992).

In addition, an individual can only make a Will if he has attained the age of eighteen.[21]

## 3-6:1 Testamentary Mental Capacity

Testamentary mental capacity has five key components. The testator must be able to comprehend the property of which he is disposing through the Will, he must know who the natural objects of his bounty are, he must understand the nature of the transaction in which he is engaging, and he must understand the relationship of each of these factors to one another; finally, he must understand the distributions that are being made under the Will.[22]

Testamentary mental capacity is a very low-level of mental capacity. While the factors sound daunting when they are listed, in actuality, requiring that an individual understand these factors is not asking for much. Basically, the testator needs to have a basic understand of his assets, know who his relatives are, know that he is signing a Will, and come up with a plan for disposing of his assets.

### 3-6:1.1 Knowledge of Assets

The testator must have a basic knowledge of his assets. While he does not have to be able to list all the assets in exacting detail, he should have a basic understanding of his worth.

### 3-6:1.2 Natural Objects of Testator's Bounty

The testator must know who the natural objects of his bounty are. In other words, he must know who his relatives are. For instance, if the testator has four children but can only remember three of them, then he does not know who the natural objects of his bounty are.

### 3-6:1.3 Nature of the Transaction

The testator must understand that he is signing a Will and what the purpose of a Will is.

---

21. N.J.S.A. 3B:3-1.

22. *Matter of Will of Liebl*, 260 N.J. Super. 519, 524 (App. Div. 1992).

### 3-6:1.4 Relationship of the Factors

The testator must be able to understand how the aforementioned factors work together. For instance, he must understand that he is signing a Will that disposes of his assets to his children.

### 3-6:1.5 Dispositional Plan

Finally, the testator must be able to come up with a plan for the disposition of his assets. Typically, this would entail telling his attorney to whom he wishes to give his property. The lawyer would put the plan in writing for him.

A dispositional plan can be quite simple ("I give everything to my children, to be divided equally among them") or it can be quite complex with multiple beneficiaries receiving varying percentages of the estate or dollar devises.

## 3-7 UNDUE INFLUENCE

A Will cannot be the product of undue influence.[23] If the Will is the product of the undue influence of another person, then the document does not reflect the will of the testator.

A testator can be influenced to make a Will, but he cannot be unduly influenced. "Undue influence" is a type of influence that robs the testator of his free agency preventing him from following his own dispositive plan and instead following the plan of another individual.[24]

A Will is called a Will because it is a document that reflects the free will of the testator, what the testator wanted with respect to his estate. If a Will is the product of undue influence, then it is not the Will of the testator; instead, it is the Will of the person exerting the undue influence over the testator.

## 3-8 PERSONAL PROPERTY MEMORANDUM

Many people wish to give items of tangible personal property to family or friends. The Probate Code permits a person to create a tangible personal property list.[25] A tangible personal property

---

23. *Haynes v. First Nat'l State Bank*, 87 N.J. 163, 176 (1981).
24. *Haynes v. First Nat'l State Bank*, 87 N.J. 163, 176 (1981).
25. N.J.S.A. 3B:3-11.

list is a document separate and apart from the Will, but it is referred to in the Will.

So, for instance, the Will may say, "I give certain tangible personal property according to a written list in my handwriting or signed by me that describes the property with reasonable certainty." The testator may or may not actually ever draft such a list, but by making that reference in the Will, the testator has the option of drafting a tangible person property list any time he wants.

As stated in the example, the list must be in the testator's handwriting or the testator must sign the list.[26] This is to be contrasted with the requirements for a holographic Will. A holographic Will, discussed above, must have its material portions in the testator's handwriting and the testator must sign the Will.[27] With the tangible personal property list, the list must be in the testator's handwriting or signed by him, not both. The list must also describe the tangible personal property being disposed of with reasonable certainty.

A person cannot devise money or real property through a tangible personal property list. Tangible personal property is, by definition, not real estate.

Referencing a tangible personal property list in a Will is very good practice. By making the reference, you give the client the opportunity to make such a list, even if the client never chooses to make such a list.

If the client does choose to make the list, the client can change the list any time he wants. So, if the client no longer owns the item of tangible personal property that he gave away through a list or if he changes his mind as to the identity of the recipient of a particular item, he can always change the list. On the other hand, if the tangible personal property were disposed of through the Will as opposed to through a list, the testator would have to change his Will to change the disposition of the item.

---

26. N.J.S.A. 3B:3-11.
27. N.J.S.A. 3B:3-2(b).

## 3-9 WHAT PROPERTY DOES A WILL CONTROL?

A Will can be a very powerful document—or not. Whether a Will controls a testator's estate or not depends, in large part, on how the testator has his assets titled.

It is important to make the client aware of the differences between probate property and non-probate property, because most people, if asked, would believe that their Will controls who gets their property after they die and this may or may not be true. Contrariwise, some people believe that a Will only controls the property that is listed in the Will; in reality, the vast majority of Wills do not list any property at all.

Whether or not a Will controls property depends on the characteristics of the property. A Will controls probate property. A Will does not control non-probate property. When a person dies, his property passes in one of three ways—either by contract, by operation of law or under his probate estate.

### 3-9:1 Non-Probate Property

A Will does not control non-probate property. Non-probate property is property that passes by contract or by operation of law.

#### 3-9:1.1 Property Passing by Contract

An example of property passing by contract would be a life insurance policy. A life insurance policy is a contract between the insurer and the insured to pay a certain sum of money upon the death of the insured. Most insurance policies provide the insured with the opportunity to name a beneficiary. If the insured does name a beneficiary, that beneficiary will receive the proceeds of the insurance. It is irrelevant what the insured's Will says about the life insurance; the life insurance company will pay out the proceeds to the named beneficiary.

#### 3-9:1.2 Property Passing by Operation of Law

An example of property passing by operation of law would be a deed held by husband and wife as tenants by the entirety.[28] If the husband were to pass away, his interest in the property would

28. N.J.S.A. 46:3-17.2.

automatically pass to his surviving wife by operation of law. It is irrelevant what the husband's Will says about who receives his interest in the property when he dies, his wife will become the owner in fee simple absolute after his death.

#### 3-9:1.3 Jointly-Held Property

Many assets that are jointly-held with another individual pass under a mixture of law and contract. For instance, a joint bank account passes to the surviving account holder by operation of law and by contract. The contract is the agreement between the account holders and the bank that directs that the account will pass to the surviving account holder upon the death of one of the account holders. The law is the Multi-Party Depositor Account Act, which directs that the account will pass to the surviving account holder upon one account holder's death.[29]

### 3-9:2 Probate Property

Property that does not pass by contract or by operation of law passes under the testator's probate estate and is controlled by his Will, if he has a valid Will. What passes under the probate estate could be a very small portion of the testator's estate or it could be a very large portion of the probate estate. It depends upon how the testator has titled his assets.

As an elder law practitioner, you are not going to title every asset that a client owns so that the asset passes under his Will. For one, the client may not want that to happen. The client may want certain assets to pass by contract or by operation of law. For another thing, the amount of time it would take an attorney to re-title each and every asset a client owns and the amount of money the attorney would have to bill his clients for that time would simply be prohibitive.

But it is good practice to give the client a heads up on how property passes after his death. A client should be informed as to how his estate passes after his death and, perhaps, disabused from the mistaken belief that a Will controls all assets (or only those assets listed in the Will).

---

29. N.J.S.A. 17:16I-2(d) (defining "joint account").

Assume that Mr. Smith owns a house worth $300,000 jointly with his wife. He also owns an IRA worth $500,000 that names his wife as beneficiary, and a bank account in his name alone worth $20,000. Mr. Smith's Will only controls the bank account, not the house or the IRA.

So, a Will could be very powerful, controlling all of a testator's estate, or relatively unimportant, controlling only a very small portion of the testator's estate.

## 3-10 TYPES OF DEVISES

A devise is the testamentary disposition of real or personal property.[30] Stated otherwise, a devise is when a testator gives some or all of his property to another person or entity through his Will. The word "devise" can be used as a noun or a verb.

There are several different types of devises, and the type of devise can matter, particularly if the estate has insufficient assets to pay all of the devises. Since, as discussed above, not all of a testator's assets pass under his Will as part of his probate estate, many testators put more devises in their Wills than their Wills control.

### 3-10:1 Specific Devise

A specific devise is a devise through which a testator gives away (devises) a specific asset to someone. A specific devise can only be satisfied by the delivery and receipt of the particular item devised.[31] For instance, "I give my car to my son" is an example of a specific devise.[32]

### 3-10:2 General Devise

A general devise is a devise of a certain sum of money. A general devise may be satisfied out of the general assets of the estate and is not paid out of specific property.[33] For instance, "I give $10,000 to my son" is an example of a general devise.

---

30. N.J.S.A. 3B:1-1 (defining "Devise").

31. *Estate of Raymond P. Lansing, by Marian E. Lansing, executrix v. State of New Jersey, Dept. of Treasury, Div. of Taxation and Sidney Glaser*, 6 N.J. Tax 137, 143 (1983).

32. *See* N.J.S.A. 3B:3-42 et seq. (establishing various rules for increases to and ademption of specific devises).

33. *Estate of Raymond P. Lansing, by Marian E. Lansing, executrix v. State of New Jersey, Dept. of Treasury, Div. of Taxation and Sidney Glaser*, 6 N.J. Tax 137, 143 (1983).

### 3-10:3 Residuary Devise

A residuary devise is a devise of the residue of the estate. A residuary devise is, essentially, giving away all of the remaining assets of the estate after the specific and general devises. For instance, "I give the remainder of my assets to my son" is an example of a residuary devise.

### 3-10:4 Abatement of Devises

What if a testator's estate is insufficient to satisfy all of the devises under his Will? For instance, assume that the testator has a probate estate that is worth $100,000, but the testator made twelve $10,000 general devises totaling $120,000 to twelve different people and two $5,000 devises to two additional people and a residuary devise to yet another person. Assume that the testator also specifically devises his car to yet another beneficiary.

Since the testator's estate is insufficient to satisfy the general devises and has no money remaining for the residuary devisee which beneficiary gets what amount of money? There is a statute dealing with the issue of abatement of devises.[34] That statute says that an estate abates in the following order:

1. First, property passing by intestacy;
2. Second, residuary devises;
3. Third, general devises; then
4. Finally, specific devises.

In our example, the decedent died with a Will, so no property passes under the intestate succession statute. Since the testator died with insufficient assets to pay the general devises, the residuary devise abates in its entirety, because residuary devises are the next to abate.

Devisees within the same class abate proportionately.[35] With the general devises, there are twelve devises of $10,000 and two devises of $5,000 and only $100,000 in estate. Each of the general devises are of an equal level of priority, that is, all of the devises are in the same class, that is, general devises, so they abate proportionately. The $5,000 devises would abate by a proportionate amount and the $10,000 would abate by a proportionate amount. Each of the

34. N.J.S.A. 3B:23-12.
35. N.J.S.A. 3B:23-12(e).

$10,000 devisees would receive approximately $7,142 and each of the $5,000 would receive approximately $3,571.

The specific devisee who received the car would not abate the devise if the car existed at the time of the testator's death.

A statute permits the testator to specify the order of abatement, thereby overriding the provisions of the standard abatement order.[36] In practice, very few Wills—none that the author has ever seen—address the order of abatement of devises. From a practical standpoint, it would be a difficult discussion to have with a client because a client thinks that his Will says these ten people are going to receive $10,000 and these two people are going to receive $5,000, so that is what is going to happen.

But then life happens. The testator goes to a nursing home for three years before he dies but after he signs his Will. His estate that was more than ample to satisfy the general devises and the residuary devise when he came to see you is now woefully insufficient. That is reality. Convincing the client of that reality, who will typically answer with a response such as "Just shoot me if that ever happens!" is easier said than done.

## 3-11 WAIVING THE PROBATE BOND

One of the most common clauses in a Will is the clause that waives the requirement that the executor post a probate bond to ensure his obligations.[37] A probate bond is similar to a policy of insurance.

If the Will fails to waive the requirement that the executor post a bond, which almost every Will does, then the executor would have to post a bond. If the estate were worth $400,000, the executor may be required to post a $400,000 bond. If the executor failed to fulfill his obligations, for instance, if the executor absconded with the estate's assets, failing to distribute assets to the beneficiaries and failing to pay creditors, the beneficiaries and creditors of the estate could request that the bonding company reimburse them for their losses that were caused by the malfeasance of the executor.[38]

A probate bond differs from a policy of insurance in that while the bonding company is obligated to compensate the beneficiaries

---

36. N.J.S.A. 3B:23-14.

37. N.J.S.A. 3B:15-1.

38. N.J.S.A. 3B:15-24 et seq.

and creditors, the bonding company has the right to sue the executor to recoup the monies they had to pay out.

While a probate bond is a good thing in that it provides insurance to the creditors and beneficiaries, it also costs the estate money. The more valuable the bond, the more money it costs the estate. For this reason, most Wills waive the requirement that the executor post a bond.

## 3-12 TESTAMENTARY TRUSTS

There are all types of trusts—revocable, irrevocable, living, testamentary—and there are even more reasons why people create a trust. A client might say to you something such as "My sister has a trust, so I thought I needed one too." The client will have no idea why her sister, who might even live in another state, has the trust. She might believe the sister's trust will eliminate estate tax or will protect the sister's money from a nursing home. Oftentimes, the client will talk about a "trust" as if there is one type of trust and the client wants that trust.

A trust is a fiduciary relationship wherein one party, the trustee, takes title to property and holds that property for the benefit of another person, aptly called the beneficiary.[39] A trust agreement or trust instrument is the legal document—typically drafted by an attorney—that details the terms of the trust.[40] A trust can be drafted to meet almost any need the grantor wants to achieve.[41]

A testamentary trust is a trust that exists in the last will and testament of the grantor.[42] As with the Will itself, a testamentary trust has no effect whatsoever until the testator dies.

From a conceptual standpoint, a testamentary trust is just additional wording in the Will. Many clients and advisors to clients (such as accountants or CPAs) after reviewing the Will say to the attorney, "I didn't see the trust," but what they fail to realize is that there is no separate trust document for a testamentary trust, in most instances. The testamentary trust agreement is simply

---

39. Restatement (Third) of Trusts §§ 2, 3.

40. Uniform Trust Code § 103(19) (defining "trust instrument"), Restatement (Third) of Trusts § 4 (defining "Terms of the trust").

41. Restatement (Third) of Trusts §§ 27, 29 (outlining purposes for which a trust can and cannot be created).

42. Restatement (Third) of Trusts § 17.

wording in the Will;[43] that wording might be one sentence in length or several pages in length.

Frequently, the Will fails to give the trust a name, so it is up to the executor or trustee (if the trustee is a different person than the executor) to give the trust a name. The trust might be contained in the third numbered paragraph of the Will, so the name might be something such as the "Article 3 Trust Under the Last Will and Testament of Jane Doe Dated September 5, 2000." Because names such as this are unwieldy and say nothing about the purpose for which the trust was created, it is probably advisable to give the trust a name in the Will, for instance, the "John Smith Special Needs Trust."

### 3-12:1 Trust for Minor

One type of trust that many people have drafted into their Wills is a trust for their minor children. As with any trust, the terms of a minor's trust can be anything the testator wants. It is the testator's money and he can put almost any term he wants on the trust that will hold his minor children's money.

The testator can direct how the money is to be spent. The testator can direct when the minor will receive the money free of trust. It is the testator's money and, as long as his limitations do not offend public policy,[44] it his money to direct any way he chooses.

It is wise to place a trust in a Will if minor children are beneficiaries under the Will. With limited exception,[45] an executor cannot distribute money directly to a minor. So, if a Will devises a substantial amount of money to a minor and fails to contain a trust for the minor, the executor will have to pay that money over to the surrogate to hold until the minor attains the age of majority or someone, typically a parent of the minor, will have to qualify as the guardian for the minor.[46]

Either solution involves cost and expense, and neither solution is as good as a trust can be. Whether the money is held with the parent as guardian for the minor or with the surrogate, the minor

---

43. Restatement (Third) of Trusts § 17(2)(c).
44. Restatement (Third) of Trusts § 29.
45. N.J.S.A. 3B:12-6.
46. N.J.S.A. 3B:12-12, N.J.S.A. 3B:12-51 et seq., *R.* 4:81-1 et seq.

has a right to the money when he attains the age of 18.[47] If, for instance, the testator devised $300,000 to a minor, the fact that the minor will receive $300,000 at the age of 18 is probably not a good thing. If the 18 year old is like many 18 year olds, that $300,000 probably will not be around by the time he is 20.

There is a statute that permits an interested party to petition the court to create a trust for a minor and that trust can be in effect long after the minor attains the age of majority; however, the statute only applies if the decedent died intestate.[48] The statute would not offer a solution for the estate of a decedent who died testate.

At the very least, assuming there are no minors who are direct beneficiaries, a well-drafted Will should contain a safety clause that permits the executor to continue to hold a minor beneficiary's inheritance in trust until the minor beneficiary attains the age of 18. If some of the direct beneficiaries are minors, the Will should contain a minor's trust.

### 3-12:2 Special Needs Trust

A special needs trust is a trust designed to preserve a disabled individual's eligibility for means-tested government programs, such as Medicaid, and to supplement the needs of the trust beneficiary.[49] Disabled individuals frequently receive needs-based governmental benefits, such as Medicaid[50] and Supplemental Security Income (SSI).[51] In order to receive these benefits, the individual must have limited assets.[52] The receipt of most any inheritance would disqualify the disabled individual from these needs-based benefits.

A special needs trust enables the beneficiary to receive his inheritance and maintain his eligibility for needs-based governmental programs. In addition, the money in the trust can be used to pay for items for which government benefits do not pay. For instance, a disabled person receiving SSI and Medicaid might

---

47. N.J.S.A. 3B:12-54, N.J.S.A. 3B:15-17.1., *R.* 4:57-2(b).
48. N.J.S.A. 3B:12-54.1.
49. 42 U.S.C. § 1396p(d)(4)(A), N.J.S.A. 3B:11-36 et seq.
50. 42 U.S.C. §§ 1396 et seq.
51. 42 U.S.C. §§ 1381 et seq.
52. N.J.A.C. 10:71-4.5.

have approximately $700 per month to pay for all of his needs. The funds in the trust can be used to supplement his needs.

The proper administration of a special needs trust is extremely important. If administered correctly, a special needs trust can be used to greatly enhance the disabled individual's life. If administered incorrectly, distributions from special needs trust can disqualify an individual from needs-based programs.

### 3-12:3 Credit Shelter Trust

A credit shelter trust is a testamentary trust commonly used for estate tax planning purposes. When planning for a married couple, a credit shelter trust—also called a by-pass trust or A/B trust—is designed to preserve the applicable exemption equivalent (the "credit") of the first spouse-to-die spouse against estate tax.[53] There are two estate taxes to which the estate of a deceased New Jersey resident may be subject, a federal estate tax and a New Jersey estate tax.

With the federal credit exemption amount now exceeding $5,000,000[54] and with a second-to-die spouse being able to elect to preserve the first spouse's credit against estate tax when filing the federal estate tax return, a concept known as "portability,"[55] credit shelter trusts have lost a lot of their utility for federal estate tax purposes. The fact of the matter is, few people die having estates in excess of $5,000,000 and of those that do, the ability of the surviving spouse to simply elect to preserve the deceased spouse's credit on the federal estate tax return removes much of the need to plan before the death of the first spouse.

But the utility of credit shelter trusts for New Jersey estate tax still exists for a great many clients. New Jersey's credit is only $675,000, and it has been at that level since 2001; moreover, unlike the federal credit that is indexed for inflation, the New Jersey credit is fixed. There are no known plans to increase the New Jersey credit. The New Jersey estate tax is based upon the federal estate tax as the federal estate tax existed on December 31, 2001,[56] so New Jersey's estate tax is, in essence, frozen in time.

---

53. N.J.S.A. 54:38-1.
54. 26 U.S.C. § 2010(c).
55. 26 U.S.C. § 2010(c)(2)(B).
56. N.J.S.A. 54:38-1.

For many New Jersey residents, $675,000 is not that much money when you consider that the house and life insurance proceeds are in the mix for purposes of calculating the gross estate that is subject to New Jersey estate tax. A person's home in New Jersey could easily be worth in excess of $400,000. Throw in a bit of life insurance and an IRA, and the decedent is over the $675,000 credit limit.

What the credit shelter trust is designed to do is preserve the credit of the first spouse to die. For instance, assume that Mr. and Mrs. Smith have an estate worth $1,000,000, including life insurance and their home. If Mr. Smith dies and has a Will that simply leaves the entirety of his estate to Mrs. Smith, then the Smiths failed to use any of Mr. Smith's credit against New Jersey estate tax.

There is no estate tax between spouses.[57] This is known as the unlimited marital deduction against estate tax. But because there is no tax, none of Mr. Smith's credit is used when he leaves his estate to Mrs. Smith.

Now, when Mrs. Smith dies and leaves her estate to the children, her estate will total $1,000,000. The New Jersey estate tax is, on average, about 10%, so a $1,000,000 estate, which exceeds the $675,000 credit by $325,000, would be subject to $33,000 in estate tax.

The Smiths could have avoided this tax by using credit shelter trusts in their Wills. The trusts would be in each of their Wills because you never know which spouse is going to die first. The trusts would be for each spouse's benefit, and as long as the trust contains an ascertainable distribution standard, meaning that the trust states that its principal can only be used for the health, maintenance, education and support of the surviving spouse, the surviving spouse could be the trustee of the trust.[58] In other words, the surviving spouse is the trustee of the trust that is for her benefit. If the trust permitted distributions to the spouse for any reason whatsoever without an ascertainable standard, then someone other than the spouse would have to be the trustee.

The assets of the Smiths would be divided so that Mr. Smith had $500,000 of assets in his name and Mrs. Smith had $500,000 of assets in her name. Now, when Mr. Smith dies, his $500,000 of

57. 26 U.S.C. § 2056.

58. N.J.S.A. 3B:11-4.1(a).

assets would pass to the trust. Since less than $675,000 passed to someone other than the spouse, that is, the trust, no tax is owed upon his passing. And, because $500,000 passed to something, the trust, other than Mr. Smith's surviving spouse, Mr. Smith's estate effectively uses $500,000 of Mr. Smith's $675,000 applicable exclusion amount.

When Mrs. Smith dies, her estate will now only be worth $500,000, not $1,000,000. Her $500,000 will pass to the children. The $500,000 from the trust will pass to the children, as remainder beneficiaries. Under this scenario, neither Mr. nor Mrs. Smith died with an estate exceeding $675,000, so no estate tax is owed.

The credit shelter trust just saved $33,000 in estate tax for the Smiths's children.

### 3-12:4 Spendthrift Trust

A spendthrift trust is a trust designed to protect the assets of the trust from the creditors of the trust's beneficiary. From time-to-time, the beneficiary of an estate has problems with creditors. The problem typically arises because the beneficiary spends more money than he makes. For this type of spendthrift beneficiary, the spendthrift trust was designed.

As long as the assets remain in the trust, the assets are protected from the creditors of the beneficiary. In a Will, the language associated with a spendthrift trust would be something such as the following:

> *Protective Provision*—All principal and income shall, until actual distribution, be free of debts, contracts, alienations, and anticipations of any beneficiary, and the same shall not be liable to any levy, attachment, execution, or sequestration while in the possession of my Executor or Trustee.

When the assets of the trust are distributed directly to the beneficiary of the trust, those assets, now in the hands of the beneficiary, become subject to the claims of the beneficiary's creditors. For this reason, the best approach would be for the trust to pay for items that the beneficiary needs directly. For instance, the trust would pay the beneficiary's rent or buy the beneficiary food.

Additional protections in the testamentary trust would include the ability of the trustee to make distributions at his absolute discretion.[59] Many testamentary trusts require the trustee to distribute assets to the beneficiary to meet the beneficiary's health, maintenance and support needs. Requiring the trustee to make these type of distributions means that the beneficiary can compel the trustee to make distributions to him for his health, maintenance and support, and if the beneficiary can compel distributions, his creditors may be able to compel distributions to him for these reasons.[60] On the other hand, if the trustee is able to make distributions (or not) at his sole discretion, then the beneficiary cannot compel distributions and his creditors, who can stand in the shoes of the beneficiary, also cannot compel the trustee to make distributions.

## 3-13 FIDUCIARIES

A fiduciary is an individual or entity that has an obligation to another to act in the best interest of that other individual or entity.[61] The fiduciary may be an executor who has an obligation to administer the estate of the decedent in the best interest of the beneficiaries. The fiduciary may be a trustee who has an obligation to invest and manage the assets of the trust in the best interest of the beneficiary, or the fiduciary may be a guardian who has an obligation to ensure the best interests of his ward.

### 3-13:1 Naming an Executor

When a testator chooses an executor, he should choose someone who is adept at handling financial matters and who is organized. Most of estate administration involves financial decisions—selling stocks, selling real estate, negotiating with creditors, accounting to beneficiaries.

Some clients will be concerned that a child whom they wish to name as an executor lives in another state, but many of the tasks that an executor performs can be accomplished from a distance. Mail can be forwarded and many financial matters can be handled online.

---

59. Restatement (Third) of Trusts § 60.

60. Restatement (Third) of Trusts § 60.

61. N.J.S.A. 3B:1-1 (defining "Fiduciary").

## 3-13:2 Naming a Trustee

Much like an executor, a trustee should be adept at handling financial matters and organized; however, because a trustee may serve for decades in his role—whereas an executor will only serve for nine months to two years, in most instances—the trustee will also need to get along with the beneficiary of the trust, so people skills are essential.

The beneficiary of the trust is going to be calling the trustee with some frequency. At times, maybe quite frequently, there will be conflicts between what the beneficiary wants and what the trustee believes to be in the best interest of the beneficiary. A good trustee will be able to resolve these conflicts and come to a resolution with the beneficiary.

Moreover, while financial affairs can be handled from afar, much as with an executor, a trustee should visit with the beneficiary to ascertain, firsthand, the needs of the beneficiary. It is difficult to be the trustee for a minor or disabled child when the trustee resides in California and the minor/disabled beneficiary lives in New Jersey. So, it would be best if the testator chose a trustee who lives near the beneficiary whenever possible.

The fact of the matter is that some things are easier said than done. A testator may not have a trusted individual who is willing to serve as trustee and lives near the beneficiary, so as the lawyer drafting the Will, that you do the best that you can given what the client has at his disposal.

## 3-13:3 Naming a Guardian

A guardian for a minor or disabled beneficiary is a surrogate parent to the beneficiary. The guardian makes decisions regarding living arrangements, healthcare, education and social matters.[62]

A testamentary guardian[63] does manage finances to some extent;[64] however, in most Wills that provide for minor beneficiaries, a testamentary trust is established for the minor and the trustee of that trust manages the assets that were devised to the minor.

---

62. N.J.S.A. 3B:12-51 et seq., N.J.S.A. 3B:12-56 et seq.

63. N.J.S.A. 3B:12-30 et seq.

64. N.J.S.A. 3B:12-52(b).

### 3-13:4 Separation of Powers

Should the testator name different people to perform each of these tasks? For instance, should the testator name one person to be the executor, another to be the trustee and yet another to be the guardian? Some attorneys believe that you should have a separation of powers, much as in accounting, where the same person doesn't perform more than one task. Designing the estate plan in this manner allows for checks-and-balances, wherein the trustee checks on the guardian and the guardian checks on the trustee, for instance.

Another line of thinking is that the fiduciaries are carrying out the duties that one person or two people as a team used to perform. Parents do not separate duties. One parent, typically, doesn't make all the financial decisions, while the other parent makes all the personal decisions. The parents share the load, each performing all the tasks of being a parent at various times.

Given the reality of life, some estate planners suggest naming the same person or persons to serve in the role of trustee and guardian. In this way, the "parent," that is, the guardian, can have access to pay for those personal decisions he has made; for instance, the guardian can pay for the soccer lessons for which he signed up the child.

The unified approach certainly has its benefits. The separation of powers approach is the safe approach but could prove unwieldy, particularly in those situations where a trust could go on for decades. There is no one right answer. The solution should be made in consultation with the client after explaining the pros and cons of each approach.

## 3-14 TAX ALLOCATION CLAUSES

No clause in a Will can be as important as the tax allocation clause, yet many attorneys overlook this clause when drafting a Will. If the estate is not subject to death taxes—federal estate, New Jersey estate or New Jersey inheritance tax—then the tax allocation clause isn't that important, but if the estate is subject to one or all of these taxes, the tax allocation clause can be extremely important.

Essentially, the tax allocation clauses, as the name suggests, allocates the death tax amongst the estate beneficiaries. The testator is devising his estate to the named beneficiaries. Since it is the testator's estate, the testator gets to decide which of the estate's beneficiaries will pay the death taxes associated with the inheritance.[65]

## 3-14:1 Proportionate Allocation

The testator can allocate the death taxes to the beneficiaries in proportion to the manner in which each beneficiary has caused tax to the estate. For instance, if beneficiary D's inheritance caused 15% of the New Jersey inheritance tax and beneficiary A's inheritance caused 0% of the tax, a tax allocation clause that allocates the tax proportionately to each beneficiary as that beneficiary's inheritance caused the tax would have beneficiary D paying 15% of the tax from his inheritance and beneficiary A paying 0% of the tax.

Perhaps because a proportionate allocation of tax appears inherently fair, this method of allocation is the default methodology by law for those Wills that fail to contain a tax allocation clause.[66] In other words, if the testator fails to state how the tax should be allocated, then the tax will be allocated proportionately to each beneficiary as that beneficiary's inheritance caused the tax. For this reason, some experienced elder law attorneys say that it would be better if the inexperienced practitioner failed to include a tax allocation clause in his Wills.

## 3-14:2 Residuary Allocation

A residuary tax allocation clause allocates the death tax caused by the estate to the residuary beneficiaries of the estate. So, for instance, if the testator devises $100,000 to one beneficiary, $200,000 to another beneficiary and the remainder of his estate to his spouse, his spouse will pay the estate or inheritance tax, if any, on the general devises even though a spouse typically inherits free of "death" tax.

A residuary tax clause can be very dangerous. Typically, the residuary beneficiaries are those individuals (or entities) whom the testator wishes to benefit the most through his estate, yet a residuary tax allocation clause could end up effectively causing the

---

65. N.J.S.A. 3B:24-2.

66. N.J.S.A. 3B:24-4.

residuary beneficiary to pay a large percentage of what would have been his inheritance in taxes to cover what the other beneficiaries received. In fact, with some estates, a residuary tax clause could end up depleting the entire residuary inheritance.

## 3-15 CREDITORS

Before a beneficiary receives his inheritance, the creditors of the estate must be paid. With most estates, this isn't an issue, but in some cases, the estate has insufficient assets with which to pay the debts of the estate. In these instances, the estate is said to be insolvent.[67]

### 3-15:1 Limitation of Creditors

In the ordinary course of administering an estate, an executor should wait nine months before distributing the assets of the estate to the beneficiaries. A statute gives creditors nine months to present their claims to the executor.[68] If an executor waits nine months before distributing the estate to the beneficiaries, creditors of the estate cannot sue the executor for distributing the estate's assets too quickly. If the executor fails to wait nine months before distributing the assets of the estate, the executor could be found personally liable for the debts of the estate because he failed to wait the statutory limitation period before making distributions to the beneficiaries.

The limitation on creditors does not limit the creditors' rights to sue on a debt owed by the decedent; the statute merely limits the ability of the creditors to sue the executor for distributing the assets of the estate too quickly. Most creditors have a contractual claim against the testator and his estate, so there would be a six year statute of limitations on such claims.[69]

### 3-15:2 Insolvency

Sometimes an estate has insufficient assets with which to pay its debts. In these circumstances, the estate is said to be insolvent. A statute establishes the priority of debts.[70] Provided the executor

---

67. N.J.S.A. 3B:22-2.
68. N.J.S.A. 3B:22-4.
69. N.J.S.A. 2A:14-1.
70. N.J.S.A. 3B:22-2.

pays the estate's debts according to this statute, the executor cannot be held liable for failing to pay some but not all of the estate's debts.

An executor would be advised to file an action in the superior court, probate part, seeking the court's judgment on the appropriateness of his proposed payment plan and putting the creditors on notice of the payment plan.[71] In this way, a creditor whom the executor has put in one priority or another has the opportunity to dispute his place in the pecking order of debt payment.

## 3-16 RELEASE AND REFUNDING BOND

Before making distributions to beneficiaries, an executor should obtain a release and refunding bond from each beneficiary.[72] A release and refunding bond is a two-part document.

The release is a declaration by a beneficiary that he releases the executor of his fiduciary obligations as executor of the estate. Since the executor is a fiduciary[73] who owes the duty of utmost care to the beneficiaries of the estate, it is appropriate that each beneficiary should release the executor his obligations before the executor makes distributions to the beneficiary.

The refunding bond is an agreement from the beneficiaries to remit to the executor their proportionate share of any debts that may become known to the executor after the distribution is made. For instance, assume that there are four beneficiaries of an estate and each beneficiary is entitled to an equal share of the estate. After the beneficiaries receive their inheritances, the executor learns of a $1,000 debt of the testator. The refunding bond, if signed by each beneficiary, obligates each beneficiary to remit his proportionate share of the debt, that is, $250, to the executor, so the executor can pay the debt.[74]

Realistically, an executor may not get the beneficiaries to remit their proportionate shares, but by waiting nine months before making distributions[75] and by having each beneficiary sign a release

---

71. N.J. Ct. R. 4:91-1 et seq. (governing procedure to declare an estate insolvent).

72. N.J.S.A. 3B:23-24.

73. N.J.S.A. 3B:1-1 (defining "Fiduciary").

74. N.J.S.A. 3B:23-41.

75. N.J.S.A. 3B:22-4.

and refunding bond,[76] the executor, as a fiduciary, has performed his duties with the utmost care, and the onus is now on the creditor to sue the beneficiaries of the estate to recover the money.

## 3-17 CONSTRUING THE WILL

From time to time, an issue arises as to the proper construction of the Will. Without going into great detail, the Probate Code devotes an article of title 3B to the proper construction of Wills, Article 4.[77]

The overarching rule of Will construction is that a Will should be interpreted in such a way as to give effect to the probable intent of the testator.[78] You can see this fact not only in case law but in the Probate Code. The writing intended to be a Will statute[79] goes far to ensure that the testator's intentions are fulfilled without regard to the formality that would typically be required when drafting a Will.[80]

## 3-18 AGREEMENT AMONG BENEFICIARIES

As discussed above, the guiding light for the interpretation of a Will is to follow the probable intent of the testator.[81] New Jersey law and its courts want to ensure that the probable intent of the testator is being followed above all else when construing a Will.

With that said, the beneficiaries of an estate are free to change the terms of the Will as they see fit, subject to the rights of creditors and taxing authorities.[82] In other words, if a beneficiary wants to disclaim his inheritance, he can.[83] If beneficiaries want to change the inheritances they will receive under the Will, and all of the beneficiaries agree to make the change, they can.[84]

Beneficiaries cannot change the rights of creditors or taxing authorities with their private agreement, but otherwise, the

---

76. N.J.S.A. 3B:23-24.
77. N.J.S.A. 3B:3-32 et seq.
78. *Engle v. Siegel*, 74 N.J. 287 (1977), *Fidelity Union Trust v. Robert*, 36 N.J. 561 (1962).
79. N.J.S.A. 3B:3-3.
80. N.J.S.A. 3B:3-2.
81. *Engle v. Siegel*, 74 N.J. 287 (1977), *Fidelity Union Trust v. Robert*, 36 N.J. 561 (1962).
82. N.J.S.A. 3B:23-9.
83. N.J.S.A. 3B:9-1 et seq.
84. N.J.S.A. 3B:23-9.

beneficiaries of an estate are free to change the terms of the Will in any manner in which they can come to agreement.

## 3-19 THE ORIGINAL WILL

It is important for an executor to present the original Will of the testator for probate. Only the original of the Will can be admitted before the surrogate of the appropriate county in common form.[85]

If the executor does not have the original of the Will, the surrogate will not act,[86] and the executor must petition the superior court, probate part, to admit the copy of the Will to probate.

### 3-19:1 Admitting a Copy of a Will to Probate

A copy of a Will can be admitted to probate, but the executor would have to petition the court to have the copy admitted to probate.[87] The executor would have to put the beneficiaries of the Will and heirs of the testator on notice of the action to probate the copy of the Will, because the interests of these individuals may be adversely affected by the admission of the copy to probate. For instance, perhaps the Will of which the executor has only a copy disinherits a person who would otherwise receive a share of the decedent's estate by way of intestate succession.

So, the admission of a copy of a Will to probate is not a sure thing. Even in those instances in which no one objects to the admission of the copy to probate, admitting a copy of a Will to probate costs far more money than admitting an original Will to probate would cost.

The lesson is that the testator should ensure the proper storage of the Will.

### 3-19:2 Storing the Will

Many elder law practitioners offer to store the original of the Will for the testator. Storing the Will properly is a valuable service for the client, because it ensures that the executor will have the original Will to admit to probate after the testator's death.

---

85. N.J.S.A. 3B:3-18, 3B:3-19.
86. N.J. Ct. R. 4:82.
87. N.J. Ct. R. 4:82.

Storing the Will is also a way to drum up future business for the elder law practitioner. The executor will need to retrieve the original Will from the attorney. If the executor has questions or needs help in administering the estate, it is highly likely that the executor will seek advice from the attorney who drafted the Will.

## 3-20 INTESTATE SUCCESSION

What if the decedent failed to have a Will drafted for him? Some people believe that if they fail to have a Will drafted, their estate will go to the State of New Jersey. While this is untrue, in this instance, fear is a good thing, because it is important for every adult to have a Will.

In the absence of a Will, a series of statutes determines the person or persons who will share in the decedent's estate.[88] These statutes are known as the intestate succession statutes. In essence, the people who will receive the decedent's estate are his closest relatives, those related to him by marriage or blood.

While the instate succession statutes are a great safety measure, intestate succession has its limitations. For one thing, the decedent may not have wished to leave his estate in the manner that the intestate succession statutes provide. Or the decedent may not have wished the beneficiaries to receive the estate in the manner in which they will under the intestate succession statutes.

A minor child will receive his inheritance directly under the intestate succession statutes, but because he is a minor, a guardian will need to be appointed to hold his assets until he attains the age of 18. A disabled child will receive his inheritance directly, causing him to lose any means-tested government benefits that he would be entitled to receive but for the inheritance.

Dying intestate is also more expensive than dying with a Will. When a person dies without a Will, an administrator will need to be appointed to handle his estate. One of the most common clauses in a Will is a clause waiving the requirement that the executor post a bond. With an intestate estate, no Will exists, so the decedent never waived the requirement to post a bond, so the administrator must post a bond, which costs the estate money, more money than it would have cost to have a Will drafted.

---

88. N.J.S.A. 3B:5-1 et seq.

# Chapter 4

# The Revocable Living Trust

## 4-1 WHAT IS A TRUST?

A "trust" is actually a fiduciary relationship regarding property.[1] A trust arises out of a manifestation of an intention to create a fiduciary relationship between the trustee and the beneficiary. A trust subjects the trustee to certain duties in dealing with the property of the trust for the beneficiary.

When a person talks about a "trust," they are often talking about the "trust agreement," the document that specifies the terms of the trust.[2] A trust agreement is the instrument that contains the terms of the trust.[3] By itself, a trust agreement is not a trust. A trust does not come into being until such time as there is property being held by the trustee for the beneficiary.[4]

A revocable trust is a trust that the grantor can revoke without the consent of the trustee or any party holding an adverse interest in the trust.[5] A revocable trust is often called a "Will substitute," because the primary purpose of a revocable trust is as a substitute for the last will and testament of the grantor.[6]

---

1. Restatement (Third) of Trusts § 2.
2. Uniform Trust Code § 103(19).
3. Restatement (Third) of Trusts § 4.
4. Restatement (Third) of Trusts § 2 cmt. (i).
5. Uniform Trust Code § 103(14).
6. Restatement (Third) of Trusts § 11 cmt. on subsection (2): (b).

### 4-1:1 Grantor/Settlor

The grantor (or settlor) is the individual who creates the trust[7] or, in most cases, who contributes property to the trust.[8] From a practical standpoint, the grantor contacts his attorney and asks his attorney to draft a trust agreement for him, establishing the terms of the trust he is seeking to create.

If more than one person contributes property to a trust, then each person is a grantor with respect to the property he contributed to the trust.[9]

### 4-1:2 Trustee

The trustee is the person or entity (such as a bank) who holds property in the trust.[10] The trustee is a fiduciary.[11] The trustee has an obligation to invest the assets of the trust in a prudent manner.[12]

The trustee can only distribute assets to the beneficiary in accordance with the terms of the trust agreement. A grantor might grant a trustee very broad (or even absolute) discretion in making distributions[13] from the trust or the grantor might establish stringent parameters for making distributions from the trust to the beneficiary.

The grantor establishes the trust and the grantor places his assets into the trust. It is the grantor's choice to establish the trust in the first instance, so it is the grantor's choice as to the terms of the trust. As long as the terms of the trust do not violate public policy and refraining from having an unlawful purpose,[14] the terms the grantor places on the trust and the extent of the trustee's authority is up to the grantor.

---

7. Restatement (Third) of Trusts § 3(1).

8. Uniform Trust Code § 103(15).

9. Uniform Trust Code § 103(15).

10. Restatement (Third) of Trusts § 3(3).

11. N.J.S.A. 3B:1-1 (defining "Fiduciary"), Restatement (Third) of Trusts § 2 cmt. b., Uniform Trust Code Article 8, *Duties and Powers of Trustee*.

12. N.J.S.A. 3B:20-11.1 et seq., Uniform Trust Code Article 9.

13. Uniform Trust Code § 504.

14. *Girard Trust Company v. Schmitz*, 129 N.J. Eq. 444, 461 (Ch. 1941), Restatement (Third) of Trusts § 29, Uniform Trust Code § 404.

### 4-1:3 Beneficiary

The beneficiary, as the word states, is the individual whom the trust was designed to benefit.[15] A beneficiary is a person who has a present or future interest in the trust.[16] A beneficiary's right to the assets of the trust is determined by the grantor when the grantor establishes the trust or upon modification of the terms of the trust if the trust is revocable.

## 4-2 CHARACTERISTICS OF TRUSTS

A trust can have various characteristics. When you meet with clients, they often speak about "a trust" as if there were only one trust or as if there were several trusts in existence and you just had to pull the trust they wanted down from a shelf in your office, much like a candy vending machine.

The fact of the matter is that a trust is (or certainly can be) a highly specific document tailored to the needs of the client. The client—who is typically the grantor of the trust—establishes the terms of the trust. The client tells you, as his lawyer, what he is trying to accomplish and it is up to you to draft the trust in accordance with those goals. It is often beneficial to ask the client "What are you trying to accomplish with a trust?"

While many clients have very similar goals (for instance, most clients seeking to establish a trust for a minor beneficiary want similar terms in the trust), a trust can be individualized to the client's and beneficiary's needs and desires.

When looking at the characteristics of a trust, there seem to be several pairs of trust characteristics. A trust can be revocable or irrevocable. A trust can be a grantor trust or a non-grantor trust. A trust can be a living trust or a testamentary trust.

These primary characteristics of a trust are discussed immediately below.

### 4-2:1 Revocable

A revocable trust is a trust the can be revoked or the terms of which can be modified in whole or in part.[17] So, for instance,

---

15. Restatement (Third) of Trusts § 3(4), Uniform Trust Code § 103(3).

16. N.J.S.A. 3B:1-1 (defining "Beneficiary").

17. Restatement (Third) of Trusts § 25, Uniform Trust Code § 103(14).

Mr. Smith establishes a trust for his benefit for the remainder of his life then for the benefit of his children after his death. Mr. Smith reserves the right to change the terms of the trust any time he wishes or to revoke the trust any time he wishes. This would be a true revocable trust.

Revocable trusts are frequently used as Will-substitutes, that is, as a substitute for the last will and testament of the grantor.[18] With a revocable trust, the grantor is reserving the right to change the trust any time he wishes during his life, but the terms of the trust can continue beyond the grantor's life. After the grantor's death, the revocable trust becomes irrevocable because the grantor, who reserved the right to modify or revoke the trust, has died, and no person has the right to modify or revoke the trust after the grantor's death.

This is very similar to a last will and testament. With a Will, the testator can change the terms of the Will at any time during his life, but after his death, the Will becomes irrevocable.

The primary difference between a living trust and a Will is that a Will is a contingent document during the testator's life. The Will only becomes effective upon the testator's death, so the effectiveness of a Will is contingent upon the testator's death. On the other hand, a revocable trust can have effectiveness during the life of the grantor, though the terms of the trust can be modified or revoked during the grantor's life. After the grantor's death, the trust becomes irrevocable.

The fact that a revocable living trust is effective during the grantor's life,[19] which is a key factor that differentiates a revocable living trust from a Will, opens up planning opportunities with a living trust that do not exist with a Will. These planning opportunities will be discussed below.

### 4-2:2 Irrevocable

An irrevocable trust is a trust the terms of which cannot be modified.[20] As with all trusts, there are various reasons why a grantor may want to create an irrevocable trust. For instance, a

---

18. Restatement (Third) of Trusts § 11(2) cmt. on subsection (2): (b).
19. Restatement (Third) of Trusts § 25.
20. Uniform Trust Code § 602(a).

grantor may wish to make a gift to a trust that will be a completed gift for purposes of federal gift tax and federal and New Jersey estate tax. A grantor may wish to make a gift to a trust that will remove assets from his name for purposes of potential Medicaid eligibility.

In addition, some trusts that start out revocable can become irrevocable. A revocable living trust that a grantor may have established as a substitute for his last will and testament becomes an irrevocable trust upon the death of the grantor.

### 4-2:3 Grantor Trust

A grantor trust, also called an intentionally defective trust, is a trust that permits the grantor of the trust to be taxed on the income that the trust earns.[21] In some cases, the grantor may wish to be taxed on the income of the trust in order to achieve a better income tax rate.

A trust pays tax at the same tax rates as an individual; however, the tax brackets of a trust are compressed, so a trust reaches the highest income tax bracket much quicker than an individual does.[22] So, a trust is effectively taxed at higher rates than individuals in most instances.

For this reason, it is sometimes advisable (as long as it does not interfere with the overall purpose of the trust) to have the grantor pay the tax on the income that the trust earns. Drafting the trust as a grantor trust can accomplish this goal.

There are various ways to make a trust a grantor trust. The grantor trust rules are found at sections 671 through 679 of the Internal Revenue Code. A revocable trust would be a grantor trust.[23] Since the grantor has reserved the right to revoke the trust, the grantor is treated as the taxable entity for purposes of income tax.

But the reservation of certain other powers over the trust can also cause the trust to be treated as a grantor trust. The reservation of a more subtle power may achieve the dual result of making the trust a grantor trust and the primary purpose of the trust, for

21. 26 U.S.C. §§ 671 to 679.

22. http://www.irs.gov/pub/irs-drop/rp-13-15.pdf.

23. 26 U.S.C. § 676.

instance, removing the assets from the name of the grantor in order to achieve potential Medicaid eligibility at a future date.

### 4-2:4 Non-Grantor Trust

If a trust is not a grantor trust, the trust, not the grantor, pays the income tax on the income the trust receives. Many trusts are non-grantor trusts. An irrevocable trust through which the grantor does not reserve any retained interest would most likely be a non-grantor trust and the income the trust receives would be taxed at income tax rates applicable to a trust.

### 4-2:5 Living Trust

A living trust is a trust that is effective during the lifetime of the grantor, hence the word "living." Because the living trust is effective during the grantor's lifetime, the grantor can use the trust during his life to accomplish a goal. A living trust can be contrasted with a testamentary trust, which is a trust contained in the last will and testament of the testator and is only effective after the death of the testator.

A grantor might place a parcel of real property in a living trust in order to avoid probate in a foreign state. For instance, if Mr. Smith owns a condo in Florida, he can re-title the condo so that the trustee of the living trust holds title to his condo, and by doing this, Mr. Smith avoids having to probate his Will in Florida. This will be discussed more extensively below, but it gives a flavor for why a grantor would establish a living trust.

A living trust could be revocable or irrevocable. A living trust could be a grantor trust or a non-grantor trust.

### 4-2:6 Testamentary Trust

A testamentary trust is a trust that is created in the last will and testament of the grantor.[24] Since a Will is only effective after the death of the testator, a testamentary trust is only effective after the death of the grantor/testator.

For instance, Mr. Smith could not re-title his Florida condo into a testamentary trust during his life in order to avoid probate in Florida because his testamentary trust is not an effective trust

---

[24] Restatement (Third) of Trusts § 17.

until after Mr. Smith dies, at which point in time it is too late to avoid probate in Florida if Mr. Smith died owning the condo in his name.

A testamentary trust is a revocable trust during the lifetime of the grantor/testator and irrevocable after the death of the grantor/testator. A testamentary trust is a non-grantor trust.

## 4-3 PROPER EXECUTION OF A TRUST

What is the proper manner of executing a trust?[25] There are statutes that instruct a testator on the proper execution of a last will and testament,[26] but no statute governs the proper execution of a trust.[27]

At a minimum, a trust should be signed by the grantor and the trustee and their signatures should be acknowledged before an individual who is authorized to take oaths, for example, a notary public or an attorney at law.[28]

If the trust is a revocable living trust designed to be a substitute for a last will and testament, then the trust should be executed in accordance with the statutes governing the execution of Wills. In other words, the trust signature section should contain self-proving language that mirrors the self-proving language from the Wills statute.[29] Both the grantor and trustee should sign the trust in the presence of two witnesses. Both witnesses should sign the trust. Finally, all of the signatures should be acknowledged by an individual authorized to take oaths.

While this type of formal execution of a revocable living trust is not necessary, it is advisable. If the trust is challenged because the grantor allegedly lacked mental capacity[30] or was being unduly influenced, having two impartial witnesses can be very helpful when defending the Will.

---

25. Except as required by the Statute of Frauds, the Restatement permits an oral trust. Restatement (Third) of Trusts § 20. Since it is unlikely that an attorney would suggest that a client use an oral trust as opposed to a written trust, a trust agreement as discussed in this book means a written trust.

26. N.J.S.A. 3B:3-1 et seq., Restatement (Third) of Trusts §§ 17, 25

27. Uniform Trust Code § 601, Comment.

28. N.J.S.A. 41:2-1.

29. N.J.S.A. 3B:3-4.

30. Uniform Trust Code § 402(a)(1).

## 4-4 WHO MAY SERVE AS A WITNESS?

The statutes governing the execution of a Will permit an interested party to be a witness to the Will.[31] The same could be said for the execution of a living trust designed to serve as a Will-substitute; however, as with the signing of a Will, if the trust is likely to be challenged (for instance, if the trust disinherits a child), then it is not advisable to use an interested party as a witness.

## 4-5 TITLING PROPERTY TO TRUST

The document that people call a "trust" is really just a trust agreement.[32] A trust does not come into being until assets are placed into the trust.[33]

You place assets in the trust by titling those assets into the trust. For instance, if Mr. Smith wanted to place his home into his revocable living trust, then he would change the deed to his house to read "Joe Smith, Trustee, of the Joe Smith Revocable Living Trust." By changing the title to his house in this manner, Mr. Smith has titled his house into the trust and has funded his trust.

Accounts at financial institutions can also be titled into the trust. Personal property does not have a title. What some practitioners do to "title" personal property into a trust is to draft a document that the grantor signs transferring ownership of his tangible personal property to his trust.

## 4-6 BENEFITS OF A LIVING TRUST: REAL AND PERCEIVED

Most of the people who come to see you for an estate planning consultation will have very little knowledge of a trust. Most client would want to avoid having a trust drafted simply because the concept scares them—they do not understand how a trust works and a trust gives them the impression that some other, unknown person is controlling their money.

A minority of the people who come to see you for an estate planning consultation will have read a book or two about living trusts or watched a television personality who advised them to get

31. N.J.S.A. 3B:3-8.

32. Uniform Trust Code § 103(19).

33. Restatement (Third) of Trusts § 2 cmt. (i), Uniform Trust Code § 401, Comment.

a living trust. Perhaps the client may have attended a seminar about living trusts, possibly given by an attorney or financial planner. These latter individuals probably believe that a living trust is the best thing since sliced bread and will want you to draft a living trust for them irrespective of your advice.

A living trust is not harmful. When a person says "I want a living trust," they are typically talking about a revocable living trust used as a Will-substitute. Since the trust is revocable, there isn't much in the way of harm that can result from the client having a living trust as opposed to a Will.

The real issue isn't one of harm, it's one of necessity. For most clients, a living trust as opposed to a Will is simply unnecessary. On the other hand, if the client really wants a living trust as opposed to a Will and having the living trust will make the client feel better, then the client should have a living trust.

Much of estate planning is about providing the client with peace of mind, so if the documents you draft accomplish the general estate planning goals of the client, then having documents that are overkill for the client's needs are appropriate if that overkill provides the client with peace of mind.

In reality, the benefits of a living trust over a Will for the vast majority of New Jersey residents are non-existent. As discussed below, the most common factual scenario in which a living trust is advisable for a New Jersey client is to help a client who owns real property in another state, such as a vacation condominium in Florida, avoid ancillary probate in the foreign state.[34] Most of the other supposed benefits that a living trust provides are illusory.

## 4-6:1 Tax Planning with a Living Trust

One touted benefit of a living trust is that the client can save taxes by employing a revocable living trust. As discussed above, a revocable living trust is a grantor trust. Since the grantor can revoke the trust at any time, the grantor has retained sufficient

34. Ancillary probate is a probate that occurs in another jurisdiction (another state, another country) than the state of domiciliary/primary probate. For instance, an individual who dies domiciled in New Jersey owning real estate in Florida would have to submit his Will for probate in New Jersey and would have to submit his Will for probate, once again, in Florida.

power over the assets of the trust that the income the trust's assets earn will be taxed to the grantor.[35]

Any "gift" to a revocable living trust would be an incomplete gift, which means that the gift would not be removed from the grantor's estate. Since the grantor can revoke the trust, he can revoke the trust and effectuate a return of the "gift," so no completed gift was made.[36]

Furthermore, since the grantor retained the right to revoke the trust up until the point of his death, the assets of the trust will be included in his estate for estate and inheritance tax purposes.

So, a revocable living trust offers no tax planning benefit. With that said, an individual could draft estate planning features into a revocable living trust that could help with estate tax; however, these are the same estate planning features that the client could draft into his last will and testament. For this reason, a revocable living trust offers no benefit over a Will for purposes of estate tax planning.

For instance, a married couple can draft credit shelter trusts (also called a by-pass trust or a A/B trusts) into their Wills in order to preserve each spouse's applicable exemption equivalent against New Jersey estate. By engaging in this type of planning in their Wills, a married couple can shelter up to $1,350,000 from New Jersey estate tax purposes. Similarly, a married couple can draft credit shelter trusts into their revocable living trusts in order to preserve their credits against New Jersey estate tax. The credit shelter trusts would be sub-trusts inside the revocable living trust proper.

There is no difference, no additional benefit between having a credit shelter trust in a last will and testament and having a credit shelter trust in a revocable living trust.

### 4-6:2 Privacy Concerns

One supposed benefit of a revocable living trust is the trust's ability to maintain the privacy of the client. Because a revocable living trust does not have to be presented to the surrogate for probate, the trust remains a private document after the death of

35. 26 U.S.C. § 676.
36. 26 U.S.C. § 2036.

the grantor. A Will that has been submitted for probate is a public document. The Will is on file with the surrogate and if any person wanted to go down to the surrogate's office and obtain a copy of the client's Will after the client's death and after the Will has been submitted to probate, he could.

Privacy is a matter of personal preference. It is not really a legal issue. A Will is not a public document until after the testator dies. A revocable living trust typically does not pass property to a person other than the grantor until after the grantor dies. People who are dead do not have privacy concerns, they are not alive. No one can embarrass or bother in any way a person who is dead, because that person is dead.

Most Wills say something such as "I give my estate to my spouse, then my children equally." There is nothing sensational about most Wills. A professionally drafted Will does not list the testator's assets, so most Wills would tell the uninformed reader very little about the affairs of the decedent.

Moreover, if a Will disinherits one of the client's children, that child is going to know he was disinherited whether the client disinherits the child through a Will or a revocable living trust.

Not only will the disinherited child know, but everyone in the family will know and probably everyone who knows the family will find out. A revocable living trust does not impose a gag order on the living, and people who are disgruntled or who benefit from the misfortune of others talk about these circumstances.

As stated, privacy is a matter of personal choice. If the privacy benefits of a living trust merit the additional costs of a living trust to the client, then the trust is worth having to that client. A good argument can be made that trying to obtain privacy with a living trust is a foolish endeavor, but if it makes the client feel better, then the juice is worth the squeeze.

### 4-6:3 Avoiding Probate

The number one benefit of a living trust, and probably the only benefit with any basis in reality as opposed to pure emotion, is the ability of a revocable living trust to avoid probate. With that said, the process of probating a Will in New Jersey is extremely simple. Submitting a Will to probate before the appropriate surrogate takes about 30 minutes from start to finish (and that is probably being very liberal in most instances) and costs about $150.

Having a living trust drafted and funding that trust will cost the client far more than $150 and will take far more time than 30 minutes. So, the benefit of avoiding probate in New Jersey is non-existent. The benefit of avoiding probate in another state for those clients who own real property in a state other than New Jersey is very real and will be discussed below.

### 4-6:3.1 Non-Probate Property

Non-probate property is property of a decedent that is not controlled by his Will. Non-probate property is property that passes by contract or by operation of law.

An example of property passing by operation of law is a parcel of real property owned by a husband and wife. Such a parcel of property would be owned as joint tenants by the entireties,[37] a form of joint tenancy with right of survivorship. If the husband passed away, his interest in the property would automatically, by operation of law, pass to his surviving wife. The deed does not need to be re-titled, the husband's Will does not need to be submitted to probate to accomplish this transfer.

An example of property passing by contract is a life insurance policy that names a beneficiary. The life insurance policy is a contract between the insured and the insurer to pay a sum certain to a designated beneficiary when the insured dies. If the insured has designated a beneficiary, then that beneficiary will receive the death benefit from the insurer upon the death of the insured.

The insured's Will does not need to be submitted to probate in order to accomplish the payout of the insurance proceeds. The life insurance policy, the contract, governs who receives the proceeds from the policy.

The terms of a revocable trust determine who receives the property of the trust after the death of the grantor. If the living trust designates individuals or entities who will receive the deceased grantor's assets held in the living trust after his death, then the trust will govern who receives those assets after the death of the grantor. The designated beneficiaries of the trust do not have to submit the

---

37. N.J.S.A. 46:3-17.2.

Will of the decedent to probate to accomplish the transfers for which the trust provides.

### 4-6:3.2 Probate Property

Most clients believe that when they die, their Will governs how their property passes. The fact of the matter is that this may or may not be true. A Will controls probate property.

Probate property is property that does not pass by operation of law or by contract, that is, probate property is all property other than non-probate property. Since a great deal of the property a client owns passes by contract or by operation of law, a client may die owning no probate property. In these cases, the client's Will is a wholly ineffective document with respect to devising his property.

For instance, assume that Mr. Smith is married. He owns a house jointly with his wife. He owns several bank accounts jointly with his wife, and he owns an IRA that names his wife as his beneficiary. Mr. Smith's estate might be worth $1,000,000. When Mr. Smith dies, not one of his assets is a probate asset, so Mr. Smith's Will controls no asset that Mr. Smith owned.

On the other hand, if Mr. Smith owned a bank account in his name alone that did not designate a beneficiary, that bank account would be a probate asset and his Will would control who receives that bank account after his death. The bank account with no beneficiary designation would be a probate asset.

### 4-6:3.3 Avoiding Primary Probate in New Jersey

As discussed above, submitting a last will and testament to probate in New Jersey takes about 30 minutes and costs about $150. There is no real benefit to avoiding probate in New Jersey. The costs that will be incurred in the hopes of avoiding probate in New Jersey far outweigh any real benefit of avoiding probate in New Jersey.

Any benefit would be psychological and emotional, not one based on the reality of the situation.

### 4-6:3.4 Avoiding Ancillary Probate with a Living Trust

A decedent's last will and testament needs to be submitted for probate in any state in which the decedent owned real property. So, for instance, if Mr. Smith dies domiciled in New Jersey but owns a condominium in Florida, then his Will first must be submitted to probate in New Jersey, his state of domicile, then in Florida. The probate proceeding in Florida would be an ancillary probate proceeding; it is ancillary to the primary probate proceeding that occurred in New Jersey, his state of domicile.[38]

In some states, such as Florida, the process of probate is quite complex and costly. Many people who are domiciled in Florida have living trusts to avoid probate, and in a state such as Florida where probate is costly and complex, having a living trust to avoid probate makes a great deal of sense.

For those clients who own real property in another state, having a living trust and titling the foreign property into the client's revocable living trust for the sole purpose of avoiding probate in the foreign state makes a great deal of sense. Since many New Jersey residents own vacation properties in other states, particularly in Florida, as an elder law practitioner, you will need to draft living trusts for these clients.

If you are not licensed in the foreign state in which the client owns his foreign real property, then you will have to engage the services of an attorney in that foreign state to re-draft the deed to the client's property in that foreign state into the client's living trust. Once titled into the living trust, the client's real property becomes intangible personal property and is not subject to probate in the foreign jurisdiction.

Avoiding probate in foreign states is the most beneficial feature of a revocable living trust.

### 4-6:3.5 No Tax Waiver

The trustee (in all likelihood the successor trustee) of a revocable living trust does not have to obtain a tax waiver[39] to release property held in the trust upon the death of the grantor, who, in all likelihood, was also the initial trustee during his life;[40] however, the property in the trust is includable in the grantor's estate for

---

38. N.J.S.A. 3B:3-26 et seq.
39. N.J.A.C. 18:26-11.4.
40. N.J.A.C. 18:26-11.13(c).

purposes of calculating the New Jersey estate and inheritance taxes, if either of those taxes are owed.[41]

Some might view the fact that the trustee does not have to obtain a tax waiver as an advantage. Of course, it could be a disadvantage as the residuary beneficiaries of the trust who received the remaining principal and income of the trust without the need to obtain a tax waiver may eschew the obligation to pay their proportionate share of any inheritance or estate tax that may be owed.

As such, this "advantage" could lead to conflict among the beneficiaries of the estate, particularly if the remainder beneficiaries of the trust differ from the beneficiaries of the probate estate.

## 4-7 DISADVANTAGES OF A LIVING TRUST

For those clients who own real property in another state, a living trust can be a very useful tool in their estate plan. For those clients who do not own real property in another state, in most instances, the disadvantages of a living trust far outweigh the benefits of a living trust.

With that said, a living trust can be the right document for a client if the client feels more comfortable with a living trust. Much of estate planning is about providing comfort to the client, so if the client feels more comfortable with a living trust, then their desire for the trust outweighs any disadvantage of a living trust.

### 4-7:1 Client Confusion

Any trust is confusing to a client, more confusing than a Will. For the most part, people who are not lawyers do not fully understand what a trust is and what a trust does.

The concept of titling assets into a trust, even if the trust is revocable and even if the client is the trustee of the trust, scares people to some extent. There is a lack-of-control aspect to a trust, even if that concept has no basis in reality.

### 4-7:2 Re-titling Assets

In order for a revocable living trust to work as a Will-substitute and to eliminate the need to submit the last will and testament to probate, the client must re-title all of their assets to the living trust.

---

41. N.J.S.A. 54:34-1c, N.J.A.C. 18:26-11.13(b).

Re-titling all the client's current assets and re-titling all future assets (which includes a need for the client to remember to re-title assets that are acquired in the future) involves a significant amount of work, both on the client's end and the attorney's end.

For a lawyer, time is money, so having the client's attorney re-title assets for the client costs the client money.

In all likelihood, a client will not re-title all of their assets. For this reason, whenever an attorney drafts a living trust for a client, he drafts a Will that works in tandem for the client. This type of Will is called a "pour over Will."[42]

A pour over Will pours over any probate assets that the client may have to the trustee of the living trust after the client's death, permitting the trust to act as the client's dispositive document or an effective Will-substitute.

The fact that a client is having a Will drafted for him at the same time that the client is having the living trust drafted should be a tip-off to the client that his family may need to probate a Will after his death. Submitting any Will to probate costs the same amount of money and takes the same amount of time in New Jersey.[43]

### 4-7:3 Level of Mental Capacity and Challenges to the Trust

One of the supposed advantages of a living trust is that the living trust is not as easy to challenge as a Will. The truth of the matter is both a revocable living trust and a Will require the same level of mental capacity.[44]

A revocable living trust is simply a Will-substitute.[45] A living trust offers no greater protection to challenge than a Will. For all intents and purposes, after the death of the grantor, a living trust is a Will.

---

42. Restatement (Third) of Trusts § 19.

43. Surrogates currently charge $5 per page to submit a Will over 2 pages in length. So, it is the length of the Will document, not the value of the estate, that determines the cost of submitting a Will to probate. Most Wills cost approximately $150 to admit to probate.

44. Restatement (Third) of Trusts § 11(2).

45. Restatement (Third) of Trusts § 11(2) cmt. on subsection (2):(b).

### 4-7:4 Complexity of a Trust

Even if a revocable living trust is not confusing to you as a lawyer, trusts are almost always confusing to a client. Clients simply do not understand how a trust works and what the purpose of the trust is.

You might explain the trust to the client in perfect detail. The client might leave your office understanding much of what you said, but at some point down the road, even the most educated client may going to forget what you said and find himself confused again.

If you are going to cause your client to be confused, there should be a legitimate reason for using the living trust.

### 4-7:5 Cost

Living trusts, if drafted and funded properly, would almost always cost substantially more money than a Will. A revocable living trust is a slightly more complex document than a Will, so for that reason, the drafting of the document should cost more than a Will costs.

In addition, in order to make a living trust work to accomplish its supposed advantages (avoiding probate, privacy, etc.), the trust must be funded with the assets of the grantor, preferably all of the assets. Re-titling all of the grantor's assets is time-consuming work. Time is money, so funding a living trust can cost a lot of money.

For most clients, paying these additional costs is wholly unnecessary and not beneficial to the client.

# Chapter 5

# Guardianship

## 5-1 WHAT IS A GUARDIANSHIP?

A guardianship is an involuntary court proceeding through which one (or more) person, called the "petitioner," seeks to have a court appoint him as the guardian of another person, called the "ward."[1] A guardian[2] is someone who manages the affairs—sometimes the financial affairs, sometimes the residential and health-related affairs, sometimes both—of the ward.

A guardianship is involuntary because the ward does not consent to the guardianship; in fact, a prospective ward cannot simply consent to a guardianship.[3] A court must adjudicate the ward as being an incapacitated individual who is incapable of handling his affairs in order for a guardian to be appointed for the ward. The court is required to follow certain procedures before it can enter a judgment of incapacity,[4] which will be discussed below.

In most instances, a well-drafted financial power of attorney document[5] and advance healthcare directive[6] can stave off the need to have a guardian appointed for a person. With a power of attorney and healthcare directive, the nominated agent can make most of the decisions that will ever have to be made for the principal, so even if the principal becomes incapacitated after signing the power

---

1. N.J.S.A. 3B:1-2 ("Ward").
2. N.J.S.A. 3B:1-1 ("Guardian").
3. *In the Matter of the Guardianship of Walter J. Macak*, 377 N.J. Super. 167, 175 (App. Div. 2005).
4. *R.* 4:86-1 et seq.
5. N.J.S.A. 46:2B-8.1. et seq.
6. N.J.S.A. 26:2H-54. et seq.

of attorney and healthcare directive, the agent can make whatever decision may need to be made for the principal.

This is not universally the case. Sometimes, a power of attorney document is not well-drafted and fails to address a certain financial transaction that the agent may need to conduct for the principal, for instance, the power of attorney document may inadequately address the agent's authority over the principal's retirement accounts and the custodian of those retirement accounts may refuse to honor the agent's request with regard to the accounts due to the power of attorney document being inappropriately drafted.

Alternatively, the principal may be engaging in actions that are dangerous to his safety or the safety of others, yet he may refuse to obtain necessary care, such as a home health aide or the services of an assisted living residence. For instance, the principal may be living alone in his home, regularly falling or leaving the gas stove on. This behavior is common for people with dementia, yet people in these circumstances often refuse care; they refuse a home health aide, they refuse to live in an assisted living residence. In these circumstances, a guardianship may be necessary even if the principal has signed a well-drafted power of attorney and advance healthcare directive. An agent under a power of attorney and advance healthcare directive cannot force the principal to do anything. In fact, even if the principal is patently mentally incapacitated, unless a court has adjudicated the principal to be incapacitated, he retains the right to revoke the power of attorney[7] and healthcare directive.[8] So, not only could the principal refuse to obey the agent's requests, the principal could simply revoke the power of attorney and advance healthcare directive, leaving the agent with no authority whatsoever.

Unless a court has adjudicated the principal as being an incapacitated person, whether the principal retains capacity is a question of fact that must be resolved by a court. An adjudication of incapacity is not something that is decided by popular decision, so while all of the principal's family members and friends may believe he is incapable of making his own decisions, if the principal does not believe that, he is free to make any decision he wants,

---

7. N.J.S.A. 46:2B-8.10.

8. N.J.S.A. 26:2H-105(a).

irrespective as to whether that decision is good or bad. People make bad decisions all the time. Sometimes, the same person continuously makes bad decisions. But bad decisions do not equate to incapacity in all circumstances, though those decisions may be an indication of a problem.

Once a court has adjudicated a ward to be an incapacitated individual, the ward lacks the legal authority to refuse the decisions that his guardian has made for him,[9] and unless the ward can prove that he has regained his capacity[10] and a court has adjudicated a return to capacity, the guardian, not the ward, makes decisions for the ward.

Now there is certainly a difference between legal authority and practical authority. For instance, if dad's home is cluttered with garbage and he continuously engages in unsafe behavior, such as leaving the gas stove running, his guardian can decide to place dad in an assisted living residence. The guardian has the legal authority to make that decision. But from a practical standpoint, if he does not want to go live in the assisted living residence, then the assisted living residence may not want him. A facility doesn't want a resident who doesn't want to be there if the resident's behavior is disruptive to staff and other residents.

So, there is a difference between legal authority and the practical application authority of which the reader should be aware. A general (or full) guardianship gives the guardian authority to make all decisions for his ward—financial decisions, healthcare decisions, and residential decisions—but the legal authority to make decisions is not necessarily the end-all and be-all to every issue that may arise regarding care decisions for an incapacitated individual.

## 5-2 DEFINING AN INCAPACITATED INDIVIDUAL

Case law concerning guardianship is fascinating if for no other reasons than the age of many of the relevant cases and the language the cases use. Many guardianship cases are quite old,

9. N.J.S.A. 3B:12-36, 3B:12-38.

10. N.J.S.A. 3B:12-28, *R.* 4:86-7.

so the language the courts used in the past to describe what we call "an incapacitated individual"[11] today are quite humorous (or shocking, depending upon your general outlook) viewed through today's sensibilities. Lunatic, imbecile, incompetent—are some of the terms you will see in these cases.[12]

Today, we say that a person is an incapacitated individual. The Probate Code defines "incapacitated individual"[13] as follows:

> "Incapacitated individual" means an individual who is impaired by reason of mental illness or mental deficiency to the extent that he lacks sufficient capacity to govern himself and manage his affairs.
>
> The term incapacitated individual is also used to designate an individual who is impaired by reason of physical illness or disability, chronic use of drugs, chronic alcoholism or other cause (except minority) to the extent that he lacks sufficient capacity to govern himself and manage his affairs.
>
> The terms incapacity and incapacitated individual refer to the state or condition of an incapacitated individual as hereinbefore defined.

It is important to note that a person who is an incapacitated individual may not be mentally incapacitated. Typically, when you think about a guardianship, you think the person is mentally incapable of handling his affairs, but this is not necessarily the case.

A court could appoint a guardian for a person who is incapable of handling his affairs as the result of physical illness or disability, or who is incapable of handling his affairs as the result of chronic alcoholism or drug use.

Putting aside for the moment guardianships brought on behalf of individuals who are developmentally disabled, most

---

11. N.J.S.A. 3B:1-2 (defining "Incapacitated individual").

12. *See, e.g., John Van Horn v. Jonathan Hann, administrator of Sarah Search*, 39 N.J.L. 207 (1876) (lunatic), *In the Matter of Anna M. Owens*, 90 N.J. Eq. 37 (Ch. 1918) (lunatic), *In the Matter of the Alleged Lunacy of Mary Ann Lindsley*, 44 N.J. Eq. 564 (E&A 1888) (imbecile).

13. N.J.S.A. 3B:1-2 ("Incapacitated individual").

guardianships are brought because the ward has some mental incapacity, for instance, dementia, but it is important to bear in mind that mental incapacity is not a necessity for a guardianship proceeding.

## 5-3 THE WARD

The "ward" is the person for whom a guardian is appointed.[14] A person is known as a ward after the court has adjudicated that person as being an incapacitated individual.

If a general (or full) guardian[15] has been appointed for the ward, then the guardian makes all decisions for the ward—decisions concerning financial matters, residential matters and health-related matters. If something less than a general guardian has been appointed, a limited guardian,[16] then the ward may retain the right to make certain decisions for himself.

The powers the ward retains authority over—for instance, the authority to make residential decisions—should be delineated in the letters of guardianship that the surrogate issues to the guardian and in the judgment adjudicating the ward to be an incapacitated individual.

## 5-4 THE GUARDIAN

The guardian is the person, or persons, whom the court has appointed to make decisions for the ward.[17] A general guardian would make all decisions for his ward—financial decisions, residential decision and health-related decisions.[18] A limited guardian makes those decisions for the ward that are not reserved to the ward in the judgment of incapacity.[19] For instance, a limited guardian might make financial decisions over a certain dollar limit (e.g., $2,000), but the ward might continue to make financial decisions under that certain dollar limit.

---

14. N.J.S.A. 3B:1-2 ("ward").
15. N.J.S.A. 3B:12-24.1(a).
16. N.J.S.A. 3B:12-24.1(b).
17. N.J.S.A. 3B:1-1 ("Guardian").
18. N.J.S.A. 3B:12-24.1(a).
19. N.J.S.A. 3B:12-24.1(b).

The court might appoint a guardian of the ward's estate (financial decisions) or a guardian of the ward's person (health care and residential decisions), or a guardian of both the person and estate of the ward. The court might appoint one individual to be guardian of the ward's estate and another individual to be guardian of the ward's person, or the court might appoint the same person to be guardian of the ward's person and estate, which is the most common scenario.

## 5-4:1 Standing

Who has standing to file a guardianship? In order to file a guardianship action, you must have an interest in the affairs of the proposed ward.[20] Persons who have an interest would include, but are not limited to, the following individuals: a spouse, domestic partner, children, other heirs and even friends that have an interest in the affairs of the ward.[21] In addition, an agent named under a financial power of attorney or an advance healthcare directive has an interest in the affairs of the ward, so he would have standing to file a guardianship action for the benefit of the ward.

The Office of the Public Guardian or the adult protective services agency serving the county of the ward's domicile may have standing in particular cases. A nursing facility in which the ward resides may have standing.[22] The lawyer for a now incapacitated person may have standing.[23]

The facts of a particular case may lend an argument for standing to other individuals, but those individuals and entities mentioned above are the most common petitioners in guardianship actions. The important thing to remember is that the individual filing for guardianship must have standing in order to bring the guardianship

---

20. *In the Matter of Jane Tierney, an Alleged Mental Incompetent*, 175 N.J. Super. 614 (Probate Part 1980), *aff'd*, 177 N.J. Super. 245 (App. Div. 1981).

21. *In the Matter of Jane Tierney, an Alleged Mental Incompetent*, 175 N.J. Super. 614 (Probate Part 1980), *aff'd*, 177 N.J. Super. 245 (App. Div. 1981) (holding that a plaintiff in a guardianship action must be a relative, creditor or a person who has a relationship of trust, contract or confidence with the proposed ward).

22. *In the Matter of Costa Nova, An Alleged Incapacitated Person*, 2011 N.J. Super. Unpub. Lexis 946 (Ch. Div. 2011), *In the Matter of Jane Tierney, an Alleged Mental Incompetent*, 175 N.J. Super. 614 (Probate Part 1980), *aff'd*, 177 N.J. Super. 245 (App. Div. 1981).

23. *In the Matter of Costa Nova, An Alleged Incapacitated Person*, 2011 N.J. Super. Unpub. Lexis 946 (Ch. Div. 2011). R.P.C. 1.14(b) (discussing when a lawyer can seek the appointment of a guardian for a client under a disability).

action. Someone who lacks an interest in the affairs of the ward cannot file for guardianship or even file a guardianship action requesting that another be appointed as the guardian for the ward.[24]

## 5-5 WHO SERVES AS GUARDIAN

In most instances, the court appoints a general or full guardian of the ward;[25] in other words, the court appoints a guardian of the estate and person of the ward. The full guardian makes all decisions for the ward—decisions involving financial matters, health-related matters and residential matters.

Being a guardian is no easy job. It involves a lot of work. Essentially, the guardian is managing his own life, his family's affairs and the affairs of his ward. Because a ward is often an individual who has physical and mental deficiencies, the typical ward requires medical assistance more frequently than a person in good health requires assistance.

A guardian can expect to get calls at 3 a.m. informing him that the ward fell out of bed at the nursing home or assisted living residence in which he resides or that the ward was taken to the hospital for a medical emergency. If the ward is residing at home, the guardian will have to hire and fire health aides. In addition, the guardian will have to ensure that he pays all of the ward's debts and applies for appropriate government benefits, such as Medicaid, if the ward's assets are depleted.

Furthermore, the guardian is often the object of criticism from family members or friends who believe (or, at least, express the opinion) that they could do a better job than the guardian is doing or who simply disagree with the guardian's decision on a given issue.

In short, being a guardian is a lot of work for very little reward. Having to file for guardianship and serving as the guardian can cause a tremendous amount of family angst. Nevertheless, serving as that person's guardian is absolutely necessary to the incapacitated persons the health and well-being of the ward.

---

24. R.P.C. 1.14(b) (discussing when a lawyer can seek the appointment of a guardian for a client under a disability).

25. N.J.S.A. 3B:12-24.1(a).

## 5-5:1 Family Members

In most instances, a family member is appointed as the ward's guardian. From a practical perspective, family members most often serve as the ward's guardian because family members are the people who file guardianship matters and because family members are the people who are most affected (after the ward himself) by the ward's incapacity.

From a legal perspective, both the statutes governing guardianship matters and the court rules governing these matters favor the appointment of family members as a ward's guardian.[26] The relevant statue directs the court to first consider the spouse or domestic partner of the ward for the role of guardian. If the spouse or domestic partner will not serve or is inappropriate to serve, then the court should consider other heirs of the ward. The statute directs the court to also consider friends of the ward; the court rule is silent on the consideration of friends, but since a statute is of greater authority than a court rule, the court should consider friends.

If no relatives or friends are willing to serve or appropriate to serve as guardian, then the court should consider the Office of the Public Guardian for Elderly Adults,[27] which is a government office that will serve as the guardian of an individual if certain criteria are met,[28] discussed below. If no family, friend or the Office of the Public Guardian is appointed, then the court can consider any other appropriate person to serve as the guardian, such as a professional guardian.

The court may give consideration to the person whom the ward has named as the agent under his power of attorney document or advance healthcare directive.

The person or institution that will serve as the guardian of the ward is always up to the court, but in most instances, a family member is appointed as the ward's guardian.

## 5-5:2 Office of the Public Guardian

The Office of the Public Guardian for Elderly Adults, commonly known as the Office of the Public Guardian, is an office under

---

26. N.J.S.A. 3B:12-25, *R.* 4:86-5(c).
27. N.J.S.A. 52:27G-20 et seq.
28. N.J.S.A. 52:27G-25(f), 3B:13A-1 et seq.

the executive branch (i.e., the governor's office) of the New Jersey government.[29] The Public Guardian for Elderly Adults Act created the Office of the Public Guardian.[30]

As stated, most people refer to the Office of the Public Guardian for Elderly Adults as the Office of the Public Guardian; however, it is important to bear in mind that the Office of the Public Guardian is only available to elderly individuals who require a guardian. The act that created the Office of the Public Guardian defines the word "elderly" as a person who is age 60 or older.[31] While age 60 isn't necessarily elderly to most people, it is the statutory definition of elderly under the relevant act. Furthermore, while 60 may be considered relatively young nowadays, the age-restriction causes problems is some situations, particularly for hospitals.

Hospitals are frequently faced with situations in which an indigent incapacitated individual who is under the age of 60 requires medical care in the short-term and a permanent guardian in the long-term. For instance, the patient may have longtime substance abuse problems and now requires medical intervention for some condition related to his longtime substance abuse problem. A short-term solution for the hospital is the appointment of a special medical guardian to make medical decisions for the patient.[32] The procedures for appointing a special medical guardian are discussed below.

Typically, the court will appoint an attorney to serve as the patient's special medical guardian. The special guardian will communicate with the health care providers regarding the care of the patient and will ensure that the patient receives the necessary acute care. Eventually, the patient will need to be discharged from the hospital, perhaps to a nursing facility or assisted living residence, but the patient may continue to be an incapacitated individual and, of course, will continue to be indigent.

If the patient is age 60 or older, the hospital can request that the Office of the Public Guardian be appointed as the patient's permanent guardian, but if the patient is under the age of 60 and if there are no family members or friends who are willing to serve

---

29. N.J.S.A. 52:27G-23.

30. N.J.S.A. 52:27G-20 et seq.

31. N.J.S.A. 52:27G-22(b).

32. *R.* 4:86-12.

as the ward's guardian, then the hospital often finds itself in a difficult position.

In many of these cases, the patient is indigent and has no money to pay a professional who might serve as his guardian, and most professionals would not want to be appointed to serve as a person's guardian, which might require substantial work, without the hope of being compensated for that work. Yet, if the person is under the age of 60, the Office of the Public Guardian cannot, according to the law that created the office, serve as the person's guardian.

The Office of the Public Guardian also will not serve if there is a willing family member or friend who will serve and whom the court determines to be appropriate to serve as the guardian.[33] The office also will not serve if their caseload is full. If the Public Guardian's caseload is full,[34] the office is required to notify the various county court houses that its caseload is full.

## 5-5:3 Professional Guardians

A professional guardian is a person who meets certain criteria defined in the act creating professional guardians.[35] In short, the act requires a professional guardian to meet the following criteria:

> § 52:27G-33. Requirements for service as guardian
>
> A person may serve as a professional guardian of an incapacitated adult if that person has been registered by the Office of the Public Guardian for Elderly Adults as a professional guardian pursuant to this act. The Office of the Public Guardian for Elderly Adults shall not register a person as a professional guardian unless that person:
>
> (1) is a full-time New Jersey resident or maintains an office in New Jersey;
>
> (2) has, prior to the effective date of this act, had a minimum of five years of work experience as a court-appointed guardian of five or more persons not related to the

---

33. N.J.S.A. 52:27G-26.
34. N.J.S.A. 52:27G-29.1.
35. N.J.S.A. 52:27G-32 et seq.

guardian; or, on or after the effective date of this act, has received a bachelor's degree and has two years of work experience in the field of care management, case management or other relevant work experience involving the management and care of elderly adults;

(3) has supplied proof of current professional liability insurance coverage to the Office of the Public Guardian for Elderly Adults;

(4) has submitted a credit check to the Office of the Public Guardian for Elderly Adults from one national credit reporting agency, which has been issued within one month of the date of the application for registration as a professional guardian;

(5) has satisfied the criminal history record background, child abuse registry and domestic violence central registry check requirements of this act;

(6) is not subject to any outstanding warrants for arrest;

(7) has completed approved initial training and biennial continuing education courses, as provided for in section 5 of this act, relating to guardianship law, procedures and ethics; and

(8) is not otherwise ineligible as set forth in section 3 of this act.

(9) Except for legal services authorized by a court, a person serving as a registered professional guardian:

   (a) shall only provide guardianship services to a ward and shall not bill the ward for other professional or licensed services while serving as guardian; and

(b) shall not contract for professional or licensed services with a person, organization or agency with which the guardian has a vested interest.

In short, a professional guardian, as the term implies, is a person who regularly serves in the role of guardian and who is not a family member or friend of the ward.

There are limitations on the amount of compensation a professional guardian can receive.[36] Frequently, when an attorney is appointed as the guardian of a ward, the lawyer-guardian can receive guardian commissions, which are discussed below, and can retain himself as attorney for the ward and bill the ward's estate for any legal work that the lawyer-guardian performs for the ward.[37] Legal work might involve preparing and filing a guardian accounting or motions to perform certain tasks, such as selling the ward's real estate.

But the professional guardianship act specifically prohibits the professional guardian from receiving compensation under licensed services or from hiring any agency (such as geriatric care manager services) if the professional guardian has a stake in the agency.[38]

Given the fact that guardian commissions are rather low[39] and being a guardian involves a substantial amount of work and the assumption of a substantial amount of liability, few individuals would probably be interested in registering as professional guardians.

## 5-6 THE COMPLAINT

The complaint to initiate a guardianship action in court—whether the action requests the appointment of a general, limited or temporary guardian[40]—must satisfy certain strict requirements. Failure of the complaint to satisfy these requirements could result in a dismissal of the complaint.[41]

---

36. N.J.S.A. 52:27G-33(e).

37. *In the Matter of the Estate of Kate Flynn, an incompetent, now deceased*, 132 N.J. Eq. 85 (Prerog. Ct. 1942), *compare* N.J.S.A. 3B:18-6.

38. N.J.S.A. 52:27G-33(e).

39. N.J.S.A. 3B:18-23 et seq.

40. *R.* 4:86-1.

41. *In the Matter of Rose Jacobs*, 315 N.J. Super. 189, 193 (Ch. Div. 1998).

## 5-6:1 Description of the Interested Parties

The complaint must state the name, age, domicile and address of the ward and the guardian. The complaint must also state the name, age, domicile and address of the ward's spouse, if the ward is married. It has been said that a person can have many residences but only one domicile, which is the place to which the person always intends to return.

The petitioner should also describe his relationship to the ward. For instance, is the petitioner the spouse of the ward? The ward's child?

The complaint should describe the petitioner's interest in initiating the action. For instance, "petitioner's interest is the health and welfare of the proposed ward."

The complaint must state the names, addresses and ages of the ward's children, if any, and the names and addresses of the ward's next-of-kin and the ward's parents, if the ward's parents are living.

If the ward is living in an institution, such as a nursing facility, the complaint must state the name of the person or place having responsibility for the care and custody of the ward. If the ward has been living in an institution, the complaint must state the period of time during which the ward has resided in the institution and the date of commitment or confinement to the institution.

Finally, the complaint must also state the name of any agent under a power of attorney that the ward has executed, any health care agent under an advance health care directive that the ward may have executed and any trustee of a trust for the benefit of the ward.[42]

## 5-6:2 Affidavit of Estate

The complaint must be accompanied by affidavits. One affidavit relates to the estate, or property, of the ward.[43] In short, the petitioner must inform the court of the assets that the ward owns.

The affidavit of the estate of the ward must list any interest that the ward owns in real estate and personal property. The affidavit should also list any income that the ward receives or may be entitled to receive, such as Social Security income and pension income.

---

42. *R.* 4:86-1.

43. *R.* 4:86-2(a).

If the person signing the affidavit does not know the assets that the ward owns or to which he is entitled, then the affiant must state that the information he has provided in his affidavit is the most information that he can secure at that time using reasonable diligence.

## 5-6:3 Physician Certifications

The complaint for a guardianship must also include the affidavits of two licensed physicians, or the affidavit of one licensed physician and the affidavit of one licensed practicing psychologist.[44]

### 5-6:3.1 Qualification of Physicians

A complaint for guardianship must be accompanied by the affidavits of two physicians having the qualifications set forth in N.J.S. 30:4-27.2(t). That statute requires the physician to be licenses in any one of the fifty states or the District of Columbia. The physicians are specifically permitted to make disclosures about the alleged incapacitated person.

### 5-6:3.2 Psychologist Certification

As an alternative to having two licensed physicians submit affidavits, the complaint can also be accompanied by the affidavit of one licensed physician and one licensed practicing psychologist. The psychologist must be licensed pursuant to New Jersey's Practicing Psychology Licensing Act.[45]

### 5-6:3.3 Timeliness of Certifications

The physicians or psychologist who examined the alleged incapacitated person must have made his examination within 30 days of the date the complaint is filed.[46] Since a person's capacity or incapacity can change over time, the Court Rules require the examination of the alleged incapacitated person to have occurred within 30 days of the date the complaint if filed.

For instance, a person may be a patient in a hospital and be quite confused and disoriented because of his medical condition

---

44. *R.* 4:86-2(b).
45. N.J.S.A. 45:14B-1 et seq.
46. *R.* 4:86-2(b).

and because he is residing in a hospital, not his home. Patients in hospitals, particularly elderly patients, are frequently disoriented when they reside in a hospital to the point where the person is mentally incapacitated. But that same person may regain most, if not all, of his capacity simply by returning home and living, once again, in a familiar environment.

The timeliness requirement is designed to weed out those instances where an alleged incapacitated person may simply have a temporary loss of capacity due to his condition and living arrangement.

### 5-6:3.3a Order to Relax

With that said, it is often difficult to get two physicians to examine a person and file a complaint with the court all in a 30-day period of time. Many incapacitated persons continue to reside in their home, but do not get out of their homes easily. The physicians often have to go to the incapacitated person's home. From a practical standpoint, the 30-day requirement can be cumbersome.

For this reason, the Court Rules permit a court to relax the 30-day requirement on an ex parte basis, meaning that the petitioner can request the court to relax the rule requiring the physicians' examination to have occurred within 30 days of the filing of the complaint without putting any other party on notice of the request to relax the requirement.[47] These request are frequently and routinely granted.

### 5-6:3.4 Content of the Affidavit

The affidavits, whether the affidavits be those of two physicians or a physician and a psychologist, must contain certain information about the alleged incapacitated person. The affidavit must state the following:[48]

(1) the date and place of the examination;

(2) whether the affiant has treated or merely examined the alleged incapacitated individual;

---

47. *R.* 4:86-2(b).

48. *R.* 4:86-2(b).

(3) whether the affiant is disqualified under N.J. Ct. R. 4:86-3;

(4) the diagnosis and prognosis and factual basis therefor;

(5) for purposes of ensuring that the alleged incapacitated person is the same individual who was examined, a physical description of the person examined, including but not limited to sex, age and weight;

(6) the affiant's opinion of the extent to which the alleged incapacitated person is unfit and unable to govern himself or herself and to manage his or her affairs and shall set forth with particularity the circumstances and conduct of the alleged incapacitated person upon which this opinion is based, including a history of the alleged incapacitated person's condition; and

(7) if applicable, the extent to which the alleged incapacitated person retains sufficient capacity to retain the right to manage specific areas, such as, residential, educational, medical, legal, vocational or financial decisions.

The affiant should also express an opinion as to whether or not the alleged incapacitated person can attend the hearing, and if not, why not. Many physicians also express an opinion as to whether or not the alleged incapacitated person would comprehend the nature of the proceedings, assuming he does attend the hearing, and be able to participate meaningfully in the proceedings.

### 5-6:3.5 What if the Physicians Cannot Gain Access?

In some cases, the alleged incapacitated person is living with someone, a friend or family member, who is attempting to thwart the guardianship action. Perhaps the family member doesn't believe dad needs a guardian. Perhaps the family member doesn't want dad to have a guardian. Perhaps the family member wants to take advantage of dad through financial exploitation and doesn't want another family member to obtain guardianship over dad and put an end to the financial exploitation. Or, perhaps the alleged incapacitated person simply doesn't want to be examined.

The Court Rules permit a physician to submit an affidavit stating that he attempted to exam the alleged incapacitated person and was refused access to the person, either by the person or by those who have custody of the alleged incapacitated person.[49] The refusal must have been within 30 days of the filing of the complaint, but the court can relax the 30-day requirement on an ex parte basis.

## 5-7 JURISDICTION AND VENUE

In the context of a guardianship action, jurisdiction involves a court's authority over the alleged incapacitated person.[50] Does a court in New Jersey have the right to decide whether or not the person is incapacitated? Venue is a question concerning the location of the action.

### 5-7:1 Jurisdiction

In most guardianship cases, jurisdiction is obvious. The alleged incapacitated person lives in New Jersey and lives in no state other than New Jersey. He may have lived in New Jersey his entire life, so there is no question that New Jersey has jurisdiction over his person.

But what if a daughter brings her mother who is obviously mentally incapacitated from Florida, where mom lives, to New Jersey because the daughter it trying to gain an advantage in litigation involving mom?[51] Does a New Jersey court have jurisdiction over mom when mom never changed her place of residence from Florida to New Jersey? The answer is no.[52]

Cases such as this happen more frequently than you would think. A family member lives in one state and brings his or her mentally incapacitated family member to another state, whether for good reasons or bad, and files for guardianship in the foreign

---

49. *R.* 4:86-2(c).

50. N.J.S.A. 3B:12B-5.

51. *See*, N.J.S.A. 3B:12B-14, *Jurisdiction declined by reason of conduct*.

52. N.J.S.A. 3B:12B-14, *In the Matter of Floretta Sutton-Logan*, 2009 N.J. Super. Unpub. Lexis 2335, *8 - *10 (App. Div. 2009), *In the Matter of Rose Jacobs*, 315 N.J. Super. 189, 193 (Ch. Div. 1998), *In the Matter of Lillian Glasser*, 2006 WL 510096 (Ch. Div. 2006).

state. The court in the foreign state must then decide whether or not it has jurisdiction to hear the case.

Questions of jurisdiction are fundamental to any action in court. A lack of jurisdiction means that the court lacks the authority to hear the case and make a decision involving the subject matter of the action.

The state in which the alleged incapacitated person is domiciled should be the state that exercises jurisdiction in a guardianship action involving that person.[53]

### 5-7:1.1 The Adult Guardianship and Protective Proceeding Jurisdiction Act

The Adult Guardianship and Protective Proceeding Jurisdiction Act (the "Uniform Act") is a uniform act that is currently enacted in all but 13 states.[54] Since many New Jersey residents are "snow birds" who spend their winters in the state of Florida, it is important to note that one of the 13 states that have not enacted the Uniform Act is Florida.

New Jersey enacted the Uniform Act in August 2012, and the Uniform Act became effective 120 days after enactment.[55]

The Uniform Act provides a methodology for courts in multiple states to determine which of the states should exercise jurisdiction in a given guardianship. In non-emergent matters, jurisdiction is laid either in the ward's "home state"[56] or in the ward's "significant-connection state."[57] The Uniform Act defines these terms and provides a methodology governing the exercise of jurisdiction.

In emergent cases, for instance, in cases where an individual who is domiciled in another state takes ill in New Jersey while on vacation, the Uniform Act permits the courts of this state to exercise jurisdiction over a ward who is physically present in New Jersey.[58]

For those states that do not participate in the Uniform Act, for instance, Florida, the provisions of the Act can serve as a guide.

---

53. *In the Matter of Rose Jacobs*, 315 N.J. Super. 189, 193 (Ch. Div. 1998).
54. N.J.S.A. 3B:12B-1 et seq.
55. N.J.S.A. 3B:12B-5.
56. N.J.S.A. 3B:12B-3(h).
57. N.J.S.A. 3B:12B-3(r), 3B:12B-9.
58. N.J.S.A. 3B:12B-11.

Since many residents of New Jersey have vacation homes in other states, there is also significant case law governing the subject. In essence, the inquiry becomes one akin to the "significant-connection" analysis under the Uniform Act.[59]

### 5-7:2 Venue

Unlike jurisdiction, which involves the very authority of a court to decide a case, venue is simply the place in which an action should be filed. While venue can be important, it is not fundamental to the court's authority to hear the case.

Generally speaking, guardianship actions are brought in the Superior Court of New Jersey, Probate Part.[60] So, the superior court, probate part, is the proper venue for guardianship actions; however, New Jersey has 15 vicinages, which are court houses located in most of the counties in New Jersey. There are 21 counties in New Jersey, so some counties share a court house.

Looking at the issue of venue more narrowly, a guardianship action should be filed in the county vicinage in which the alleged incapacitated person is domiciled at the time of the filing of the complaint.[61]

So, as with the question of jurisdiction, the issue of venue comes down to the same domicile test; however, unlike with the question of jurisdiction, issues regarding venue are not fundamental to the action. A court cannot hear a matter if it lacks jurisdiction, but the superior court, Monmouth County vicinage, could continue to hear a guardianship matter even if the domicile of the alleged incapacitated person, and thus the correct venue, ultimately turns out to be Ocean County.

Domicile is the place to which the person always intends to return. Since many incapacitated people are mentally incapacitated, questions about domicile could arise. For instance, assume that Mr. Smith is living in a nursing home in Monmouth County, and his family has decided that he never will return home. Mr. Smith, on the other hand, has a home in

---

59. *In the Matter of Floretta Sutton-Logan*, 2009 N.J. Super. Unpub. Lexis 2335, *8 - *10 (App. Div. 2009), *In the Matter of Rose Jacobs*, 315 N.J. Super. 189, 193 (Ch. Div. 1998), *In the Matter of Lillian Glasser*, 2006 WL 510096 (Ch. Div. 2006).

60. *R.* 4:83-1.

61. *R.* 4:83-4(b).

Ocean County, and if you ask Mr. Smith, he'll tell you that he wants to go home.

Mr. Smith has not been adjudicated as a mentally incapacitated person. His family might not even have a power of attorney or living will for him. So, given these facts, is Mr. Smith's domicile Monmouth County or Ocean County? Probably Ocean County because Mr. Smith intends to return home, he never changed his domicile and no person with authority (such as a legal guardian) ever changed his domicile.

From a practical standpoint, it probably doesn't matter in which county the action is filed, as both counties would probably entertain the action. Since Mr. Smith is physically located in Monmouth County and since the intention is that he never will leave the nursing home in Monmouth County, it is probably better to file the action in Monmouth County.

Of course, Monmouth and Ocean counties are coterminous counties, so the choice of Monmouth County or Ocean County does seem academic. But what if Mr. Smith were in the New Jersey Veterans' Home located in Vineland, New Jersey (Cumberland County) and his family and his home is located were Bergen County?

Here, the choice of county can have some far reaching practical implications. If the action is filed in Bergen County, the place to which Mr. Smith intends to return—if you were to ask him—then the court-appointed attorney must travel hours to visit with his client and charge his client many hundreds of dollars to make that trip. If Mr. Smith wants to attend the hearing and his court-appointed counsel believes he should attend the hearing, then Mr. Smith needs to travel many hours to get to the court house, perhaps by ambulance.

In an extreme example such as this, you can see how choice of venue could have a big impact on the litigation. Filing in Bergen County, Mr. Smith's true domicile until such time as he is adjudicated an incapacitated individual could actually be a big disadvantage to Mr. Smith. His family lives in Bergen County, so they can easily get to the court house and gain access to their attorney. Mr. Smith lives in Cumberland County. He probably does not have ready access to a phone, the internet or the mail. He probably cannot drive a car and may not be able to get around without the assistance of an ambulance. His attorney's office would be hundreds of miles away and the court house would be hundreds of miles away.

Though, technically, Mr. Smith is domiciled in Bergen County, the best place to file a guardianship action against him would be Cumberland County for many practical reasons.

If an alleged incapacitated person is not domiciled in the state of New Jersey, then the action for a guardianship should be filed in any county in which the alleged incapacitated person has property.[62]

## 5-8 COUNSEL FOR PETITIONER

Most guardianship actions are filed by private individuals who are seeking to be appointed the guardian of a family member or friend who is now incapable of handling his affairs as the result of a physical or mental infirmity. In most instances, the petitioner will retain his own attorney to assist him with the filing of the guardianship action.

Private counsel will prepare the complaint for the petitioner and the various other legal documents that need to accompany the complaint. Counsel will typically assist the petitioner with arranging for two physicians to exam the alleged incapacitated person. In most cases, the physicians will prepare their own affidavits and reports. In some cases, counsel will prepare a blank physician's affidavit for the examining or treating physician to complete.

Counsel will file the action in court, arrange for the filed complaint to be served upon the alleged incapacitated person and attend any court appearances with the petitioner.

## 5-9 COURT-APPOINTED COUNSEL

When an action for guardianship is filed, the court is required to appoint an attorney for the alleged incapacitated person.[63] The reason for this is simple: A petitioner files an action for guardianship typically alleging that as the result of a mental infirmity the alleged incapacitated person is incapable of handling

---

62. *R.* 4:83-4(b).

63. *R.* 4:86-4(b).

his own affairs. Given this allegation, the alleged incapacitated person probably lacks the mental capacity to understand the nature of the action that has been filed against him and the mental capacity to understand that he can retain his own attorney to fight the guardianship action.

Furthermore, since an attorney-client relationship is a contractual relationship whereby the client contractually retains the attorney to represent him, an alleged incapacitated person may lack sufficient mental capacity to retain an attorney.[64] In other words, even if the alleged incapacitated person wanted to retain his own attorney, he may lack the requisite contractual mental capacity to retain an attorney. Each attorney needs to make his own assessment as to whether or not a potential client has the mental capacity to engage his services.

Court-appointed counsel is the attorney for the alleged incapacitated person. Attorneys are advocates for their clients, so court-appointed counsel's duty is to advocate for his client.[65] In any attorney-client relationship, the client is the boss. While an attorney may refrain from advocating for a client's position in certain circumstances (for instance, if a client wants an attorney to help the client cover up on-going or future criminal activity or to assist the client with fraudulent conveyances), for the most part, the client is the boss and his attorney must advocate for his position.

The same is true for court-appointed counsel. Court-appointed counsel is the advocate for the client, the alleged incapacitated person, and must advocate for his client's position, unless his client's position is patently absurd or poses an undue risk of harm to the alleged incapacitated person.[66]

With that said, court-appointed counsel has certain duties that no private counsel has. The requirement that court-appointed counsel perform these duties has led to confusion as to the role of court-appointed counsel. Is the role of court-appointed counsel

---

64. *In the Matter of William Schiller*, 148 N.J. Super. 168, 180 (Ch. Div. 1977), citing 17 C.J.S., Contracts § 133(1) (discussing contractual mental capacity).

65. *In the Matter of M.R., an Alleged Incompetent or Mentally Retarded Adult*, 135 N.J. 155 (1994) (detailing the role of a court-appointed attorney in the context of a guardianship action).

66. *In the Matter of M.R., an Alleged Incompetent or Mentally Retarded Adult*, 135 N.J. 155, 176 (1994).

that of advocate for the client's wishes or that of advocate for the client's best interests?

The Supreme Court of New Jersey in the seminal case of *M.R.*[67] clearly came down on the side of advocate for the client's wishes; nevertheless, the duties of court-appointed counsel can, in some cases, serve as landmines for court-appointed counsel who may feel that he is being pulled between his duties to the client and his duties under the court rules.

## 5-9:1 Court-Appointed Counsel's Duties

The Court Rules[68] prescribe certain duties that the court-appointed counsel must perform. Those duties are as follows:

**(1) Personally interview the alleged incapacitated person[69]**

Note that court-appointed counsel must personally interview the alleged incapacitated person. Counsel cannot simply pick up the phone and call the alleged incapacitated person. Court-appointed counsel must meet with his client, where that meeting occurs is at the discretion of counsel, but an actual meeting must occur.

In many cases, the alleged incapacitated person is not easily movable. He may be living in a nursing home or he may be homebound, so court-appointed counsel must go to the client. If the alleged incapacitated person were to drive himself to his court-appointed attorney's office, court-appointed counsel may want to advocate for a complete and immediate dismissal of the action.

**(2) Make inquiry of persons having knowledge of the alleged incapacitated person's circumstances, his or her physical and mental state and his or her property[70]**

Unlike with his client, court-appointed counsel need only make inquiry of other persons having knowledge of the alleged incapacitated person. Court-appointed counsel does not have to meet personally with these people. Counsel may call them or write letters to them.

---

67. *In the Matter of M.R., an Alleged Incompetent or Mentally Retarded Adult*, 135 N.J. 155 (1994).

68. *R.* 4:86-4(b).

69. *R.* 4:86-4(b)(1).

70. *R.* 4:86-4(b)(2).

Counsel is not obligated to make inquires of every person having knowledge of the alleged incapacitated person. Sometimes, family members or friends may complain that the court-appointed attorney didn't make an inquiry to them, but that is not the obligation of counsel. Counsel may wish to make inquiry of as many people as he can, but he may obtain an adequate picture of the alleged incapacitated person's circumstances by inquiring into far fewer than all the people who have knowledge of the alleged incapacitated person's circumstances.

**(3) Make reasonable inquiry to locate any will, powers of attorney, or health care directives previously executed by the alleged incapacitated person or to discover any interests the alleged incapacitated person may have as beneficiary of a will or trust**[71]

If an alleged incapacitated person has a power of attorney and a living will, the guardianship action may simply be unnecessary. For instance, if Mr. Smith named his daughter as his power of attorney agent and health care agent and that daughter is willing to serve as Mr. Smith's agent, then Mr. Smith may not need a guardian.[72] His daughter can simply make decisions for him using those documents that Mr. Smith put in place when he had mental capacity.

In addition the person Mr. Smith nominated to serve as his agent or as the executor of his estate can be very relevant as to who, if anyone, should serve as Mr. Smith's guardian. If Mr. Smith named his daughter to serve as his executor and agent and if Mr. Smith's son files to be appointed as his guardian, the fact that Mr. Smith nominated his daughter as his executor and agent is relevant as to whether or not the son or daughter should be appointed his guardian, if a guardian needs to be appointed.

Whether Mr. Smith is the beneficiary of a trust is relevant to Mr. Smith's estate. If Mr. Smith is the beneficiary of a trust with assets worth $1,000,000, that fact can be relevant to Mr. Smith's ability to care for himself by paying for appropriate care.

The Court Rule specifying court-appointed counsel's duties compels counsel to file a report with the court and those individuals who have entered a formal appearance in the guardianship action

---

71. *R.* 4:86-4(b)(3).
72. N.J.S.A. 3B:12-25, *R.* 4:86-6(c).

at least three days before the hearing date. Counsel's report must contain certain items:[73]

Court-appointed counsel typically details his conversations with his client and those having knowledge of his client's circumstances. In this regard, the duties of court-appointed counsel are quite different than those of private counsel.[74]

Obviously, a primary obligation of an attorney is the duty of confidentiality. An attorney does not have a conversation with a client then detail that conversation in a report to the court and to the adversaries of his client. Nonetheless, court-appointed attorneys do this all of the time. A typical report to the court might state something such as the following: "I met with Mr. Smith at the nursing home. Mr. Smith did not know where he was, the month, day or time. Mr. Smith told me that he did not want his daughter to serve as his guardian and asked me to advocate on his behalf against the guardianship action that his daughter filed. Mr. Smith wanted to leave the nursing home and return to his home."

Now, the client wants the attorney to advocate against the guardianship action. At the same time, Mr. Smith's court-appointed counsel is informing the court and the daughter that Mr. Smith was disoriented, failing to know where he was and the date.

So, there is clearly a pull on court-appointed counsel who is both an advocate and a reporter, to some extent. Private counsel is not constrained by the same duties as court-appointed counsel. An experienced attorney who is frequently appointed as court-appointed counsel can, in most cases, navigate around court-appointed counsel's obligation as advocate and the duties court-appointed counsel owes to the court, but there is little question that the requirements of the Court Rules can pose issues for an unfamiliar or inexperienced attorney.

### (1) Recommendations concerning the court's determination on the issue of incapacity

As with court-appointed counsel's obligation to report to the Court and the parties who have filed appearances in the case, counsel's obligation to make recommendations concerning the

---

73. *R.* 4:86-4(b).

74. R.P.C. 1.6, *Confidentiality of Information.*

court's determination of incapacity can pose issues that private counsel does not face.

Private counsel does not inform the court and his adversaries that he believes his client is an incapacitated individual and recommend the appointment of a guardian for his client. Perhaps the client told court-appointed counsel that he doesn't want a guardian and that he wants counsel to fight the guardianship action. How does court-appointed counsel reconcile his client's desire with that of his obligation?

Counsel may believe that his client does need a guardian, but he also may believe that his client's desires are not patently absurd or pose a risk of *undue* harm to his client.[75] Perhaps Mr. Smith tells his court-appointed counsel that he wants to leave the nursing home, return home and hire a home aide to care for him. Given his statements (whether or not Mr. Smith will hire an aide may be another question, but that is the statement he is making to his court-appointed counsel), counsel may not believe that Mr. Smith's preferences pose a risk of undue harm to him or are absurd.

In this case, counsel is obligated to make his recommendations (as opposed to the preferences of his client) to the court, advocate for his client's desires and, perhaps, make a recommendation to the court to appoint a guardian ad litem, which is discussed below.

For now, it is important to bear in mind that the role of court-appointed counsel is an appointment that is not very straightforward and can be fraught with opposing obligations and duties.

**(2) May make recommendations concerning the suitability of less restrictive alternatives such as a conservatorship or a delineation of those areas of decision-making that the alleged incapacitated person may be capable of exercising**

As an advocate for his client, court-appointed counsel may wish to make recommendations for less restrictive alternatives, such as a limited guardian[76] or a conservatorship,[77] if the client

---

75. *In the Matter of M.R., an Alleged Incompetent or Mentally Retarded Adult*, 135 N.J. 155, 176 (1994).

76. N.J.S.A. 3B:12-24.1(b).

77. N.J.S.A. 3B:13A-1 et seq.

would consent to a conservatorship.[78] Counsel may believe that the alleged incapacitated person can handle small amounts of cash or participate in decisions as to where he lives or participate in medical decisions. Reservations of authority, such as these examples, makes a guardianship a limited guardianship.

A general or full guardianship is a guardianship through which the guardian makes all decisions for his ward—decisions concerning health care, financial matters and residential matters.[79] The ward has no legal input into any of these decisions.

A limited guardianship is a guardianship through which the guardian makes some but not all of the decisions for the ward.[80] A ward for whom a limited guardian has been appointed may retain the right to do certain things for himself, such as those outlined above. He may be able to vote for politicians or to marry.

A permanent guardian that does not have general powers is a limited guardian. There is no one definition of what a limited guardian can and cannot do for his ward; it is highly case-specific.

Counsel may also wish to advocate for a conservatorship for his client, if his client will consent to a conservator. Conservatorships are discussed below. A conservatorship, unlike a guardianship, is a consensual arrangement.[81] Typically, a conservator makes financial decisions for the conservatee, not decisions involving health or residence. The conservatee retains the right to make financial decisions for himself.

### (3) Whether a case plan for the incapacitated person should thereafter be submitted to the court

Court-appointed counsel may recommend that a care plan for the incapacitated person be submitted to the court. A growing number of social workers are becoming geriatric care managers. A geriatric care manager assesses a person and makes recommendations as to their care. Do they need to live in a nursing home? Can they live at home with a home health aide?

---

78. N.J.S.A. 3B:13A-2.
79. N.J.S.A. 3B:12-24.1(a).
80. N.J.S.A. 3B:12-24.1(b).
81. N.J.S.A. 3B:13A-2.

A geriatric care manager may also arrange for services to be provided to a person. For instance, a geriatric care manager may arrange for home health aides for the incapacitated person.

Note that this requirement states "for the incapacitated person" as opposed to "for the alleged incapacitated person." The requirement also uses the word "thereafter." Both of these speak to a recommendation as to an action that will take place post-declaration of incapacity.

The court rules permit court-appointed counsel to make a recommendation as to whether or not such a care plan should be submitted to the court.

**(4) The report shall further state whether the alleged incapacitated person has expressed dispositional preferences and, if so, counsel shall argue for their inclusion in the judgment of the court**

The Court Rules require court-appointed counsel to indicate whether or not the alleged incapacitated person has expressed dispositional preferences. In other words, has the incapacitated person indicated whom he would wish to receive his estate after his death. The rule also requires the count-appointed counsel to argue for the inclusion of those dispositional preferences in the judgment of incapacity.

This is an interesting requirement. From a practical standpoint, few reports of court-appointed counsels address these issues. If a guardian is appointed for a ward, the court cannot grant the guardian the power to make a last will and testament for the ward, though a court can grant a ward the authority to enter a trust agreement that can be revocable or irrevocable and the terms of which could continue after the death of the ward.[82]

So, for instance, it would appear to be within the court's authority to grant a guardian the authority to create an irrevocable life insurance trust for the ward or to create a revocable living trust the terms of which might include post-death dispositional preferences. But a court cannot grant the guardian the power to draft a last will and testament for his ward.

---

[82] N.J.S.A. 3B:12-49.

On the other hand, the Court Rules compel court-appointed counsel to state whether or not the alleged incapacitated person has expressed dispositional preferences and to argue for the inclusion of those preferences into the judgment of incapacity. So, a judgment of incapacity might state the persons or entities that will receive the ward's estate after his death, if the ward expressed preferences to his court-appointed counsel.

This is a very interesting requirement that very few reports address.

**(5) The report shall also make recommendations concerning whether good cause exists for the court to order that any power of attorney, health care directive, or revocable trust created by the alleged incapacitated person be revoked or the authority of the person or persons acting thereunder be modified or restricted**

Assume that Mr. Smith signed a power of attorney and a living will or that he signed a revocable living trust that now holds most of his estate and names a successor trustee to serve if Mr. Smith ever were to become incapacitated, which he now is. Should those documents remain in full force and effect?

What if the power of attorney and living will and trust name Mr. Smith's daughter as agent/successor trustee, but court-appointed counsel if recommending that Mr. Smith's son serve as his guardian? Perhaps there is evidence that the daughter used some of Mr. Smith's funds in an inappropriate manner.

Court-appointed counsel should recommend whether or not these documents should be revoked or, in some manner, modified. In the example above, it would probably be best if the power of attorney, living will and revocable trust were simply revoked. A court shouldn't appoint the son as guardian and permit the daughter to continue to serve as agent/trustee. How would the son account for the daughter's actions? Whose decision would control on a given issue?

Perhaps the documents name the daughter as agent and the son as alternate agent, so court-appointed counsel could recommend that the documents be modified to eliminate the daughter and to permit the son to serve as agent despite the fact that the daughter is willing to serve.

From a practical standpoint, even if the documents named the son as agent/successor trustee, courts typically revoke any power of attorney or living will because the court doesn't want a conflict between the powers of the guardian and the powers of the agent under the power of attorney or living will document.[83] In most cases, this is the prudent course of action.

## 5-10 THE GUARDIAN AD LITEM (GAL)

If "special circumstances" come to the attention of the court at any time prior to the entry of a judgment, the court may appointed a guardian ad litem for the alleged incapacitated person.[84] A party to the action can make a formal motion requesting the court to appoint a guardian ad litem or the court might decided to appoint a guardian ad litem on its own accord.

The rule requires "special circumstances" to exist, so a guardian ad litem is not something that should be appointed in every case.

### 5-10:1 Definition

A guardian ad litem is not a guardian, so the name is a bit of a misnomer. The Probate Code defines the word "guardian" to include a person who has qualified as a guardian of the person or estate, or both, of a minor or incapacitated individual pursuant to a testamentary or court-appointment, but the definition specifically excludes a person who is merely a guardian ad litem.[85]

### 5-10:2 Role of the GAL

The role of a guardian ad litem is to express what he believes to be in the best interest of the alleged incapacitated person and to report to the court on his opinion.[86] The role of the guardian ad litem differs from that of the court-appointed counsel.[87]

---

83. N.J.S.A. 46:2B-8.4(c).

84. *R.* 4:86-4(d).

85. N.J.S.A. 3B:1-1 ("Guardian").

86. *R.* 4:86-4(d).

87. *In the Matter of M.R., an Alleged Incompetent or Mentally Retarded Adult*, 135 N.J. 155, 172-178 (1994), *In the Matter of the Guardianship of Walter J. Macak*, 377 N.J. Super. 167, 176 (App. Div. 2005).

As stated above, court-appointed counsel is an advocate for the alleged incapacitated person.[88] While the duties of court-appointed counsel to the court and to the parties who have entered an appearance in the action can be fraught with pitfalls for the inexperienced attorney, the fact remains that court-appointed counsel, like all attorneys, is an advocate for his client.

A guardian ad litem is not an attorney. While courts frequently appoint attorneys to serve as guardians ad litem, there is no requirement that an appointed guardian ad litem be an attorney. The guardian ad litem could be a social worker or any person the court chooses to appoint.

Most importantly, unlike an attorney who is an advocate for his client's wishes, a guardian ad litem expresses *his* opinion as to what is in the best interest of the alleged incapacitated person.

The alleged incapacitated person might be saying that he doesn't want a guardian, that he just wants to go home and that he wants the guardianship action dismissed. The alleged incapacitated person's desires may not be patently absurd or necessarily pose a risk of undue harm to him; nevertheless, the guardian ad litem can report to the court that, in his opinion, a guardian should be appointed and the alleged incapacitated person should remain in a nursing home. The guardian ad litem must express the reasons for his opinion, but the opinion of the guardian ad litem is in no way constrained by the wishes of the alleged incapacitated person.

A guardian ad litem can be helpful because a judge simply isn't going to visit the alleged incapacitated person in his environment. Perhaps the person is living in a home that is full of garbage. While the court can hear testimony as to the facts of a case, in a close case, actually seeing how the alleged incapacitated person is living and hearing from the alleged incapacitated person in his home environment can be helpful.

## 5-11 SERVICE OF THE PLEADINGS

The Court Rules compel the plaintiff to provide the court with an affidavit prior to the hearing attesting to the fact that the

---

88. *In the Matter of M.R., an Alleged Incompetent or Mentally Retarded Adult*, 135 N.J. 155 (1994).

alleged incapacitated person has been personally served with the complaint and accompanying papers (affidavit of estate, affidavits of physicians, etc.).[89] The plaintiff must provide proof by affidavit of the fact that the alleged incapacitated person was afforded the opportunity to either personally appear before the court or to appear by attorney before the court.

The plaintiff is required to inform the alleged incapacitated person that if he chooses, he may demand trial by jury on the issue of his capacity.[90] Finally, the plaintiff must provide proof by affidavit of the fact that the alleged incapacitated person was given or offered assistance to communicate with friends, relatives or attorneys.[91]

The court is free to direct the manner in which service must be made upon the interested parties other than the alleged incapacitated person. Typically, the court will sign an order to show cause that compels the plaintiff to serve the complaint and accompanying papers on the interested parties (relatives, court-appointed counsel) by certified mail and regular mail.

## 5-12 THE RETURN DATE

The complaint and accompanying papers (affidavit of estate, affidavits of physicians, etc.) are filed with the surrogate of the county in which the alleged incapacitated person is domiciled. Either the surrogate or a judge of the Superior Court, Probate Part, will sign an "order to show cause" or order for hearing, which appoints an attorney as court-appointed counsel for the alleged incapacitated person and establishes an initial return date.[92] Unless the court shortens the timeframe in the order to show cause and states the reason why it shortened the timeframe, the order to show cause must provide at least 20 days' notice of the return date to the alleged incapacitated person.[93]

Litigants believe that the return date is the date on which the issue of capacity or incapacity and who, if anyone, should be appointed the guardian will be decided. Whether the court will

---

89. *R.* 4:86-5.
90. N.J.S.A. 3B:12-24, *R.* 4:86-6, 4:86-6(a).
91. *R.* 4:86-5.
92. *R.* 4:86-4(a).
93. *R.* 4:86-4(a).

decide the issue of capacity and who should be the guardian on the return date depends on whether or not the guardianship action is contested or uncontested. Most courts set the return date on a motion day for the court, so the court is entertaining many different cases on the return date.

If the guardianship is "contested," meaning that the alleged incapacitated person or one of the interested parties is contesting an issue in the guardianship action, then the court simply doesn't have time to conduct a trial on the return date and decide the contested issues. The court might have ten or more cases with various issues pending before it on the day fixed for hearing. There might be twenty or more attorneys and their clients sitting in the court on the return date waiting for their case to be heard.

If the guardianship is contested in any way, the court will probably establish a discovery schedule on the return date and set the matter down for a trial date, which could be several months in the future.

If the guardianship is uncontested—meaning that the alleged incapacitated person, his court-appointed counsel or any interested party does not contest any issue in the guardianship—then the court will decide the matter on the return date. Courts across New Jersey conduct matters differently.

Unless a trial by jury is demanded by or on behalf of the alleged incapacitated person, the court decides the issue of incapacity after taking testimony in open court.[94] With the consent of court-appointed counsel, the court may take the testimony of the physicians who filed affidavits by telephone or may dispense with their testimony all together.[95]

From a practical standpoint, the issue of capacity is very rarely decided by a jury.[96] Most probate judges have never presided over a trial by jury on the issue of capacity.

From a practical standpoint, on the return date of an uncontested guardianship, most judges take very little testimony. Some may ask the plaintiff to testify as to the allegations in the complaint and may question the plaintiff somewhat as to his understanding of the role

---

94. *R.* 4:86-6(a).

95. *R.* 4:86-6(a).

96. N.J.S.A. 3B:12-24.

of a guardian (the duties and obligations of a guardian, the proposed guardian's willingness to accept these duties, etc.).[97] In most instance, the "hearing" takes no more than five minutes.

In fact, while the Court Rules require a hearing,[98] some counties do not even require the appearances of counsel in court if the matter is uncontested. If the court-appointed counsel and the physicians all agree as to the incapacity of the alleged incapacitated person and if everyone agrees that the plaintiff should be appointed as the guardian of the alleged incapacitated person, then, while not technically in compliance with the Court Rules, it seems appropriate that the court should forego the hearing.

The appearance of court-appointed counsel and plaintiff's counsel in court only costs the alleged incapacitated money, as it is the alleged incapacitated person's estate that, in most cases, pays the fees of these attorneys.[99] Making them appear in court to repeat what is already before the court by way of affidavits and the report of court-appointed counsel seems unnecessary, and more and more counties agree with this fact and are foregoing appearances on the return date of uncontested guardianship matters. Technically, though, the court rules do require the appearance of counsel even if the matter is uncontested.

Most guardianship matters are uncontested. Even those that are contested frequently resolve themselves through settlements.

## 5-13 CONTESTED VERSUS UNCONTESTED HEARINGS

Elder law practitioners frequently discuss a guardianship matter in terms of whether or not it is contested or uncontested. Most guardianship actions are uncontested, but since a guardianship is an adversarial action, it could easily become contested.

An uncontested guardianship is one in which no one contests the incapacity of the proposed ward and no one contests the appointment of the person who is seeking to be appointed as the guardian for the ward.

---

97. *R.* 4:86-6(d).
98. *R.* 4:86-6(a).
99. *R.* 4:86-4(e).

In the vast majority of guardianship actions, the proposed ward is truly incapacitated, typically mentally incapacitated. Moreover, most guardianship actions are filed by one spouse seeking to be appointed guardian of the other spouse or by a child seeking to be appointed guardian of her parent. In most instances, the need to file for guardianship is discussed amongst the closest family members before it is filed, and the family comes to a decision that a guardianship is necessary.

This is not to say that all guardianship actions are uncontested. In some instances, the proposed ward, perhaps through counsel, contests the need for a guardianship. In other cases, family members fight over who should be appointed as guardian for the ward; a guardianship can be a very emotional matter.

Perhaps the guardianship involves a mother of four children. The idea that the children now have to declare their mother as being mentally incapacitated can be an extremely emotional event. Even if all of the children believe in their heart that mom can no longer handle her affairs, one or two of the children may not want to have mom declared incapacitated by a court.

## 5-13:1 Contesting Incapacity

In some cases, the issue of capacity is contested. The proposed ward may receive a copy of the pleadings and become quite angry that someone, perhaps one of his children, believes he needs a guardian and has filed for guardianship over him. Even if the proposed ward has some issues with dementia and some physical limitations, he may still retain the wherewithal to comprehend the general nature of a guardianship and to seek out and to retain the services of an attorney.

The ward can retain his own attorney and contest the guardianship, contending that he is capable of handling his own affairs and doesn't need a guardian. Or, the court-appointed attorney could contest the issue of capacity on behalf of the ward.

The Court Rules compel court-appointed counsel to meet personally with the ward.[100] Case law compels court-appointed counsel to advocate for the ward and to adhere to the ward's

---

100. *R.* 4:86-4(b)(1).

directions, unless the desires of the ward are patently absurd or pose a risk of undue harm to the ward.[101] The Rules of Professional Conduct contain a similar provision.[102]

Court-appointed counsel could meet with the ward, personally believe that the ward would benefit from the appointment of a guardian, but the ward could express his desire to fight the guardianship. The ward could be managing his affairs in a marginal manner, not quite to the point where he is a danger to himself, and the proposed ward could say to his court-appointed counsel that he doesn't want a guardian.

In cases such as this, court-appointed counsel is compelled to advocate for his client and to request that the court dismiss the guardianship action.

Since most guardianship cases are brought for legitimate reasons, whether or not a proposed ward decides to contest the issue of capacity often turns on how counsel approaches the proposed ward. As discussed above, an incapacitated person is someone who can no longer handle his affairs as the result of physical or mental infirmity.[103]

The fact of the matter is that some older individuals, can no longer handle their affairs as the result of a combination of physical and mental infirmities. The proper question for counsel is: If left to his own devices, could the proposed ward handle his own affairs? Does he have the wherewithal to comprehend the nature of his limitations? Does he have the wherewithal to retain the services of others, such as a home health aide, to assist him in those areas he can no longer handle for himself?

Once counsel—whether court-appointed or private counsel—has resolved those questions for himself, he can then counsel his client. As attorneys, our job is to advise our clients, and sometimes the best advice may be that the client does require the assistance of a guardian. After all, in order for a court-appointed counsel to be appointed in the first place, two physicians have had to examine the ward and opine that the ward requires the assistance of a guardian.

---

101. *In the Matter of M.R., an Alleged Incompetent or Mentally Retarded Adult*, 135 N.J. 155 (1994).

102. R.P.C. 1.14.

103. N.J.S.A. 3B:1-2 ("Incapacitated person").

A ward cannot consent to a guardianship;[104] only a court of competent jurisdiction can adjudicate an individual as being incapacitated. The client always has the final say, unless his intentions are patently absurd or pose a risk of undue harm, but counsel should not forget about his obligation to advise the client.

Luckily for court-appointed counsel, the vast majority of guardianships do not involve judgment calls. From the start to the finish of the action, it is typically evident that the ward is an incapacitated individual and requires the assistance of a guardian.

### 5-13:2 Contesting Who Should Be the Guardian

In some cases, it is not the capacity of the ward that is in question but the choice of who should be the guardian. Perhaps mom has four children and two of those children never got along. Both might seek to be named as the guardian of mom. There is a statute that creates an order of priority as to who should be appointed as the guardian of a ward,[105] but when there are two children fighting over the position, both would have equal priority to be appointed as the guardian.

In cases such as this, the matter could result in a trial to determine who should be appointed as guardian. Evidence might be presented as to the mother's past predilections. One son might claim that mom named him as her power of attorney agent. The other son might claim that the power of attorney was the product of undue influence and was signed when mom lacked the capacity to execute the power of attorney.

In the end, the court will have to determine what the mother would have wanted and what is in the mother's best interest.

### 5-13:3 Conservatorship

A conservatorship is a consensual arrangement through which one person, called the conservatee, consents to the appointment of another individual, called the conservator, to manage his estate.[106]

---

104. *In the Matter of the Guardianship of Walter J. Macak*, 377 N.J. Super. 167, 175 (App. Div. 2005).

105. N.J.S.A. 3B:12-25, *see also R.* 4:86-6(c).

106. N.J.S.A. 3B:13A-1 et seq., *R.* 4:86-11.

A court cannot appoint a conservator for a person if the proposed conservatee objects to the appointment.[107]

A conservatorship action, like a guardianship action, is governed by a set of statutes that are part of New Jersey's Probate Code. Those statutes forbid a court from appointing a conservator if the proposed conservatee objects to the appointment.

A court is permitted to appoint counsel for the conservatee, if the court believes that counsel is necessary to protect the interests of the conservatee,[108] but unlike in a guardianship action, the court is not compelled to appoint counsel.

The conservatee must attend the hearing appointing his conservator unless it is established to the satisfaction of the court that the conservatee is unable to attend the hearing.[109] If the conservatee is unable to attend the hearing, the court should order an investigation to ensure that the conservatee does not object to the conservatorship, unless the court believes that the interests of the conservatee are adequately protected by counsel who is representing the conservatee.

As with a guardianship, the court can compel the conservator to post a bond,[110] to file an inventory,[111] and to file an accounting.[112] Because of the court's ability to require a bond, an inventory, and an accounting—a conservatorship offers court-supervision over the actions of the conservator that do not typically exist when a person signs a power of attorney.

In most instances, a conservator manages the estate (the property) of the conservatee, not his health or residential related matters;[113] however, in certain instances the powers of a conservator can

---

107. N.J.S.A. 3B:13A-2, *In the Matter of the Conservatorship of William C. Halley*, 342 N.J. Super. 777 (App. Div. 2001). The statutes governing conservatorship actions establish a priority for the appointment of individuals to serve as conservator, first priority is given to a person or financial institution of the conservatee's choosing. N.J.S.A. 3B:13A-8(a). But the statute also permits the court to deviate from that priority for good cause. N.J.S.A. 3B:13A-8. So, a question may arise, What if the court does not appoint the person the conservatee has chosen? Since a conservator cannot be appointed if the conservatee objects to the appointment, N.J.S.A. 3B:13A-2, then the action would have to be dismissed.

108. N.J.S.A. 3B:13A-3.

109. N.J.S.A. 3B:13A-4, *R.* 4:86-11(b).

110. N.J.S.A. 3B:13A-13.

111. N.J.S.A. 3B:13A-17.

112. N.J.S.A. 3B:13A-25, *R.* 4:86-11(d).

113. N.J.S.A. 3B:13A-1(b).

be expanded to include the health and residential affairs of the conservatee.[114] Some attorneys involved in contested guardianship actions use the ability to expand the powers of the conservator to include health and residential related matters to create a de facto guardianship that is more palatable to all involved in the contested guardianship action.

In practice, very few straight conservatorship actions are filed. If a person retains his capacity, he typically has a financial power of attorney document drafted and nominates an agent to make financial decisions for him. For that matter, if a person retains his capacity, he also signs a living will and nominates someone as his healthcare agent to make healthcare decisions for him.

Few people know or understand about conservatorship or understand them, and fewer still would want to incur all the legal fees associated with a conservatorship when a power of attorney and living will can accommodate their needs for far less money and in a far more comprehensive manner than a conservatorship.

A person might want a conservatorship if he has no one whom he feels comfortable naming as his agent under a power of attorney or living will. Perhaps he wants the court-supervision that is inherent with a conservatorship. The Office of the Public Guardian for Elderly Individuals will serve as a conservator if requested,[115] though the name of the office seems to be a bit of misnomer in this situation. The fact that the public guardian will serve provides an option for those people who simply have no one they trust who could handle their finances if they were unable to handle those matters for themselves.

With all of that said, the way most conservatorships come into being is the result of a settlement from a matter that was initially filed as a guardianship. Perhaps the ward contests the need for a guardian and his children simply don't want to fight with their father over whether or not he needs a guardian. The children might feel comfortable enough if one of them is named as conservator for the father. As mentioned above, the powers of the conservator might be expanded to include health and residential matters, creating a de facto guardianship.

---

114. N.J.S.A. 3B:13A-24.

115. N.J.S.A. 52:27G-25(f).

The fact of the matter is that the father might consent to the conservatorship (even with expanded powers) then never handle his own affairs again in a meaningful manner. His son, who is now his conservator, might take over his affairs and the goal of the guardianship—which may have been to prevent the father from being financially exploited or abused, whether by others or through his own neglect—can be accomplished in a manner that is more palatable to the father.

In some cases, changing the tone of the action (from guardianship to conservatorship) can go far in resolving the matter.

## 5-14 DISCOVERY

In contested matters, counsel for plaintiff, court-appointed counsel and counsel for any other party will appear in court on the return date of the order to show cause. In all likelihood, the court will establish a preliminary date for a hearing/trial and will discuss a discovery schedule with counsel.[116]

In guardianship actions, the full panoply of discovery is available. The court and counsel will discuss the discovery schedule, and the court will sign a case management order that establishes the schedule of discovery, sets a date for a pre-trial conference and establishes the hearing date.

## 5-15 THE HEARING

Assuming the guardianship action is contested and has not resolved itself, a hearing, or trial, will be held before a judge.[117] The Court Rules and statutes permit the alleged incapacitated person or someone acting on his behalf to request a trial by jury on the issue of capacity,[118] but very few guardianship cases are ever tried before a jury. (Most judges sitting in the probate part probably have never presided over a guardianship jury trial on the issue of capacity.)

In the absence of a legitimate jury demand, the court decides the issue of capacity, after taking testimony in open court.[119]

---

116. *R.* 4:10-1 et seq.
117. *R.* 4:86-6.
118. N.J.S.A. 3B:12-24.
119. *R.* 4:86-6(a).

The incapacitated person should be present at the hearing, unless the plaintiff and court-appointed attorney certify that the incapacitated person is unable to attend the hearing as the result of physical or mental incapacity.[120] In such a case, the court must find that it would be prejudicial to the health of the incapacitated person to attend the hearing or unsafe for the incapacitated person to attend the hearing.

In a contested guardianship, the hearing would be conducted like any other trial, with testimony taken and evidence admitted into the record. At the end of the hearing, the court will decide the issue of capacity and will decide who should serve as the guardian, if the proposed ward is adjudicated to be incapacitated.

## 5-16 APPOINTMENT OF GUARDIAN

The court decides who should serve as the guardian of the incapacitated person.[121] There are several different types of guardians: pendente lite guardian, limited guardian, general guardian, guardian of the person, guardian of the property, sole guardian and co-guardians.[122] (There are also special medical guardians, but that is discussed below.[123])

In most guardianship actions, the plaintiff is filing to be appointed the sole, general (or full) guardian of the person and estate of the incapacitated person. With that said, something less than a full guardian of the person and estate does present itself in guardianship actions with regularity.

Most guardianship actions involve an elderly ward who suffers from dementia or some other disease associated with aging that is progressive and renders the ward incapacitated. But a fair number of guardianships involve developmentally disabled individuals.[124] Particularly when dealing with a developmentally disabled person, a limited guardianship—something less than a general guardianship—may be appropriate.

---

120. *R.* 4:86-6(a).
121. *R.* 4:86-6(c).
122. N.J.S.A. 3B:12-24.1, *R.* 4:86-6(c).
123. *R.* 4:86-12.
124. N.J.S.A. 30:4-165.7, *R.* 4:86-10.

Perhaps the person retains the right to perform certain life tasks, and his right to perform those tasks should be preserved and nurtured. The best way to do that is through a limited guardianship that retains for him his autonomy over his own life in certain ways yet protects him in the ways, in which he needs protection.

### 5-16:1 Guardian of the Person

The guardian of the person of the incapacitated person makes decisions affecting the health and residence of the incapacitated person. For instance, the guardian of the person makes medical decisions for the incapacitated person. The guardian of the person makes decisions about where the incapacitated person will live and with whom he can socialize.

### 5-16:2 Guardian of the Estate

The guardian of the estate of the incapacitated person (also called the guardian of the property) manages and controls the property of the incapacitated person.

### 5-16:3 Sole Guardian

A sole guardian (*pendente lite*, general or limited) is a guardian who serves alone. A sole guardian can be contrasted with a co-guardian, which typically involves two persons serving as the guardian for an incapacitated person.

A court could appoint one person (say the ward's son) to serve as the sole guardian of his person and another person (say the ward's daughter) to serve as the sole guardian of his property. In most cases, the court appoints one person to serve as the sole guardian of the person and estate of the ward.

### 5-16:4 Co-Guardians

Co-guardians are two or more persons who serve as the guardian of a ward at the same time. Typically, no more than two people are appointed to serve at any one time, as having three or more persons serve as someone's guardian is simply unwieldy.

Co-guardians could be appointed for any number of reasons; perhaps, the plaintiffs requested co-guardians or perhaps appointing co-guardians was a means to settle a contested guardianship.

When filing guardianships for developmentally disabled individuals, co-guardians are rather typical as both the mother and father want to serve as the guardian of their child, who may have recently attained the age of majority and now needs a guardian.

## 5-16:5 General Guardian

A general (or plenary) guardian is a guardian who makes all decisions (financial, residential, healthcare) for the ward.[125]

## 5-16:6 Limited Guardian

A court can appointed a limited guardian of the person, a limited guardian of the estate or a limited guardian of both the person and estate.[126] A limited guardianship is a guardianship through which the ward retains capacity to perform some, but not all, of his life tasks. For instance, the ward might not be able to handle large financial transactions, but he may be able to handle transactions involving small amounts of money, perhaps transactions under $1,000. Or a ward may not be able to make any financial decisions, but he may be able to participate in health and residential related decisions.

The court is required to make specific findings into those areas for which the ward retains capacity and those areas for which the ward does not retain capacity. The judgment should state those areas in which the ward retains capacity and those areas in which the ward lacks capacity.[127]

## 5-16:7 Pendente Lite Guardian

A pendente lite guardian is a guardian who is appointed on a temporary basis to serve as guardian for the incapacitated person during the guardianship litigation.[128] An incapacitated person might need immediate help, for instance, he may be a patient in a hospital and he might need someone who can place him in a nursing facility and apply for Medicaid benefits for him.

---

125. N.J.S.A. 3B:12-24.1(a).
126. N.J.S.A. 3B:12-24.1(b).
127. N.J.S.A. 3B:12-24.1(b).
128. N.J.S.A. 3B:12-24.1(c).

By court rule, at least twenty days' notice of the hearing must be given to the alleged incapacitated person, so a general or limited guardian isn't going to be appointed for a person for several weeks, perhaps several months if the matter is contested.[129] Because the incapacitated person might need immediate help, the statutes permit the court to appoint a guardian on a temporary basis to serve during the pendency of the litigation. This type of guardianship is known as a pendente lite guardian.

The powers granted to the pendente lite guardian must be necessary to deal with the critical needs of the incapacitated person or to avoid substantial harm befalling him.[130] The appointment of a pendente lite guardian must be in the best interest of the incapacitated person. The powers of the guardian should be crafted as necessary to protect the incapacitated person or his estate. For instance, the court might permit the pendente lite guardian to access a limited amount of the incapacitated person's assets ("no more than $30,000") and direct how those funds are to be used ("to pay for the care of the incapacitated person in an appropriate long-term care facility, such as a nursing home").

The order appointing the pendente liteguardian can permit the incapacitated person to move before the court on 2 days' notice (or even shorter notice as the court prescribes) to dissolve the guardianship.[131] The incapacitated person would serve the plaintiff and pendente lite guardian with notice of his request to dissolve the guardianship.

The order appointing the pendente lite guardian shall have no effect on the adjudication of the incapacity of the alleged incapacitated person.[132] Furthermore, the order shall not limit the rights of the incapacitated person except to the extent provided in the order.[133]

An order appointing a pendente lite guardian without notice to the incapacitated person expires within 45 days unless the court extends the appointment for good cause.[134] The pendente lite

---

129. *R.* 4:86-4(a).
130. N.J.S.A. 3B:12-24.1(c)(2), (4).
131. N.J.S.A. 3B:12-24.1(c)(7).
132. N.J.S.A. 3B:12-24.1(c)(6).
133. N.J.S.A. 3B:12-24.1(c)(6).
134. N.J.S.A. 3B:12-24.1(c)(8).

guardian shall furnish a bond, unless the court relieves him of this obligation.[135]

## 5-17 PAYMENT OF COUNSEL FEES

Who is going to pay for this? A guardianship action is expensive. Even an uncontested guardianship can cost $5,000 between the lawyers' fees (court-appointed counsel, plaintiff's counsel) and the doctors' fees for the examinations and affidavits and the court costs.

Despite the fact that a guardianship is an adversarial proceeding, through which the plaintiff is seeking to wrest control over the affairs of the ward, a guardianship is also for the ward's benefit. The plaintiff is attempting to protect the ward from himself and from potential or actual exploitation by others. For that reason, in most guardianship actions, the person who pays the costs of the guardianship (counsel fees, physician fees and court costs) is the ward.

There is a Court Rule that specifically permits the court to compensate plaintiff's counsel, court-appointed counsel and a guardian ad litem, if any, from the estate of the ward.[136] Note that the guardianship court rule does not permit the court to compensate any attorneys other than plaintiff's counsel and court-appointed counsel.

Nevertheless, if a guardianship matter has other attorneys involved (for instance, counsel for a family member who is contesting the guardianship or private counsel for the incapacitated person), courts frequently compensate all counsel from the ward's estate. The American Rule regarding counsel fees is that a litigant pays his own attorney's fees, unless there is a specific exception to the American Rule.[137] The guardianship compensation Court Rule provides such an exception for plaintiff's counsel and court-appointed counsel. There is another Court Rule that permits a court to award counsel fees from a "fund in court."[138]

Since a guardianship action is for the benefit of the ward, who is a third-party to most of the litigants in a guardianship action with the exception of the ward, a court can award fees to other attorneys out of the fund in court that is the ward's estate. The idea is that the

---

135. N.J.S.A. 3B:12-24.1(c)(10).

136. *R.* 4:86-4(e).

137. *In the Matter of the Estate of Elizabeth Hull Vayda, deceased*, 184 N.J. 115 (2005).

138. *R.* 4:42-9(a)(2).

litigants were advocating for the protection of the ward's estate and should be compensated from that estate for their efforts.

The Court Rule on compensation in a guardianship action also permits the court to compensate court-appointed counsel and plaintiff's counsel "in such other manner as the court shall direct."[139] So, under the guardianship compensation rule, which is an exception to the American Rule on counsel fees, the court could direct that someone other than the ward's estate compensate plaintiff's counsel and court-appointed counsel. For instance, the court may direct that plaintiff compensate his own attorney and court-appointed counsel.

## 5-18 GUARDIAN BOND

A guardian bond is designed to protect the ward's estate from the potential wrongful acts of the guardian. For instance, if a guardian steals the ward's money, the guardian's bond will reimburse the ward's estate or the ward's creditors for the money the guardian stole.

The bonding company would have a cause of action against the guardian who stole the money. In other words, the bonding company could sue the guardian for the money he stole and for which the bonding company had to reimburse the estate of the ward or the ward's creditors.

In guardianship cases, with limited exceptions, a bond is required.[140] The court in its discretion is free to set the amount of the bond and the conditions of the bond, for instance, compelling the guardian to account to the court as a condition of the bond.

### 5-18:1 Requests To Increase or To Decrease the Bond

A bond is typically set on the value of the liquid assets of the estate, not the real property, which the guardian is not free to sell or mortgage without a court order.[141] For instance, if the ward has a house worth $400,000 and bank/brokerage accounts worth $300,000, the court will typically set the bond at $300,000.

The judgment appointing the guardian will typically state that the guardian cannot sell or mortgage the ward's real property

---

139. *R.* 4:86-4(e).

140. N.J.S.A. 3B:15-1.

141. *R.* 4:94-1 et seq.

without further order of the court. Since the guardian cannot sell or mortgage the real estate, there is no reason for the court to bond the guardian for the value of the real property.

If the guardian later applies to sell the real property and is granted permission, the court will, in all likelihood, increase the amount of the bond. For instance, if the ward's real estate does sell for $400,000 and the ward's liquid assets are now worth $700,000, then the court may increase the guardian's bond from $300,000 to $700,000.

Guardians are typically required to account to the court.[142] Many wards reside in long-term care facilities, such as nursing homes or assisted living residences. Over time, the ward's estate will decrease in value, because the guardian is paying the nursing home $10,000 a month.

If the guardian submits the accounting and the ward's liquid assets have decreased from $300,000 to $200,000 because of long-term care costs, the guardian could request the court to decrease the bond from $300,000 to $200,000. The larger the bond, the more the bond costs the estate, so it is good to lower the amount of the bond when possible.

## 5-19 LIABILITY OF GUARDIAN FOR DEBTS OF THE WARD

The guardian of the person of a ward is not obligated to provide for the ward from the guardian's own funds.[143] It is the guardian of the person who would make healthcare and residential decisions for the ward. For instance, the guardian of the person is the guardian who would make the decision to place the ward in a nursing home or assisted living residence.

The statutes assure the guardian of the person that he is not financially obligated for his ward.[144]

## 5-20 INVENTORY

A court may require a guardian to file an inventory of the real and personal property of the ward; however, the court cannot require

---

142. N.J.S.A. 3B:12-63, N.J.S.A. 3B:17-3.

143. N.J.S.A. 3B:12-56.

144. N.J.S.A. 3B:12-56(a).

the guardian to file an inventory until three months after letters of guardianship were granted.[145] An inventory is not mandatory in all guardianship cases, but many courts do require a guardian to file an inventory.

An inventory is a very simple document that simply lays out the real and personal property that the ward owns.

## 5-21 ACCOUNTING

A guardian shall file accountings with the court at intervals as the court requires.[146] Some courts require a guardian to file an accounting every year. Some courts might permit the guardian to file his accounting every other year if the size of the ward's estate does not warrant an annual accounting.

In some instances, the court might require the guardian to file his accounting formally. In other cases, the court may require the initial accounting to be filed formally and permit informal accountings thereafter.[147] When and how an accounting must be filed is at the discretion of the court.

### 5-21:1 Format of an Accounting

A formal must follow certain formatting procedures which are prescribed by court rule. A summary of the formal accounting must be filed with the complaint to the court in the action for the settlement of the account.[148] That summary must contain the following pieces of information:

> (1) in the case of a first accounting, the amount for which the accountant was chargeable as of the date the . . . obligation devolved upon him or her, or where an inventory is on file, the amount of the inventory; or in the case of a second or later accounting, the balance remaining in the hands of the accountant as shown in the last previous account;
>
> (2) the amount for which the accountant became chargeable in addition thereto;

---

145. *R.* 4:86-6(d).
146. N.J.S.A. 3B:17-3.
147. http://www.judiciary.state.nj.us/forms.htm.
148. *R.* 4:87-2(b).

(3) the total of the first two items;

(4) the amount of the allowances claimed in the account; and

(5) the balance in the accountant's hands. Charges and allowances sought on account of corpus and income shall be stated separately both in the summary and in the account.

### 5-21:2 Formal Accounting

A formal accounting is an accounting that is filed with the court pursuant to the Court Rule governing the settlement of accounts. The surrogate's office audits formal accountings and charges an audit fee.[149] After the accounting has been audited, the complaint to settle the account and the accounting are filed with the Superior Court.

Interested parties have an opportunity to file exceptions to the accounting,[150] and the Superior Court reviews the accounting and exceptions, if any, and accepts the accounting, accepts the accounting with exceptions or rejects the accounting.

Assuming that the court accepts the accounting, the liability of the guardian for the period of time covered in the accounting is settled for all time.[151]

Since a formal accounting is filed with the court and audited by the surrogate, there are more fees and costs involved with a formal accounting as opposed to an informal accounting.

### 5-21:3 Informal Accounting

An informal accounting is an accounting that is not filed with the court. An informal accounting may be sent into the surrogate's office, but it is not audited and the superior court does not review the accounting.

There are no formatting rules for an informal accounting, since the accounting is not being filed with the court. Most practitioners who file informal accountings for their clients simply follow the formatting rules applicable for an accounting that is being filed formally with the court.

---

149. N.J.S.A. 22A:2-30.

150. *R.* 4:87-8.

151. N.J.S.A. 3B:17-8.

The filing of an informal accounting does not resolve the guardian's potential liability for acts performed during the time period covered in the accounting, since a final judgment is not entered approving the accounting.

## 5-22 GUARDIAN COMMISSION

For the work that the guardian performs on behalf of the ward and for the liability that the guardian assumes, the guardian is entitled to a commission.[152] The guardian is entitled to an annual commission on the corpus and income of the estate.[153] The guardian is also entitled to a termination commission when the guardianship is terminated, in most cases upon the death of the ward.[154]

### 5-22:1 Corpus Commission

A guardian is entitled to an annual corpus or principal commission, which is based upon the principal balance of the ward's estate.[155] The annual commission to which the guardian is entitled is as follows: $5 per thousand dollars of corpus on the first $400,000 of principal value of the estate and $3 per thousand dollars of corpus on the value of the estate in excess of $400,000.

So, if a ward's estate is worth $600,000, the guardian would be entitled to an annual corpus commission of $2,000 on the first $400,000 in value (400 x $5.00 = $2,000) and $600 on the remaining $200,000 in value (200 x $3.00 = $600).

#### 5-22:1.1 Valuing the Estate

How do you value the principal of the estate for purposes of calculating the corpus commission? In most instances, the guardian uses the "presumptive value" of the estate.[156] The presumptive value of an asset is the value of the asset when the guardian received the asset or, at the option of the guardian, the value of the asset at the end of the accounting period.

---

152. N.J.S.A. 3B:18-23 et seq.
153. N.J.S.A. 3B:18-25, 3B:18-24.
154. N.J.S.A. 3B:18-28.
155. N.J.S.A. 3B:18-25.
156. N.J.S.A. 3B:18-18, 3B:18-30.

So, if a guardian receives a bank account of the ward worth \$100,000 and uses the money from that account to pay the ward's bills and, at the end of the accounting period, the account is worth \$50,000, the guardian can take a commission on the historic \$100,000 value, not the current \$50,000 value.

### 5-22:2 Income Commission

The guardian is also entitled to an annual income commission, which is 6% of the value of the income received by the guardian.[157]

### 5-22:3 Termination/Distribution Commission

A guardian is also entitled to a distribution/termination commission.[158] He is entitled to a commission on all distributions (or payments) he makes on behalf of the ward, and he is entitled to a termination commission based upon the value of the estate upon the termination of the guardianship. The amount of this commission depends upon how long the guardian has served. The longer the guardian has served the greater the commission.[159] The distribution/termination commission is in addition to the annual income and corpus commissions.[160]

If the distribution of assets or the termination of the guardianship occurs within five years of the date the court appointed the guardian, then the guardian is entitled to a termination commission of 2% of the presumptive value of the distribution or the estate (if the guardianship is being terminated). If the distribution of assets or termination of the guardianship occurs after five years but before the termination of the tenth anniversary of the guardian's appointment, then the guardian is entitled to a commission of 1.5% of the value of the distribution or the estate. Finally, if the distribution or termination of the guardianship occurs more than ten years after the guardian receives the ward's property, the guardian is entitled to a distribution/termination commission of 1% of the value of the estate.

---

157. N.J.S.A. 3B:18-24.
158. N.J.S.A. 3B:18-28.
159. N.J.S.A. 3B:18-28(a) - (c).
160. N.J.S.A. 3B:18-28.

The termination/distribution commission permits the guardian to take a termination/distribution commission either upon the termination of the guardianship or upon the distribution of the ward's assets, for instance, when the guardian actually makes the distributions to pay the ward's expenses.[161] Many guardians wait until the termination of the guardianship to claim the distribution/termination commissions.

This may be bad practice given the graduated scale of the commission based upon the length of time serving as a ward's guardian. A more appropriate procedure would be to put in for the distribution commission annually along with the income and corpus commissions and to seek a termination commission upon the termination of the guardianship based upon the presumptive value of the assets remaining in the ward's estate at that time.

## 5-23 COMMON POST-JUDGMENT MOTIONS

There are several, common post-judgment motions that guardians make. These are motions to approve the sale of the ward's real estate, to gift the ward's assets, or to reduce the guardianship bond.

### 5-23:1 Motion for Sale of Real Estate

A guardian cannot sell or mortgage a ward's home without the court's permission,[162] yet wards frequently do not live in their homes. A ward might live in a nursing home or an assisted living residence, so his home is sitting vacant.

Most judgments appointing a guardian for a ward contain a line that says "the guardian cannot sell or mortgage the ward's real property without the permission of the court." Assuming the guardian wants to sell the ward's home, the guardian will file a motion with the court in order to gain permission to sell the ward's home.

The guardian might seek approval before listing the house and asks the court's permission to sell the home within a certain dollar-value range. For instance, the guardian might have the home appraised and the appraised value might be $120,000, so the

---

161. *In the Matter of Herbert Reutlinger, an Incompetent, now Deceased*, 140 N.J. 231, 235-236 (1995).

162. *R.* 4:94-1 et seq.

guardian will ask the court's permission to sell the house if the sales price is within a 10% value range from $120,000.

Or the guardian might wait until he enters a contract for the sale of the home. When signing the contract, the guardian might indicate in the contract that the sale is subject to court approval. The guardian would then have the home appraised by two real estate appraisers and submit those appraisals and the contract of sale to the court for its approval.

### 5-23:2 Motion for Gifting by the Guardian of Ward's Assets

A guardian might want to gift the assets of the ward for Medicaid planning purposes or for tax-planning purposes or the guardian may simply want to carry on a charitable gifting program in which the ward had engaged prior to his incapacity. Whatever the purpose, the guardian must obtain the court's permission in order to make gifts of the ward's estate.

Both the statutes governing guardianship actions and the case law concerning gifts by a guardian of the ward's assets require a guardian to seek the court's permission before making a gift of the ward's estate.[163] Case law dictates that the guardian satisfy five criteria before the guardian will be permitted to gift the assets of the ward.[164] Those criteria are as follows:

(1) the mental and physical condition of the incompetent are such that the possibility of her restoration to competency is virtually nonexistent;

(2) the assets of the estate of the incompetent remaining after the consummation of the proposed gifts are such that, in the light of her life expectancy and her present condition of health, they are more than adequate to meet all of her needs in the style and comfort in which she now is (and since the onset of her incompetency has

---

163. N.J.S.A. 3B:12-50, 3B:12-58, *In the Matter of Mildred Keri, a Mentally Incompetent Person*, 181 N.J. 50 (2003).

164. *In the Matter of Mildred Keri, a Mentally Incompetent Person*, 181 N.J. 50, 58-59 (2003).

been) maintained, giving due consideration to all normal contingencies;

(3) the donees constitute the natural objects of the bounty of the incompetent by any standard;

(4) the transfer will benefit and advantage the estate of the incompetent by a reduction of death taxes;

(5) there is no substantial evidence that the incompetent, as a reasonably prudent person, would, if competent, not make the gifts proposed in order to effectuate a saving of death taxes.

The experienced elder law practitioner finds himself making motions to gift the ward's assets with some regularity. A great number of people fail to plan for their disability or plan for their disability in inadequate ways. For instance, many people do not have powers of attorney or do not have well-drafted powers of attorneys. If a person has failed to plan and is incapacitated, then no one else can make decisions for him. Someone will have to become his guardian. If that guardian wants to engage in Medicaid planning for the ward, that planning will almost invariably involve gifting the ward's assets.[165]

If the guardian wants to engage in this type of planning for his ward, the guardian will have to seek the court's permission to gift the ward's assets.

Similarly, many powers of attorney fail to permit the agent to gift the principal's assets or fail to adequately address this issue. The power of attorney might only permit the agent to gift an amount equal to the annual exclusion for federal gift tax purposes, currently $14,000. Because the power of attorney document fails to address gifting by the agent in any manner or fails to adequately address the agent's ability to gift the principal's assets, a guardianship may be necessary in order to permit the agent to engage in Medicaid planning.

A guardian may wish to gift the ward's assets because the ward has an estate that will be subject to federal or New Jersey estate tax. The assets the ward will retain after the gift may be more than adequate to provide for his care, so the guardian may think it

---

165. N.J.S.A. 46:2B-8.13a.

prudent to make annual exclusion gifts to the family members of the ward. To make these gifts, the guardian will need to seek the approval of the court.

### 5-23:3 Motion To Reduce Bond

As discussed above, a common request from a guardian is to reduce the guardian bond. Guardians are required to post a bond in order to insure their faithful performance.[166] If a guardian commits wrongful acts (for instance, embezzles money from his ward's accounts), the guardian bond is there to make the ward whole for the guardian's wrongful act.

A court will typically require the guardian to post a bond equal to the value of the liquid assets of the estate. Since the guardian cannot sell or mortgage the real property of the ward without further permission of the court, courts typically do not require the guardian to post a bond on the value of the real property.

But bonds cost a ward's estate money. The larger the bond ($200,000, $300,000, $400,000), the more the bond costs the ward's estate. In the end, the ward's estate pays for the bond, because the bond is there to insure the ward's estate.

Many wards reside in long-term care facilities, such as nursing homes or assisted living residences. These facilities cost a great deal of money, as much as $12,000 a month. With costs such as those, there is no question that the estate of most wards will be rapidly depleted. As the value of the ward's estate is reduced, the value of the guardian's bond should also be reduced, thereby reducing the attendant cost of the bond.

So, motions to reduce the guardian's bond are not uncommon.

## 5-24 DELEGATION OF THE GUARDIAN'S POWERS

A little used provision of the guardianship act is the right of the guardian to delegate his powers to another person.[167] The guardian of the person of an incapacitated person (the statute does not mention guardian of the estate of an incapacitated

---

166. N.J.S.A. 3B:15-1 et seq.

167. N.J.S.A. 3B:12-39.

person) can delegate to another person any of his powers regarding the care, custody or property of the incapacitated person.

Interestingly, the statute speaks in terms of the "guardian of the person," yet it permits the guardian to delegate powers relating to the property of the ward, which would typically be the purview of the guardian of the estate.

The delegation of power(s) must be accomplished through a duly executed power of attorney document. The delegation cannot last longer than a period of 6 months.

## 5-25 REMOVAL OF GUARDIAN FOR CAUSE

Most guardians serve until they are no longer needed. In the vast majority of cases, this means that the guardian serves until the ward dies.[168] A few guardianships terminate because the ward regains mental capacity.[169]

Some guardianships terminate because the guardian is removed for cause.[170] When the guardian is removed for cause, a substituted guardian would need to be appointed.[171]

Cause for the removal of a guardian may arise in a variety of circumstances. The seminal case for the removal of a fiduciary is *Wolosoff v. CSI Liquidating Trust*.[172] Removal of any fiduciary should be granted sparingly.[173]

The removal of a fiduciary may be based upon misconduct (for instance, a breach of the duty of loyalty)[174] or it may be because of extreme disharmony between the fiduciary and the beneficiary/ward.[175]

The disharmony that must exist to warrant the removal of a guardian would have to be such as to materially interfere with the guardian's duties to the ward.[176] The disharmony may arise out of the misconduct of the guardian but proving the existence

168. N.J.S.A. 3B:12-64(a)(2).
169. N.J.S.A. 3B:12-28, 3B:12-64(a)(3), *R.* 4:86-7.
170. N.J.S.A. 3B:12-64(a)(1).
171. N.J.S.A. 3B:12-65 et seq.
172. *Wolosoff v. CSI Liquidating Trust*, 205 N.J. Super. 349 (App. Div. 1985).
173. *Wolosoff v. CSI Liquidating Trust*, 205 N.J. Super. 349, 360 (App. Div. 1985).
174. *Wolosoff v. CSI Liquidating Trust*, 205 N.J. Super. 349, 359 (App. Div. 1985).
175. *Wolosoff v. CSI Liquidating Trust*, 205 N.J. Super. 349, 360-361 (App. Div. 1985).
176. *Wolosoff v. CSI Liquidating Trust*, 205 N.J. Super. 349, 360-361 (App. Div. 1985).

of misconduct is not a prerequisite to the removal of a fiduciary based upon an allegation of disharmony.[177]

## 5-26 DEATH OF GUARDIAN

Sometimes, the guardian dies before the ward. If that happens, the court will need to appoint a substitute guardian.[178]

### 5-26:1 Nomination of Substitute Guardian in Will

Some guardians may nominate a person to serve as a substitute guardian in their last will and testament. The nomination of a substitute guardian in the last will and testament of the initial guardian is not binding upon the court; the court has jurisdiction over the appointment of a guardian for an incapacitated person.

But the court may give some weight to the person whom the initial guardian nominated to be the substitute guardian. For instance, if a husband is serving as the guardian for his wife and if he nominates one of his sons to serve as the wife's/mother's guardian in the event that he dies, the Court may give some weight to the fact that the husband wanted that son to serve as the ward's guardian.

More importantly, other family members may give the nomination some weight. If there are four children and the father/guardian nominated one of the children in his Will as a substitute guardian in the event of his death, the other children may not fight that nomination. So, the nomination in the Will could serve a very important practical purpose.

## 5-27 DEATH OF WARD

The authority and responsibility of the guardian terminates upon the death of the ward;[179] however, termination of the guardianship does not affect the guardian's liability for prior acts or his obligation to account for the funds of the ward.[180]

---

177. *Wolosoff v. CSI Liquidating Trust*, 205 N.J. Super. 349, 361 (App. Div. 1985).

178. N.J.S.A. 3B:12-65 et seq.

179. N.J.S.A. 3B:12-64(a).

180. N.J.S.A. 3B:12-64(b).

## 5-27:1 Power of Guardian After Death

If the body of the ward remains unclaimed for a period of five days, the guardian can arrange for the ward's funeral and pay for the ward's funeral from the assets of the ward's estate.[181] The guardian can also pay the surrogate's fees of administration (for instance, to have the last will and testament of the ward admitted to probate and the cost of the administrator's bond, if any) and the cost of the guardian bond.

## 5-27:2 Arranging the Funeral

If the ward's body remains unclaimed for five days, the guardian can arrange for the ward's funeral and pay for the ward's funeral from the ward's estate.[182] This sometimes happens when a professional has been appointed as the guardian for an individual on application of a facility such as a hospital or nursing home.

The professional may initially be appointed as a temporary guardian to make medical decisions for an incapacitated person and that temporary guardianship may eventually become a permanent general guardianship. The incapacitated person may have no known family or friends who are willing to serve as his guardian, so the court will appoint a professional, such as an attorney, to serve as the ward's guardian.

Eventually, the ward may pass away, and having no known family, his body may remain unclaimed. The guardian can arrange for his funeral and pay for his funeral even though the guardianship was terminated for most other purposes due to the ward's death.

In cases such as this, the guardian would be advised to have the ward's body embalmed and interned or buried, as opposed to having the body cremated. Even if the ward has no assets and is the recipient of Medicaid benefits (for instance, perhaps the ward was indigent and living in a nursing facility), the Medicaid program will pay for the cost of an inexpensive burial.

Family members may present themselves after the funeral and disagree with the funeral arrangements that the guardian made. A burial can be undone, a cremation cannot be reversed.

---

181. N.J.S.A. 3B:12-64(c).
182. N.J.S.A. 3B:12-64(c).

### 5-27:3 Guardian's Duty with Respect to Ward's Will

If the guardian is in possession of the original last will and testament of the ward, the guardian must deliver the original Will to the surrogate of the county in which the ward died domiciled upon the death of the ward.[183] The guardian must also notify the executor nominated in the Will or a beneficiary named in the Will that he (the guardian) has delivered the Will to the surrogate. The guardian must retain the assets of the ward to await delivery of those assets to the nominated executor once the executor has qualified as executor before the surrogate.

#### 5-27:3.1 Guardian's Power To Act as Personal Representative

If within 40 days after the death of the ward no other person has been duly appointed as the personal representative of the ward's estate and no action for appointment is pending in the superior court, the guardian may apply to the superior court for appointment as the personal representative of the estate of the ward.[184]

The guardian must put the heirs or named beneficiaries under the Will, if any, on notice of his action to be appointed as the personal representative of the estate.

## 5-28 RETURN TO COMPETENCY

Though it is somewhat rare, in some instances, a ward regains his capacity. This happens more frequently with younger people who have been rendered incapacitated perhaps as the result of an accident or a medical event (such a heart attack or a surgery that went awry) or with a person who was incapacitated as the result of chronic alcoholism or drug use.

Both a Court Rule and a statute permit the superior court to declare that an incapacitated person has regained his capacity.[185] The action to declare that an individual has regained his capacity must be "supported by an affidavit … setting facts the fats evidencing that the previously incapacitated person no longer is

183. N.J.S.A. 3B:12-60.
184. N.J.S.A. 3B:12-61.
185. N.J.S.A. 3B:12628, *R.* 4:86-7.

incapacitated."[186] Notice must be given to the persons who had an initial interest in the guardianship action.

An action to declare that the ward has regained capacity could be an action to declare that he has regained his full capacity or only partial capacity. For instance, a general guardianship could be terminated in its entirety or a general guardianship could be converted to a limited guardianship. The issue is very fact-sensitive.

Because a return to competency action is somewhat rare and because the statute and rule are somewhat vague as to what evidence is necessary in order to adjudicate a return to competency ("supported by an affidavit"), the procedure for such actions can vary from county to county. One county might want affidavits from two physicians attesting to their belief that the ward has regained his capacity. Another county might accept an affidavit from one physician.

But the statute and rule do not say anything about physicians' affidavits. Moreover, how does a ward arrange for and pay for two physicians to examine him and draft/execute affidavits attesting to the fact that the ward has regained his capacity? Most wards do not have access to their money. Many wards reside in long-term care facilities without the means to transport themselves to a doctor's office. These are real-life issues.[187] [See APP Article].

If the guardian is amendable to the return to competency action, then obtaining and paying for one or two physician affidavits probably would not be an issue. If the guardian is not amendable to the return to competency action, then the ward should be able to file a summary action in the superior court supported by an affidavit that he executes setting forth the facts and reasons why he believes he has partially or fully regained his capacity.

## 5-29 SPECIAL MEDICAL GUARDIANSHIP

A special medical guardianship (SMG) is a creature of court rule, not statute.[188] A special medical guardianship can be initiated

---

186. *R.* 4:86-7.

187. *See, e.g.*, Asbury Park Press story about an man fighting to declare himself competent. http://www.app.com/article/20130901/NJNEWS2001/309010033.

188. *R.* 4:86-12.

by a hospital, nursing home, treating physician, relative or other appropriate person.[189] A special medical guardianship is requesting the appointment of a guardian of the person, not the estate. The SMG acts in a manner consistent with the court's order, so the powers of a guardian are defined by the order appointing him.

The procedure for filing an application to appoint a SMG should comply with the procedure to appoint a general or limited guardian as much as is practicable under the circumstances;[190] however, because SMG applications are often emergent in nature (for instance, the ward may be a patient in the hospital awaiting life-saving surgery), the court is permitted to accept an oral complaint and oral testimony, either by phone or in court, of the physicians and witnesses. The appointment of court-appointed counsel is not required but a court-appointed counsel should be appointed "[w]henever possible"; in most instances, an attorney is appointed as court-appointed counsel.[191]

If the court renders an oral order appointing the SMG, the order should be reduced to writing as promptly as possible and shall recite the facts upon which the appointment was made.[192] So, the rules make it clear that SMGs may be appointed on a wholly verbal record—verbal complaint, verbal testimony, verbal order.

The court rule fails to state the procedure relating to the termination of a special medical guardian. Typically, the plaintiff (in many cases, a hospital) will file an order to terminate the SMG once the patient has received the appropriate care and a care plan for the patient has been put in place. For instance, perhaps the ward has been discharged to a nursing home for rehabilitation.

---

189. *R.* 4:86-12(a).
190. *R.* 4:86-12(c).
191. *R.* 4:86-12(c).
192. *R.* 4:86-12(d).

# Chapter 6

# What Is Long Term Care?

## 6-1 TYPES OF LONG TERM CARE

In the past 20 years, the business of long term care has seen explosive growth. In short, the provision of long term care services is big business.

As a result of this growth and the concomitant competition that comes with the expansion of an industry, long term care services have become more diverse and those services have become much more pleasant for the end user.

Gone are the days of dirty "retirement homes" or nursing homes that merely warehouse elderly individuals. Those facilities have been replaced with assisted living residences, nursing homes that seek to provide a home-like setting and continuing care retirement communities (known as CCRCs). While most people will say they want to stay in their homes, a large percentage of people who change their residence to a long term care facility grow to like, or love, their new living arrangements.

For those who do stay in their homes, the business of providing home health aides to elderly individuals has become a highly competitive business. In any given area, there are numerous businesses that provide home health aides to elderly individuals.

### 6-1:1 Home Health Aides

Home health aides are individuals who provide long term care services to elderly (or disabled) individuals in their homes. There are many businesses that provide home health aides in a given area of this state.

### 6-1:1.1 Live-in Aide

A live-in home health aide is an aide who comes to live in the client's home. The idea is that the aide will be in the client's home, 24 hours a day, 7 days a week, to ensure that the client is all right and that his needs are being met. Obviously, we all must sleep, so a live-in aide is not going to be watching the elderly individual all day long, but the idea is that the aide will be there if something does go wrong. Sometimes, it is necessary—and probably optimal, if the family can afford it—to have a live-in aide and an aide that comes at night, so the live-in aide can sleep.

The elderly individual pays the live-in aide and provides the aide with room and board.

### 6-1:1.2 Hourly Aide

An hourly home health aide is an aide who provides services to an elderly individual on an hourly basis. The aid might work anywhere from 2 hours to 12 hours a day. The aide does not live with the elderly individual.

Sometimes, an elderly individual might need assistance literally 24 hours a day, 7 days a week, and some families will arrange for shifts of hourly aides to provide services to the elderly family member. A live-in aide simply could not physically meet the needs of the elderly individual who requires constant care. So, for instance, the family might arrange for three, eight hour shifts of aides to come to the home to care for their mother.

### 6-1:1.3 Employer-Provided Aides

Some home health aide agencies employ the aides that work for them. The aides are employees of the business. The business pays employment taxes for the aide. The business provides workers' compensation insurance.

The family hires the home health aide company to provide its employees to care for their family member. Because the aide is an employee of the company and because the company has additional expenses that are not associated with simply being a placement agency, such as worker's compensation insurance, home health businesses that provide employee-aides typically charge higher rates than home health businesses that are merely placement agencies.

### 6-1:1.4 Home Health Aide Agencies

Most home health aide businesses are placement agencies. The business does not employ the aides that it provides to clients. The home health aide agency is merely a placement agency and tends to be less expensive than home health aide businesses that provide aides who are employees of the company.

There is a debate as to whether or not the aide is an employee of the family, for whom the family should be paying employer-employee payroll taxes, or an independent contractor. If the aide were an employee of the family, then the family should pay employer-employee payroll taxes and obtain workers' compensation insurance.[1] If the aide were an independent contractor, the family is responsible for paying the aide and the family is responsible for issuing an IRS Form 1099 to the aide.[2] The aide is responsible for paying her own income tax on his earnings.

Whether the aide is an employee of the family or an independent contractor depends upon the amount of control the aide exercises over her work.[3] A full-time aide of the family is probably an employee of the family. An argument could be made that a part-time aide is an independent contractor, since the aide has more control over her schedule.

The duties that an aide performs are menial, perfunctory duties, so the fact that the aide would have control over her work, as opposed to being directed by the family, is a difficult argument to make. So, the general nature of an aide's duties militates in favor of finding that the aide is an employee of the family. This is an interesting point that from a practical standpoint is almost wholly ignored.

Almost every family that employs an aide from a placement agency treats the aide as an independent contract or, but most never issue 1099 Forms to the aide. Legally, though, most aides from placement agencies are employees of the family, so there are a great number of families in this country that are failing to pay the necessary employer taxes and that are failing to obtain workers'

---

1. http://www.irs.gov/Businesses/Small-Businesses-&-Self-Employed/Independent-Contractor-Self-Employed-or-Employee
2. www.irs.gov/pub/irs-pdf/i1099msc.pdf
3. http://www.irs.gov/Businesses/Small-Businesses-&-Self-Employed/Independent-Contractor-Self-Employed-or-Employee

compensation insurance. This fact opens up these families to potential liability issues of which they are simply ignorant.

### 6-1:1.5 Payment "Under the Table"

The reality is that a great number of families simply hire an aide "under the table." Either through word of mouth or through an ad in a paper, they find an individual who is an aide and hire that person either on an hourly basis or a live-in basis to care for their family member.

Because these aides have no affiliation with an employer or a placement agency, they tend to be much less expensive than obtaining an aide through legitimate avenues. Hence the attraction families have to paying an aide under the table.

### 6-1:1.6 Tax Consequences

If you hire an aide who is an employee of the company that provided the aide, then the company is responsible for paying the employment taxes associated with the aide's services.

With an aide who is provided through a placement agency, at best the aide is an independent contractor, so the family should issue an IRS Form 1099 to the aide. Some would argue that the aide is not an independent contractor, because the aide is merely following the directions of his employer. If this is the case, then the family is the employer and must pay employment taxes for the aide.

When a family pays an aide under the table, in cash, they are neither withholding taxes nor issuing a Form 1099 to the aide. The family is engaged in tax evasion with the aide, so as an attorney, you cannot advise the client to pay an aide under the table.

### 6-1:1.7 Liability Issues

An issue that is often overlooked or simply ignored-because the family doesn't know how to address the issue is liability. The family is bringing a third person, the aide, into their parent's home. The aide might live with the parent.

What if the aide falls down and hurts himself? The aide is often put in precarious positions as he tries to assist the elderly family member with walking or showering, for instance. An aide has a very physical job attempting to maneuver the elderly individual about and could easily be hurt in the course of his job.

If the aide is an employee of the business that provided the aide, then the aide is covered by workers' compensation insurance.[4] If the aide is injured assisting the family member, the aide is hurt on the job and can file a workers' compensation claim.

If the aide is an independent contractor or is simply being paid under the table, then the aide would have to have private insurance that covers his work. Most, if not all, of the individuals who work as aides through placement agencies or under the table would not have this insurance, so there is a huge liability issue of which families should be aware. In reality, this risk is almost completely ignored.

### 6-1:1.8 Turnover Issues

There is often a high turnover rate with aides. Being an aide can be hard work and is often low-paying for the aide. Given these two facts, many families will be faced with a high turnover rate among aides, so the family should be aware of this fact.

Furthermore, the elderly family member might not like the aide. The elderly individual might not want any aide or he may not like the race or nationality of the aide. For whatever reason, the elderly individual may cause a constant rotation of aides as he, essentially, chases the aides out of his house.

Home health aide businesses will arrange for new aides when one aide leaves, but even home health aide businesses experience shortages with aides or may not be able to obtain the "right" aide for the elderly individual. If the family arranged for the aide themselves, then they will have to find a new aide if one aide leaves.

## 6-1:2 Adult Day Care

Much like day care for children, there are companies that provide adult day care for elder or disabled individuals. Many of these facilities have vans that are handicapped accessible. The van will pick the elderly individual up in the morning at his house, take him

---

4. http://lwd.dol.state.nj.us/labor/wc/wc_index.html

to the day care center during the daytime hours and return him to his home at night.

This type of facility appeals to families who have an elderly individual living with them and the "caregiver" in the home (perhaps a son or daughter) works during the daytime. In order to enable the daughter-caregiver to go to her job, the father will spend his day in a day care facility. Or, the family might send the elderly individual to the daycare for socialization purposes.

In many instances, the facility will ensure that the elderly individual receives the appropriate care, including the administration of medication, and that he is engaged socially.

## 6-1:3 Residential Health Care Facilities

Though rare, there are still "retirement homes" or "old folks' homes" in New Jersey, technically called residential healthcare facilities.[5] These facilities are not nursing homes or assisted living residences. Essentially, they are boarding homes for elderly individuals.

## 6-1:4 Assisted Living Residences

An assisted living residence is a facility that provides differing levels of assistance to its residents.[6] Most assisted living residences have the look and feel of a hotel. As with hotels, the rooms in assisted living residences do not have kitchens, but may have a microwave oven and a sink.

The facility will have a nurse on staff, though a nurse may not be present 24 hours a day, 7 days a week. The facility will have numerous aides.

Some residents may be receiving little to no care and merely reside in the facility for socialization and safety reasons. Other residents may be receiving extensive care.

A great number of assisted living residences have units for residents who suffer from dementia or other neurological issues associated with aging. The dementia unit may be called the "memory care unit" or some other euphemism such as "The Cottages." These

---

5. N.J.S.A. 30:11A-1.
6. N.J.S.A. 26:2H-7.15.

units are typically secure, meaning that you need to enter a code in a keypad in order to gain ingress or egress from the unit.

Residents of assisted living residences pay on a month-to-month basis, though there may be a one- or two-month notice period before the resident can terminate the rental agreement.

## 6-1:5 Nursing Facilities

A nursing facility is commonly known as a nursing home.[7] Nursing homes typically have one or more nurses on premises 24 hours a day, 7 days a week. Nursing homes have aides on premises at all times. Nursing homes also have a physician who is a staff physician, though the physician is not on premises at all times but merely visits the facility from time-to-time.

In recent years, there has been a trend whereby nursing homes are trying to look more like assisted living residences (carpeting on the floor, nice curtains on the windows, etc.) and assisted living residences are trying to provide services such as those provided by a nursing home (a nurse on staff, a visiting physician, etc.).

In general, long term care facilities want to offer potential residents an "aging in place" option, meaning that once the resident enters the facility, the resident will not have to leave the facility and can receive whatever care he might need in that facility for the remainder of his life.

Residents and families do not want to continuously move because they cannot receive the care they need where they are; they like the idea that the facility can provide whatever care they need as their needs increase. So, assisted living residences and nursing homes are trying to provide more and more care and to provide it in a home-like environment.

### 6-1:5.1 Skilled Nursing Facilities

A nursing home typically has two sections, the skilled nursing facility section[8] and the nursing facility section.[9] A skilled nursing facility is a facility that provides rehabilitative services

---

7. N.J.S.A. 30:13-2 (defining "nursing home); 42 U.S.C. § 1396r(a) (defining "nursing facility").

8. 42 U.S.C. § 1395i-3(a).

9. 42 U.S.C. § 1396r(a).

to its residents. A skilled nursing facility, or SNF (pronounced "sniff"), is a short-term care facility, designed to rehabilitate the resident as best as that can be accomplished, then send the resident somewhere else. That somewhere else may be to a long term care facility (nursing facility or assisted living residence) or return the person to his home, depending upon the abilities of the resident after the rehabilitation.

Many of the residents of skilled nursing facilities are having their care paid for by the Medicare program.[10] Most people who are receiving skilled nursing facilities services within a nursing facility do not believe they are in a nursing home. The client's family will come to you and say, "Mom is in a rehab facility." You might say, "What nursing home is she in?" The family member will respond, "Mom's not in a nursing home."

A skilled nursing facility is part of a nursing home or nursing facility, but because the services the SNF provides are designed to be short-term, most people do not believe they are in a nursing home. The fact of the matter is that they are in a nursing home.

#### 6-1:5.2 Nursing Facilities

A nursing facility,[11] as opposed to a skilled nursing facility,[12] is the long term care section of the nursing home. A nursing facility, as stated above, is what people think of when they think of nursing homes. Most nursing homes have a skilled nursing facility section and a nursing facility section.

Residents pay nursing facilities on a daily basis, though they are billed monthly. So, for instance, if the resident leaves the facility in the middle of the month, he will only be billed for those days he was actually in the facility and may receive a refund if he paid the facility the month in advance.

### 6-1:6 Continuing Care Retirement Communities

Continuing Care Retirement Communities, or CCRCs, are facilities that are designed to provide "aging in place."[13] The facility will have

10. 42 U.S.C. §§ 1395 et seq.
11. 42 U.S.C. § 1396r(a).
12. 42 U.S.C. § 1395i-3(a).
13. N.J.S.A. 54:4-8.58

an independent living section, an assisted living residence section and a nursing facility section. The nursing facility may have a skilled nursing facility section and a straight nursing facility section.

Most residents enter CCRCs in the independent living section. As the resident's needs increase, he may move to the assisted living section or the nursing facility section. The idea is that the resident will not have to leave the facility to receive the care he needs, unless he needs to go to a hospital.

CCRCs tend to be the most expensive form of long term care. Not only does the resident pay the facility on a monthly basis, but most CCRCs have a high entrance fee that may be fully or partially refundable. These entrance fees, which range anywhere from $100,000 to $400,000, require the resident to come up with a very large sum of cash that the facility will hold and on which it will earn interest.[14]

In many instances, the entrance fee will only be refunded after the resident vacates the facility, after the room is refurbished and after the room has been re-let. The refurbishment of the room will be taken from the entrance fee before it is refunded to the resident. The entrance fee is fully available to the CCRC to pay the resident's rent and to pay for the resident's care until the resident vacates the facility;[15] so, when the resident expends all of his assets other than the entrance fee, the facility will begin to use the entrance fee to pay the resident's charges.

If the resident relocates and the resident has not expended the entrance fee on his care, the entrance fee may be partially refundable, fully refundable or not refundable at all. It depends upon the terms of the agreement that the resident entered into with the facility.

## 6-2 THE ACTIVITIES OF DAILY LIVING

Defining long term care is a point of contention between the client and the programs that will assist with the payment of long term care services, such as the Medicaid program.[16] Many clients will come to your office and state that their parent requires long term care services, or something to that effect. Viewed at its most

---

14. N.J.S.A. 52:27D-342.
15. 42 U.S.C. § 1396p(g).
16. 42 U.S.C. §§ 1396 et seq.

basic level, long term care is care that is provided consistently over a long period of time. It could be anything from basic housekeeping to meal preparation to hands-on assistance with bathing.

The type of long term care that an elderly individual requires is important, because the Medicaid program, which is the largest single payer of long term care services in this country, will only pay for assistance if the applicant for benefits requires assistance with certain, defined tasks.

These tasks are known as the activities of daily living. There are the basic activities of daily living (ADL), which the Medicaid program examines to determine if an applicant will qualify for benefits, and the instrumental activities of daily living (IADL), which are much less important in determining whether the applicant will receive assistance in paying for his long term care services.

The instrumental activities of daily living are what many clients think of as long term care—housekeeping, medication administration, ability to shop, ability to cook, etc.—but that the Medicaid program does not equate with a need for long term care. For instance, a client's mother might be living alone, but she is unable to clean her house, cut her lawn, administer her medications properly or cook a meal. The mother might be leaving pots on the stove, causing the pots to burn.

The son, who is now sitting in your office, might be worried that his mother is going to burn her house down with her inside of it, as she tries to cook her dinner. This is a very common scenario that a family member will present to you.

Nevertheless, though most people would say the mother requires long term care services, if the mother can cloth herself, bath herself, toilet herself and ambulate on her own, she may be disqualified from receiving Medicaid assistance to pay for her long term care services. So, as an elder law practitioner, you must be mindful of what long term care is and whether or not the prospective client requires what the government will consider to be long term care.

Moreover, the New Jersey Medicaid program requires an applicant for institutional Medicaid care services (such as nursing facility or assisted living residence service) to need "hands-on" assistance with three of the basic activities of daily living—clothing, bathing, toileting, ambulating, transferring, eating—before the applicant for institutional level Medicaid care services in New Jersey will qualify for the Medicaid program. When an applicant for Medicaid benefits in New Jersey satisfies the health criterion for Medicaid eligibility, the beneficiary is issued a PreAdmission Screen, or PAS (pronounced "pass").[17] A PAS is a creature of New Jersey law, not the federal laws governing the Medicaid program.

Hands-on assistance means that another individual must be required to put his hands on the elderly individual in order to accomplish those tasks.[18] In the alternative, the elderly individual must have cognitive impairments such that he requires constant cueing to accomplish three activities of daily living. For instance, does the elderly individual need to be continuously reminded to dress, to toilet, to bathe, to clothe?

### 6-2:1 Clothing

Clothing is the ability to choose the appropriate clothes given the weather and to put those clothes on your body. Some people simply do not have the physical or mental wherewithal to pick out appropriate clothing and to put that clothing on themselves. If they require hands-on assistance with these activities from another individual, then they require assistance with this activity of daily living.

### 6-2:2 Bathing

Bathing is the ability to get in and out of the shower or tub and to bathe yourself. The Medicaid program does not view the inability to wash one's own hair as being an inability to bathe. Washing one's hair is viewed as a grooming issue (as odd as that may seem).

---

17. N.J.S.A. 30:4D-17.10.

18. N.J.A.C. 8:85-2.1. ("Individuals requiring NF services may have unstable medical, emotional/behavioral and psychosocial conditions that require ongoing nursing assessment, intervention and/or referrals to other disciplines for evaluation and appropriate treatment. Typically, adult NF residents have severely impaired cognitive and related problems with memory deficits and problem solving. These deficits severely compromise personal safety and, therefore, require a structured therapeutic environment. NF residents are dependent in several activities of daily living (bathing, dressing, toilet use, transfer, locomotion, bed mobility, and eating).") As used in the regulation, the word "several" has been interpreted to mean 3 or more by Office of Community Choice Options, which is the agency responsible for determining if an applicant for Medicaid benefits qualifies from a health perspective for the Medicaid program.

### 6-2:3 Toileting

Toileting is the ability to recognize that you need to relieve your bowels and bladder and completing the acts of relieving yourself.

### 6-2:4 Transferring

Transferring is the ability to move from a bed to a chair or from a bed or chair to a standing position.

### 6-2:5 Mobility

Mobility is the ability to ambulate.

### 6-2:6 Eating

Eating involves the hand-to-mouth movement of food from plate to mouth and swallowing the food. Eating is not meal preparation. Many family members will say that an elderly person cannot eat, but they merely mean that the elderly person cannot prepare his own meals.

## 6-3 INSTRUMENTAL ACTIVITIES OF DAILY LIVING

There are a great number of instrumental activities of daily living (known as IADLs). Examples of IADLs are the following: food preparation, shopping, administration of medication, housekeeping and laundry. If a person could not perform his IADLs, most people would agree that the person needs long term care services. For instance, if a person could not shop for himself, do his laundry, clean his house or take his medication, most people would agree that he needs long term care. But if that person could perform his basic activities of daily living without hands-on assistance (clothing, bathing, toileting, etc.), then he would not qualify for Medicaid long term care services.

So it is vitally important to understand what the client's needs are, because even if the client meets the financial criteria for Medicaid eligibility, he may not meet the health criterion for eligibility. If the client does not meet the health criterion for Medicaid eligibility (that is, qualify for a PAS), he will not qualify for institutional level Medicaid care services under the Medicaid program in New Jersey.

## 6-4 ADMISSION AGREEMENT

When a person enters a long term care facility, he will inevitably be asked to sign an admission agreement. Particularly when entering an assisted living residence or a continuing care retirement community, the client will be asked to sign an admissions agreement *before* he enters the facility.

With nursing homes, many residents are asked to sign the admission agreement *after* the resident enters the facility. Because most people enter a nursing facility for rehabilitative care after being discharged from the hospital, most nursing home residents are asked to sign an admissions agreement *after* they enter the facility.

A client may ask you to review the admission agreement before he will sign the agreement. Some facilities will negotiate over the terms of the agreement more than others will. The occupancy rate of the facility at the time your client enters the facility will influence the facility's willingness to change the terms of its standard admission agreement: the more residents the facility has, the less willing they will be to negotiate the terms of their admissions agreement.

### 6-4:1 Failure to Sign Admissions Agreement

As stated, most assisted living residences and continuing care retirement communities have the prospective resident sign the admission agreement before the resident enters the facility, so a refusal to sign the agreement will result in the prospective resident's failure to gain admission to the facility. With a nursing home, because the facility typically presents the admission agreement after the resident is admitted, the failure to sign the agreement is far less impactful.

The law requires a nursing facility to present an admissions agreement to the resident; however, there is no law that permits a nursing facility to discharge a resident for failing to sign the admissions agreement. There are only six defined reasons why a nursing facility can discharge a resident, and the failure to sign an admissions agreement is not on that list.[19] Stated otherwise, a nursing facility cannot discharge a resident for failing to sign the admissions agreement.

---

19. 42 U.S.C. §§ 1396r(c)(2)(A)(i) to (vi).

So, with a nursing facility resident who is currently residing in a nursing facility, the request from the facility to sign their admissions agreement—and admissions agreements are always drafted in favor of the facility (after all, it is the facility that drafted the agreement)—can be met with a refusal, and the facility cannot do anything about that refusal.

### 6-4:2 Liability of Elderly Individual Under Admission Agreement

The resident is responsible for the expenses he incurs in a facility whether he signs the admissions agreement or not. Facilities are in the business of providing long term care. Facilities understand the industry far better than the average resident. Facilities also have their attorneys draft the agreements, so without question, the admissions agreement favors the facility.

Admissions agreements smooth out many issues for the facility—late payment fees, interest, legal fees, arbitration. All of these issues are smoothed out through the admissions agreement in a manner that favors the facility.

### 6-4:3 Liability of Responsible Party Under Admission Agreement

Most facilities request that a third-party sign the admissions agreement on behalf of the resident as the "responsible party." The responsible party is a third-person, typically a family member of the resident, who agrees to be responsible for the resident's bills if the resident fails to pay those bills.

What typically happens is that mom enters a nursing home. Her family is very distraught and wants mom to receive all the care that she needs. The facility presents the daughter with a 20 page admissions agreement and tells her that she has to fill out the admissions agreement and get it back to them. If the daughter doesn't sign the admissions agreement promptly, the staff of the facility will remind the daughter frequently to sign the agreement and get it back to them.

The admissions agreement contains many "responsible party" lines. The daughter will sign the agreement as the responsible party because her mother is incapable of signing the agreement or because the daughter doesn't want to bother her mother given her current health condition.

If, at some point, mom lacks the ability to pay the facility and, for some reason or other, mom doesn't qualify for Medicaid, the facility will look to the daughter to pay the facility as the "responsible party." The facility may sue the daughter as the responsible party if the facility is not being paid for one reason or the other.

### 6-4:3.1 Lack of Consideration

There are several arguments that can be made against responsible party agreements, but the best argument is that the agreement lacks consideration.[20] If a daughter signs as the responsible party for her mother because the facility requires the daughter to sign before they will permit the mother to enter the facility or under threat that the mother will be discharged if the daughter does not sign the agreement, what consideration does the daughter receive in return?

The daughter has no responsibility to support or care for her mother. While the daughter probably would never abandon her mother and leave her helpless and forlorn, that is because the daughter loves the mother, not because the daughter has a legal obligation to care for and support her mother.

Since the daughter has no legal obligation to support or care for her mother, there is no consideration to support the daughter's obligation to be responsible for her mother's debts.

## 6-4:4 Liability of Power of Attorney Agent Under Admission Agreement

What if the resident's power of attorney agent signs the admissions agreement and clearly delineates his status as the resident's agent. Is the power of attorney agent responsible for the resident's bills? Facilities do, from time-to-time, threaten to sue power of attorney agents, claiming that the agent is responsible for the resident's bills because he signed the agreement.

A power of attorney agent for a resident is responsible for using the principal's income and assets prudently. In this regard, the

---

20. No contract is enforceable, of course, without the flow of consideration both sides must "get something" out of the exchange. *Friedman v. Tappan Development Corp.*, 22 N.J. 523, 533 (1956) (quoting 1A. Corbin, Contracts § 110 (1963 ed.).

agent must ensure that the principal's bills are paid to the extent that the principal has money to pay those bills.

So, does an agent have a responsibility to apply for Medicaid benefits at the appropriate time and to ensure that the principal's Medicaid application is approved? From time-to-time, a power of attorney agent may fail to cooperate with the county board of social services and the principal's Medicaid application may be denied. Is the agent liable to the facility because he failed to cooperate in processing the resident's Medicaid application?

There is no definitive answer at this time, but some facilities are attempting to test these areas of liability. If the agent started the application for Medicaid benefits but failed to diligently follow up with the various requests the county board of social services made during the application and the application is denied, then the nursing facility may have a cause of action against the agent. (On the other hand, an agent who never applies for Medicaid benefits probably would not be liable since he was under no legal obligation to act as the power of attorney agent in the first place.)

### 6-4:5 Continuing Care Retirement Community Admission Agreement

Continuing Care Retirement Communities (CCRCs) are facilities that provide independent living facilities, assisted living facilities and nursing facilities all under the same roof or within the same campus. There are very few CCRCs in the state of New Jersey, probably fewer than twenty.

CCRCs typically have very comprehensive admissions agreements because the resident may live in the facility for many years, progressing from an independent living resident to nursing home resident. The facilities also tend to require prospective residents to deposit a very large entrance fee with the facility. Typically, the entrance fee is either partially or wholly refundable after the resident leaves the facility.

In 2006, the CCRC lobby was able to have a provision written into the Medicaid Act that makes the entrance fee an available resource to the resident if the entrance fee meets certain criteria.[21] The entrance fee must be partially or wholly refundable, it must be

---

21. 42 U.S.C. § 1396p(g).

available to pay for the resident's fees at the CCRC and it must not convey an ownership interest in the facility to the resident. Most CCRCs' entrance fees will meet these three criteria.

The extent to which the entrance fee is refundable may affect the monthly charge the resident pays. The greater the refundable portion of the entrance fee, the more the resident may pay on a monthly basis, though this is not always the case.

Many of the CCRCs' admissions agreements will contain a provision that prohibits the resident from gifting assets after he enters the facility. Essentially, the facility is making the resident agree to the fact that the CCRC relied upon the assets that the prospective resident disclosed to them in the admissions process and now wants the prospective resident to agree, contractually, to refrain from disposing gratuitously of those assets that he disclosed to the facility.

## 6-5 ABILITY OF NURSING FACILITY TO DISCHARGE RESIDENT

Nursing facilities that accept Medicare and Medicaid, which is almost every facility in the state of New Jersey, can only discharge a resident for certain, defined reasons.[22] If the facility attempts to discharge for a reason other than these defined reasons, the facility is violating the law.

### 6-5:1 Federal Rules on Discharge

The federal laws governing the Medicaid and Medicare programs provide six defined reasons why a nursing facility can discharge a resident.

#### 6-5:1.1 Necessary for Resident's Welfare

If the discharge is necessary for the resident's welfare, then the nursing facility can discharge the resident.[23] The facility may simply be unable to handle the health issue from which the resident suffers. If this is the case, the facility can discharge the resident.

---

22. 42 U.S.C. §§ 1396r(c)(2)(A)(i) to (vi).
23. 42 U.S.C. § 1396r(c)(2)(A)(i).

### 6-5:1.2 Resident's Health Has Improved

If the resident's health has improved to an extent where he no longer requires a nursing facility level of care, then the facility can discharge the resident.[24] Obviously, we do not want people living in nursing homes who do not need the level of care provided by the nursing home, and most people would not want to be in a nursing home if they did not have to be there.

### 6-5:1.3 Safety of Others

The resident may pose a safety risk to other residents.[25] For instance, some residents act out and become violent. Such behavior is fairly common with dementia. If the resident's behavior cannot be controlled in the facility to such an extent that it poses a risk to the safety of others in the facility (the staff, other residents, visitors), then the facility can discharge the resident.

### 6-5:1.4 Health of Others

The resident may have a contagious disease that cannot be properly treated in the nursing facility and that poses a risk to the health of others in the facility (staff, other residents, visitors).[26] In cases such as these, the facility can discharge the resident.

### 6-5:1.5 Failure to Pay After Notice

If the resident fails to pay after reasonable notice, the facility is justified in discharging the resident.[27] A resident may be paying the facility privately or Medicaid may be paying the facility for the resident because the resident qualified for Medicaid benefits. Whether the resident is paying privately or if the Medicaid program is paying for him, he is paying the facility, so he cannot be discharged for non-payment.

On the other hand, if the resident is simply not paying the facility or doesn't have money to pay the facility yet has failed to qualify for Medicaid benefits, then the resident is not paying the facility

---

24. 42 U.S.C. § 1396r(c)(2)(A)(ii).
25. 42 U.S.C. § 1396r(c)(2)(A)(iii).
26. 42 U.S.C. § 1396r(c)(2)(A)(iv).
27. 42 U.S.C. § 1396r(c)(2)(A)(v).

and the facility can discharge the resident for non-payment after reasonable notice to the resident.

Failure to pay also occurs when the resident is a Medicaid beneficiary and fails to turn his income over to the facility. A Medicaid beneficiary has an obligation to pay his income to the facility on a monthly basis, less certain deductions. If the resident fails to pay his income to the facility, he is failing to pay the facility and can be discharged after reasonable notice.

#### 6-5:1.5.a Reasonable Notice

Reasonable notice of a failure to pay is commonly held to be thirty days' notice.[28]

### 6-5:1.6 Closure of the Facility

If the facility ceases to operate as a licensed nursing facility, then it can discharge the residents of the facility.[29]

## 6-5:2 State Rules on Discharge

New Jersey has its own rules on discharges from nursing facilities, which are contained in regulations. New Jersey's discharge rules explain and expound upon the federal rules.[30] Most importantly, the New Jersey rules on discharge expand the application of the discharge rules contained in the federal Medicaid Act to current Medicaid beneficiaries and to those individuals who have merely applied for Medicaid benefits but have not been approved to receive such benefits.[31]

A resident who is merely an applicant for Medicaid benefits is likely to feel the most "heat" from the facility regarding payment. Residents who have sufficient assets to pay the facility will receive few complaints from the facility if the facility is getting paid. Residents who are actual Medicaid beneficiaries also will receive few complaints from the nursing home because the Medicaid program is paying the facility.

---

28. Medicare and Medicaid, Requirements for Long Term Care Facilities, 56 Fed. Reg. 48,826, 48,840 (1991).

29. 42 U.S.C. § 1396r(c)(2)(A)(vi).

30. N.J.A.C. 8:85-1.10.

31. N.J.A.C. 8:85-1.10(d).

The Medicaid program pays the facility about 30% less, on average, than a facility charges a privately-paying resident. Given this, nursing homes have a love-hate relationship with Medicaid; nursing homes don't like receiving 30% less, but the facilities know that they need the Medicaid program for the vast number of individuals who simply cannot pay or cannot pay any longer for their care from private funds.

When a resident is neither privately paying or receiving Medicaid benefits, the facility is not getting paid, so the facility is not happy during the period of time it is not getting paid. Including those residents who are Medicaid-pending within the definition of "Medicaid beneficiary" means that the Medicaid-pending resident cannot be treated as a non-paying resident subject to discharge upon reasonable notice. This is a big safety shield for these residents.

## 6-5:3 Discharge Plan

Even if one of the six reasons for discharge exists, the facility still must put together a plan for safe discharge of the resident-a discharge plan. A safe discharge plan would include, at a minimum, the proposed location to which the resident is being discharged, and it must state how the resident's health and social needs will be met in the location to which it is proposed the resident be discharged.

The fact that the facility must safely discharge the resident is often a large impediment to the facility's ability to discharge the resident. For instance, assume that the resident fails to pay the facility and the facility provides the resident with reasonable notice of the resident's failure to pay, now what?

If the resident fails to pay even after reasonable notice, but the resident still needs a nursing home level of care, can the facility discharge the resident? Yes, but only if the facility can discharge the resident safely, which would mean that the facility needs to discharge its non-paying resident to another nursing facility. What nursing facility is going to accept this non-paying resident? The answer is no facility, so the facility that would like to discharge the resident is effectively stuck with the resident.

### 6-5:3.1 Notice of Discharge

The facility must provide the resident with notice of its intention to discharge and must provide the resident with its safe discharge plan.[32] Unless there is an issue involving safety or health, the facility will give 30 days' notice of its intent to discharge and its safe discharge plan.[33]

## 6-6 DISCHARGE FROM ASSISTED LIVING RESIDENCES

Unlike nursing facilities that have a significant number of rules regarding discharge, discharge from an assisted living residence is handled under standard landlord-tenant eviction rules. In short, there are no specific rules regarding when an assisted living residence can discharge a resident and what procedures it must follow.

Without question, laws governing when and how an assisted living residence can discharge a resident should be put in place, but currently no such laws exist.

## 6-7 TAX DEDUCTIBILITY OF LONG TERM CARE

Long term care that is a medical necessity is a deductible expense for federal income tax purposes.[34] The entire cost of a nursing facility is a deductible medical expense. With a nursing home, the resident's room and board is so closely associated with the necessary medical care the resident is receiving that the entire cost of the facility is a deductible medical expense.

With assisted living residences, only the care for which the resident is paying is deductible, not the room and board.

The cost of a home health aide may also be deductible if the care is medically necessary.

The deductibility of medical expenses can be very helpful. If the elderly individual has money in qualified accounts (401(k)s, IRAs, etc.), the ability to write-off the cost of the elderly individual's care against the money that is removed from his qualified accounts can be helpful. At least the resident isn't being hit with a double-whammy—the cost of his care and the taxes for removing money from his qualified accounts.

---

32. N.J.A.C. 8:39-5.4(b).
33. 42 U.S.C. § 1396r(c)(2)(B)(ii).
34. 26 U.S.C. §§ 213, 7702B(c)(2).

### 6-7:1 Certification of Chronic Illness

If the elderly individual is paying for a home health aide or is residing in an assisted living residence, it can be helpful to have the elderly individual's physician sign a certification of chronic illness. Essentially, the certification is a document through which the individual's physician certifies that the elderly individual is in need of long term care services either for physical or for cognitive reasons.[35]

Having the physician sign such a certification can be helpful if the elderly individual claims the payment of the aide or assisted living residence as a deduction on his tax return and there is an audit of his return.

Obviously, the elderly individual would need to have paid the aid "over the table" in order to claim the payment of the aide as a medical deduction. Furthermore, only a portion of an assisted living residence bill is deductible. A portion of every assisted living residence invoice is for room and board, which is not deductible, and a portion is for health care that is being provided to the elderly individual, which is deductible.

---

35. 26 U.S.C. § 7702B(c)(2).

# Chapter 7

# Paying for Long-Term Care

## 7-1 PRIVATE PAYMENT

Paying for long term care privately is a rather simple concept—the elderly or disabled individual pays for his care from his funds. If the client chooses this course of action, he will continue to pay until such time as he runs out of money or no longer requires long term care.

### 7-1:1 Home Health Aide

As discussed above in Chapter 6, there are all types of home health aide "companies"; there are placement agencies, companies for which the aide is an employee and aides who work "under the table." Currently, an aide costs about $20 to $25 per hour. A live-in aide costs approximately $165 to $200 per day, plus room and board.

An elderly individual who requires a live-in aide will pay approximately $5,000 per month for the care he needs. If the elderly individual is paying from his own funds for the aide, he will simply pay for the aide from those funds.

### 7-1:2 Adult Day Care

Adult day care facilities, like day care facilities for children, provide a safe haven for elderly individuals during the daytime hours when their caregiver is at work. These facilities cost approximately $75 to $90 per day.

### 7-1:3 Residential Health Care Facilities

In New Jersey, there are still residences that might be thought of as "old folks homes." These are simply boarding houses that cater to elderly individuals. Technically, these facilities are called Residential Health Care Facilities.[1]

### 7-1:4 Assisted Living Residence

Assisted living residences are hotel-like facilities that provide care and socialization for elderly individuals.[2] These facilities might cost anywhere from $3,500 to $8,500 a month depending upon the level of care the resident is receiving.

Most facilities have various levels of care that equate to the hours of care service the resident receives in a given day or the type of services that the resident receives. Many of these facilities also have sections for memory-impaired residents. These sections might be referred to as the "memory care unit" or by some other euphemism. The memory care units typically cost more than the part of the facility that does not cater to residents with memory impairment issues.

### 7-1:5 Nursing Facility

A nursing facility, or nursing home,[3] in New Jersey costs anywhere from $8,500 per month to $12,000 per month. The average monthly nursing home cost in this state is approximately $9,500.

### 7-1:6 Continuing Care Retirement Community

Payment of a Continuing Care Retirement Community, or CCRC, is complicated. Most CCRCs require prospective residents to provide an entrance fee to the community. The entrance fee may be anywhere from $100,000 to $400,000, depending upon the facility, the size of the room and the number of residents (a single resident or a couple). The entrance fee may be partially or wholly refundable upon the termination of the resident's stay at the facility. Typically, even if wholly refundable, an amount necessary to refurbish the apartment is deducted from the entrance fee.

In addition to the entrance fee, most CCRCs charge a monthly rental amount. The monthly rental amount is often different

---

1. N.J.S.A. 30:11A-1.
2. N.J.S.A. 26:2H-7.15.
3. N.J.S.A. 30:13-2 (defining "nursing home"); 42 U.S.C. § 1396r(a) (defining "nursing facility").

depending upon whether the resident is residing in the independent living section of the facility, the assisted living section or the nursing facility section of the CCRC. The monthly charge for the assisted living residence and nursing facility in a CCRC is typically commensurate with the charge for stand-alone facilities of that nature.

The monthly rental charge for the independent living section may or may not include one or more meals a day.

## 7-2 LONG TERM CARE INSURANCE

Long term care insurance is a form of private insurance designed to pay for long term care services.[4] As with most policies of insurance, the basic concept of long term care insurance is that the insured pays a premium and the insurance company agrees to cover a loss if the insured incurs that loss. In this case, the loss is the cost of long term care, such as care at home, in an assisted living residence or in a nursing home.

Most policies of long term care insurance require the insured to need hands-on assistance with two or more of the activities of daily living (clothing, bathing, toileting, etc.) before the insurance will begin to assist with the payment of the care. Some policies of long term care insurance narrow the number of activities of daily living thereby reducing the opportunity for the insured to qualify for payment.

For instance, the definition of "activities of daily living" contained in the policy might not contain toileting, because toileting is one of the activities that people tend to lose first. By excluding toileting from the list of activities of daily living, the insurance company is reducing the likelihood that the insured will qualify for coverage, so this is something to look for in the policy your client is seeking to purchase.

Assuming that the insured does qualify for benefits under the policy, the policy will pay a given amount of money for a specified period of time. For instance, the policy might pay $150 per day for five years if the insured is residing in a nursing home or $100 per day

---

[4] For more information on long-term care insurance, visit the website of the American Association for Long Term Care Insurance. http://www.aaltci.org/

if the insured is residing in an assisted living residence or receiving care at home.

The primary deterrent for people interested in purchasing long term care insurance is the cost of the insurance. The insurance could cost the insured $2,000 a year. Since most people do not believe they will ever require long-term care services, the thought of paying $2,000 a year for something they believe they will never need proves too much for most people. (The reality is a fair percentage of people will require long-term care, but this is one issue on which reality and perception diverge.)

There are a number of factors that affect the amount of the premium.

### 7-2:1 Elimination Period

The elimination period is the period of time during which the insured qualifies for payments under the policy (for instance, when the insured requires assistance with two or more activities of daily living) but during which the policy will not pay for the insured's care. A ninety-day elimination period means that for 90 days after the insured requires assistance with two activities of daily living, the policy will not pay the insured for his care.

There are statistics that say a high percentage of individuals will require long-term care in their lifetime; however, what these statistics fail to tell you is that included in that percentage are people who require rehabilitative services for three months of less.[5] Many people will, at some point in their lives, require rehabilitation, for instance, because they suffered a stroke or broke a hip. A far lesser percentage of individuals will require true long term care, that is, custodial care for years.

On the other hand, as long term care services become better and better—and they are—and more and more diverse—and they are—people will be receiving long-term care for a lot longer. In olden days, long-term care was a dirty word. Today, people welcome moving to a senior community and enjoy their stays in assisted living residence. Even nursing homes are becoming more home-like.

---

5. http://www.aaltci.org/long-term-care-insurance/learning-center/probability-long-term-care.php

So, people will be receiving long term care services for a lot longer than they did in the past. Yet, despite the improvements, long term care continues to have a bad reputation with many people and the mentality of "I can do it on my own" is still pervasive.

What the elimination period is designed to do from the perspective of the insurance company is eliminate those individuals who are only receiving rehabilitative or short-term services, which is a large percentage of individuals who receive "long-term care" during their lives. If the insurance company eliminates the first 90 days during which the insured requires care, the insurance company is excluding most people who require care from having that care paid by the insurance.

The longer the elimination period, the lower the premium for the insured.

### 7-2:2 Daily Benefit Amount

The daily benefit amount is the amount the insurance company will pay the insured on a daily basis once the insured qualifies for coverage. Most policies of insurance have one daily benefit amount if the insured is residing in a nursing home and another daily benefit amount if the insured is residing at home or in an assisted living residence. For instance, the insurance might pay $200 a day if the insured is in a nursing home and $100 a day if the insured is residing at home or in an assisted living residence.

### 7-2:3 Duration of Coverage

The duration of coverage issue concerns the period of time during which the insurance will pay. A long-term care policy might pay the daily benefit amount for two years or three years or for the insured's lifetime. The longer the duration of coverage, the higher the premium.

Policies frequently have a pool of money from which the insured draws down. If the policy will pay the insured a daily benefit amount of $200 per day for three years, the pool of money might be $218,400, which would be sufficient to pay the $200 daily benefit amount for three years. If the insured is residing at home and only drawing down $100 per day, the duration of coverage will actually be six years, not three, because the insured is drawing down on the pool of money more slowly than if he were taking the maximum daily benefit amount.

### 7-2:4 Inflation Rider

An inflation rider automatically increases the daily benefit amount on an annual basis. If an insured purchases a policy of insurance that pays a daily benefit amount of $200, or a monthly benefit of approximately $6,000, that would be a fairly good policy of insurance based upon the cost of long-term care today, which can range from $5,000 to $12,000 a month. An insured would have the $6,000 from the insurance and his fixed income (Social Security benefit and pension) to pay for his care. Even if the insured had a $2,000 or $3,000 a month deficit, that deficit isn't devastating in most instances.

But would $6,000 a month in insurance be sufficient 20 years from now? Probably not. While no one knows what the cost of long-term care will be 20 years from now, an estimated range of $15,000 to $30,000 a month probably would not be that far off.

So, an automatic inflation rider that increases the daily benefit amount by 5% a year could be helpful. Of course, the existence of the inflation rider and the higher the percentage of the rider, the higher the insured's premiums will be.

### 7-2:5 Partnership Program

The Partnership for Long Term Care Program offers a unique policy of long term care insurance to an insured.[6] As discussed more extensively in Chapter 8, in order to qualify for Medicaid benefits, an applicant for Medicaid benefits must have a limited amount of assets.

An insurance policy under the Partnership Program not only provides the insured with cash to pay privately for his long term care but also increases the amount of assets that the Medicaid applicant can retain and still qualify for Medicaid.[7] For instance, if the insured purchases $200,000 in long-term care insurance through a qualified partnership policy, then when that insured applies for Medicaid benefits, he can retain an additional $200,000 in resources and still qualify for Medicaid benefits.

---

6. http://www.aaltci.org/long-term-care-insurance/learning-center/long-term-care-insurance-partnership-plans.php

7. 42 U.S.C. § 1396p(b)(1)(C).

Partnership Program long-term care insurance policies are available in New Jersey.

## 7-3 VETERANS BENEFITS

There are a slew of benefits offered to veterans. As an elder law attorney practicing in New Jersey, the two most common benefits you will encounter are Aid and Attendance, which is a cash assistance benefit offered to a veteran or the widow or a veteran, and the benefits offered by the New Jersey veterans homes.

### 7-3:1 Aid and Attendance

Until recently, most individuals in the legal community and the general public were unaware of the Aid and Attendance (A&A) benefit. In recent years, there has been a growing awareness of A&A.

A&A is a cash assistance program offered through the Veterans Administration to certain veterans or their survivors.[8] In 2014, A&A will pay the veteran a maximum monthly benefit of $1,759 and the survivor of a veteran a maximum monthly benefit of $1,130.[9]

In order to be eligible for A&A, the applicant (veteran or survivor of a veteran) must be eligible for a veterans pension. In order to be eligible for a veterans pension, the veteran must have served at least 90 days in active duty service and at least one of those days must have been during a wartime period. The applicant must also be 65 or older or disabled or a resident of a skilled nursing facility. The applicant must also require the assistance of another individual with his activities of daily living or be bedridden or be a resident in a nursing home.

In addition to these requirements, there are some general financial guidelines. Generally speaking, a married veteran must have $80,000 in assets or less other than the home. A single veteran or survivor must have $40,000 or less in assets other than the home. These asset guidelines are not a hard-and-fast number but a general guideline to applicants.

---

8. 38 U.S.C. § 1114(l).

9. In a recently decided, unpublished opinion, the United States District Court for the District of New Jersey held that A&A obtained because the applicant had unusual medical expenses, such as assisted living expenses, cannot be treated as income for purposes of determining the individual's eligibility for the Medicaid program. *Galletta v. Velez*, 1:13-cv-532 (June 13, 2014). Most individuals receive A&A as the result of unusual medical expenses, such as the need to pay for an assisted living residence or a home health aide.

### 7-3:2 New Jersey Veterans Homes

There are three New Jersey Veterans Memorial Homes in the state. The homes are located in Paramus, Menlo Park and Vineland.[10]

The homes are open to veterans who served in active duty and were honorably discharged as well as to the spouses of such individuals.[11] A spouse must be at least 50 years of age and must have been married to the veteran for not less than 10 years.[12] Preference is given to those applicants seeking admission who have been residents of New Jersey for two years or more prior to admission.[13]

The facilities have certain asset eligibility criteria.[14] The amount a veteran or the spouse pays for his care is based upon an income criterion.[15] The regulations governing eligibility create a three-year lookback period during which the memorial homes will look to see if a prospective resident has made any uncompensated asset transfers in order to qualify for residence in the memorial home.[16]

The homes are very well kept and offer an excellent option for veterans or the spouse of a veteran who requires long term care services. The only downside to the facilities is that there are only three facilities throughout the state, and a family member often wants the nursing home in which his loved one resides to be within 20 minutes of the family member's home.

## 7-4 MEDICARE

Medicare is a federal health insurance program for qualified aged and disabled individuals.[17] Medicare is funded through deductions from a future beneficiary's wages. Generally speaking, Medicare is available to individuals who are 65 years of age or older and who are entitled to Social Security benefits.[18] Medicare is also available

---

10. http://www.state.nj.us/military/veterans/health.html.
11. N.J.A.C. 5A:5-2.1.
12. N.J.A.C. 5A:5-1.2.
13. N.J.A.C. 5A:5-1.2.
14. N.J.A.C. 5A:5-2.1.
15. N.J.A.C. 5A:5-5.3.
16. N.J.A.C. 5:5-3.1(a)1.v.(2).
17. 42 U.S.C. §§ 1395 et seq.
18. 42 U.S.C. § 1395p(f).

to individuals who are disabled and who have been receiving Social Security disability benefits for not less than 24 months.[19]

Medicare coverage is broken down into parts. Each part provides a different bundle of coverage for health care costs.

## 7-4:1 Part A

Part A provides in-patient hospital care, in-patient care in a skilled nursing facility, home health care services and hospice care.[20] As an elder law attorney, the skilled nursing facility (SNF) coverage will be the Part A Medicare coverage with which you and your clients will have the most interaction.

### 7-4:1.1 Skilled Nursing Facility Services

A skilled nursing facility is, in most instances, the rehabilitative section of a nursing facility or nursing home.[21] The family member of a client will come to you and say, "Mom is in a rehab center right now, but we are thinking about moving her to a nursing home." The fact of the matter is that mom is already in a nursing home, she's simply in the wing or section of the nursing home that the nursing home has designated as its skilled nursing/rehabilitative care section.

### 7-4:1.2 Days of Coverage

Medicare Part A coverage will provide up to 100 days of SNF care per spell of illness for in-patients requiring skilled or rehabilitative services.[22] A spell of illness begins when the patient received Medicare covered services as an in-patient in a hospital and ends when the patient has spent 60 days outside of the hospital or SNF or ceased receiving Medicare-covered services in the nursing facility.[23]

In order to receive SNF coverage, the patient must have been hospitalized for at least three days and must enter the SNF within 30 days of being discharged from the hospital for skilled

19. 42 U.S.C. § 1395p(g).
20. 42 U.S.C. § 1395x.
21. 42 U.S.C. § 1395i-3(a).
22. 42 U.S.C. § 1395x(h).
23. 42 U.S.C. § 1395x(a).

or rehabilitative care.[24] From a practical standpoint, most of your clients will be discharged directly from the hospital to the SNF. A physician must certify that the skilled or rehabilitative care in the SNF is necessary.

Assuming these criteria are met, during a spell of illness, the patient is entitled to full coverage for days 1 through 20. For days 21 through 100 there is a co-payment that is the responsibility of the patient. The co-payment typically increases on an annual basis. In 2014, the daily co-payment is $152.

#### 7-4:1.3 Maintenance Versus Improvement

Skilled or rehabilitative services can be contrasted with custodial care. Skilled care is care that is designed to improve the patient's current condition or to maintain the patient's present condition; however, there are limits on Medicare's SNF coverage.

Medicare's Part A program will not pay for care designed to improve or maintain the patient for more than 100 days. If the patient requires care designed to maintain his present condition for greater than 100 days, that patient has effectively become a long-term custodial care resident of the nursing home, since the Medicare program will no longer cover the cost of his care.

#### 7-4:1.4 Full Time Rehabilitation

In order to receive Part A coverage in a SNF, the patient must require skilled or rehabilitative services on a daily basis and the care must only be available in a SNF. A daily basis means five days per week.

### 7-4:2 Part B

Medicare Part B provides coverage for physician services, durable medical equipment, home health care not provided under Part A and a slew of other services.[25] Individuals entitled to Part A benefits are automatically enrolled in Part B coverage unless they specifically decline the coverage.[26]

---

24. 42 U.S.C. § 1395x(i).
25. 42 U.S.C. § 1395x.
26. 42 U.S.C. § 1395i-2; 42 C.F.R. § 407.17(b).

### 7-4:3 Part C

Medicare Part C, also known as Medicare Advantage, deals with the financing of Medicare covered services.[27] A Medicare Part C plan must offer the basic benefits available under Parts A and B plus some additional benefits. An example of a Medicare Part C plan would be a Medicare HMO plan.

### 7-4:4 Part D

Medicare Part D is the Medicare prescription drug plan.[28] The Medicare Part D program establishes certain co-payments, deductibles and out-of-pocket limitations that a Part D plan can have; however, the plans themselves are offered by private insurance companies. It is up to those companies to establish what drugs their plans will cover. The covered package of drugs is called a drug formulary.

## 7-5 MEDIGAP INSURANCE

Medigap insurance policies are a type of standardized insurance policy that private insurance companies offer to potential insureds.[29] There are ten standardized policies of Medigap insurance, denoted with the letters A through J.

In short, Medigap insurance is designed to fill the gaps of Medicare, the co-payments and deductibles. Each standardized policy of Medigap insurance fills a different bundle of gaps in the Medicare program. The more gaps the policy fills, the more expensive the policy of insurance.

## 7-6 MEDICAID

Medicaid is a federal-state cooperative health insurance program for needy individuals.[30] The federal government offers the various states the opportunity to participate in the Medicaid program. A state is not required to participate in the program. Of course, if a state does not participate in the program, then the State will not receive federal monies for Medicaid. The federal government

---

27. 42 U.S.C. § 1395w-21.
28. 42 U.S.C. § 1395w-101.
29. 42 U.S.C. § 1395ss.
30. 42 U.S.C. §§ 1396 et seq.

often contributes more than 50% of the costs associated with the Medicaid program. New Jersey does participate in the Medicaid program and offers various programs of Medicaid to its citizenry.

In order to qualify for Medicaid, an applicant must have limited assets and income. The assets figure is typically very low, frequently no more than $2,000 countable assets. The income figures vary widely depending upon the program of Medicaid from which the applicant seeks benefits.

There are many different programs of Medicaid. To break down the Medicaid program into broad categories for purposes of this limited discussion, there are community Medicaid programs and institutional (or long-term care) Medicaid programs.

Community Medicaid is essentially Medicaid as traditional health insurance only. In other words, much like private health insurance and Medicare, community Medicaid provides traditional health insurance to needy individuals.

As an elder law attorney, you will be primarily focused on those programs of Medicaid that pay for institutional or long-term care services. Institutional Medicaid pays for care in a nursing home or in an assisted living residence. Institutional Medicaid pays for a home health aide in the person's home or for an adult daycare program.

As is discussed more thoroughly in Chapter 8, institutional Medicaid programs have transfer of asset provisions. If the applicant has disposed of assets within the five-year lookback period leading up to the date of the application, then the applicant will be ineligible for institutional level Medicaid services for a period of time. Community Medicaid programs, unlike institutional Medicaid programs, do not have transfer of asset penalty provisions.

# Chapter 8

# The Medicaid Program

## 8-1 THE MEDICAID PROGRAM

As an elder law attorney, a large part of your practice will involve working with the Medicaid program. The Medicaid program is a health insurance program for needy individuals.[1] Medicaid is a federal-state cooperative program.[2] The various states voluntarily participate in the Medicaid program; however, if a state chooses to participate in the program, it must comply with the federal Medicaid Act and its implementing regulations.[3] New Jersey does participate in the program.[4]

Some programs of Medicaid—the ones with which you will be working the most—assist with the payment of long-term care services, such as care in a nursing home or an assisted living residence.[5] Because the cost of long-term care can be exceedingly high, anywhere from $3,500 to $12,000 per month, many people who never thought they would need assistance from the government to pay for their daily needs turn to Medicaid to pay for the costs associated with their care.

This chapter will focus on institutional level care services provided under the Medicaid program, as opposed to community

---

1. 42 U.S.C. §§ 1396 et seq.; *West Virginia Univ. Hosps., v. Casey*, 885 F.2d 11, 15 (3d Cir. 1989).

2. *Wilder v. Virginia Hospital Ass'n.*, 496 U.S. 498, 501 (1990).

3. *Sabree v. Richman*, 367 F.3d 180, 182 (3d Cir. 2004).

4. N.J.A.C. 30:4D-1 et seq.; N.J.A.C. 10:71-1.1 et seq.

5. 42 U.S.C. §§ 1396a(a)(10)(A)(ii)(V), (VI). In Medicaid parlance, when the Medicaid program assists with the payment of nursing home care, care in an assisted living or home health aide care, the Medicaid program is providing "institutional level care" services to the beneficiary, as opposed to care in the community.

Medicaid services. Institutional level care services are long-term care services (home health aides, adult day care services, assisted living residences and nursing homes). Community Medicaid services are pure health insurance services for needy individuals.

## 8-2 COMMUNITY MEDICAID

There are various Medicaid programs.[6] Community Medicaid programs are for those individuals who need a pure health insurance program. Individuals who are seeking to qualify for community Medicaid benefits do not need long-term care services, such as nursing home services or assisted living residence services. For the most part, individuals seeking to qualify for community Medicaid programs are not potential elder law clients.

Community Medicaid programs do not have transfer of asset penalty provisions. Transfer of asset penalty provisions will be discussed extensively, below.

## 8-3 INSTITUTIONAL LEVEL MEDICAID

In New Jersey, there are two Medicaid programs that provide institutional level care services, such as a home health aide at home, adult daycare, an assisted living residence or a nursing facility.[7] As an elder law attorney, your focus will be on these programs of Medicaid, which provide institutional level care services to your clients.

The primary distinguishing feature of these two programs (Medicaid Only and Medically Needy Medicaid) is the fact that the Medicaid Only program has an income cap for eligibility whereas the Medically Needy program does not have an income cap. As discussed in greater detail, Section 8-15:1, this distinction between the programs will soon be eliminated.

### 8-3:1 Medicaid Only Medicaid

The Medicaid Only Medicaid program provides institutional level care services at home, in an assisted living residence or in a nursing facility.[8] The eligibility criteria for this program are discussed below.

---

6. N.J.A.C. 10:72-1.1 et seq.

7. N.J.A.C. 10:70-1.1 et seq. (Medically Needy Medicaid); N.J.A.C. 10:71-1-1 et seq. (Medicaid Only Medicaid).

8. N.J.A.C. 10:71-1.1 et seq.

### 8-3:2 Medically Needy Medicaid

The Medically Needy Medicaid program is a Medicaid program that provides institutional level care services in a nursing facility only.[9] Those applicants who qualify for the Medically Needy Medicaid program cannot receive institutional care services at home or in an assisted living residence.

## 8-4 FEDERAL RULES

The federal Medicaid Act is an extremely complex and elaborate Act.[10] There are numerous quotes from federal courts describing the complexity of the law and the manner in which the law is frequently amended.[11] In short, the Medicaid Act is difficult to understand.

As an elder law practitioner, your primary focus will be on two provisions of the Medicaid Act—the transfer of asset rules and the spousal impoverishment rules. Since Medicaid is only available to needy individuals, the program contains provisions that punish individuals who dispose of assets before applying for benefits. These rules will be discussed in greater detail below. The spousal impoverishment provisions set aside a certain amount of assets and income for the well spouse; these rules will be discussed more extensively below.

In addition to the Medicaid Act, the federal law also consists of regulations that implement the Act. The federal regulations implementing the Medicaid Act are found at 42 C.F.R. Parts 430-456.

Finally, for the day-to-day practice, there is the Program Operations Manual System (or POMS),[12] which is a field manual that federal caseworkers use for the Supplemental Security

---

9. N.J.A.C. 10:70-1.1 et seq.

10. 42 U.S.C. §§ 1396 et seq.

11. *Rehabilitation Ass'n of Virginia v. Kozlowski*, 42 F.3d 1444, 1450 (4th Cir. 1994) ("There can be no doubt but that the statutes and provisions in question, involving the financing of Medicare and Medicaid, are among the most completely impenetrable texts within human experience. Indeed, one approaches them at the level of specificity herein demanded with dread, for not only are they dense reading of the most tortuous kind, but Congress also revisits the area frequently, generously cutting and pruning in the process and making any solid grasp of the matters addressed merely a passing phase.").

12. https://secure.ssa.gov/apps10/poms.nsf/chapterlist!openview&restricttocategory=05

Income Program, or SSI.[13] SSI is the cash-assistance program most closely related to the Medicaid program. SSI provides cash assistance (that is, money) to needy individuals. If an individual qualifies for SSI, he automatically is enrolled in a community Medicaid program.[14]

The fact that SSI is the federal cash assistance program that is most closely akin to Medicaid has significance under the Medicaid Act. Essentially, it means that many of the rules that govern the SSI program govern the Medicaid program; specifically, those rules governing income and resource eligibility.[15] This is called "comparability."

The rule of comparability can be stated as follows: Medicaid's asset and income eligibility rules must be comparable to those of the SSI program. Comparability is only achieved if the rules governing income and resource eligibility for New Jersey's Medicaid programs are no more restrictive than the rules governing income and resource eligibility for the SSI program.[16] "No more restrictive" means that by using the income or resource methodology that the state uses for its Medicaid program more individuals may be made eligible for that state's Medicaid program than would be eligible if the SSI income or resource methodology were used but no individual who would be eligible if the SSI methodology were used, is made ineligible.[17]

The POMS offers practical advice to the caseworker, and the Medicaid practitioner, as to how the Medicaid program should work. Most New Jersey Medicaid caseworkers have never heard of the POMS and probably none of them have ever seen the POMS. As stated, federal caseworkers working with the SSI program use the POMS, not New Jersey Medicaid caseworkers, but the rules and examples expressed in the POMS can be very helpful when confronted with an issue involving New Jersey Medicaid. This is because New Jersey's Medicaid program can be no more restrictive than the federal government's SSI program in granting eligibility,

---

13. 42 U.S.C. §§ 1381 et seq.

14. The federal regulations implementing the Supplemental Security Income program are found at 20 C.F.R. Part 416.

15. 42 U.S.C. §§ 1396a(a)(10)(C)(i)(III), 1396a(r)(2).

16. 42 U.S.C. §§ 1396a(a)(10)(C)(i)(III), 1396a(r)(2).

17. 42 U.S.C. § 1396a(r)(2)(B); *Sable v. Velez*, 388 Fed. Appx. 235, 237 (3d Cir. 2010).

at least with respect to the rules the Medicaid program uses in assessing income and resource eligibility.

Knowing about the POMS will put you one step ahead of the caseworkers with whom you are working on behalf of your client.

Finally, though not technically a law, in 1994 the Centers for Medicare and Medicaid Services (CMS)[18]—the agency of the United States Department of Health and Human Services that is responsible for administering the Medicaid program—published a template State Medicaid Manual (SMM) for the various states to use as a model when setting up their Medicaid programs. At the time the SMM was published, CMS was known as the Health Care Finance Administration or HCFA. The sections of the SMM that address transfer of asset rules and trusts, which are the most relevant sections for an elder law attorney, was the 64th revision to the SMM. The revisions were made by "transmittals" to the states; accordingly, the section of the SMM to which elder law attorneys frequently find themselves turning is commonly known as HCFA Transmittal 64 or simply the State Medicaid Manual (SMM).[19]

## 8-5 STATE RULES

New Jersey has voluntarily chosen to participate in the Medicaid program. New Jersey enacted the New Jersey Medical Assistance and Health Services Act when it chose to participate.[20] There are a few practical rules that a person can draw from New Jersey's Medicaid Act.

Pursuant to New Jersey's Medicaid Act, the Department of Human Services is responsible for administering New Jersey's Medicaid program.[21] Within the department, the Division of Medical Assistance and Health Services, or DMAHS (pronounced Da Mas), is responsible for administering the program.[22] DMHAS contracts with the various county boards of social service to administer the Medicaid program at the local level;[23] accordingly,

---

18. In 1994, CMS was known as the Health Care Finance Administration (HCFA).

19. http://www.cms.gov/Regulations-and-Guidance/Guidance/Manuals/Paper-Based-Manuals-Items/CMS021927.html (relevant sections are section 3257 and section 3258).

20. N.J.S.A. 30:4D-1 et seq.

21. N.J.S.A. 30:4D-3, 30:4D-4.

22. N.J.S.A. 30:4D-4; N.J.A.C. 10:71-1.5.

23. N.J.A.C. 10:71-1.5.

an applicant for Medicaid benefits will apply at the county board of social services in the county in which the applicant is domiciled.[24]

Most of the rules governing the Medicaid program in New Jersey come from the regulations that DMHAS promulgates.[25] In addition to the regulations, DMAHS periodically transmits letters, called Medicaid Communications or MedComms, to the county boards of social services implementing various rules and policy procedures that affect the Medicaid program. These MedComms are available on DMAHS's website.[26]

## 8-6 DEFINED: ASSET

The Medicaid Act, like many comprehensive Acts, contains definitions of various words and phrases. In Medicaid parlance, a "resource" and "income" are both "assets."[27] This definition of the word "asset" is important for the Medicaid program's transfer of assets rules, because an applicant for Medicaid benefits can be rendered ineligible for those benefits if he transferred a resource or an income item prior to applying for benefits within a certain period of time.[28] This concept will be discussed more fully below.

The distinction between resources and income is also important for the spousal impoverishment provisions of the law,[29] which, like the transfer of assets rules, will be discussed more fully below.

### 8-6:1 Resources

A resource is what most people think of as an asset (real estate, cash, stocks, bonds, etc.).[30] A resource is something the applicant currently owns and can convert to cash for his support.[31] For eligibility purposes, a resource can take many forms; it could be countable, non-countable, available or unavailable.

---

24. N.J.A.C. 10:71-2.5.
25. N.J.A.C. 10:70-1.1 et seq., 10:71-1.1 et seq.
26. http://www.state.nj.us/humanservices/dmahs/info/resources/medicaid/.
27. 42 U.S.C. § 1396p(h).
28. 42 U.S.C. § 1396p(c)(1).
29. 42 U.S.C. § 1396r-5.
30. 42 U.S.C. § 1382b.; N.J.A.C. 10:71-4.1.
31. 42 C.F.R. § 416.1201(a) ("resources means cash or other liquid assets or any real or personal property that an individual (or spouse, if any) owns and could convert to cash to be used for his or her support and maintenance."); 42 C.F.R. § 416.1201(b) (defining liquid resource); N.J.A.C. 10:71-4.1(b).

### 8-6:1.1 Non-countable Resources

A non-countable resource is a resource that does not count against the eligibility of the applicant for Medicaid benefits.[32] There are limited non-countable resources. The primary non-countable resources are the following: a home, a car, personal effects and household goods, certain small policies of life insurance and an irrevocable prepaid funeral.[33]

In most instances, the home is only a non-countable resource if the applicant is residing in the home. If the applicant is residing in a nursing facility or in an assisted living residence and is unlikely to return home, then the home must be listed for sale. In New Jersey, a six month absence from the home raises a presumption that the applicant does not intend to return to the home.[34] The only exception to this rule is if the applicant proves—for instance, through a doctor's certification—that his condition is expected to improve and he will be returning to the home despite his being absent from the home for more than six months.[35]

There are certain equity limitations on these non-countable resources, but for the most part, these equity limitations are either not encountered or unenforced by the county boards of social services. For instance, there is a $750,000 limitation on the equity value of the home.[36] This equity limitation is indexed for inflation each year beginning in 2007.[37]

The home equity limitation does not apply if the spouse of the applicant is residing in the home or if a child of the applicant who is under age 21 is residing in the home or if a child of any age who is disabled is residing in the home.[38] Moreover, even if the applicant were single and did not have a child under the age of 21 or a disabled

---

32. 42 U.S.C. § 1382b.; N.J.A.C. 10:71-4.4.

33. 42 C.F.R. § 416.1210; N.J.A.C. 10:71-4.4.

34. 42 C.F.R. § 416.1212(c) (requiring an intent to return to the home for the home to remain excluded if the applicant is not currently residing in the home); N.J.A.C. 10:71-4.4(b)(1)(i) (providing that a six-month absence from the home raises a presumption that applicant does not intend to return to the home).

35. N.J.A.C. 10:71-4.4(b)(1)(i).

36. 42 U.S.C. § 1396p(f)(1), N.J.A.C. 10:71-41.(d)(1)(v), Medicaid Communication No. 11-01.

37. Medicaid Communication 11-01. In 2014, the equity limitation for a home is $814,000.

38. 42 U.S.C. § 1396p(f)(2); Medicaid Communication 11-01.

child residing in the home, the home equity limitation would have little impact on the application from a practical standpoint.

If a person is applying for institutional level Medicaid services, the applicant is, in most instances, residing in a nursing home or an assisted living residence. When that occurs, the applicant's home needs to be sold unless the applicant can prove that he will be returning to the home within six months.

So, unless an unmarried applicant who does not have a child under the age of 21 or who is disabled is applying for institutional level Medicaid services at home and is living in a home with an equity value greater than $750,00, the equity value limitation has no affect on the application. From a practical standpoint, as an elder law practitioner, you will encounter so few clients who are unmarried, applying for institutional services at home and have a home with an equity value greater than $750,000, that the equity limitation on the home has little practical consequence.

Similarly, there is a $2,000 limitation on the value of personal effects and household goods that the applicant can own,[39] but the county boards never enforce this limitation.

A prepaid funeral is a non-countable resource irrespective of the value of the prepaid fund;[40] however, money remaining in the fund after payment for funeral services must be remitted to DMAHS to reimburse the Division for Medicaid benefits paid on behalf of the now-deceased Medicaid beneficiary.

One automobile, irrespective of value, is excluded if used to transport the applicant or a member of his household.[41]

The cash surrender value of life insurance policies having an aggregate face value of no more than $1,500 is exempt.[42] If the applicant owns a life insurance policy or policies with an aggregate face value of more than $1,500, then the cash surrender value of the life insurance is a countable resource.

---

39. 42 U.S.C. § 1382b(a)(2)(A); 42 C.F.R. § 416.1216; N.J.A.C. 10:71-4.4(b)(3).
40. 42 U.S.C. § 1382b(a)(2)(A); N.J.A.C. 10:71-4.4(b)(9)(i)(3).
41. 42 C.F.R. § 416.1218; N.J.A.C. 10:71-4.4(b)(2)(i).
42. 42 C.F.R. § 416.1230; N.J.A.C. 10:71-4.4(b)(4).

### 8-6:1.2 Countable Resources

Countable resources are all resources other than non countable resources. For instance, cash, bank accounts, stocks, bonds, mutual funds, real estate other than the home, etc.[43] As discussed above, the cash surrender value of certain small policies of life insurance are non-countable resources.[44] The cash surrender value of all other life insurance policies is a countable resource. This is important to bear in mind because many people do not think about life insurance as being a resource, but to the extent the policy has cash surrender value, it often is a resource for purposes of determining Medicaid eligibility.

If a given Medicaid program imposes a resource limitation for purposes of eligibility, that resource limitation is for countable resources. Non-countable resources, as the phrase would imply, do not count towards the resource eligibility limitations.

### 8-6:1.3 Unavailable/Non-liquid Resources

If a resource is unavailable (or non-liquid) to the applicant, then it does not count towards the resource eligibility limitation of the Medicaid program.[45] An unavailable resource is a resource that cannot be converted to cash within 20 days excluding certain non-work days.[46] The burden is the applicant's to prove that the resource cannot be converted to cash within 20 days, though certain resources, such as the home are assumed to be unavailable in those instances in which the applicant must sell the home.[47]

For instance, if the applicant is residing in a nursing facility but owns a home, his home must be listed for sale. The county board of social services will assume that the home is unavailable and will grant the applicant conditional eligibility provided the applicant

---

43. 42 U.S.C. § 416.1201; N.J.A.C. 10:71-4.1.

44. 42 U.S.C. § 416.1230; N.J.A.C. 10:71-4.4(b)(4).

45. 42 C.F.R. § 1201(a)(1) ("If a property right cannot be liquidated, the property will not be considered a resource of the individual (or spouse)."); 42 C.F.R. § 1201(b), (c) (defining liquid and nonliquid resources); *compare with* N.J.A.C. 10:71-4.1(b) ("Both liquid and nonliquid resources shall be considered in the determination of eligibility, unless such resources are specifically excluded under the provisions of N.J.A.C. 10:71-4.4(b)."). New Jersey's regulation may be in violation of the federal rule on comparability, discussed above. 42 U.S.C. §§ 1396a(a)(10)(C)(i)(III), 1396a(r)(2).

46. 42 C.F.R. § 1201(c).

47. Medicaid Communication 87-26 (discussing the liquidation of non-liquid resources).

agrees to list his home for sale and does in fact list the home for sale. The applicant will enter a liquidation agreement with the county through which the applicant agrees to liquidate the unavailable resource, to wit, the home.

Until the home is sold, the applicant is granted conditional eligibility,[48] that is, eligibility is granted despite the fact that the applicant owns a valuable countable resource (an unoccupied home) on the condition that the applicant lists the home for sale. When the home does sell, the Medicaid benefits of the applicant will be terminated, as the applicant will now have an available, countable resources that puts the applicant over the resource limit, that is, the proceeds derived from the sale of the home, which was an unavailable countable resource while it was being listed for sale.

### 8-6:2 Income

Income is cash the applicant *receives* that can be used to pay for the applicant's food or shelter.[49] As with resources, there are countable income items[50] and non-countable income items.[51] From a conceptual standpoint, the key distinction between a resource and income item is that a resource is something the applicant currently owns, whereas income is cash the applicant receives that can be used to pay for food or shelter.

#### 8-6:2.1 Non-countable Income

There are a number of income exclusions listed in the New Jersey regulations.[52] The exclusions that are listed are derived from the federal SSI program. From a practical standpoint, very few of these exclusions will ever apply to your elderly client who is seeking institutional care level Medicaid services.

---

48. POMS SI § 01150.200.

49. 42 C.F.R. § 416.1102; N.J.A.C. 10:71-5.1(b), *compare with* 42 C.F.R. § 416.1201(a) ("resources means cash or other liquid assets or any real or personal property that an individual (or spouse, if any) owns and could convert to cash to be used for his or her support and maintenance."); 42 C.F.R. § 416.1201(b) (defining liquid resource); N.J.A.C. 10:71-4.1(b). A resource is something the applicant currently *owns* that can be used for his support; income is something the applicant *receives* that can be used for his support.

50. 42 C.F.R. § 416.1102; N.J.A.C. 10:71-5.2.

51. 42 C.F.R. § 416.1103; N.J.A.C. 10:71-5.3.

52. N.J.A.C. 10:71-5.3.

The one exclusion that may apply is the exclusion of the first $20 of monthly income.[53] If the applicant is over the income cap (discussed below) by $20, this exclusion may come in handy.

#### 8-6:2.2 Countable Income

Countable income is all cash the applicant receives that can be used for food and shelter and to which a specific exclusion does not apply.[54] From a practical standpoint, that's almost all the cash the applicant receives. Most elderly individuals receive Social Security and, perhaps, a pension. These items are countable income items.

## 8-7 NEEDY INDIVIDUAL

Medicaid is a health insurance program for needy individuals.[55] In order to be needy, the applicant must satisfy certain financial and health-related criteria.

### 8-7:1 Financial Eligibility

Financial need for institutional level Medicaid services focuses on the resources and income of the applicant.

#### 8-7:1.1 Resources

In New Jersey, there are two programs of Medicaid that provide institutional levels of services—the Medicaid Only program[56] and the Medically Needy program.[57] For the Medicaid Only program, the applicant must have less than $2,000 in countable resources.[58] For the Medically Needy program, the applicant must have less than $4,000 in countable resources.[59] Note that the limits apply to countable resources, not to non-countable resources. Non-countable resources do not count against the resource limits; that is why they are called non-countable resources.

---

53. N.J.A.C. 10:71-5.3(a)(18).
54. N.J.A.C. 10:71-5.2.
55. 42 U.S.C. § 1396(b)(2)(B).
56. N.J.A.C. 10:71-1.1. et seq.
57. N.J.A.C. 10:70-1.1. et seq.
58. N.J.A.C. 10:71-4.5(c).
59. N.J.A.C. 10:70-5.1(a).

### 8-7:1.2 Income

The resource limitation differential between the Medicaid Only program and the Medically Needy program is inconsequential, $2,000 versus $4,000. It is the income differences that separate the programs.

The Medicaid Only program has an income cap. In order to qualify for the Medicaid Only program, the applicant's income must be below the income cap. The income cap is set through a formula; the cap is 300% of the federal SSI monthly benefit rate. In 2014, the federal monthly benefit rate for SSI is $721,[60] so the income cap is $2,163.[61]

In most years, the federal benefit rate is increased due to its cost of living increase adjustment feature (COLA),[62] so in most years, the income cap will receive a 300% COLA increase. Most elderly individuals receive Social Security benefits. Social Security benefits also increase based upon the same COLA the SSI program utilizes;[63] accordingly, while the client's income is increasing by 100% of the COLA, the income cap is increasing by 300% of the COLA.

The rate of increase can be important for some clients, because if a client's gross income (and the income cap uses the gross income of the client, not his net income) is one penny above the income cap, he will not qualify for the Medicaid Only program. To gross up the client's income, you need to add back any deductions from Social Security for the Medicare program and you need to add back any deductions from his pension income (taxes, health insurance premiums, etc.). As stated, if the client's gross income is one penny above the income cap, he cannot qualify for the Medicaid Only program.

For this reason, for those clients who are on the margin of being able to qualify for Medicaid Only but who have income just slightly too high, the fact that the income cap increases by 300% of the COLA can be of some help.

Qualifying for Medicaid Only is extremely important for those clients who seek to qualify for institutional level Medicaid services at home or in an assisted living residence. In both of those settings,

---

60. http://www.ssa.gov/OACT/COLA/SSI.html.
61. N.J.A.C. 10:71-5.6(a).
62. 20 C.F.R. § 416.405.
63. 20 C.F.R. § 404.272.

the Medicaid Only program is the only program that will provide an institutional level of services. So, if a client presents to you with gross income of $2,200, even though he is only $37 over the income cap, he will not qualify for the Medicaid Only program, so he will not qualify for institutional level Medicaid services at home or in an assisted living residence. Even if the client had zero resources, if his income is over the cap, he is ineligible for Medicaid Only.

Currently, the State is seeking to implement amendments to its Medicaid program that will eliminate the income cap for care at home or in an assisted living residence, but as of this date, those amendments have not been implemented.[64]

The Medically Needy program is an income spend down program. From a practical standpoint, what this means is, as long as the client's income is insufficient to pay for the cost of his care, he will qualify for Medically Needy Medicaid.[65]

The Medically Needy Medicaid program is only available to pay for care in a nursing facility. Those clients seeking to qualify for Medicaid at home or in an assisted living residence will not benefit from the Medically Needy program.

Technically, a beneficiary of the Medically Needy program spends down his income every month, then qualifies for Medicaid benefits after he accomplishes the spend down.[66] For instance, assume the following facts: Mr. Smith resides in a nursing home costing $300 per day, or $9,000 per month. His income is $3,000 a month. Mr. Smith qualifies for Medically Needy Medicaid. For the first 10 days of every month, Mr. Smith is paying for his care privately at the rate of $300 per day ($300 x 10 = $3,000). For the remaining 20 days, Medicaid is paying.

### 8-7:2 The Pre-Admission Screen (PAS)

In addition to the financial criteria (resources and income), an applicant for institutional level care services must have a need for

---

64. The New Jersey Comprehensive Waiver is designed to modify New Jersey's Medicaid program by, in part, eliminating the income cap for institutional care services in the home or assisted living residence setting. http://www.state.nj.us/humanservices/dmahs/home/waiver.html. The Comprehensive Waiver is a Section 1115 waiver, 42 U.S.C. § 1315, that CMS approved at New Jersey's request in October 2012. To date, New Jersey has failed to implement its own Comprehensive Waiver, so the income cap remains in place.

65. Medicaid Communication 95-11.

66. Medicaid Communication 95-11.

care from a health perspective. The law that imposes this criterion is the Pre-Admission Screen Act.[67] A Pre-Admission Screen is called a PAS (pronounced Pass).

### 8-7:2.1 Activities of Daily Living

A PAS is issued to an applicant if the applicant either requires hands-on assistance with three or more activities of daily living (ADLs) or has cognitive impairments that affect his ability to perform independently three or more ADLs.[68] There are six ADLs: clothing, bathing, toileting, eating, transferring, and mobility. These are the only activities of daily living that matter when making the PAS assessment.

There are also instrumental activities of daily living (IADLs). IADLs are activities such as meal preparation and medication administration. Most people believe that if a person cannot prepare their own meals or cannot take their medications properly they need help, but the inability to perform IADLs does not get an applicant for Medicaid a PAS.

The Office of Community Choice Options (OCCO)[69]—which is an office of the Division of Aging Services, part of the Department of Health and Senior Services—employs nurses who make the assessment as to whether or not an applicant for Medicaid benefits qualifies for a PAS. From a practical standpoint, OCCO believes that it is the only entity that can make such an assessment. In other words, even if the applicant's physician attested to the fact that the applicant required hands-on assistance with three or more ADLs, OCCO believes that it is the one and only entity that can make that determination and if that office does not believe that the applicant requires hands-on assistance with three ADLs, then the applicant does not qualify for Medicaid benefits.

This can be confusing because the county board of social services will ask the applicant to have his physician complete a medical assessment form called a PA-4.[70] Essentially, the PA-4 is just a preliminary screening tool. The physician is attesting to the fact

67. N.J.S.A. 30:4D-17.10.

68. N.J.A.C. 8:85-2.1.

69. N.J.A.C. 8:85-1.2. (defining Office of Community Choice Options or OCCO).

70. N.J.A.C. 8:85-1.8€(3).

that the applicant may require care in a nursing facility or assisted living residence within the next 30 days.

The PA-4, though, is really an elimination tool, not an eligibility tool. If the physician attests that the applicant will not require care in a nursing home or assisted living residence in the next 30 days, then his application will be denied; however, if the physician attests to the fact that the applicant may need such care in the next 30 days, then the application can proceed, and OCCO will make its own assessment.

### 8-7:2.2 Telephone Screen

For those individuals applying for an institutional level of services at home, for instance, a home health aide or adult day care services, there is a phone screen assessment tool that the applicant must satisfy. Through the phone screen, the area agency on aging (AAA) performs a telephone screen asking the applicant questions about his ability to perform some of the instrumental activities of daily living, the basic activities of daily living, his living arrangements and his communication and behavior skills.

As with a PA-4, the phone assessment tool is an elimination tool. If the applicant fails to meet the eligibility criteria on the phone screening tool, he will be disqualified from benefits. If the applicant satisfies the eligibility criteria on the phone assessment, the application will proceed. Satisfying the phone assessment tool does not mean the applicant is eligible for Medicaid institutional level care services; it simply means the applicant will not be denied those benefits at that stage of the application process.

### 8-7:2.3 The Assessment Tool

When the nurse from OCCO comes to see the applicant (at home or in the assisted living residence or in the nursing facility), the nurse will use a standardized assessment tool. For all intents and purposes, the section of primary purpose in this assessment tool is the section addressing the ADLs.

If the applicant does not require hands-on assistance with three ADLs or have cognitive impairments that substantially affect his ability to perform three ADLs, then he will not receive a PAS and he will not be eligible for institutional level Medicaid care services.

## 8-8 INSTITUTIONALIZED INDIVIDUAL

The federal Medicaid Act uses the phrase "institutionalized individual" in various locations throughout the Act. An individual who is an inpatient in a nursing facility or who is receiving a level of home- and community-based services (for instance, a home health aide or assisted living residence) that allow the individual to reside in the community as opposed to residing in a nursing facility is an "institutionalized individual."[71]

## 8-9 INSTITUTIONALIZED SPOUSE

The federal Medicaid Act uses the phrase "institutionalized spouse" in various locations throughout the Act. An institutionalized spouse is the spouse who is receiving an institutional level of services (for instance, home- and community-based Medicaid services or nursing facility services).[72] In addition, in order to be an institutionalized spouse, the person must not be married to a spouse who is living in a medical institution or nursing facility.[73]

If a married couple is residing in a nursing home, neither spouse is an institutionalized spouse. Both of the spouses would simply be institutionalized individuals.

## 8-10 COMMUNITY SPOUSE

The community spouse is the spouse of the institutionalized spouse. In order to be a community spouse, the community spouse must not be living in a medical institution or nursing facility.[74]

### 8-10:1 Who is a Spouse

A community spouse must be legally married to the institutionalized spouse.[75] This fact had great relevance with respect to homosexual couples and is part of the reason why our judicial system entered an injunction compelling the State to permit homosexual couples to marry.[76]

---

71. 42 U.S.C. § 1396p(h)(3).
72. 42 U.S.C. § 1396r-5(h)(1).
73. 42 U.S.C. § 1396r-5(h)(1).
74. 42 U.S.C. § 1396r-5(h)(2).
75. 42 U.S.C. § 1396r-5(h)(2).
76. *Garden State Equal. v. Dow*, 216 N.J. 314 (2013).

## 8-11 COMMUNITY SPOUSE RESOURCE ALLOWANCE

The community spouse resource allowance or CSRA (pronounced Cezra) is an amount of countable resources that the community spouse can retain without affecting the institutionalized spouse's eligibility for Medicaid benefits.[77] The CSRA came into being as part of the Medicare Catastrophic Coverage Act of 1988 or MCCA (pronounced Mecca).[78]

The purpose of the CSRA is to prevent the community spouse from being impoverished after the institutionalized spouse qualifies for Medicaid benefits. For this reason, the MCCA is said to have put spousal impoverishment provisions (the CSRA and the minimum monthly maintenance needs allowance, discussed below) into the Medicaid Act.

When dealing with a married couple, the Medicaid program deems the assets of each spouse to be available to the institutionalized spouse;[79] accordingly, it is irrelevant in which spouse's name a resource is titled. All resources are available to pay for the institutionalized spouse's care.

Stated otherwise, the Medicaid Act treats a married couple as one economic unit, so which spouse actually owns the resource is of no importance. For instance, if the community spouse has all of the resources in her name, those resources will still be deemed to the institutionalized spouse for purposes of determining his eligibility for Medicaid benefits.

The CSRA is important to avoid spousal impoverishment because the institutionalized spouse can only have $2,000 in countable resources in order to qualify for Medicaid benefits. The problem the deeming of resources creates for the community spouse is the fact that if the institutionalized spouse needs to have no more than $2,000 in resources in his name, then because of deeming, the community spouse along with the institutionalized spouse would need to have no more than $2,000 in resources in her name.

Before the MCCA's spousal impoverishment provisions, this fact presented a very big problem for the community spouse who

---

77. 42 U.S.C. § 1396r-5(f)(2).
78. 42 U.S.C. § 1396r-5.
79. 42 U.S.C. § 1396r-5(c)(2).

would be living in the community with, essentially, no money. The Medicaid program is providing for the institutionalized spouse's needs—the institutionalized spouse is residing in a nursing home, getting the care he needs, having a roof provided for him and receiving three meals a day. On the other hand, the community spouse is still living at home with no one providing for her needs. The purpose of the CSRA is to permit the community spouse to maintain her needs, to permit her to remain self-sufficient.

The CSRA only applies to countable resources;[80] the community spouse is free to retain all of the non-countable resources (such as the home, a car, household goods and personal effects).[81] The CSRA has a maximum amount and a minimum amount.[82] In 2014, the maximum CSRA is $117,240 and the minimum CSRA is $23,448.[83]

## 8-11:1 Snapshot Date

The snapshot date is the date on which a couple's assets are assessed for purposes of determining the amount of the CSRA the community spouse can retain. The snapshot date is the beginning of the first continuous period of institutionalization of the institutionalized spouse.[84]

From a practical standpoint, the county boards of social services use the first day of the month during which the institutionalized spouse enters the nursing home or the assisted living residence. For instance, if the institutionalized spouse enters a nursing home on December 15th, most county boards of social services will look at the combined resources of the couple as of December 1st and use that date as the snapshot date. For individuals applying for institutional services at home, most county boards will use the first day of the month in which an application for Medicaid benefits is filed.

Once a snapshot date occurs for a client, it is fixed in time forever. For instance, if an institutionalized spouse who is residing in a nursing facility returns home and is no longer receiving

80. 42 U.S.C. § 1396r-5(c)(5).
81. 42 U.S.C. § 1382b.
82. 42 U.S.C. § 1396r-5(f)(2).
83. Medicaid Communication 14.01.
84. 42 U.S.C. § 1396r-5(c).

Medicaid benefits at home then goes back to a nursing facility, the snapshot that occurred on his first admission is the snapshot date that would be used for purposes of determining the community spouse's CSRA.[85]

### 8-11:2 Minimum CSRA

The minimum CSRA establishes a floor-level of countable resources that the community spouse can retain.[86] In 2014, the minimum CSRA is $23,448.[87] If the couple has anything less than $23,448 multiplied by 2 ($23,448 x 2) or $46,896, then the community spouse can retain the minimum CSRA.

So, for instance, if the couple has $45,000 in countable resources when the institutionalized spouse enters the nursing home, the community spouse can retain the minimum CSRA, or $23,448. If the couple has $30,000 in countable resources, the community spouse can retain $23,448. If the couple has $20,000 in countable resources, then the community spouse can retain the entire $20,000, as that amount of countable resources is below the minimum level.

### 8-11:3 Maximum CSRA

The maximum CSRA establishes a ceiling-level of countable resources that the community spouse can retain.[88] In 2014, the maximum CSRA is $117,240.[89] If the couple has anything more than $117,240 multiplied by 2 ($117,240 x 2), or $234,480, then the community spouse can retain the maximum CSRA.

### 8-11:4 CSRA Calculation Examples

The calculation of the CSRA can be somewhat of a mystery to the client, though it really is rather straightforward. Most clients believe that they can retain half of the countable resources no matter the value. For instance, a client with $1,000,000 in countable resources will typically believe that he can retain $500,000 of those

---

85. 42 U.S.C. § 1396r-5(c) ("There shall be computed (as of the beginning of the *first* continuous period of institutionalization (beginning on or after September 30, 1989) of the institutionalized spouse)") (emphasis added).

86. 42 U.S.C. § 1396r-5(f)(2)(A)(i).

87. Medicaid Communication 14-01.

88. 42 U.S.C. § 1396r-5(f)(2)(A)(ii).

89. Medicaid Communication 14-01.

resources. Alternatively, clients believe that they can retain all of the resources that are titled in their names. For instance, a wife with all of the resources titled in her name will believe that she can retain all of those resources.

But how is the CSRA calculated? Let's explore a few examples.

If the couple has $230,000 in countable resources, the community spouse can retain the maximum CSRA or $117,240. If the couple has $500,000 in countable resources, the community spouse can still only retain the maximum CSRA or $117,240. If the couple has less than the maximum CSRA times 2 or $234,480 ($117,240 x 2 = $234,480) but more than the minimum CSRA times two or $46,896 ($23,488 x 2 = $46,896), then the community spouse can retain one-half of the countable resources.

For instance, if the couple has $200,000 in countable resources, then the community spouse can retain $100,000 in countable resources. If the couple has $150,000 in countable resources, then the community spouse can retain $75,000 in countable resources. If the couple has $100,000 in countable resources, then the community spouse can retain $50,000. If the couple has $50,000, then the community spouse can retain $25,000.

The MCCA established a maximum and a minimum level of countable resources that the community spouse can retain, not an absolute figure. Remember that the community spouse can still retain the non-countable resources, the house, a car, the personal goods and household effects.

### 8-11:4.1 Increasing the CSRA

There are provisions in both the federal and state laws that pertain to increasing the CSRA under certain circumstances.[90] If an increase in the CSRA is necessary to bring the community spouse's income up to the minimum monthly maintenance needs allowance or MMMNA, discussed immediately below, then the institutionalized spouse or the community spouse can request an increase in the CSRA in order to generate sufficient income to bring the community spouse's income up to the MMMNA.[91] In short, the MMMNA is a spousal income allowance whereby

---

90. 42 U.S.C. §§ 1396r-5(e)(2)(C), 1396r-5(f)(3); N.J.A.C. 10:71-4.8(a)(4), (5).
91. 42 U.S.C. § 1396r-5(e)(2)(C).

the community spouse is entitled to retain a certain amount of the institutionalized spouse's income in order to meet her monthly needs.

The CSRA-increase provision can best be demonstrated by way of example. Assume that the community spouse is entitled to a MMMNA, or spousal income allowance, of $2,000, but she can only receive $1,000 of that monthly income by way of a divergence of the institutionalized spouse's income to her.[92] Let's further assume that the couple has $500,000 in countable resources, which means that the community spouse can retain the maximum CSRA or $117,240.[93]

An attorney for the couple might contend that the community spouse needs to retain all of the remaining countable resources or $382,760 ($500,000 - $117,240 = $382,760) in order to generate sufficient income to bring her up to her MMMNA. In this example, the community spouse is entitled to a $2,000 spousal income allowance. She is receiving $1,000 from the institutionalized spouse. The additional countable resources of $382,760 are still inadequate to generate the additional $1,000 a month in income that she can retain if the county board of social services imputes a 2% rate of return to those assets [($382,760 x 2% = $7,655)/12 = $637.93 per month].

This provision of the law is interesting in that it permits either the institutionalized spouse or the community spouse to request the increase in the CSRA.[94] This is one of the few provisions of the Medicaid Act that gives a right to both the applicant and his spouse.

There is a provision in the law called the "income-first rule," which requires the income of the community spouse to be diverted to the community spouse in order to bring her up to the MMMNA before additional resources can be retained by the community spouse to bring her income up to the MMMNA.[95]

---

92. 42 U.S.C. § 1396r-5(d)(3).

93. 42 U.S.C. § 1396r-5(f)(2)(A)(ii)(II); Medicaid Communication 14-01.

94. 42 U.S.C. § 1396r-5(e)(2)(C).

95. 42 U.S.C. § 1396r-5(d)(6); *Wisconsin Dept. of Health and Family Services v. Blumer*, 534 U.S. 473 (2002).

### 8-11:4.2 Forum for Increasing the CSRA

An increase in the CSRA must be made by way of a fair hearing, which, from a practical standpoint, means that a request for an increased CSRA must be made after the applicant has received an approval letter and after the community spouse has received her initial CSRA award.[96] From a practical standpoint, this makes increasing the CSRA very difficult.

Taking the hypothetical above, the community spouse would be requesting that she be permitted to retain all of the countable resources, yet she is only guaranteed the right to retain the maximum CSRA, which is $382,760 less than the amount of resources she is claiming she can retain. In order to request the increased CSRA, the institutionalized spouse will need to apply for Medicaid, be denied benefits because of the excess resources above the maximum CSRA, then take a fair hearing from the denial through which the community spouse requests the right to retain all the countable resource, or $500,000.

The fair hearing process will be discussed below, but for purposes of discussion at this point, it can be assumed that the fair hearing process is very much slanted in favor of the State and can take years to resolve. Meanwhile, the community spouse is paying the nursing home in which the institutionalized spouse resides $10,000 a month. By the time the fair hearing is resolved and even assuming that the community spouse wins her appeal, there may not be sufficient resources remaining to permit the community spouse to retain even the maximum CSRA let alone the $500,000 in resources she was initially requesting.

For this reason, very few applications to increase the CSRA are ever made; probably no such application has ever been made by an applicant for benefits who was not represented by counsel.

## 8-12 MINIMUM MONTHLY MAINTENANCE NEEDS ALLOWANCE

The minimum monthly maintenance needs allowance or MMMNA is a spousal income allowance for the community spouse.[97] In short, the community spouse may be entitled to retain

---

96. 42 U.S.C. § 1396r-5(e).
97. 42 U.S.C. § 1396r-5(d).

a certain amount of the institutionalized spouse's income in order to pay her monthly bills.

There is a formula for calculating the MMMA. The formula takes into consideration the basic needs of the community spouse (food, clothing, medical expenses, etc.)[98] and certain excess shelter needs (rent, mortgage, utilities, real estate taxes, homeowner's insurance) that exceed an established threshold.[99]

### 8-12:1 Basic Allowance

The basic allowance of the MMMNA is designed to pay for the basic, monthly needs of the community spouse—food, clothing, medical expenses, etc.[100] The basic allowance is adjusted each year for inflation on or about July of that year.[101] For the July 2013 through July 2014 time period, the basic allowance is $1,938.75.

### 8-12:2 Excess Shelter Allowance

The excess shelter allowance portion of the MMMNA calculation is designed to take into consideration certain shelter expenses that exceed an established base-level.[102] The base-level of shelter expenses is also adjusted each year in July.[103] For the July 2013 through July 2014 time period, the base level for the excess shelter allowance is $581.62.

If the community spouse's monthly shelter expenses (rent, mortgage, real estate taxes, homeowner's insurance, homeowner's association fee, etc.) exceed $581.62, then the community spouse can retain an amount of the institutionalized spouse's income needed to cover this excess amount.

### 8-12:3 Maximum MMMNA

The federal law establishes a maximum MMMNA.[104] For the 2013-2014 period, the maximum MMMNA is $2,841. As with

---

98. 42 U.S.C. § 1396r-5(d)(3).
99. 42 U.S.C. § 1396r-5(d)(4).
100. 42 U.S.C. § 1396r-5(d)(3).
101. 42 U.S.C. § 1396r-5(g).
102. 42 U.S.C. § 1396r-5(d)(4).
103. 42 U.S.C. § 1396r-5(g).
104. 42 U.S.C. § 1396r-5(d)(3)(C).

the basic allowance amount and the excess shelter base-level, the maximum MMMNA amount is adjusted annually around July.

From a practical standpoint, the state of New Jersey does not enforce the maximum MMMNA and will award a MMMNA above the maximum to a community spouse if the calculation of the MMMNA warrants an award above the maximum.

## 8-12:4 Calculating the MMMNA

The calculation of the MMMNA is based upon the following formula:

| | | |
|---|---|---|
| | $1,938.75 | Basic Allowance Amount |
| – | $______ | Community Spouse's Gross Income |
| | $______ | Basic Allowance |
| | | |
| | $______ | Shelter Expenses |
| – | $581.62 | Excess Shelter Base Level |
| | $______ | Excess Shelter Allowance |
| | | |
| | $______ | Basic Allowance |
| + | $______ | Excess Shelter Allowance |
| | $______ | Total MMMNA |

Let us assume that the community spouse has gross monthly income of $1,000 from Social Security and a pension. Let's further assume that the community spouse has monthly shelter expenses of $1,200. The calculation of the MMMNA would be as follows:

| | |
|---|---|
| $1,938.75 | Basic Allowance Amount |
| $1,000.00 | Community Spouse's Gross Income |
| $938.75 | Basic Allowance |
| | |
| $1,200.00 | Shelter Expenses |
| $581.62 | Excess Shelter Base Level |
| $618.38 | Excess Shelter Allowance |
| | |
| $938.75 | Basic Allowance |
| $618.38 | Excess Shelter Allowance |
| $1,557.13 | Total MMMNA |

The MMMNA comes from the institutionalized spouse's income. Assume that the institutionalized spouse has monthly income of $2,000. The community spouse's MMMNA of $1,557.13 will come from his monthly income of $2,000, leaving him with $442.87 ($2,000 - $1,557.13 = $442.87).

If the institutionalized spouse had income of only $1,000 a month and the community spouse were entitled to a MMMNA of $1,557.13, or $557.13 more than the institutionalized spouse's total income, the community spouse may be able to retain countable resources above the CSRA to increase her MMMNA, as discussed above.

## 8-12:5 Increasing the MMMNA

### 8-12:5.1 Court-Ordered MMMNA

The Medicaid Act establishes the above-referenced methodology for calculating the MMMNA.[105] The Medicaid Act also states that if a court has entered an order of support to the community spouse, then the State must honor that support order as the MMMNA if the order for support provides for a higher amount than the statutory methodology would provide.[106]

In other words, assume that under the standard methodology for calculating the MMMNA the community spouse is entitled to $557.13, but further assume that the community spouse has a support order from the Superior Court of New Jersey, Family Part, that provides for his receiving, by way of a support order, $1,000 per month from his wife who is now residing in a nursing home. The Medicaid Act holds that the State must honor that support order and permit the community spouse to retain $1,000 of the institutionalized spouse's income.

Some practitioners have attempted to utilize this provision of the Act to increase the MMMNA. Both the institutionalized spouse and the community spouse will retain counsel. The community spouse will file an action in the Superior Court of New Jersey, Family Part, seeking an order of support from the institutionalized spouse. The community spouse will obtain the support order.

---

105. 42 U.S.C. § 1396r-5(d).
106. 42 U.S.C. § 1396r-5(d)(5).

The action in the Family Part must be filed prior to applying for Medicaid benefits. In addition, DMAHS must be notified of the action and the action must be adversarial. The Court should be made aware of the fact that an application for Medicaid benefits will be filed in the near future and an evidentiary hearing as to the needs of the community spouse should be held.

The State will not honor an order entered without notifying DMAHS and without evidence being presented as to the community spouse's needs, and our courts have upheld the fact that DMHAS does not have to honor such an order.[107]

### 8-12:5.2 Forum for Increasing the MMMNA

Because the county board of social services has to adhere to a court order of spousal support, an applicant for benefits might receive a higher MMMNA than he would following the ordinary application procedures if his spouse files for a spousal income award from the Superior Court, Family Part, before filing for Medicaid benefits. If the community spouse is going to take this option, she must file and receive the spousal award before filing the application for Medicaid benefits.[108]

Most community spouses do not file a support action in the Family Part before filing a Medicaid application; in fact, very few elder law attorneys employ this procedure. If the community spouse has not received a spousal support award from the Family Part, the federal and state laws establish a procedure for increasing the MMMNA.[109]

The standard procedure for increasing the MMMNA is to file for a fair hearing of the award after the institutionalized spouse is awarded benefits and after the community spouse receives the award of the MMMNA using the standard formula.[110] The community spouse must prove that exceptional circumstances exist for an increased MMMNA.[111] Our courts have interpreted the phrase

107. *R.S. v. Div. of Medical Assistance and Health Services*, 434 N.J. Super. 250 (App. Div. 2014).

108. *M.E.F. v. A.B.F.*, 393 N.J. Super. 543 (App. Div. 2007).

109. 42 U.S.C. § 1396r-5(d).

110. 42 U.S.C. § 1396r-5(e)(2).

111. 42 U.S.C. § 1396r-5(e)(2)(B).

"exceptional circumstances" very narrowly, nearly foreclosing the ability to increase the MMMNA in most instances.[112]

In essence, our courts have held that the word "exceptional" means unusual, so only unusual expenses can result in an increase in the MMMNA under the fair hearing methodology. Most elderly individuals do not have unusual expenses (the nursing home would not be an unusual expense because the Medicaid program is now paying for the institutionalized spouse's care); their lives and their spending patterns are fairly established.

## 8-13 TRANSFER OF ASSETS RULES

Medicaid is a health insurance program for needy individuals.[113] With regard to an applicant for Medicaid benefits, a large part of his being "needy" is being unable to pay for his care. Being unable to pay for care means that the applicant has few resources from which to pay for his care and insufficient income to pay for his care.

Because the Medicaid program looks at both the resources and income of the applicant in order to assess eligibility, the law imposes a punishment if the applicant gratuitously disposes of either a resource item or an income item within a specified period of time prior to applying for Medicaid benefits.[114] The specified period of time is 60 months before the filing of the application for Medicaid benefits.[115] This period of time is commonly known as the "lookback period."

Medicaid classifies resources and income as an "asset."[116] If the applicant makes an uncompensated transfer of any asset within the 5 years prior to applying for Medicaid benefits, the applicant will be rendered ineligible for Medicaid benefits for a period of time and will have to find another means of paying for the care he requires.

The specified period of time is supposed to be equivalent to the amount of time during which the applicant could have paid

---

112. *K.L. v. Div. of Medical Assistance and Health Services*, 2012 N.J. Super. Unpub. Lexis 515 (App. Div. 2012); *Dorn v. Div. of Medical Assistance and Health Services*, 2006 N.J. Super. Unpub. Lexis 2109 (App. Div. 2006).

113. 42 U.S.C. § 1396.

114. 42 U.S.C. § 1396p(c).

115. 42 U.S.C. § 1396p(c)(1)(B).

116. 42 U.S.C. § 1396p(h)(1).

privately for his care if he had not made the uncompensated transfer of an asset.[117]

The asset transfer rules only apply to Medicaid institutional level care services (such as care in a nursing home or assisted living residence), not to community Medicaid services (such as Medicaid as a pure health insurance program).[118] So, an applicant for Medicaid could be rendered ineligible for institutional level care services for a period of time yet still receive community Medicaid services during the period of ineligibility that results from his having made an uncompensated transfer of an asset during the lookback period.

## 8-13:1 Penalty Period

Medicaid punishes an individual who has made an uncompensated transfer of an asset within the lookback period by making the individual ineligible for institutional level care services for a period of time.[119] The calculation of this period of ineligibility or penalty period will be discussed in detail below.

## 8-13:2 Uncompensated Transfer

The Medicaid Act punishes all uncompensated transfers that occur during the lookback period. It is important to realize that uncompensated transfers, not necessarily gifts, are punished if made within the lookback period. An uncompensated transfer includes a gift but also captures any transfer for which the applicant failed to receive value irrespective of the intention of the person making the transfer. A gift requires an intention to make a gift;[120] an uncompensated transfer has no intention requirement.

Most people speak in term of gifts when talking about Medicaid uncompensated transfers. A great number of clients are reluctant to classify the transfers they made during the lookback period as gifts. For instance, you may ask a client if he made any gifts during the lookback period. The client may respond in the negative, but later, in the interview process, the client will tell you about a bank

---

117. 42 U.S.C. § 1396p(c)(1)(E)(i)(II).

118. 42 U.S.C. § 1396p(c)(1)(C)(i).

119. 42 U.S.C. § 1396p(c)(1)(E).

120. *Trenton Savings Fund Society v. Byrnes*, 110 N.J. Eq. 617 (Ch. 1932).

account of his that he transferred to his son's name or about a car that he gave his son.

These transfers are the types of uncompensated transfers that the Medicaid program punishes, but the client, for whatever reason, fails to think of these transfers as gifts and will fail to inform you of them when asked directly. You will need to give the client examples when you ask if the client has given away any assets within the lookback period. "Have you transferred any bank accounts to your family?" "Have you given a family member a car in the past 5 years?"

## 8-13:3 Lookback Period

Because Medicaid is only available to needy individuals, Medicaid will disqualify an applicant from receiving institutional level care services (e.g., nursing home services, home health aide services, assisted living residence services) if the applicant makes an uncompensated transfer of an asset within a specified period of time-the look back period. The specified period of time is 60 months (or 5 years) before the applicant is both (1) an institutionalized individual and (2) applies for Medicaid benefits.

Each uncompensated transfer within the lookback period triggers its own five-year lookback period. For instance, assume that Mr. Smith transferred $10,000 on November 1, 2008, $20,000 on March 16, 2011, and $10,000 on January 26, 2012. Mr. Smith is residing in a nursing home. He applies for Medicaid benefits on December 1, 2013. Mr. Smith is an institutionalized individual because he is residing in a nursing facility and because he has applied for Medicaid benefits.[121]

The Medicaid program will look back 60 months before the date of the application, which was December 1, 2013, in this example. Sixty months before December 1, 2013, is a period of time beginning January 1, 2009, and ending December 2013.

In this hypothetical case, all of Mr. Smith's uncompensated transfers with the exception of the November 1, 2008, transfer occurred within the lookback period. The Medicaid Office will aggregate the two transfers that occurred within the lookback period (the $20,000 March 16, 2011 transfer and the $10,000 January 26, 2012 transfer) and will assess a penalty period or period

---

121. 42 U.S.C. § 1396p(h)(3).

of ineligibility for Medicaid institutional level care services against Mr. Smith.

If Mr. Smith were to wait out the lookback period for each transfer, he would have to wait until April 1, 2016, for the March 16, 2011 transfer and until February 1, 2017, for the January 26, 2012, transfer.

## 8-13:4 Aggregating Transfers

The Medicaid Act compels the State to aggregate the uncompensated transfers that are made during the lookback period.[122] So, if an applicant transfers $10,000, $20,000, and $10,000 within the lookback period, the Medicaid Act requires those transfers to be aggregated. In this example, the aggregate of the transfers is $40,000. The applicant will be penalized for having made $40,000 in uncompensated transfers.

## 8-13:5 The Divisor Figure

There are two factors to consider when calculating a penalty period for institutional level care services due to an uncompensated asset transfer that occurs within the lookback period: the aggregate of the transfers that were made during the lookback period and the divisor figure.[123] The divisor figure is the weighted-average cost of a nursing home room in the state of New Jersey at the time of application.[124]

The State conducts a survey of all nursing homes throughout the state. The number of beds in each facility is taken into consideration when the State makes this calculation, hence the average is weighted to take into consideration that fact that facilities have differing numbers of beds and differing costs of care. The county board uses the divisor figure to calculate the penalty period given the aggregate transfers that the applicant made during the lookback period.

The theory behind the penalty period is that the applicant could have used the assets he gave away to pay privately for his care. For this reason, the State is compelled to use an accurate divisor figure when calculating the penalty period because an accurate divisor figure allows the penalty period to reflect the fact that the applicant

---

122. 42 U.S.C. § 1396p(c)(1)(i)(I).
123. 42 U.S.C. § 1396p(c)(1)(i).
124. 42 U.S.C. § 1396p(c)(1)(i)(II).

could have used the assets he disposed of to pay for his care for the length of the penalty period.[125]

The current monthly divisor figure is $313.50 per day.

## 8-13:6 Transferring Income

The Medicaid transfer of asset rules punish the transfer of a resource item (cash, stocks, bonds, mutual funds, cars, real estate, etc.) and income items (Social Security, pensions, annuity income, rental income, etc.). Since the vast majority of elderly clients only have two sources of income (Social Security and pension income) and since these forms of income cannot be transferred due to anti-alienation provisions in the Social Security Act and various pension plans, few, if any, clients will ever transfer an income item.

With that said, you should bear in mind the fact that the transfer of an income item can be punished as a transfer of an asset. If, for instance, the client disposed of an income item that paid him $200 a month and the client were an 80 year old male, you would calculate the aggregate uncompensated transfer that the client made as follows:

| | | |
|---|---|---|
| | $200 | Per month transfer |
| x | 97 | # of months of life expectancy of 80 year old male[126] |
| | $19,400 Aggregate Transfer | |

## 8-13:7 Transferring Resources

Most individuals who make uncompensated transfers dispose of a resource item. The fair market value of the resource on the date the resource is transferred is the value of the uncompensated transfer for purposes of calculating a penalty period.[127] An automobile is valued at the Kelley Blue Book trade-in value. A share of common stock should be valued at the average of the high and low on the date of transfer. Real estate is valued using the tax assessed value and the equalization ratio, which is a figure that the New Jersey Division of Taxation publishes annually for each municipality in

---

125. Medicaid Communication 14-06.

126. Use the life expectancy tables published by the Chief Actuary of the Social Security Administration. These tables can be found at http://www.ssa.gov/OACT/STATS/table4c6.html.

127. N.J.A.C. 10:71-4.1.

the state and is designed to equalize the tax assessed value to the fair market value.

When dealing with an unmarried client who owns a stock, bank account or brokerage account jointly with another individual, the form in which the resource is held is important. If the form of ownership is an "and" account, meaning that both owners must sign in order to sell the asset, then the applicant owns one-half the resource. Jointly owned real estate is, in most instances, an "and" form of ownership since both owners must sign any documents necessary to sell the real estate.

If the form of ownership is an "or" account, meaning that either owner can sell the entire account, then the applicant owns the entire account unless the applicant or co-owner/non-applicant can prove to the satisfaction of the county board of social services the contributions to the account of the non-applicant account owner.[128] For instance, if a father and son own a bank account worth $10,000 and the son can prove that he contributed $5,000 to that account, then the county board of social services should treat the account as being owned 50% by the father and 50% by the son.

If the applicant disposes of a resource during the lookback period, the county board should punish the applicant for disposing of his value of the resource. With the bank account discussed immediately above, if the father removed his name from the bank account thereby transferring the account to his son in its entirety, then the county should assess a penalty period against the father based upon a $5,000 uncompensated transfer.

## 8-13:8 Otherwise Be Receiving

The State cannot begin a penalty period until such time as the applicant is an institutionalized individual (for instance, resides in a nursing facility and files an application for Medicaid benefits) and would otherwise be receiving an institutional level of care services but for the application of the penalty period.[129] In other words, the applicant must be in a nursing facility, resource-eligible, income-eligible and file an application for institutional level

---

128. *K.R. v. Somerset County Board of Social Services*, docket number OAL No. HMA 12343-07.

129. 42 U.S.C. § 1396p(c)(1)(D)(ii).

care services. If all of these facts exist and if the only reason the applicant is not receiving Medicaid institutional level care services is because he made an uncompensated transfer of an asset within the lookback period, then the county board of social services should begin the penalty period as of the first day of the month in which the application was filed.

The "otherwise be receiving" requirement came into being as part of the Deficit Reduction Act of 2005,[130] which modified various provisions of the Medicaid Act. This requirement makes starting a penalty period quite complex. Most applicants for Medicaid benefits are unaware of this requirement and go about their way expecting to receiving Medicaid benefits after they have spent down their assets on their care.

For instance, if Mr. Smith made uncompensated transfers on January 1, 2010, and applies for benefits on December 1, 2013, after having spent down his assets on his nursing home care, the penalty period for his January 1, 2010, transfer will not even begin until Mr. Smith is out of money and applies for benefit. Obviously, this poses a serious problem for Mr. Smith, because the penalty period begins just when he has no money to pay for his care.

Since many elder individuals make uncompensated transfers to family members, there are a great number of individuals who need assistance to correct issues they created because they made uncompensated transfers years before they applied for Medicaid benefits.

### 8-13:9 Calculating a Penalty Period

Let's assume that Mr. Smith made uncompensated transfers totaling $50,000 within the lookback period. Mr. Smith resides in a nursing facility and files an application for Medicaid benefits. Mr. Smith would otherwise be receiving institutional level care services but for the fact that he made the $50,000 uncompensated transfer within the lookback period.

The county board of social services will calculate the penalty period by taking the $50,000 uncompensated transfer and dividing the $50,000 figure by the divisor figure.[131] As of the

---

130. Public Law 109-171 (February 8, 2006).

131. 42 U.S.C. § 1396p(c)(1)(E).

writing of this book, the divisor figure is $313.50 per day, or approximately $9,535 per month. The result of the calculation is 5.3 ($50,000/$9,535 = 5.2). That is the number of months during which Mr. Smith will be ineligible for institutional level care services, 5.2, beginning with the month he files an application for Medicaid benefits.

The lookback period is 60 months, but the penalty period can be unlimited in duration.[132] For instance, if Mr. Smith transferred $1,000,000, he would be ineligible for 104.8 months ($1,000,000/$9,535 = 104.8), if he filed an application for Medicaid benefits. The solution to this problem is for Mr. Smith to simply wait-out the lookback period. If Mr. Smith waits 61 months after the transfer to apply for benefits, the $1,000,000 transfer will not be within the lookback period, so the county board cannot assess a penalty period against him for the uncompensated transfer.

### 8-13:9.1 Tolling a Penalty Period

Once a penalty period begins to run, it cannot be tolled or stopped.[133] So, if the applicant has a penalty period imposed against him, the fact that he may at a later date be ineligible for institutional level care services will not toll the penalty period that was assessed against him and that is currently running.

For instance, if the applicant would otherwise be receiving institutional level care services and has a penalty assessed against him but later receives an inheritance, the fact that he is now resource-ineligible does not toll the running of the penalty period that has already been assessed and has begun running.

### 8-13:9.2 Withdrawing a Premature Application

What if an applicant files an application at an imprudent time given uncompensated transfers that he made during the lookback period? For instance, assume that Mr. Smith made an uncompensated of $1,000,000 on January 1, 2010, and he imprudently applies for Medicaid benefits on December 1, 2013,

---

132. 42 U.S.C. § 1396p(c)(1)(E).

133. Centers for Medicare and Medicaid Services, New Medicaid Transfer of Assets Rules Under the Deficit Reduction Act of 2006, Sections 6011 and 6016, II.A.

meaning that the $1,000,000 transfer is within the lookback period. Can Mr. Smith simply withdraw the application and wait out the lookback period before re-applying without the State assessing a penalty period against him based upon his $1,000,000 uncompensated transfer?

There is no clear answer on this question. If the county board of social services did not already assess a penalty period against Mr. Smith, probably. If the county did assess a penalty period against Mr. Smith, probably not, because the penalty period does not toll once it begins to run.

### 8-13:10 Transfer Exclusively for Reasons Other Than to Qualify for Medicaid

The Medicaid Act punishes uncompensated transfers that were made to qualify for Medicaid benefits. So, if an applicant can prove to the satisfaction of the county board of social services that the applicant made an uncompensated transfer exclusively for reasons other than to qualify for Medicaid benefits, then the transfer will not result in a penalty period.[134] From a practical standpoint, proving that a transfer was made exclusively for reasons other than to qualify for Medicaid benefits is very difficult.

The law presumes that any uncompensated transfer made within the lookback period was made to qualify for Medicaid benefits. Reading the Final Agency Decisions of the Director of the Division of Medical Assistance and Health Services that address this issue leads you to believe that if the applicant is elderly, which most applicants for institutional level care services are, then there is a presumption that the transfer was made to qualify for Medicaid benefits.

There are several factors that the state regulation lists that lend credibility to the applicant's contention that the transfer was made for reasons other than to qualify for Medicaid benefits,[135] but these factors are not conclusive on the issue.[136] For instance, the applicant may show the sudden onset of an illness that caused him

134. 42 U.S.C. § 1396p(c)(2)(C)(ii); N.J.A.C. 10:71-4.10(j), (k).

135. N.J.A.C. 10:71-4.10(k).

136. *V.M. v. Dep't. of Human Services*, 2011 N.J. Super. Unpub. Lexis 1307 (App. Div. 2011).

to require a nursing home level of services and, eventually, to apply for Medicaid benefits, but the fact that the applicant suffered the sudden onset of an illness is not conclusive as to his claim that he made any uncompensated asset transfers for reasons exclusively other than to qualify for Medicaid benefits.

### 8-13:11 Eliminating a Penalty Period

If an applicant seeks to eliminate a penalty period or a potential penalty period due to uncompensated asset transfers that occurred during the lookback period, then each of the individuals who were the recipients of the asset transfers must return the entirety of all assets that were transferred.[137] For instance, if Mr. Smith gave $10,000 to John, $5,000 to Mary and $2,000 to Jane, then in order for Mr. Smith not to be punished for those transfers, John must return $10,000 to Mr. Smith, Mary must return $5,000 to Mr. Smith and Jane must return $2,000 to Mr. Smith. If John and Mary return their money but Jane refuses, Mr. Smith will be punished for all of the transfers, not just the $2,000 he gave to Jane.

If Mr. Smith transferred $1,000,000 to his son and his son returns $999,999 to him, Mr. Smith will be punished for the entire $1,000,000 transfer. All of the assets from each recipient who received an asset must be returned in order to eliminate a penalty period.

## 8-14 EXCEPTIONS TO THE TRANSFER OF ASSET RULES

The law provides certain exceptions to the transfer of assets rules.[138] If the asset transfer falls into one of these exceptions, then the asset transfer cannot result in a penalty period.

### 8-14:1 The Home

There are certain exceptions to the transfer of assets rules that relate directly to the home.[139] Of note, the law refers to the "home," not a house. The word "home" is not defined in the Medicaid

137. 42 U.S.C. § 1396p(c)(2)(C)(iii); Medicaid Communications 10-06, 10-02.
138. 42 U.S.C. §§ 1396p(c)(2)(A), (B).
139. 42 U.S.C. § 1396p(c)(2)(A).

Act, but it can be assumed that the law is referring to the primary principal residence of the institutionalized individual, and not all real estate the institutionalized individual may own.

### 8-14:1.1 Transfer of Home to Community Spouse

Because the resources owned by either the community spouse or the institutionalized spouse are attributed to the eligibility of the institutionalized spouse with the exception of the CSRA,[140] resource transfers between spouses do not trigger penalty periods.[141] A resource owned by the community spouse is, for purposes of determining the eligibility of the institutionalized spouse, owned by the institutionalized spouse.

In line with this concept, the Medicaid Act does not punish the institutionalized spouse for transferring an interest in the home to the community spouse.[142]

### 8-14:1.2 Transfer of Home to Sibling with Equity Interest

The home can be transferred to a sibling who has an equity interest in the home and who has resided in the home for at least one year before the individual becomes an institutionalized individual.[143] If the sibling satisfies the criteria of the exception, the home can be transferred to the sibling without triggering a penalty period.

#### 8-14:1.2.a What Is an Equity Interest?

This exception uses the phrase "equity interest" when referring to the form of ownership interest the sibling must have in the home. The use of this phrase is of some note. The POMS gives examples of equitable interests.[144] A sibling who has made mortgage payments or paid real estate taxes, for instance, could be found to have had an equitable interest in the home. In fact, a sibling who has put sweat equity (labor and time) into the home could be found to have an equity interest.

---

140. 42 U.S.C. § 1396r-5(c)(2).

141. 42 U.S.C. §§ 1396p(c)(2)(A)(i), (B)(i).

142. 42 U.S.C. § 1396p(c)(2)(A)(i).

143. 42 U.S.C. § 1396p(c)(2)(A)(iii).

144. POMS SI § 01110.515.C.

Certainly, holding legal title in the real property in some fashion would be an interest sufficient to satisfy the equitable interest requirement, though real estate scholars may debate the differences between an equitable interest in real estate and a legal interest in real estate.

#### 8-14:1.2.b Timing of Transfer

The sibling must have resided in the home for at least 1 year before the individual becomes an institutionalized individual. From a practical standpoint, it may be best to wait until the individual enters the nursing facility and applies for Medicaid benefits or until the individual applies for home- and community-based services to transfer the home to the sibling, as the individual only becomes an "institutionalized individual" at that time.

### 8-14:1.3 Transfer of Home to Disabled or Blind Child

The home can be transferred to a child of the institutionalized individual who is totally and permanently disabled or who is blind.[145]

#### 8-14:1.3.a What Does It Mean To Be Disabled?

The child must be totally and permanently disabled. A determination from the United States Social Security Administration that the individual is totally and permanently disabled is conclusive as to the issue of disability.[146] The Social Security Administration defines "disability" as the "inability to engage in any substantially gainful employment by reason of any medically determinable physical or mental impairment which can be expected to result in death, or has lasted or can be expected to last for a continuous period of not less than 12 months."[147]

#### 8-14:1.3.b What Does It Mean To Be Blind?

The Medicaid Act defines "blindness" as follows: "central visual acuity of 20/200 or less in the better eye with the use of

145. 42 U.S.C. § 1396p(c)(2)(A)(ii)(II). The home can also be transferred to a child under the age of 21, 42 U.S.C. § 1396p(c)(2)(A)(ii)(I), but from a practical standpoint, this rarely happens.

146. N.J.A.C. 10:71-4.10(d)(2).

147. 42 U.S.C. § 416(i).

a correcting lens."[148] A determination of the United States Social Security Administration on the issue of blindness is conclusive on this issue.

#### 8-14:1.3.c Who Is a Child?

This exception applies to a transfer to a child of the institutionalized individual or the community spouse. The child could be born to or adopted by the institutionalized individual or the community spouse. The exception does not apply to transfers to stepchildren or grandchildren. As a practitioner, you may find yourself hoping to prove that a disabled grandchild or stepchild should be permitted to receive an exempt transfer under this provision. Legally speaking, a grandchild or stepchild does not satisfy the requirements of this exception.

If your client is a married couple and the marriage is a second marriage, each spouse may have children from first marriages. If the disabled child is the child of the institutionalized individual, then you want to ensure that only the institutionalized individual transfers the home to his disabled child, not the community spouse. If the disabled child is the child of the community spouse, then you want to ensure that only the community spouse transfers the home to her disabled child. So, for instance, assume that the couple jointly own an asset and the disabled child is the child of the community spouse.

Good practice would call for the asset to be transferred to the sole name of the community spouse (this transfer is exempt because it is a transfer between spouses), then the community spouse transfers the asset to her disabled child. Since the disabled child is only a stepchild of the institutionalized individual, a transfer from him to the disabled child would not satisfy the requirements of the disabled child transfer exemption.

#### 8-14:1.3.d Timing of Transfer

The transfer to a blind or disabled child can be made at any time prior to the passing of the institutionalized individual. The transfer could occur before the individual is an institutionalized individual or after the individual becomes an institutionalized individual.

---

148. 20 C.F.R. § 404.1581.

### 8-14:1.3.e Outright Transfer

The home can be transferred outright to the blind or disabled individual, free of any trust.

### 8-14:1.3.f Transfer to a Sole Benefit of Trust

In addition to an outright transfer to a blind or disabled child, the home could be transferred to a trust for the sole benefit of the disabled child. The only definition of what it means for a trust to be "for the sole benefit of" an individual is found in HCFA Transmittal 64 of CMS's State Medicaid Manual (SMM).[149]

### 8-14:1.3.f.1 Definition of Sole Benefit

HCFA Transmittal 64 of the SMM defines "sole benefit of" or sbo as follows: "A *transfer* is considered to be for the sole benefit of a spouse, blind or disabled child, or a disabled individual if the transfer is arranged in such a way that no individual or entity except the spouse, blind or disabled child, or disabled individual can benefit from the assets transferred in any way, whether at the time of the transfer or at any time in the future."[150] An outright transfer to a disabled or blind child clearly meets the definition because *the transfer* is solely for the benefit of the blind or disabled child. What the disabled child does with the transferred asset after *the transfer* is another matter, but *the transfer* itself is clearly for the sole benefit of the blind or disabled child with an outright transfer.

The transfer to a trust for the sole benefit of a blind or disabled child can be accomplished in two ways.

### 8-14:1.3.f.2 Disability Annuity Trust

If the trust is an annuity trust that will pay out to the blind or disabled child in a manner that is actuarially sound based upon the life expectancy of the child, then the trust will be considered a sole benefit of trust. To determine actuarial soundness, you would use the actuarial tables published by the Office of the Chief Actuary of the United States Social Security Administration.[151]

---

149. SMM § 3257.B.6.

150. SMM § 3257.B.6.

151. http://www.ssa.gov/OACT/STATS/table4c6.html.

If the term of the annuity trust is less than or equal to the life expectancy of the child as provided in the actuarial tables based upon the child's age at the time of the transfer to the trust, then the trust is actuarially sound. If the trust is actuarially sound and pays to no one other than the child during the life of the child, then the trust satisfies the sbo requirement. Typically, the trust would payout in equal installments; those installments may be monthly, quarterly or annually, but the entirety of the trust must be paid out to the disabled child over a period of time that is equal to or less than the child's life expectancy.

For instance, assume that Mr. Smith enters a nursing home. Mr. Smith has a totally and permanently disabled son who is 50 years of age. Based upon the life expectancy tables of the Chief Actuary of the Social Security Administration, the son's life expectancy is 29.35 years.

If Mr. Smith transfers his assets to a trust that pays the son the amount transferred in equal installments (monthly, annually) that result in the entirety of the trust being paid out to the son over a period of time that is equal to or less than 29.35 years, then the trust is actuarially sound.

### 8-14:1.3.f.3 Payback Trust

Another method of achieving the sbo requirement is to insert a payback provision into the trust for the disabled child.[152] A payback provision essentially provides that any state that provided Medicaid benefits to the child will be reimbursed (or reimbursed proportionately if the assets of the trust are insufficient to pay back the various states that provided benefits to the child in full) for the amount of Medicaid benefits paid on behalf of the child during the child's life before any distribution will be made to others.

For instance, if the child is receiving Medicaid benefits and the parent transfers his assets to a special needs trust for the child that contains a payback provision for any Medicaid benefits the son receives during his life, this trust will satisfy the sbo requirement. Assume that the parent transfers $400,000 to a special needs trust for the son that contains a payback provision. The son is receiving

---

152. SMM § 3257.B.6.

Medicaid benefits. The trust names the state of New Jersey as first remainder beneficiary for any Medicaid benefits paid on behalf of the son. The parent's other children are named as contingent beneficiaries.

Assume further that the son dies after having received $200,000 of Medicaid benefits during his life. New Jersey, specifically the Division of Medical Assistance and Health Services, will be paid back for the $200,000 it paid for the son's benefit. The remainder of the trust, if any, will pass to the parent's other children.

#### 8-14:1.3.f.4 Federal Rules on Payback

Under the federal rules, which are contained in HCFA Transmittal 64 to the State Medicaid Manual, a sbo trust must either be actuarially sound or contain a payback provision. Either solution is acceptable to achieve sbo status as long as the trust benefits no one other than the disabled child during the child's lifetime.

#### 8-14:1.3.f.5 State Rules on Payback

New Jersey's regulations require that in order for a transfer to a trust for the sole benefit of a disabled child to satisfy the requirements of this exception, the trust must contain a payback provision.[153] Stated otherwise, if you want a transfer of the home to a trust for a disabled child to be exempt from a penalty period, the transferor must transfer the home to a trust for the sole benefit of the disabled child that contains a payback provision.

This is not the federal law on the issue. As stated, under the federal law, the transfer to a disability annuity trust or a payback trust will satisfy the sbo requirement as long as the trust benefits no one other than the child during the child's lifetime.

Federal rules trump state rules where those rules conflict on an issue as federal law preempts the field in this area of the law.[154] This concept is called federal preemption. The Medicaid Act is a very comprehensive law. When federal law and state law conflict in this area, the federal law controls.

---

153. N.J.A.C. 10:71-4.10(f).

154. *Weatherbee v. Richman*, 351 Fed. Appx. 786, 788 (3d Cir. 2009).

From a practical standpoint, however, what are you to advise your clients? One piece of advice would be to transfer to a disability annuity trust without a payback provision and sue the state in federal court if the state fails to grant exempt status to the trust transfer. The best forum for such a suit would be the federal court system.

Another piece of advice, and one with which the client would probably more readily agree, is to draft wording into the trust that says the state will receive payback to the extent required by federal and state law in order for the trust to satisfy the sbo requirement. If the trust is a disability annuity trust, the extent to which payback is required under federal law to meet the requirements of a sole benefit of trust is non-existent.

Moreover, the child may not be and may never receive Medicaid benefits. Many disabled individuals receive Social Security Disability Income and Medicare, not Medicaid, so payback does not come into play for these individuals. If the child never received Medicaid benefits, then payback is unnecessary after his passing.

### 8-14:1.4 Transfer of Home to Caregiver Child

The home can also be transferred to a child who resided in the individual's home for at least 2 years immediately before the individual became an institutionalized individual and who provided a level of care to the individual that permitted the individual to remain in his home instead of in a nursing facility.[155]

#### 8-14:1.4.a Level of Care

The level of care that the child provided to the parent must be a high level of care.[156] The parent's physical or mental state must have been such during the two-year period of time that the parent

155. 42 U.S.C. § 1396p(c)(2)(A)(iv).

156. *Compare* POMS SI § 01150.122.C. (discussing the provision of care requirement as it relates to the SSI program) *with* N.J.A.C. 10:71-4.10(d)(4)(i) ("The care provided by the individual's son or daughter for the purposes of this subchapter shall have exceeded normal personal support activities (for example, routine transportation and shopping)."). Comparability, 42 U.S.C. §§ 1396a(a)(10)(C)(i)(III), 1396a(r)(2), does not apply to the transfer of assets rules, 42 U.S.C. § 1396a(a)(10)(G), so the State is free to be more restrictive than the federal rules governing the exceptions to the transfer of assets rules.

required special attention or care.[157] A child who provides to the parent assistance only with the instrumental activities of daily living (shopping, routine transportation, etc.) will not satisfy the "level of care" requirement. The assistance should be with some of the activities of daily living (clothing, bathing, toileting, mobility, walking, dressing) supplemented by assistance with some of the instrumental activities of daily living (e.g., medication administration).

### 8-14:1.4.b What Makes Someone a Caregiver Child

A caregiver child is a child who provides to her parent hands-on assistance with some of the activities of daily living supplemented by assistance with some of the instrumental activities of daily living. Many children will tell you that they provided care to their parent for two years or more, but when you inquire more extensively with the child, you will realize that the child only provided assistance with some of the basic instrumental activities of daily living (shopping, cooking, etc.) While assistance with IADLs can be of some benefit to boost the assistance with the ADLs that a true caregiver child would have provided to her parent, assistance with the IADLs alone does not a caregiver child make.

The child should have provided hands-on assistance with some of the ADLs, because that is the type of care that a true institutionalized individual requires and would receive had he been residing in a nursing facility.

### 8-14:1.4.c Duration of Care

The care the child provides must be for a duration of two years or more before the date the individual became an institutionalized individual. In English, what that means is, the child must provide a high level of care to the parent for at least two years prior to the parent either entering a nursing facility and applying for Medicaid benefits or applying for home- and community-based institutional level care services.

---

157. N.J.A.C. 10:71-4.10(d)(4)(i) ("The individual's physical or mental condition shall have been such as to require special attention and care. The care provided by the son or daughter shall have been essential to the health and safety of the individual and shall have consisted of activities such as, but not limited to, supervision of medication, monitoring of nutritional status, and insuring the safety of the individual.").

If the care has been provided for longer than two years, that is great, but two years is good enough. The child must reside with the parent during the period of time for which the care is provided. The care should be provided in consecutive months. There is no mention of tacking months if there are breaks in the care/living arrangements. If push comes to shove, there may be an argument for tacking time periods together, but for the cleaner case, consecutive months of care/living are best.[158]

#### 8-14:1.4.d Evidence of Being a Caregiver

With a disabled or blind child, a determination of disability or blindness from the United States Social Security Administration is conclusive as to the issue of the child's disability or blindness.[159] With a case involving a caregiver child, there is no standard of proof provided in the law as to the issue of whether or not a child has satisfied the caregiver child requirements. There is no single standard to prove this issue. Through experience, a practitioner learns of those proofs that may satisfy the various county board of social services, and evidence that satisfies one county board may not satisfy another county board.

#### 8-14:1.4.d.1 Physician Certification

One piece of evidence any application containing a caregiver transfer of the home should have is a certification from the treating physician of the applicant. You will want the institutionalized individual's physician to certify that for at least the two years immediately preceding the date of application the individual required a nursing facility level of care. Moreover, if the individual's medical records for the past two years support the contention that the individual required a nursing facility level of care during the past two years, you may want to submit the individual's medical records with the application. The more technical and voluminous the proofs you submit to support the transfer, the more likely it is that the caseworker will simply accept the contention that the individual required a nursing facility level of care.

---

158. *M.J. v. Div. of Medical Assistance and Health Services*, 2008 N.J. Agen. Lexis 1317 (Final Agency Decision 2008).

159. N.J.A.C. 10:71-4.10(d)(2).

The certification of the physician should outline the individual's care needs and the care the child provided, if that care is known to the physician.

#### 8-14:1.4.d.2 Witnesses' Certification

Another piece of information that an application should have if the applicant is claiming an exception to the transfer of assets rules based upon the caregiver child exception is certifications from witnesses—family, friends and neighbors. The best witnesses are disinterested witnesses, such as neighbors, since they have no stake in the transfer or less of a stake than family members. The more certifications you can obtain, particularly those from disinterested third-parties, the better.

The certification of the witnesses should outline the individual's living arrangement for the past two years, his care needs and the type of care the caregiver child provided to the individual during the past two years (or more) that permitted the individual to remain at home instead of in a nursing facility.

#### 8-14:1.4.d.3 Caregiver Child Certification

The caregiver child him/herself should also submit a certification in support of the transfer. The certification of the caregiver child should outline the individual's living arrangement for the past two years, his care needs and the type of care the caregiver child provided to the individual during the past two years (or more) that permitted the individual to remain at home instead of in a nursing facility.

#### 8-14:1.4.e The Working Caregiver Child

What if the putative caregiver child works? Some county boards will argue that a caregiver child who works a fulltime job cannot be a caregiver child because the child is not providing care to the parent while the child is at work.[160] This contention becomes more prevalent with the county boards when the putative caregiver child works more than one job, even if none of those jobs are fulltime jobs.

---

160. The POMS provides that the care must be substantial, but not necessarily full-time. POMS SI § 01150.122.C.

There is no guide for proving that a child is a caregiver child, so the various county boards of social services tend to make up their own standards of proof. Few caregivers provide care to their patient on a twenty-four-hour-a-day/seven-day-a-week basis. Providing that type of care simply is not physically or mentally possible, so the argument that a caregiver child cannot have a job or jobs is false. (Many parents of young children, for instance, view their paying jobs as a break from taking care of the kids, and the same can be said for adult children who are taking care of an elderly parent.)

The applicant and his putative caregiver child must prove that the care the caregiver child provided to the institutionalized individual permitted the individual to reside at home instead of in a nursing facility. So, the real question is: If the care the child provided were not provided would the parent have been in a nursing facility during the two year period of time immediately preceding the date of institutionalization? If the answer to that question is "yes," then the child is a caregiver child.

So, for instance, if the child worked a fulltime job from 8 a.m. to 5 p.m., Monday through Friday, and the parent was cared for by a paid home health aide during those times and by the child the other times of the day/week and if the care the child provided permitted the parent to reside at home instead of in a nursing home for at least the last two years, then the child is a caregiver child.

#### 8-14:1.4.f Timing of Transfer

When should the individual transfer his home to the caregiver child? Since the caregiver child must provide a level of care that permitted the parent to reside at home instead of in a nursing facility for at least two years prior to the date the individual became an institutionalized individual, the best time to make the transfer is when an application for Medicaid benefits has been filed. At that time, the individual is an institutionalized individual[161] and the two-year care period is an ascertainable period of time.

---

161. 42 U.S.C. § 1396p(h)(3).

## 8-14:2 Exemptions to the Transfer of Asset Penalty Provision

The federal Medicaid Act and the state regulations contain specific exemptions to the transfer of asset penalty provisions of the Medicaid program. The exemptions discussed immediately above apply only to the home. The exemptions listed immediately below apply to all assets, including the home.[162]

### 8-14:2.a Transfer of Assets to the Community Spouse

As with the transfer of the home, the transfer of any assets to the community spouse is exempt from the transfer of asset penalty rules. The reason for this exemption is simple, since the resources of a couple are pooled for purposes of determining the institutionalized spouse's eligibility for Medicaid benefits, it is irrelevant in which spouse's name the resources are titled.

As for income items, which are not pooled for purposes of determining the institutionalized spouse's eligibility for Medicaid benefits, it is very rare that a pure income item, that is, an income item not associated with a resource (such as a privately-purchased annuity) can be transferred from one individual to another. For instance, you cannot transfer Social Security income and you cannot transfer most defined pension benefits.

### 8-14:2.b Transfer of Assets to Blind or Disabled Child

As with the home, any asset can be transferred to the blind or disabled child of the institutionalized individual or the community spouse.[163] A determination by the United States Social Security Administration is conclusive as to the issue of whether or not a child is blind or disabled.[164]

An institutionalized individual could transfer $1,000,000 to a blind or disabled child and the transfer would be exempt from the transfer of assets penalty rules. Depending upon the government benefits the child is receiving, the transfer may or may not affect his eligibility for the benefits he is receiving.

---

162. 42 U.S.C. § 1396p(c)(2)(B).
163. 42 U.S.C. § 1396p(c)(2)(B)(iii).
164. N.J.A.C. 10:71-4.10(d)(2).

For instance, if the disabled child is receiving Supplemental Security Income or Medicaid benefits, both of which are means-tested government benefits, then the child will lose his benefits if the assets are transferred directly to the child free of a trust. If the child is receiving Social Security disability income or Medicare, the receipt of the assets will not disqualify him from government benefits. The child's circumstances need to be taken into consideration when making the asset transfer.

The child's circumstances may not be as important when transferring the home, if the home also serves as the child's home, because a home is an exempt resource for purposes of determining eligibility for SSI or Medicaid.[165] The transfer of other assets, though, could negatively impact the child's eligibility for means-tested government benefits.

#### 8-14:2.b.1 Who Is a Child?

This exception applies to transfer to a child of the institutionalized individual or the community spouse. The child could be born to or adopted by the institutionalized individual or the community spouse. The exception does not apply to transfers to stepchildren or grandchildren. As a practitioner, you may find yourself hoping to prove that a disabled grandchild or stepchild should be permitted to receive an exempt transfer under this provision. Legally speaking, a grandchild or stepchild does not satisfy the requirements of this exception.

If your client is a married couple and the marriage is a second marriage, each spouse may have children from first marriages. If the disabled child is the child of the institutionalized individual, then you want to ensure that only the institutionalized individual transfers the asset to his disabled child, not the community spouse. If the disabled child is the child of the community spouse, then you want to ensure that only the community spouse transfers the asset to her disabled child. So, for instance, assume that the couple jointly own an asset and the disabled child is the child of the community spouse.

Good practice would call for the asset to be transferred to the sole name of the community spouse (this transfer is exempt because

---

165. 42 U.S.C. § 1382b.

it is a transfer between spouses),[166] then the community spouse transfers the asset to her disabled child. Since the disabled child is only a step child of the institutionalized individual, a transfer from him to the disabled child would not satisfy the requirements of the disabled child transfer exemption.

### 8-14:2.b.2 Timing of Transfer

The transfer to a blind or disabled child can be made at any time prior to the passing of the institutionalized individual. The transfer could occur before the individual is an institutionalized individual or after the individual becomes an institutionalized individual; however, because assets other than the home may affect the institutionalized individual's eligibility for Medicaid benefits in the first instance, the assets would probably need to be transferred to the blind or disabled child before he achieves eligibility for Medicaid benefits.

### 8-14:2.b.3 Outright Transfer

The assets can be transferred outright to the blind or disabled individual, free of any trust.[167]

### 8-14:2.b.4 Transfer to a Sole Benefit of Trust

In addition to an outright transfer to a blind or disabled child, all assets can be transferred to a trust for the sole benefit of the disabled child. The only definition of what it means for a trust to be "for the sole benefit of" an individual is found in HCFA Transmittal 64 of CMS's State Medicaid Manual.[168]

### 8-14:2.b.4.a Definition of Sole Benefit

HCFA Transmittal 64 of the SMM defines "sole benefit of" or sbo as follows: "A transfer is considered to be for the sole benefit of a spouse, blind or disabled child, or a disabled individual if *the transfer* is arranged in such a way that no individual or entity except the spouse, blind or disabled child, or disabled individual can benefit from the assets transferred in any way, whether at the

---

166. 42 U.S.C. §§ 1396p(c)(2)(A)(i), 1396p(c)(2)(B)(i).
167. *Sorber v. Velez*, 2009 U.S. Dist. Lexis 98799 (D. N.J. 2009).
168. SMM § 3257.B.6.

time of the transfer or at any time in the future."[169] An outright transfer to a disabled or blind child clearly meets the definition because *the transfer* is solely for the benefit of the blind or disabled child. What the disabled child does with the transferred asset after the transfer is another matter, but *the transfer* itself is clearly for the sole benefit of the blind or disabled child with an outright transfer.

The transfer to a trust for the sole benefit of a blind or disabled child can be accomplished in two ways.

### 8-14:2.b.4.b Disability Annuity Trust

If the trust is an annuity trust that will pay out to the blind or disabled child in a manner that is actuarially sound based upon the life expectancy of the child, then the trust will be considered a sole benefit of trust. To determine actuarial soundness, you would use the actuarial tables published by the Office of the Chief Actuary of the United States Social Security Administration.

If the term of the annuity trust is less than or equal to the life expectancy of the disabled individual as provided in the actuarial tables based upon the disabled individual's age at the time of the transfer to the trust, then the trust is actuarially sound. If the trust is actuarially sound and pays to no one other than the disabled individual during his life, then the trust satisfies the sbo requirement. Typically, the trust would pay out in equal installments; those installments may be monthly, quarterly or annually, but the entirety of the trust must be paid out to the disabled individual over a period of time that is equal to or less than his life expectancy.

For instance, assume that Mr. Smith enters a nursing home. Mr. Smith has a totally and permanently disabled stepson who is 50 years of age. Based upon the life expectancy tables of the Chief Actuary of the Social Security Administration, the stepson's life expectancy is 29.35 years.

If Mr. Smith transfers his assets to a trust that pays the stepson the amount transferred in equal installments (monthly, annually) that result in the entirety of the trust being paid out to the stepson over a period of time that is equal to or less than 29.35 years, then the trust is actuarially sound.

---

169. SMM § 3257.B.6.

### 8-14:2.b.4.c Payback Trust

Another method of achieving the sbo requirement is to insert a payback provision into the trust for the disabled individual. A payback provision essentially provides that any state that provided Medicaid benefits to the disabled individual during the disabled individual's life will be reimbursed (or reimbursed proportionately if the assets of the trust are insufficient to pay back the various states that provided benefits to the child in full) after the disabled individual's death for the amount of Medicaid benefits paid before any distributions will be made to others.

For instance, if the disabled stepson is receiving Medicaid benefits and the institutionalized individual transfers his assets to a special needs trust for the benefit of his disabled stepson that contains a payback provision for any Medicaid benefits the stepson receives during his life, this trust will satisfy the sbo requirement. Assume that the institutionalized individual transfers $400,000 to a special needs trust for his stepson and the trust contains a payback provision. The stepson is receiving Medicaid benefits. The trust names the State of New Jersey as first remainder beneficiary for any Medicaid benefits paid on behalf of the stepson. The disabled individual's children are named as contingent beneficiaries.

Assume further that the stepson dies after having received $200,000 of Medicaid benefits during his life. New Jersey, specifically the Division of Medical Assistance and Health Services, will be paid back for the $200,000 it paid for the stepson's benefit. The remainder of the trust, if any, will pass to the institutionalized individual's children.

### 8-14:2.b.4.d Federal Rules on Payback

Under the federal rules, which are contained in HCFA Transmittal 64 to the State Medicaid Manual, a sbo trust must either be actuarially sound or contain a payback provision. Either solution is acceptable to achieve sbo status as long as the trust benefits no one other than the disabled child during the child's lifetime.

### 8-14:2.b.4.e State Rules on Payback

New Jersey's regulations require that in order for a transfer to a trust for the sole benefit of a disabled child to satisfy the requirements of the exception to the transfer of assets rules, the trust must contain a payback provision.[170] Stated otherwise, if you want a transfer of an asset to a trust for a disabled child to be exempt from a penalty period, the transferor must transfer the asset to a trust for the sole benefit of the disabled child that contains a payback provision.

This is not the federal law on the issue. As stated, under the federal law, the transfer to a disability annuity trust or a payback trust will satisfy the sbo requirement as long as the trust benefits no one other than the child during the child's lifetime.

Federal rules trump state rules where those rules conflict on an issue involving the Medicaid program as federal law preempts the field in this area of the law. This concept is called federal preemption. The Medicaid Act is a very comprehensive law. When federal law and state law conflict in this area, the federal law controls.

From a practical standpoint, however, what are you to advise your clients? One piece of advice would be to transfer the assets to a disability annuity trust without a payback provision and sue the state in federal court if the state fails to grant exempt status to the trust. The best forum for such a suit would be the federal court system.

Another piece of advice, and one with which the client would probably more readily agree, is to draft wording into the trust that says the state will receive payback to the extent required by federal and state law in order for the trust to satisfy the sbo requirement. If the trust is a disability annuity trust, the extent to which payback is required under federal law to meet the requirements of a sole benefit of trust is non-existent.

Moreover, the child may not be and may never receive Medicaid benefits. Many disabled individuals receive Social Security Disability Income and Medicare, not Medicaid, so payback does not come into play with these individuals. If the child never receives Medicaid benefits, then payback is unnecessary.

---

170. N.J.A.C. 10:71-4.10(f).

### 8-14:2.c Transfer of Assets to a Trust for a Disabled Individual Under Age 65

Any asset can be transferred to a sbo trust for any disabled person who is under the age of 65.[171] There is no limitation on the value of the assets that can be transferred to such a trust and there is no limitation on the type of asset that can be transferred to such a trust.

In addition, there is no limitation regarding the relationship of the disabled individual and the transferor. Stated otherwise, the disabled person does not need to be related to the institutionalized individual in any manner whatsoever.

From a practical standpoint, few clients would want to transfer assets to an individual who bears no relationship to them, but they could and not be subject to a Medicaid asset transfer penalty if the transfer is made to an sbo trust for a disabled individual who has failed to attain the age of 65. This exception would allow a transfer to an sbo trust for a disabled stepchild, a grandchild or an in-law.

#### 8-14:2.c.1 Disabled

The applicable statute that creates this exemption from the transfer of assets penalty provisions requires the individual to be disabled. No mention is made of a blind individual being eligible for this exemption. A determination of disability by the United States Social Security Administration is conclusive as to the issue of disability.

#### 8-14:2.c.2 Under Age 65

The disabled individual must have failed to attain the age of 65. If the disabled individual has attained the age of 65 (if he is age 65 or older), then the transfer to an sbo for such a disabled individual would not be exempt from the transfer of assets penalty provisions.

#### 8-14:2.c.3 Sole Benefit of Trust

HCFA Transmittal 64 of the SMM defines "sole benefit of" or sbo as follows: "A transfer is considered to be for the sole benefit of a spouse, blind or disabled child, or a disabled individual if

---

171. 42 U.S.C. 1396p(c)(2)(B)(iv).

the transfer is arranged in such a way that no individual or entity except the spouse, blind or disabled child, or disabled individual can benefit from the assets transferred in any way, whether at the time of the transfer or at any time in the future."[172] The transfer to a trust for the sole benefit of a disabled individual can be accomplished in two ways.

#### 8-14:2.c.4 Disability Annuity Trust

If the trust is an annuity trust that will pay out to the disabled individual in a manner that is actuarially sound based upon the life expectancy of the disabled individual, then the trust will be considered a sole benefit of trust. To determine actuarial soundness, you would use the actuarial tables published by the Office of the Chief Actuary of the United States Social Security Administration.[173]

If the term of the annuity trust is less than or equal to the life expectancy of the disabled individual as provided in the actuarial tables based upon the disabled individual's age at the time of the transfer to the trust, then the trust is actuarially sound. If the trust is actuarially sound and pays to no one other than the disabled individual during the life of the individual, then the trust satisfies the sbo requirement. Typically, the trust would pay out in equal installments; those installments may be monthly, quarterly or annually, but the entirety of the trust must be paid out to the disabled individual over a period of time that is equal to or less than the individual's life expectancy.

For instance, assume that Mr. Smith enters a nursing home. Mr. Smith has a totally and permanently disabled nephew who is fifty years of age. Based upon the life expectancy tables of the Chief Actuary of the Social Security Administration, the nephew's life expectancy is 29.35 years.

If Mr. Smith transfers his assets to a trust that pays the nephew the amount transferred in equal installments (monthly, annually) that result in the entirety of the trust being paid out to the nephew over a period of time that is equal to or less than 29.35 years, then the trust is actuarially sound.

---

172. SMM § 3257.B.6.

173. http://www.ssa.gov/OACT/STATS/table4c6.html.

### 8-14:2.c.5 Payback Trust

Another method of achieving the sbo requirement is to insert a payback provision into the trust for the disabled individual. A payback provision essentially provides that any state that provided Medicaid benefits to the disabled individual will be reimbursed (or reimbursed proportionately if the assets of the trust are insufficient to pay back the various states that provided benefits to the disabled individual in full) for the amount of Medicaid benefits paid on behalf of the disabled individual during the individual's life before any distribution will be made to others.

For instance, if the disabled individual is receiving Medicaid benefits and the applicant transfers his assets to a special needs trust that contains a payback provision for any Medicaid benefits the disabled individual receives during his life, this trust will satisfy the sbo requirement. Assume that the applicant transfers $400,000 to a special needs trust with payback provision for his nephew. The nephew is receiving Medicaid benefits. The trust names the State of New Jersey as first remainder beneficiary for any Medicaid benefits paid on behalf of the nephew. The parent's other children are named as contingent beneficiaries.

Assume further that the nephew dies after having received $200,000 of Medicaid benefits during his life. New Jersey, specifically the Division of Medical Assistance and Health Services, will be paid back for the $200,000 it paid for the nephew's benefit. The remainder of the trust, if any, will pass either to those individual whom the applicant named as contingent beneficiaries in the trust or to the applicant's intestate heirs if the applicant were not competent to name contingent beneficiaries.

#### 8-14:2.c.5.a Federal Rules on Payback

Under the federal rules, which are contained in HCFA Transmittal 64 to the State Medicaid Manual, a sbo trust must either be actuarially sound or contain a payback provision. Either solution is acceptable to achieve sbo status as long as the trust benefits no one other than the disabled individual during the disabled individual's lifetime.

### 8-14:2.c.5.b State Rules on Payback

New Jersey's regulations require that in order for a transfer to a trust for the sole benefit of a disabled individual to satisfy the requirements of the exception to the transfer of assets rules, the trust must contain a payback provision.[174] Stated otherwise, if you want a transfer of asset to a trust for a disabled individual to be exempt from a penalty period, the transferor must transfer the asset to a trust for the sole benefit of the disabled individual that contains a payback provision.

This is not the federal law on the issue. As stated, under the federal law, the transfer to a disability annuity trust or a payback trust will satisfy the sbo requirement as long as the trust benefits no one other than the disabled individual during the individual's lifetime.

Federal rules trump state rules where those rules conflict on an issue federal law preempts the field in this area of the law. This concept is called federal preemption. The Medicaid Act is a very comprehensive law. When federal law and state law conflict in this area, the federal law controls.

From a practical standpoint, however, what are you to advise your clients? One piece of advice would be to transfer to a disability annuity trust without a payback provision and sue the state in federal court if the state fails to grant exempt status to the trust. The best forum for such a suit would be the federal court system.

Another piece of advice, and one with which the client would probably more readily agree, is to draft wording into the trust that says the state will receive payback to the extent required by federal and state law in order for the trust to satisfy the sbo requirement. If the trust is a disability annuity trust, the extent to which payback is required under federal law to meet the requirements of a sole benefit of trust is non-existent.

Moreover, the disabled individual who is the beneficiary of the sbo trust may not be and may never receive Medicaid benefits. Many disabled individuals receive Social Security Disability Income and Medicare, not Medicaid, so payback does not come into play with these individuals. If the disabled individual never receives Medicaid benefits, then payback is not necessary.

---

174. N.J.A.C. 10:71-4.10(f).

## 8-14:3 Special Needs Trusts

A special needs trust is a trust that is created pursuant to federal statute.[175] There are three special needs trusts that are creatures of the federal Medicaid Act—a d(4)(A) Trust or self-settled special needs trust,[176] a pooled trust or a d(4)(C) Trust,[177] and a Miller Trust.[178] With that said, when a clientmentions a special needs trust, they are, in most instances, talking about a d(4)(A) trust, which is also commonly known as a self-settled special needs trust. All special needs trusts are sbo trusts.[179]

### 8-14:3.a The d(4)(A) Trust

A d(4)(A) trust, called such after its statutory cite, 42 U.S.C. § 1396p(d)(4)(A), is a sbo trust into which the disabled individual's assets are placed. Because the assets of the disabled individual are placed into the d(4)(A) trust, a d(4)(A) trust is a self-settled special needs trust.

#### 8-14:3.a.1 Self-Settled

Oddly, you would think that a self-settled trust was a trust that the disabled individual created for himself and into which he placed his own assets, but you would be incorrect. A d(4)(A) trust must be established for the disabled individual by the individual's legal guardian, parent, grandparent or a court of competent jurisdiction.[180] The disabled individual cannot be the grantor (the person who establishes the trust) of his own self-settled special needs trust.

As of the writing of this book, the National Academy of Elder Law Attorneys is attempting to change this oddity in the law, so a disabled individual can be the grantor of his self-settled special needs trust into which his assets will be placed. But currently, only a legal guardian, parent, grandparent or a court can establish a d(4)(A) trust for the benefit of a disabled individual. The disabled individual cannot establish his own trust.

---

175. 42 U.S.C. §§ 1396p(d)(4)(A) to (C).
176. 42 U.S.C. § 1396p(d)(4)(A).
177. 42 U.S.C. § 1396p(d)(4)(C).
178. 42 U.S.C. § 1396p(d)(4)(B).
179. SMM § 3257.B.6.
180. 42 U.S.C. § 1396p(d)(4)(A); N.J.S.A. 3B:11-36.

### 8-14:3.a.2 Disabled

The individual for whom the self-settled special needs trust is established must be disabled. A determination of disability by the United States Social Security Administration is dispositive on the issue of disability.

### 8-14:3.a.3 Under Age 65

The disabled individual for whom the trust is established must be under the age of 65. If the disabled individual is age 65 or older, a self-settled special needs trust cannot be established for the disabled individual's benefit.

A question arises as to whether or not additional assets can be placed into a self-settled special needs trust *after* the individual attains the age of 65 if the trust was *established* before the individual attained the age of 65. For instance, if a disabled individual establishes a d(4)(A) trust when he is 56 and places a settlement award in the trust, can that individual place an inheritance he receives when he is 70 into that trust without the transfer of the inheritance to the trust being subject to the transfer of assets penalty provisions? The answer is no. The additional transfers will be subject to transfer of assets penalties.

The result would be different if the additions were from an asset that was irrevocably assigned to the trust before the disabled individual attained the age of 65. For instance, assume that a disabled individual is the beneficiary of an annuity that will continue to pay him a monthly benefit until well after he has attained the age of 65. If that disabled individual has irrevocably assigned the payments from that annuity to a d(4)(A) trust before he attained the age of 65, then the additions will not be subject to punishment because for all intents and purposes, the payments were assigned before the disabled individual attained the age of 65.

### 8-14:3.a.4 Payback

A payback provision is a provision that after the death of a Medicaid beneficiary, reimburses a state for medical assistance (i.e., Medicaid benefits) that the state paid out on behalf of the individual during his life. If the beneficiary received Medicaid benefits in more than one state, then each state receives proportionate reimbursement.

A self-settled special needs trust must contain a payback provision; accordingly, when the beneficiary of the trust dies, Medicaid will be reimbursed for any benefits that it paid on behalf of the individual during his life irrespective of the age of the trust beneficiary at the time he received the benefits. After the state is reimbursed, the remainder of the assets can be paid either to the contingent beneficiaries whom the disabled individual named or to the disabled individual's intestate heirs if the disabled individual lacked the mental capacity to name beneficiaries.

Absent a payback provision, a state can only seek estate recovery from a deceased Medicaid beneficiary's estate for Medicaid benefits paid on behalf of the beneficiary after the Medicaid beneficiary attains the age of 55.[181] For this reason, a practitioner sometimes must decide whether or not an asset should be placed into a special needs trust that must contain a payback provision.

For instance, if a 20 year old disabled individual inherits the home he lives in, the home will be exposed to payback if placed into a d(4)(A) trust for all benefits paid on behalf of that 20 year old individual. On the other hand, if the 20 year old disabled individual owned the home, a non-countable resource, in his own name and died before he attained the age of 55, then the home would not be subject to estate recovery.

#### 8-14:3.a.5 State Regulations

The State of New Jersey has published a series of regulations specifically devoted to self-settled special needs trusts.[182] These regulations form, essentially, a checklist that all self-settled special needs trust must satisfy in order to pass muster with the state. A practitioner would be well-advised to follow the checklist these regulations create.

### 8-14:3.b Pooled Trust

A pooled special needs trust is a trust into which the disabled individual's assets are placed and those assets are pooled with the assets of various other disabled individuals for purposes of investment and management. A separate account for purposes of

---

181. 42 U.S.C. § 1396p(b).
182. N.J.A.C. 10:71-4.11.

accounting is maintained for the disabled individual's funds, but his assets are pooled with the assets of other disabled individuals.[183]

### 8-14:3.b.1 Pooled But Separate

The basic principal of a pooled trust is that more interest can be earned on money when that money is pooled together. This is actually a basic concept of finance. Banks, for instance, pool their deposits together for purposes of investment, yet every bank maintains a separate account for the individual investor so the investor knows how much money he has on deposit.

The same concept exists with a pooled trust. Like a bank, the disabled individual's money is not an island; the individual's account is maintained for accounting purposes but the money is pooled for investment purposes.

### 8-14:3.b.2 Disabled

The individual for whom a pooled special needs trust is established must be disabled. A determination of disability by the United States Social Security Administration is dispositive on the issue of disability.

### 8-14:3.b.3 Age Limitations

Unlike with a self-settled special needs trust, the statute that creates pooled special needs trusts does not contain an age limitation. Nowhere in the statute that creates a pooled special needs trust is the requirement that the disabled individual place his assets in the trust before the disabled individual has attained the age of 65.

This fact has caused many elder law practitioners to argue that transfers to a pooled special needs trust after the individual has attained the age of 65 should not trigger penalty periods. To date, these arguments have fallen on deaf ears with the courts and the Centers for Medicare and Medicaid Services, the federal agency responsible for administering the Medicaid program. The New Jersey Medicaid program will punish transfers made to a pooled special needs trust if the disabled individual has attained the age of 65; accordingly, individuals will be subject to transfer of

183. 42 U.S.C. § 1396p(d)(4)(C).

assets penalties if they transfer assets to a pooled special needs trust if the transfer occurs after the individual has attained the age of 65.

#### 8-14:3.b.4 Payback

A payback provision is a provision that after the death of the trust beneficiary mandates reimbursement to the state for medical assistance (i.e., Medicaid benefits) that the state paid out on behalf of the individual during his life. If the beneficiary received Medicaid benefits in more than one state, then each state receives proportionate reimbursement.

A pooled special needs trust must contain a payback provision; however, unlike a self-settled special needs trust, a pooled special needs trust must pay back the state up to the amount of Medicaid benefits provided to the disabled individual only to the extent the remaining funds are not retained by the trust.[184] In other words, the pooled trust can retain some, none or all of the assets remaining in the disabled individual's account after the trust beneficiary's death; the amount that remains in the individual's account after the trust retains whatever amount it chooses to retain must be paid to the state to reimburse the state for any medical assistance (i.e., Medicaid benefits) that the state paid out on behalf of the disabled individual during his life.

The issue of how much a pooled special needs trust can retain was litigated in the Third Circuit Court of Appeals, and in that case, the Court held that a Pennsylvania statute that limited the amount to no more than 50% of the amount remaining in the disabled individual's account at the time of his death was invalid as contradicting, and being preempted by, federal law.[185]

### 8-14:3.c Miller Trust

A Miller Trust, named after a Colorado federal court case, is a trust designed to hold income, not resources, of a Medicaid beneficiary.[186] In states that do not have Medically Needy Medicaid

184. 42 U.S.C. § 1396p(d)(4)(C)(iv).

185. *Lewis v. Alexander*, 685 F.3d 325 (3d Cir. 2012).

186. 42 U.S.C. § 1396p(d)(4)(B), SMM § 3259.7.C.

programs (and New Jersey is currently not one of those states),[187] an individual can place excess income into a Miller Trust by re-directing or by depositing that income into the trust after the Medicaid beneficiary receives the income. The re-direction/deposit of the income into the Miller Trust will remove the excess income from the Medicaid beneficiary's name; accordingly, the individual will no longer be ineligible for Medicaid benefits based upon his having excess income.

Pursuant to the federal statute that creates Miller Trusts, a Miller Trust must be an irrevocable trust composed only of pension, Social Security and other income of the Medicaid beneficiary.[188] Upon the death of the Medicaid beneficiary, the State must receive an amount equal to the amount that the State paid on behalf of the individual for medical assistance during his life; in other words, a Miller Trust must have a payback provision.[189]

It should be noted that the Medicaid beneficiary can re-direct his income to the Miller trust; however, he cannot irrevocable assign his income to the trust.[190] In other words, the Medicaid beneficiary can request that his income be deposited into an account in the name of the trust, but the beneficiary cannot irrevocably assign the income to the trust, making the trust the owner of the income. The income must remain the income of the Medicaid beneficiary.

Because New Jersey currently has a Medically Needy program,[191] the State is barred from permitting Miller Trusts;[192] however, it is anticipated that New Jersey will be eliminating its Medically Needy program for institutional level care services effective October 31, 2014, in order to permit the State to use Miller Trusts in conjunction with the Comprehensive Medicaid Waiver.[193]

The use of a Miller Trust can best be explained by example: Assume Mr. Smith has income of $2,300 a month and can only have $2,163 a month in income in order to qualify for the state's Medicaid program. Mr. Smith could place $137 of his income

---

187. 42 U.S.C. § 1396p(d)(4)(B)(iii).

188. 42 U.S.C. § 1396p(d)(4)(B)(i).

189. 42 U.S.C. § 1396p(d)(4)(B)(ii).

190. SMM § 3259.7.C.

191. N.J.A.C. 10:71-1.1 et seq.; *Miller v. Ibarra*, 746 F. Supp. 19 (D. Colo 1990).

192. 42 U.S.C. § 1396p(d)(4)(B)(iii).

193. *See* Section 8-15:1 for discussion of Comprehensive Waiver.

into a Miller Trust and Mr. Smith's income will now be below the State's income cap for Medicaid eligibility.

The income placed in the Miller Trust no longer counts against Mr. Smith's eligibility for Medicaid;[194] however, the deposit of the income into the Miller Trust could result in a transfer of asset penalty unless the income is spent in a certain manner within a specified period of time for the benefit of Mr. Smith or his wife.[195]

Continuing with our example, Mr. Smith must use the $137 he has placed into the Miller Trust within that month (or at the option of the State, before the end of the following month) to pay for specified items for himself or his spouse. For instance, Mr. Smith might use the income to pay for additional home health aide services or for his nursing home care. The key is that the income must be used within the time period that the State establishes for the sole benefit of Mr. Smith or his spouse in order for no asset transfer to have occurred.[196]

In short a Miller Trust eliminates excess income from counting against the applicant for purposes of determining his initial eligibility for Medicaid;[197] however, in order to remain eligible, the excess income directed to the trust must be spent for the sole benefit of the Medicaid beneficiary or his spouse within a specified period of time, typically within the month the income is placed in the trust or no later than the end of the following month.[198]

A Miller Trust creates a legal fiction through which the Medicaid beneficiary no longer has the excess income that was disqualifying him from Medicaid. The trust and the laws governing the trust then establish a methodology through which an income spend down occurs each and every month of the excess income that was placed into the trust. In essence, this income spend down through the Miller Trust is no different than the income spend down that occurs each month for current Medically Needy Medicaid beneficiaries.

---

194. 42 U.S.C. § 1396p(d)(4); SMM § 3259.7.C.3.

195. SMM § 3259.7.C.3.

196. SMM § 3259.7.C.3.

197. 42 U.S.C. § 1396p(d)(B).

198. SMM § 3259.7.C.

## 8-15 GLOBAL OPTIONS

The Global Options program (or GO) provides home- and community-based waiver services (commonly known as a "HCBS waiver") in the State of New Jersey. Any HCBS waiver program, in whichever State the program may exist, is a Medicaid program that provides institutional level Medicaid care services outside the settings mandated by the Medicaid Act.[199]

For instance, states that participate in the Medicaid program must provide Medicaid benefits to certain individuals. These individual are known as the "categorically needy," because if an individual meets the requirements for eligibility, he must receive those services if those services are needed by the individual.[200] Other services can be provided to individuals at the option of the state. Individuals who qualify in states that choose to provide these services are known as the "optionally categorically needy."[201]

A state can also request a change to the mandates of the Medicaid program or for an expansion of those individuals for whom Medicaid services can be provided. These changes or expansions are known as "waivers."[202] One specific waiver for which the Medicaid Act provides is HCBS waivers, so a State can provide institutional level care services to a beneficiary at home (a lesser restrictive setting) as opposed to in a nursing home (a more restrictive setting).[203]

The GO program is a HCBS waiver that the State of New Jersey applied for with the federal government and received permission to implement. Through GO, New Jersey provides various HCBS waiver services (such as adult daycare and home health aides) to individuals at home who but for the provision of those services would be residing in a nursing facility. Both in-home and assisted living services are provided under the GO program in New Jersey.

The GO program has a monthly income cap, which is currently $2,163 or 300% of the 2014 Supplemental Security Income

199. 42 U.S.C. § 1396n(d).
200. 42 U.S.C. § 1396a(a)(10)(A)(i).
201. 42 U.S.C. § 1396a(a)(10)(A)(ii).
202. 42 U.S.C. § 1396n.
203. 42 U.S.C. § 1396n(d).

program's federal benefit rate. If an applicant's income exceeds the income cap by one penny, he will not be able to qualify for the GO program.

## 8-15:1 New Jersey Comprehensive Waiver

New Jersey has obtained approval for a Section 1115 Demonstration Waiver.[204] Demonstration waivers are typically granted for a period of five years and are designed to allow the various states to experiment with their Medicaid programs in a manner that promotes the program but could also lead to improving the program. New Jersey's Section 1115 waiver is called the New Jersey Comprehensive Waiver.[205] In brief, the comprehensive waiver combines various HCBS waiver programs that New Jersey has implemented through the years into one, comprehensive waiver program.

One of the most anticipated aspects of the Comprehensive Waiver is the elimination of the income cap for those individuals seeking institutional level care services at home or in an assisted living residence. In other words, those individuals who are looking to qualify for Medicaid at home or in an assisted living residence will not be denied benefits simply because their income is above the income cap, which is currently $2,163 or 300% of the 2014 Supplemental Security Income program's federal benefit rate.

CMS approved New Jersey's Comprehensive Waiver in October 2012. To date, New Jersey has failed to implement fully its own Comprehensive Waiver for inexplicable reasons; most notably, New Jersey has, to date, failed to implement the provision of the Comprehensive Waiver that eliminates the income cap for HCBS services, such as assisted living and home health care services.

With that said, it is anticipated that New Jersey will implement the provision of the Comprehensive Waiver that eliminates the income cap effective November 1, 2014. In order to implement this provision of the Comprehensive Waiver, New Jersey will permit

---

204. 42 U.S.C. § 1315.

205. The New Jersey Comprehensive Waiver is designed to modify New Jersey's Medicaid program by, in part, eliminating the income cap for institutional care services in the home or assisted living residence setting. http://www.state.nj.us/humanservices/dmahs/home/waiver.html. The Comprehensive Waiver is a Section 1115 waiver, 42 U.S.C. § 1315, that CMS approved at New Jersey's request in October 2012. To date, New Jersey has failed to implement its own Comprehensive Waiver, so the income cap remains in place.

the use of Miller Trusts[206] to hold the income of a Medicaid beneficiary whose income exceeds the income cap, currently $2,163, for institutional level care services.

Because Miller Trusts cannot be used in States that have a Medically Needy program for individuals in a nursing facility,[207] New Jersey is closing out its Medically Needy program effective October 31, 2014. Beginning November 1, 2014, individuals with income in excess of the income cap ($2,163) who are seeking institutional level care services in the home, an assisted living residence or a nursing facility will need to place their income in excess of the cap (or all of their income if they so chose) into a Miller Trust in order to qualify for those institutional level care services.[208]

It is anticipated that the State will publish guidelines for the use of Miller Trusts and will provide the template of a Miller Trust for those applicants for Medicaid services who do not retain the services of an elder law attorney. In this regard, New Jersey will follow the lead of the state of Indiana, which has published similar material on its website for Medicaid applicants.[209]

## 8-16 NURSING FACILITY SERVICES

New Jersey's Medicaid program will pay for nursing facility services. Both the Medicaid Only[210] and Medically Needy[211] programs will assist with the payment of nursing facility services.

## 8-17 ESTATE RECOVERY

In certain situations, Medicaid will seek reimbursement for those funds the program expended for the benefit of a Medicaid beneficiary.[212] In most instances, Medicaid only seeks reimbursement (or recovery) of benefits after the beneficiary

---

206. 42 U.S.C. § 1396p(d)(4)(B), *Miller v. Ibarra*, 746 F. Supp. 19 (D. Colo 1990).

207. 42 U.S.C. § 1396p(d)(4)(B)(iii).

208. *See generally* SMM § 3259.7.C. discussing Miller Trusts, also known as Qualified Income Trusts or QITs.

209. http://www.in.gov/fssa/ddrs/4860.htm.

210. N.J.A.C. 10:71-1.1 et seq.

211. N.J.A.C. 10:70-1.1 et seq.

212. 42 U.S.C. § 1396p(b); N.J.S.A. 30:4D-7.2, N.J.A.C. 10:49-14.1.

dies; for this reason, Medicaid seeking reimbursement is called estate recovery.

Medicaid will seek asset recovery by placing a lien, the Medicaid lien, on the estate of a deceased Medicaid beneficiary.[213]

## 8-17:1 Incorrectly Paid Benefits

The Medicaid program will seek recovery of incorrectly paid Medicaid benefits.[214] For instance, if a Medicaid beneficiary fails to disclose an asset and ownership of that asset would have made the beneficiary ineligible for benefits and the state later discovers that the beneficiary owns the asset, then the state will find that the beneficiary received incorrectly paid benefits. The beneficiary was receiving Medicaid when he should not have been receiving Medicaid benefits.

When benefits have been incorrectly paid, Medicaid will seek recovery against the beneficiary's estate, if the beneficiary is no longer living,[215] or from the beneficiary himself,[216] if the former beneficiary is still living.

## 8-17:2 Correctly Paid Benefits

With correctly paid benefits, Medicaid will only seek recovery after the Medicaid beneficiary dies;[217] furthermore, Medicaid will only seek recovery for those benefits paid after the Medicaid beneficiary attained the age of 55.[218] Medicaid will not seek estate recovery for benefits paid on behalf of the beneficiary before he attained the age of 55.

When dealing with a younger Medicaid beneficiary and a sbo trust that contains a payback provision, it is important to bear in mind that estate recovery is only for benefits paid after the Medicaid beneficiary attains the age of 55, but a payback provision in a trust would mandate payback for all benefits the Medicaid beneficiary received, including those he received before attaining the age of 55. For instance, assume that a 40 year old Medicaid beneficiary

---

213. N.J.S.A. 30:4D-7.2(c).
214. N.J.A.C. 10:49-4.4.
215. N.J.S.A. 30:4D-7.2a(a).
216. N.J.A.C. 10:49-14.4.
217. N.J.A.C. 10:49-14.1.
218. 42 U.S.C. § 1396p(b), N.J.S.A. 30:4D-7.2, N.J.A.C. 10:49-14.1.

inherits a home. Do you place the home in a self-settled, d(4)(A) special needs trust or leave the home in the name of the disabled individual?

The home is an exempt resource,[219] so the Medicaid beneficiary could own the home and continue to receive Medicaid benefits.

As a practitioner, you should inform the client of these facts and bear in mind the fact that if the disabled individual dies and the home was titled into his d(4)(A) trust, then Medicaid must be reimbursed for all benefits that it paid on behalf of the individual, including those benefits paid before the beneficiary attained the age of 55.[220] However, if the home were in the individual's name at the time of his death, Medicaid can only seek recovery for those benefits paid after he attained the age of 55.

Medicaid will only seek recovery if the estate of the beneficiary exceeds $3,000.[221] Since, in most instances, a Medicaid beneficiary cannot have more than $2,000 in countable resources, the largest single resource from which Medicaid seeks recovery is the home. A Medicaid beneficiary living at home can retain the home, an exempt resource, and still qualify for benefits. When that beneficiary dies owning the home, his estate has a resource of significant value against which estate recovery can be had made.

Medicaid will not seek estate recovery if the Medicaid beneficiary is survived by a spouse, a child under the age of 21 or a child who is blind or totally and permanently disabled.[222]

## 8-17:3 Challenges to Estate Recovery

A challenge to the propriety or amount of the Medicaid lien must be brought in the Superior Court of New Jersey.[223] The Medicaid lien is a preferred debt in an action to declare an estate insolvent.[224]

---

219. 42 U.S.C. § 1382b.
220. 42 U.S.C. § 1396p(d)(4)(A).
221. N.J.A.C. 10:49-14.1.
222. 42 U.S.C. § 1396p(b)(2), N.J.S.A. 30:4D-7.2a(a), 10:49-14.1(j).
223. N.J.S.A. 30:4D-7.8.
224. N.J.S.A. 30:4D-7.2(d)(2), N.J.S.A. 3B:22-2(c).

## 8-18 FAIR HEARING PROCESS

An applicant for Medicaid benefits who is negatively affected by a decision of the county board of social services has the right to appeal that decision. The process for appealing the decision is called a "fair hearing."[225]

In short, an applicant has 20 days to appeal an adverse decision. The process for beginning an appeal is to fill out the application for a fair hearing on the back of the county's notice form. The appeal application is forwarded to the Division of Medical Assistance and Health Service or DMHAS. DMHAS forwards the application to the Office of Administrative Law (OAL).

OAL schedules a date for an administrative hearing before an Administrative Law Judge (ALJ). The hearing is conducted much like any other hearing with several differences. The person representing the county board may not be an attorney. Instead, the Medicaid supervisor and caseworker may be "representing" the county board of social services in the hearing. The rules of evidence are followed; however, the rules are relaxed when necessary.[226]

After the hearing, the ALJ will issue a decision.[227] The ALJ's decision is merely a recommendation to the Director of DMAHS, because the Director of DMAHS can accept the ALJ's decision, reject the ALJ's decision or fail to comment on the ALJ's decision in which case the ALJ's decision will become the final agency decision after 45 days.[228] In most instances, the Director will render a decision of her own, which is the Final Agency Decision or FAD.

Once the Director has rendered a decision, the applicant has the right to appeal the Director's decision to the Appellate Division of the Superior Court of New Jersey, if the applicant believes the Director's decision is incorrect. The Appellate Division must give the Director's decision substantial deference. In short, the Appellate Division can only overturn the decision of the Director if the Appellate Division holds the Director's final agency decision to be arbitrary and capricious.[229]

---

225. N.J.A.C. 1:1-1.1 et seq.
226. N.J.A.C. 1:1-15.1 et seq.
227. N.J.A.C. 1:1-18.1 et seq.
228. N.J.A.C. 1:1-18.6.
229. *Russo v. Bd. Of Trs., Policemen and Firemen's Ret. Sys.*, 206 N.J. 14, 25 (2011).

The bottom line is that the fair hearing process is heavily weighted against the applicant who is appealing an adverse decision. Many elder law practitioners joke that the phrase "fair hearing" is a misnomer as that there is nothing fair about the hearing.

The Director issues her FAD and once that is done, the FAD is entitled to substantial deference. Obviously, the Director has a strong inclination to support the actions of her agents at the county boards of social services. Furthermore, an applicant who wishes to appeal a FAD must wait 18 months to two years before receiving a decision from the Appellate Division, something that few people residing in nursing homes and racking up $10,000 a month in bills without knowing whether or not Medicaid will pay for their care have the intestinal fortitude to withstand. Not to mention the fact that an attorney will want to be paid a substantial retainer to engage in this type of litigation, that may last anywhere from two to three years.

The net result is that few clients will go the distance with an appeal of an adverse decision. Of those that do appeal such adverse decision, very few will win their appeals given how the system is weighted against them.

## 8-19 FEDERAL COURT

An applicant for Medicaid benefits who has been adversely affected by a decision of the county board of social services may have the right to sue the Director of DMHAS in her official capacity in federal court in order to enjoin her, through her agents at the county board, from engaging in the conduct that is alleged to have been improper.

Medicaid is a federal law.[230] As such, violations of the Medicaid Act frequently give rise to a federal cause of action.[231] The fundamental question that the litigant must ask "Did the actions of the county board of social service infringe upon the applicant's rights as specified in a federal law, such as the Medicaid Act or the regulations implementing the Act?" If so, the applicant probably

---

230. 42 U.S.C. §§ 1396 et seq.

231. 28 U.S.C. §1331.

has the right to sue in federal court to enjoin the actions of the county board.[232]

Elder law practitioners have been fairly successful litigating various issues affecting the Medicaid Act in federal court. In fact, some of these suits have changed the course of how the Medicaid Act is administered in the state of New Jersey.

232. *Dultz v. Velez*, 727 F. Supp. 2d 480 (D.N.J. 2010).

# Chapter 9

# Medicaid Planning

## 9-1 PLANNING AHEAD

Medicaid planning is a process through which an individual attempts to preserve a portion or all of his assets for his benefit or the benefit of his family and to qualify for Medicaid benefits sooner than he would qualify for Medicaid if he failed to plan for his eligibility. No single issue differentiates an elder law attorney from other attorneys than the ability of the elder law attorney to advise a client effectively on issues surrounding the Medicaid program.

When planning for Medicaid, there are two primary modes of planning—emergency planning and non-emergency planning. Emergency planning involves a client who is currently receiving long term care and who is seeking to qualify for Medicaid as quickly as possible so that the Medicaid program can assist with the payment of his bills. Non-emergency planning (or "planning ahead") involves planning for a client who does not currently require assistance, who may never require assistance, and who is not seeking to qualify for Medicaid benefits in the foreseeable future.

As an elder law practitioner, when planning ahead for a client, you are often trying to make transfers that take advantage of the five-year lookback period for asset transfers.[1]

---

1. 42 U.S.C. § 1396p(c)(1).

## 9-2 THE LOOKBACK PERIOD

As discussed in Chapter 8, the Medicaid program is for needy individuals.[2] As such, the program punishes individuals seeking to qualify for Medicaid benefits who have made uncompensated asset transfers by making those individuals ineligible for institutional level Medicaid services for a period of time.[3] The greater the value of assets that the individual transferred, the longer the period of ineligibility.

With that said, only asset transfers that occur during the lookback period are punished. The lookback period is the 60-month period of time that precedes an application for Medicaid benefits.[4] If an uncompensated asset transfer is made at any time during the lookback period, that uncompensated transfer will result in a period of ineligibility for Medicaid benefits, commonly known as a penalty period.

The period of ineligibility that results from an uncompensated transfer that occurs during the lookback period can be of unlimited duration.[5] If an uncompensated asset transfer is made *before* the lookback period, the asset transfer cannot result in any period of ineligibility for Medicaid benefits.

For instance, if Mr. Smith were to transfer $10,000 to his son three years before applying for Medicaid benefits, that $10,000 transfer will result in a period of ineligibility for Medicaid benefits. On the other hand, if Mr. Smith were to transfer $1,000,000 in assets to his son 61 months before applying for Medicaid benefits, that $1,000,000 transfer will not result in a period of ineligibility for Medicaid benefits.

In short, the lookback period is, quite literally, the period of time that the county board of social services is looking at to see if the Medicaid applicant has made any asset transfers. Uncompensated transfers outside the lookback period cannot be punished. All uncompensated asset transfers during the lookback period can be punished.

---

2. 42 U.S.C. § 1396.
3. 42 U.S.C. § 1396p(c)(1).
4. 42 U.S.C. § 1396p(c)(1)(B).
5. 42 U.S.C. § 1396p(c)(1)(E).

## 9-3 THE FIVE-YEAR PLAN

A five-year plan is really just a plan that takes advantage of the lookback period. The "plan" could be as simple as the client transferring money to his child by way of a check, then waiting five years for the lookback period to expire. Or the plan could be more complex and involve transfers to a trust. Either way, the plan is designed to take advantage of the lookback period.

Some "emergency plans" involve a five-year plan. A five-year plan is not exclusively for those clients who are planning ahead; however, in order for a five-year plan to work for a client who currently requires long term care services, the client must have sufficient assets to enable him to transfer a portion of those assets to his children and retain sufficient assets to pay for his care for the next 5 years.

For instance, if Mr. Smith is currently in a nursing home costing him $100,000 per year after applying his income to the cost of his care, then Mr. Smith will need more than $500,000 (given inflation) in order to transfer a portion of his assets to his children and wait five years before applying for benefits. In fact, applying an inflation factor of 5% per year to account for the inevitable increase in the cost of long term care, Mr. Smith would probably need more than $550,000 before he could transfer any portion of his estate and wait five years before applying for benefits.

### 9-3:1 Client Pays for Care During Five-Year Period

There are two ways of structuring a five-year plan where the client currently requires long term care. Under one scenario, the client transfers a portion of his assets to his family and retains a sufficient amount of assets to pay for his care for the next 5 years.

For instance, if Mr. Smith has $1,000,000 and needs $550,000 to pay for his care for the next five years, he can transfer $450,000 to his son and retain $550,000 in his own name. Mr. Smith can use the $550,000 he retained to pay for his care for the next five years.

The benefit of arranging the plan in this manner is that Mr. Smith is assured he will have the money in his name to pay for his care. Mr. Smith is saving a portion of his assets for his family's benefit, but he is not putting his own care at risk in any way.

### 9-3:2 Children Pay for Care During Five-Year Period

Under another scenario, the five-year plan would have Mr. Smith transfer the entirety of his assets to his son, and his son would pay for Mr. Smith's care with a portion of the money that Mr. Smith transferred to the son. This methodology has two benefits.

Mr. Smith is still preserving a portion of his estate for his family, that is, $450,000. In addition, the son can deduct the amounts the son is now paying for Mr. Smith's care on the son's income tax return. A family member who pays more than 50% of another family member's medical expenses can claim the ill family member's expenses as a medical deduction.[6]

## 9-4 OUTRIGHT TRANSFERS

An outright asset transfer is a transfer from one individual to another individual outright and free of trust. For instance, Mr. Smith writes a check to his son for $20,000. The son deposits the check into the son's checking account. This is an outright transfer.

### 9-4:1 Advantages

There are several advantages to an outright transfer. These advantages are discussed below.

#### 9-4:1.1 Simplicity

An outright transfer of an asset is simple. If Mr. Smith writes a check for $20,000 to his son and his son deposits that check in the son's bank account, that transfer is extremely simple. In fact, it is so simple that the client's reaction will be something such as the following: "Really? I can just write a check for $20,000 to my son and he can deposit it into his account? That's it? Doesn't he have to pay tax on it? Do I have to pay tax?"

You will then find yourself explaining to the client that a person can gift $5,340,000 during their lifetime without paying gift tax,[7] and in addition, the person can gift $14,000 per year, the annual exclusion gift amount, without reducing their $5,340,000 lifetime exclusion amount.[8] Since every Medicaid planning client has less

---

6. 26 U.S.C. § 152(c).
7. 26 U.S.C. § 2505.
8. 26 U.S.C. § 2503.

than $5,340,000 (no person with more money than that would seriously consider engaging in Medicaid planning or need to engage in Medicaid planning since the person can self-insure against the cost of long term care), no Medicaid planning client will ever pay gift tax on an uncompensated transfer.

The receipt of a gift is never taxable. So, there is no chance that the son will pay gift tax for the $20,000 that he receives from his father.

After you explain all of this to the client, the client will probably be wondering what they are doing in your office. You just told them that all they have to do is write a check to their son and wait slightly more than five years before applying for Medicaid benefits. The "plan" is so simple that the client will no longer see the need for an attorney.

Of course, nothing is ever that simple with Medicaid and planning for Medicaid. The chance that a person without knowledge of the program will do something incorrect is always far higher than the likelihood that the client will navigate the Medicaid system without issue, but it may be difficult to convince the client of this fact if they now believe that they simply have to write a check and wait slightly more than five years.

#### 9-4:1.2 Untraceable Transfer

An outright transfer to a third-party, such as a child, is completely untraceable to the applicant for Medicaid benefits after 60 months. For instance, if Mr. Smith transferred $100,000 to his son 61 months before applying for Medicaid benefits, there is no chance that the county board of social services could ever see that transfer.

Depending on how a trust to which assets are transferred is structured, a transfer to a trust may result in the county board of social services claiming that the assets of the trust are available to the applicant. For instance, if the trust is a grantor trust and the applicant has been claiming the income that the trust's assets earned on his tax return, the county may claim that the assets of the trust are available to the applicant. While such a claim may have no basis in the actual facts or the law, a practitioner should bear in mind that he cannot always count on the facts or the law to help his client when it comes to the Medicaid program.

Once the county board of social services makes a claim about an issue—such as, the assets of the trust are available to the applicant—the county will deny benefits to the applicant and make the applicant fight for eligibility. Discussed in Chapter 8, any such fight is weighted against the applicant. Being right on a legal issue may not result in a win for a Medicaid applicant if forced into a situation where the applicant has to appeal the county board's decision.

#### 9-4:1.3 Ease of Undoing Transfer

Another advantage of an outright transfer is the ease of undoing the transfer if need be. A penalty period will not be imposed against an applicant if all of the assets that were transferred during the lookback period are returned to the applicant by the recipient of the asset transfer(s).[9] So, if Mr. Smith transfers $100,000 to his son, and his son returns the entire $100,000 to Mr. Smith, the transfer penalty for the $100,000 transfer will be eliminated.

An asset return only works if (1) all of the assets that were transferred during the lookback period are returned to the applicant and (2) the assets that were transferred are returned to the applicant by the recipient of the asset transfer(s). For instance, if Mr. Smith transfers $100,000 to his son James and Mr. Smith's son Robert gives Mr. Smith $100,000, the assets transfer was not undone by Robert's gift of $100,000 to Mr. Smith. Instead, the county will simply find that Mr. Smith gifted $100,000 to James and Robert gifted $100,000 to Mr. Smith. The transfer penalty for the $100,000 uncompensated transfer will still be imposed.

Furthermore, if Mr. Smith gifts $100,000 to his son James, and James returns $99,999 to Mr. Smith, the county will still impose a transfer penalty for the full $100,000 transfer. All of the assets transferred must be returned to Mr. Smith. The county will not partially abate a transfer if some of the assets are return, and the county will not eliminate a penalty period unless all of the assets are returned.

With an outright transfer, it is easy for the recipient of the gift to simply return the transferred assets to the applicant. This may not be the case with a transfer to a trust.

If Mr. Smith transfers $100,000 to an irrevocable trust for the benefit of his children, not for his benefit in any manner whatsoever, then the transfer will be a completed asset transfer for purposes of Medicaid eligibility. But what if Mr. Smith needs nursing home

---

9. Medicaid Communications 10-02, 10-06.

care a year later and the kids want to give Mr. Smith back the $100,000 to undo the transfer?

The very terms of the trust do not permit a transfer from the trust to Mr. Smith's, the trust is for the children's benefit, not Mr. Smith, so the trust cannot transfer assets to Mr. Smith. Furthermore, if the assets of the trust are distributed to the children and the children return the assets to Mr. Smith, then the county could hold that the recipient of the transfer (the trust) did not return the assets to Mr. Smith. Instead, the county could hold that there was a $100,000 transfer to an irrevocable trust and a $100,000 gift from the children to Mr. Smith; the county could then still impose a penalty period for the $100,000 uncompensated transfer.

Now, all the beneficiaries of the trust and the trustees of the trust may enter an agreement to change the terms of the trust and return the assets to Mr. Smith,[10] but if the county is challenging the return, the applicant may be in trouble given how the Medicaid appeals process is weighted against the applicant. Certainly, an outright transfer has an ease for undoing the transfer that does not exist with a transfer to a trust.

### 9-4:2 Disadvantages

There are several disadvantages to outright transfers.

#### 9-4:2.1 Death of Donee

What if Mr. Smith transfers $100,000 to his son James and James dies? Mr. Smith may have expected James to hold the $100,000 and to return the money to him if he ever needed the money—a moral obligation, not a legal obligation.

Now that James has died, James's wife probably will inherit her husband's estate. Maybe James's wife, who now is left without a husband, doesn't want to return any of the money to Mr. Smith. Perhaps the wife is financially insecure and believes she needs the money to support her own needs. Perhaps the wife never liked her father-in-law and simply doesn't want to give him anything.

There are a slew of scenarios that could happen if the recipient of the gift predeceases the applicant, but the bottom line is that the applicant will have no control over what happens with his money

---

10. N.J.S.A. 3B:23-9.

once he transfers the money to his son. The money is now the son's money, and if the son predeceases the father, the money will be part of the son's estate.

#### 9-4:2.2 Creditors of Donee

If Mr. Smith transfers $100,000 to his son James and James owes people money, the creditors of James might attach the $100,000 gift that the father made to his son. The $100,000 is now part of James's assets. The money is subject to the claims of James's creditors.

#### 9-4:2.3 Divorce of Donee

If Mr. Smith transfers $100,000 to his son James and James or his wife file for divorce, Mr. Smith's $100,000 might become embroiled in the divorce litigation. While a gift is exempt from equitable distribution,[11] litigants in divorce cases have very strong, often negative, feelings about their soon-to-be ex-spouse. The son's wife may assert a claim for the $100,000 just to gain leverage to get something else that she wants and to which she truly believes she is entitled.

In addition, while a gift is exempt from equitable distribution, the judge in the Family Part may take the assets of James into consideration when establishing an appropriate alimony award for his ex-spouse.[12]

### 9-4:3 Gift Tax on Transfers

The Medicaid Act subjects applicants to a penalty period, or period of ineligibility for Medicaid benefits, if the applicant makes an uncompensated transfer of an asset during the lookback period.[13] While an uncompensated transfer does not have to rise to the level of a gift, most uncompensated transfers are gifts.

When clients think about gifts, they immediately believe that there are limits on the amount they can gift in any one year. Most believe that the amount they can gift in any one year is limited

---

11. N.J.S.A. 2A:34-23(h).
12. N.J.S.A. 2A:34-23(b)(10).
13. 42 U.S.C. § 1396p(c)(1).

to the annual exclusion amount,[14] or what they believe to be the annual exclusion amount at that time.

The fact of the matter is that every person receives a lifetime exclusion against gift tax equivalent to $5,000,000. This sum is indexed for inflation, so the present lifetime exclusion is $5,340,000.[15] In addition, a person can give $14,000 each and every year to an unlimited number of people without reducing their lifetime exclusion.[16] In other words, Mr. Smith could give $14,000 to 100 people without reducing his lifetime exclusion of $5,340,000. If Mr. Smith gave $15,000 to the 101st person, his lifetime exclusion would be reduced from $5,340,000 to $5,339,000.

From a practical standpoint, most clients who are planning for Medicaid have between $20,000 and $700,000 in assets. No individual seeking to qualify for Medicaid benefits has in excess of $5,340,000, so no individual seeking to qualify for Medicaid would ever pay gift tax. In short, no individual seeking to qualify for Medicaid benefits will ever pay gift tax as a result of the transfers he makes in order to qualify for Medicaid benefits.

### 9-4:4 New Jersey Inheritance Tax on Transfers

Most individuals seeking to qualify for Medicaid benefits are transferring assets to their spouse or to their children, but from time-to-time, a client may wish to transfer assets to a more distant relative, such as a nephew, niece, brother or sister. If the client transfers assets to an individual who would be considered a Class C or D beneficiary for purposes of the New Jersey Inheritance Tax and if that client dies within three years of the transfer, that transfer will need to be brought back into the inheritance tax return of the client.[17]

You should make the client and the transferee aware of this fact. Most people who receive gifts are quick to treat the money as their money and will resent the need to return a portion of the money to pay a tax of which they were unaware.

---

14. 26 U.S.C. § 2503.
15. 26 U.S.C. § 2505.
16. 26 U.S.C. § 2503.
17. N.J.S.A. 54:34-1 et seq.

## 9-5 TRANSFERS TO TRUST

For reasons discussed immediately below, many clients who engage in Medicaid planning will prefer to transfer their assets to a trust. When making a transfer to a trust for purposes of Medicaid planning, the trust must contain certain features in order for the transfer to the trust to be a completed transfer.

It is of paramount importance that the transfer be considered a completed transfer, because if the transfer is incomplete, then the applicant still owns the asset for purposes of Medicaid eligibility. For instance, if an applicant transfers $100,000 to a trust and the terms of the trust permit the applicant to receive $10,000 of the trust's assets if the applicant needs a heart transplant, then $10,000 of the trust is available to the applicant even if the probability of his ever needing a heart transplant are extremely remote.[18] The State Medicaid Manual provides that if there is any circumstance under which the assets of the trust can be returned to the applicant, then to the extent the assets can be returned to the applicant, the assets that can be returned are available to the applicant.

In some cases, it is a delicate balancing act between retaining certain rights for the client to achieve a purpose and making the transfer complete for purposes of achieving Medicaid eligibility. For various reasons, a client may wish to retain an interest in a trust that he established to achieve Medicaid eligibility.

### 9-5:1 Features of a Medicaid Planning Trust

From a pure Medicaid planning aspect, having the applicant retain no interest in the trust is optimal; however, such a trust could be too narrowly drafted for many Medicaid planning clients and their families.

If the applicant retains no interest whatsoever in the trust, transfers to the trust will effectively divest the assets from the applicant. If the applicant makes an uncompensated transfer to such a trust and waits 61 months after having made the transfer, then the county board cannot see that a transfer was made.

If an applicant transfers assets to a trust but retains the right to the income those assets generate, then the income of the trust

---

18. 42 U.S.C. § 1396p(d)(3)(B), SMM § 3259.6.B.

will be deemed available to the applicant.[19] In addition, even after 60 months, the county board will be able to see the trust as the applicant is receiving income from the trust. The county board will have the right to review the trust to ascertain the exact nature of the applicant's retained interest. Obviously, such a review opens the trust up for scrutiny and the results of that scrutiny may or may not have a proper foundation in the facts or the law.

So, there is risk inherent in retaining an interest in the trust. Oftentimes, it is the fear that the county board will take a position not based on the facts of the case or the law that should concern the elder law practitioner the most.

### 9-5:1.1 Irrevocable

Any trust used to achieve Medicaid eligibility must be irrevocable. An irrevocable trust is a trust the terms of which cannot be modified or revoked. If the grantor/applicant could modify or revoke the trust and have the assets (or a portion of the assets) returned to him, then the assets (or that portion of the assets) of the trust remain available to the applicant.[20]

The trust should be irrevocable. In this way, as long as the dispositive provisions of the trust refrain from naming the applicant as a beneficiary, there can be no argument that the applicant can achieve a return of the assets under any circumstance whatsoever.[21]

### 9-5:1.2 Under No Circumstances Whatsoever

If there is any circumstance under which the applicant can receive the assets of the trust or any portion of the assets of the trust, then the assets of the trust or that portion of the assets of the trust is available to the applicant for purposes of determining his eligibility for Medicaid.[22] It is irrelevant how remote the circumstances triggering the return may be. If the trust permitted a return of the assets to the applicant if pigs could fly, then the assets of the trust are available to the applicant.

---

19. *J.S. v. Division of Medical Assistance and Health Services*, OAL docket number HMA 4896-06.

20. 42 U.S.C. § 1396p(d)(3)(A).

21. 42 U.S.C. § 1396p(d)(3)(B), SMM § 3259.6.B.

22. SMM § 3259.6.B.

A properly drafted trust for purposes of achieving Medicaid eligibility will state that the assets of the trust are available to the applicant and his spouse under no circumstance whatsoever. Because assets owned by one spouse are deemed available to the institutionalized spouse for purposes of determining his eligibility for Medicaid,[23] it is prudent to draft the trust so that the assets of the trust are unavailable to the grantor and his spouse even if the applicant is not married. Even an elderly client could remarry, so it is prudent to draft the trust with this fact in mind.

### 9-5:1.3 Access to Income

From a legal perspective, it may be advisable for the client to retain no interest in the assets of the trust under any circumstance whatsoever. With that said, for practical reasons, a Medicaid trust will often be drafted in a manner that retains for the client certain rights. One common interest that clients wish to retain is the right to the income from the trust.

If the client transfers a brokerage account worth $400,000 to an irrevocable trust, the client may still need the income his investments earn to pay his bills. It is one thing for the client to give up access to the $400,000 of principal the client may never have needed to tap into those assets anyway but the client may be living off the income his assets generate.

Many trusts used for purposes of Medicaid planning retain for the client the right to the income of the trust. These trusts are known in the field as "income-only trusts." The client (and his spouse) has no access to the principal of the trust, but he is entitled to the income the assets of the trust generate.

The advantages of income-only trusts are two-fold. For one, the client retains the income from his assets. This makes the client feel good. He feels in control of his money, even though he is not, and he continues to benefit from his money.

Secondly, because the client retained the right to the income from the trust for the remainder of his life, the retained income interest can form the basis for including the assets of the trust in the estate of the client when he passes away.[24] By including the

---

23. 42 U.S.C. § 1396r-5(c)(2).

24. 26 U.S.C. §§ 677, 1014, 2036.

assets in his estate, the assets will receive a stepped-up basis. So, for instance, if the brokerage account that was transferred to the trust contained stocks with a low cost basis, the basis in those stocks will be stepped-up upon the client's death because of his retained income interest.

Since most clients seeking to qualify for Medicaid benefits do not have estates that would be subject to federal or even New Jersey estate tax, the inclusion of the assets in the estate of the client is positive. The client's estate will receive a stepped-up basis with no estate tax being owed in most instances.

### 9-5:1.4 Access to Principal

While you can never say never when it comes to Medicaid/estate planning, it would be an extremely rare case in which you would leave a Medicaid planning client with access to the principal of a trust designed to achieve Medicaid eligibility. If the client retains access to the principal of the trust under any circumstance whatsoever, then those assets are available to the client for purposes of determining his eligibility for benefits.

With that said, as an elder practitioner, you will be asked to review trusts that another lawyer informed the client would help achieve Medicaid eligibility for the client and that trust will permit the client to access the principal of the trust. The trust may state that the client can access the trust for his health, maintenance and support, yet his former attorney told him the trust would help achieve Medicaid eligibility for him.

Just know that this is untrue. As stated above, the best Medicaid trust would prohibit the client from accessing the principal and income of the trust under any circumstance whatsoever. Anything less than that exposes a portion of the trust to the client's long term care costs or exposes the client to arguments as to why the trust's assets are available to the client. While there may be good reason to leave the client with some retained interest, leaving the client with access to the principal of the trust probably cannot be justified under any circumstance if Medicaid eligibility is the goal of the client.

### 9-5:1.5 Grantor Trust

A trust can be its own separate entity for tax purposes or the income from the trust can be taxed to the grantor. Several provisions of the Internal Revenue Code establish the circumstances under which the income of a trust will be taxable to the grantor of the trust.[25] Because income tax rates for trusts are effectively higher than income tax rates for individuals due to the compression of the tax brackets for trusts, it is often beneficial to have a trust treated as a grantor trust.

Furthermore, if the trust owns the personal residence of the client/applicant, having the trust treated as a grantor trust can retain the exclusion from gain that the client will receive upon the sale of the home, if the home served as the client's primary principal residence for two of the last five years.[26] For instance, assume that Mr. Smith purchased his home in 1960 for $20,000. Over the years, he made $50,000 in capital improvements, giving him a cost basis in the home of $70,000. The home is worth $230,000 in today's market.

If Mr. Smith were to sell his home, he would pay no capital gains tax; Mr. Smith is receiving $230,000 in proceeds, but his basis is $70,000 and he can exclude $250,000 of gain on the sale of his primary principal residence. Between his basis and the exclusion there is more than enough coverage to eliminate any tax.

On the other hand, if Mr. Smith transferred his house outright to his son and his son sold the house, the son would only have the $70,000 basis, not the $250,000 exclusion from gain on the sale of the primary residence because Mr. Smith's home is not his son's home. The son would pay capital gains tax on the difference between the $70,000 basis he received upon the gift from his father and the net proceeds derived from the sale of the house.

If Mr. Smith transferred his home to a grantor trust, even if Mr. Smith retained no access to the principal or income of the trust for purposes of determining his eligibility for Medicaid benefits, then the sale would be a reportable event on Mr. Smith's taxes, not his son's. Because the sale is still reportable on Mr. Smith's taxes, the regulations implementing the relevant section of the Internal Revenue Code[27] permit Mr. Smith to use his $250,000 exclusion from gain on the sale of his primary principal residence. In this

---

25. 26 U.S.C. §§ 671 to 679.

26. 26 U.S.C. § 121.

27. 26 U.S.C. § 121, 26 C.F.R. §§ 1.121-1 et seq.

instance, between his basis of $70,000 and the $250,000 exclusion, Mr. Smith will not owe capital gains tax as the result of the sale of his primary principal residence.

### 9-5:2 Advantages

Aside from the advantages already discussed, the transfer to a trust has certain advantages over outright transfers to individuals. In a nutshell, when a client transfers assets outright the client retains no protection whatsoever for his assets. It is as if the client is tossing the assets into the air and hoping they find a safe home.

The client can do little or nothing to ensure his asset will be protected from potential problems the recipient of the transferred assets may have. With a trust, the client can retain a certain level of control without running afoul of the rules governing Medicaid eligibility.

#### 9-5:2.1 Death of Donee

A client may feel completely comfortable with transferring assets to his children. "I trust my children without hesitation," the client will say. The thing many clients do not consider is if the client's child dies before the client.

For instance, assume that Mr. Smith transfers his home to his son. A year after the transfer, the son dies. The son has a Will that leaves his entire estate to his wife, Mr. Smith's daughter-in-law. Mr. Smith comes to you and says that he doesn't want his house to be owned by his daughter-in-law, he wants his house to go to his grandchildren, his son's children.

Obviously, Mr. Smith should have considered the possibility of his son predeceasing him when he made the transfer of the home. His attorney should have made him aware of this contingency as well.

With a trust, the client can address this contingency. The terms of the trust can provide for what happens with the house in the event Mr. Smith's son predeceases Mr. Smith. In fact, the trust could address this issue in great detail, perhaps creating a sub-trust for any beneficiary who may be under the age of majority.

#### 9-5:2.2 Creditors of Donee

If Mr. Smith transfers assets directly to his children, he subjects his assets to the creditors of his children. Even if the children presently have no creditors, fortunes can turn and a child may be unable to pay his debts at some point in the future.

The likelihood that a donee will have creditor problems increases with the number of donees. For instance, if Mr. Smith has six children as opposed to one or two children there is a greater probability that one of the six children will have credit issues.

A trust can protect the transferred assets from the creditors of the children. For instance, assume that the trust contains a spendthrift clause;[28] a spendthrift clause is designed to protect the assets of the trust from the creditors of the trust's beneficiaries as long as the assets remain in the trust.[29]

Further assume that the trust has co-trustees[30] and neither trustee can distribute assets to himself.[31] So, in other words, only trustee #1 can transfer assets to trustee #2 and vice versa and only both trustees can transfer assets to a trust beneficiary who is not also a trustee. The trust is also a discretionary trust that permits the trustees of the trust to distribute the assets of the trust to their sole and absolute discretion; no beneficiary can compel the trustees to make a distribution of the assets.[32]

If the provisions of the trust are drafted in this manner, then the assets of the trust are protected from the creditors of the beneficiaries as long as the assets remain in the trust. Since the idea of the trust is to hold the assets until Mr. Smith dies or qualifies for Medicaid benefits, the assets of the trust will remain protected from his children's credit problems or potential credit problems as long as those assets remain in the trust.

### 9-5:2.3 Divorce of Donee

What if Mr. Smith transfers his assets to his son and his son ends up embroiled in a divorce? While a gift is exempt from equitable distribution in a divorce,[33] the son's soon-to-be ex-wife may make a claim for the gifted assets simply to gain leverage for something

---

28. N.J.S.A. 25:2-1.

29. Uniform Trust Code, § 502, Comment.

30. N.J.S.A. 3B:11-3, *Trustees Construed To Be Joint Tenants*.

31. N.J.S.A. 3B:11-4.1.

32. Uniform Trust Code, § 504(b).

33. N.J.S.A. 2A:34-23(h).

else that she wants. In addition, the assets the son owns may form a basis for the wife getting a higher level of alimony from the son.[34]

If the assets are held in a trust and the trust is drafted in such a way as to prevent the son from accessing the assets without the consent of another, for instance, the co-trustee,[35] then the wife would not be able to claim that the assets are available for distribution to the son or that the income from the assets should be taken into consideration when computing the wife's alimony.

### 9-5:3 Disadvantages

#### 9-5:3.1 Complication of Transfer

One of the main disadvantages of a trust is that a trust is complicated when compared to an outright transfer. Many clients will be intimidated by a trust. No matter how well you may explain the workings of the trust and the advantages of a trust over an outright transfer, the client may still be confused by the trust and intimidated by the trust.

Adding to the complication the client perceives about the trust is the fact that many trusts need to file their own income tax returns to report the income the trust generates.[36] Telling a client that they need to file a separate tax return for the trust each and every year only adds to the complexity of the trust for the client; moreover, to the client, the perceived expense associated with retaining the services of an accountant every year to draft the trust's income tax return is a concern.

These disadvantages are far more perceived than real, but it is difficult to explain reality to the client.

## 9-6 TRANSFER OF THE HOME

The single most important asset to a client is his home. Most of the individuals who come to see an elder law attorney for purposes of Medicaid planning are interested in protecting their home. In a pre-planning mode, that is, a plan where the client will transfer the

---

34. N.J.S.A. 2A:34-23(b)(10).

35. N.J.S.A. 3B:11-4.1.

36. IRS Form 1041. *See* http://www.irs.gov/pub/irs-pdf/i1041.pdf (explaining when a trust must file a Form 1041).

home and wait five years before applying for Medicaid benefits, there are a number of ways in which the transfer of the home can be accomplished.

### 9-6:1 Life Estate

Having a client transfer his home to his children and retain a life estate in the home is one of the oldest and simplest ways in which to protect the home in a pre-planning mode. The client has a deed drafted for him through which he transfers the home from himself as fee simple owner to himself as life tenant with his children as remaindermen.[37]

When a Medicaid applicant owns real property with another individual and that other individual refuses to sell the property, the county board will treat the property as unavailable.[38] Technically, a life tenant could sell his interest in the property (the life estate) without the consent of the remainderman, but there is no readily available market for the sale of a life estate.[39] Accordingly, only if the remainderman will consent to the sale of his interest in the property (the remainder interest), too, would the property be marketable. So—from a practical standpoint, if not a legal standpoint—the property is unavailable when all the Medicaid applicant owns is a life estate and the remainderman refuses to sell.

Furthermore, upon the applicant's death, DMAHS will not seek estate recovery against the property. The New Jersey regulations governing estate recovery do not permit recovery against a life estate created during the applicant's life.[40]

Given the foregoing, if the client transfers his home subject to a retained life estate then waits 61 months before applying for Medicaid benefits, the home will no longer count against him for purposes of determining his eligibility for Medicaid benefits, and DMAHS will not seek estate recovery against the home after his death for any Medicaid benefits that may have been paid.

---

37. N.J.S.A. 46:3-13.

38. POMS SI § 01110.515; N.J.A.C. 10:71-4.1(c).

39. The sale would be of an estate pur autre vie, a life estate measured by the life of another, that is, the Medicaid applicant's life. *See, e.g., Robeson v. Duncan*, 74 N.J. Eq. 745 (Ch. 1908). So, the buyer of the life estate would be purchasing a life estate measured by the life of an elderly, sickly individual, whose life expectancy is greatly diminished.

40. N.J.A.C. 10:49-14.1(l)(2)(i).

### 9-6:2 Life Tenancy

The difference between a true life estate and a life tenancy is that with a life tenancy, the client is simply retaining the right to use and occupy the home during his life. He is not retaining the right to the proceeds of sale if the home is sold during his life.

The advantage of a life tenancy over a life estate is that if the home is sold during the client's life, then the client is not entitled to any of the proceeds of sale. Because the remaindermen are often interested in selling the home once the client begins to reside in a nursing home, retaining less than a full life estate for the client can be beneficial.

### 9-6:3 Tax Basis in Home

When an individual makes a lifetime gift of an asset, the recipient of the gift typically receives a carryover basis.[41] Basis is the amount of money the client paid for the asset plus capital improvements. Capital gains tax is calculated by subtracting the individual's basis from the net proceeds of sale.

Assume that Mr. Smith purchased his home for $20,000. Assume further that Mr. Smith made $50,000 in capital improvements to his home, giving him a $70,000 basis in the home. Finally, assume that Mr. Smith's home currently is worth $300,000.

If Mr. Smith were to gift his home to his children retaining a life estate for himself, his children will own the home worth $300,000 subject to Mr. Smith's life estate. The children will receive a portion of Mr. Smith's basis at the time of the gift based upon Mr. Smith's age. This is called a "carryover basis."

For instance, assume that Mr. Smith was seventy-five years of age at the time he gifted his house to his children subject to his retained life estate. Based upon his age and the applicable IRS's actuarial tables, the gift of the remainder interest was worth 79.318% of the house.[42] So, the children would have received 79.318% of Mr. Smith's $70,000 basis, or a $55,522 carryover basis.

If Mr. Smith's children sell the home during Mr. Smith's life, the children will have to pay capital gains tax on the difference

---

41. 26 U.S.C. § 1040.

42. http://www.irs.gov/Retirement-Plans/Actuarial-Tables

between their share of the proceeds of sale and their basis in the property.

### 9-6:4 Step-Up in Basis

If a client dies owning a life estate or a life tenancy in his home, the home will receive a stepped-up basis at the time of his death.[43] The retained lifetime interest in the property includes the property in his estate for estate tax purposes and gives the home a stepped-up basis. When the children of the client sell the home after the death of the client, the children probably will not have any capital gains tax to pay because their basis in the property will meet or exceed the net proceeds of sale.

### 9-6:5 Section 121 Exclusion

When an individual owns and uses a house as his primary principal residence for two of the five years preceding the sale of the house, that individual is entitled to a $250,000 exclusion from the gain realized on the sale of the house.[44] This is the Section 121 exclusion, named after the section of the Internal Revenue Code in which the exclusion is found. A married couple can exclude up to $500,000 of gain.

If a client transfers his home to his children and retains a life estate, the client continues to own a portion of the home. If the home is sold during his lifetime, the client is entitled to a portion of the proceeds of sale. The portion of the proceeds of sale to which the client is entitled differs depending on the actuarial table you use.

The county board of social services will look at the tables found in the State Medicaid Manual to ensure that the client received the appropriate portion of the proceeds of sale.[45] The county board is looking to see if an uncompensated asset transfer happened upon the sale of the house. As long as the client received the appropriate portion of the proceeds of sale based upon the sales price, his age and the actuarial table, no uncompensated asset transfer occurred at the time of the sale of the house.

---

43. 26 U.S.C. §§ 1014, 2036.
44. 26 U.S.C. § 121.
45. SMM § 3258.9.

The Internal Revenue Service uses a different actuarial table to determine the portion of the proceeds of sale that are properly attributable to the client for purposes of taxation.[46]

When determining the portion of the sales proceeds to which the client's Section 121 exclusion can be applied, the client would use the IRS actuarial tables. The children would have to pay capital gains tax on the remainder of the proceeds of the sale to the extent those proceeds exceed the carryover basis that they received in the property when the property was gifted to them.

If the client retained a life tenancy, so that the client is not entitled to any portion of the proceeds of sale, then no portion of the proceeds of sale is attributed to the client and the client cannot use his Section 121 exclusion.

Capital gains tax on the sale of the house during the client's lifetime can be avoided (or greatly reduced) by placing the remainder interest in the house in a grantor trust[47] that would preserve the client's Section 121 exclusion on the sale.[48]

## 9-6:6 Exclusions to the Transfer of Asset Rules

There are a number of exclusions to the transfer of assets rules that are found in the Medicaid Act.[49] These exclusions are discussed in great detail in Chapter 8.

The statutory exclusions include the caregiver child exception to the transfer of the applicant's home[50] and the transfer of the home to a sibling of the applicant who owns an equity interest in the home with the applicant.[51] The statutory exclusions also include the transfer of assets to a blind or disabled child of the applicant[52] or the transfer of assets to a trust for the sole benefit of a disabled individual under the age of 65.[53]

---

46. http://www.irs.gov/Retirement-Plans/Actuarial-Tables.
47. 26 U.S.C. §§ 671 to 679.
48. 26 U.S.C. § 121, 26 C.F.R. § 1-121-1 et seq.
49. 42 U.S.C. § 1396p(c)(2).
50. 42 U.S.C. § 1396p(c)(2)(A)(iv).
51. 42 U.S.C. § 1396p(c)(2)(A)(iii).
52. 42 U.S.C. § 1396p(c)(2)(B)(iii).
53. 42 U.S.C. § 1396p(c)(2)(B)(iv).

## 9-7 PLANNING WITH WILLS

Most married individuals have traditional Wills that devise the entirety of their estates to each other, then to their children after the death of both spouses. For example, both the husband's and wife's Wills provide for the following: "I devise my entire estate to my spouse. If my spouse predeceases me, I devise my entire estate to my children."

This type of Will is known as an "I Love You" Will, because each spouse leaves the entirety of his/her estate to the other spouse to the exclusion of all others. For many married couples, these Wills are quite appropriate; however, as individuals age, the wisdom of drafting these traditional Wills wanes.

What if the married couple with whom you are meeting is 85 years of age or older and are in poor health? Are "I Love You" Wills appropriate for this couple? Probably not, because if one spouse were to die, the other spouse will only be older, probably more sickly and will now no longer have the support of the other spouse. There is a much higher probability that the surviving spouse will require care in a long term care facility after the death of his spouse.

Assume that a married couple of advanced age comes to see you. The couple owns a home worth $300,000 and a bank account worth $200,000, giving the couple a gross estate of $500,000. The couple lives very modestly and there is no real chance that either spouse will ever spend all of their assets, unless those assets are consumed by long term care costs.

If you draft traditional Wills for this couple and the wife dies a year later, the husband will now own assets in his name worth $500,000. If the husband enters a nursing home one year after that, the entirety of his estate, $500,000, will be exposed to the costs of his long term care. This did not need to happen.

Instead of drafting traditional Wills for this couple, the attorney could have drafted Wills that allow for elective share planning.[54] A spouse is the only person a client cannot effectively disinherit. If one spouse disinherits the other spouse, then the surviving spouse can file a claim against the deceased spouse's estate. This claim is called the elective share.

---

54. N.J.S.A. 3B:8-1 et seq.

The elective share is a formula and certain assets are excluded from the calculation, but most people describe the elective share as one-third of the couple's combined estate. In brief, the calculation takes into account what the deceased spouse owned and what the surviving spouse owns, and the surviving spouse is entitled to one-third of the aggregate.

So, assume the same married couple comes into your office. You suggest that each spouse drafts a Will through which he or she leaves the surviving spouse what the surviving spouse would be entitled to under the statutes governing the elective share. You then divide the couple's estate so that each spouse owns one-half the estate. The wife owns $100,000 in bank accounts in her name and one-half the house as tenant-in-common. The husband owns the same.

Now, one year later the wife dies. The husband already owns one-half the aggregate estate, so he is entitled to no portion of the wife's estate.[55] Instead, the wife's estate passes to the children, not the husband. When the husband enters a nursing home one year after the death of his wife, he only has an estate worth $250,000, not $500,000.

Through this relatively simple planning technique, you have preserved one-half of the couple's estate; furthermore, because the husband received everything he was entitled to receive from his wife estate (in this case, nothing), no uncompensated asset transfer occurred.[56] Without further planning, if the husband spent down his $250,000, he would qualify for Medicaid benefits and the children would have one-half of their parent's estate.

## 9-8 EMERGENCY PLANNING

Planning with a couple's Wills or a plan involving waiting out the lookback period are all pre-planning techniques (or emergency planning for clients who have somewhat significant assets and can afford to pay their long term care costs for five years yet still transfer a portion of their assets to their children). The client is not in need of long-term care services, is not currently receiving

---

55. N.J.S.A. 3B:8-18.

56. N.J.A.C. 10:71-4.10(b)(3)(ii).

long term care services and/or will not be qualifying for Medicaid benefits in the near future.

For purposes of this book, the phrase "emergency planning" involves planning for a client who currently requires long term care and who needs to qualify for Medicaid benefits as soon as possible but excludes those individuals whose only option is to engage in a five-year plan. For instance, if the client is in a nursing home and has $100,000 in total assets, the client cannot engage in a five-year plan in order to preserve a portion of her estate; she simply does not have sufficient assets to pay for her care for five years let alone transfer a portion of her estate to her children and wait five years before applying for Medicaid benefits.

## 9-9 INCREASING THE CSRA

The community spouse is entitled to retain a portion of the couple's countable resources.[57] This portion of the assets is called the Community Spouse Resource Allowance, or CSRA. In 2014, the maximum CSRA is $117,240 and the minimum CSRA is $23,448.[58]

As discussed more extensively in Chapter 8, the community spouse may retain an amount of countable resources somewhere between the maximum and minimum figure. For instance, if the institutionalized spouse enters a nursing home and the couple owns $150,000 in countable resources, then the community spouse will be entitled to retain $75,000 of the countable resources, or one-half the total countable resources.

If the institutionalized spouse has not entered a nursing home and the community spouse comes to your office telling you that he is thinking about placing his wife in a nursing home, a planning opportunity exists to increase the CSRA the community spouse can retain. For instance, if the couple owns a home and $150,000 in cash, then the community spouse can retain the home and $75,000. If the couple borrows $90,000 against their home before the wife enters the nursing home, then the couple will have $240,000 in countable resources when the wife enters the nursing home.

---

57. 42 U.S.C. § 1396r-5(f)(2).

58. Medicaid Communication 14-01.

Based upon the couple owning $240,000 in countable resources at the time the wife enters the nursing home, the community spouse can now retain the maximum CSRA of $117,240 and the house. Sometime after the wife enters the nursing home and an application for Medicaid benefits has been filed, the husband can use the $90,000 he borrowed to repay the loan against the home.

The repayment will reduce the couple's countable resources to $150,000 again, with the husband being able to retain $117,240 of that amount as his CSRA.

## 9-10 INCREASING THE MMMNA

The community spouse may be entitled to a portion (or all) of the institutionalized spouse's income as an income allowance.[59] This income allowance is called the Minimum Monthly Maintenance Needs Allowance or MMMNA. As discussed more extensively in Chapter 8, the MMMNA is established through a two-part formula.

The standard two-part formula has a basic allowance and an excess shelter allowance. Pursuant to federal law, the MMMNA has a maximum allowance that cannot exceed $2,841 per month. In short, under no circumstance can the community spouse receive more than $2,841 per month from the institutionalized spouse's income under the standard MMMNA formula.

A community spouse may be disappointed with the income allowance to which he is entitled under the standard formula. If the community spouse files for a support order in the Superior Court of New Jersey, Family Part, before filing for Medicaid benefits, the county board must honor the support order that the Superior Court entered.[60] Some practitioners find that they can achieve a higher income allowance in this manner.

It is important to file and receive the support order before the application for Medicaid benefits is filed.[61] The county board is an interested party to the support action and should receive notice of the action, even if no application for benefits is currently pending. The court should conduct an evidentiary hearing to determine the

---

59. 42 U.S.C. § 1396r-5(d).

60. 42 U.S.C. § 1396r-5(d)(5).

61. *M.E.F. v. A.B.F.*, 393 N.J. Super. 543 (App. Div. 2007).

amount of the community spouse's income allowance and both the husband and wife should present evidence supporting and defending against the request for the allowance.[62]

## 9-11 THE SPEND DOWN

The concept of spending down an applicant's assets simply means what it says—the client is spending their money. The applicant may be paying his bills, such as credit card bills, or he may be purchasing non-countable resource. Purchasing non-countable resources effectively converts a countable resource, for instance, cash, into a non-countable resource, for instance, an automobile.

### 9-11:1 Irrevocable Funeral

One common spend down/conversion purchase is the purchase of an irrevocable prepaid funeral. Once a client qualifies for Medicaid benefits, he will no longer have any significant countable resources in his name. At some point in time, the client will die and will need a funeral, so it is a good idea to prepay for this need at a time when the client still has assets from which to pay for the service.

The funeral must be an irrevocable prepaid funeral. An irrevocable prepaid funeral is a funeral that the client cannot change or revoke and receive a partial or full refund of the purchase price. The county board will insist that the funeral be irrevocable in order to ensure that the client no longer has access to the funds used to purchase the funeral.

Under the regulations governing prepaid funerals, such a funeral can only be established if the purchaser is anticipating Medicaid eligibility within the next six months.[63] Any funds remaining in the funeral fund that are not used to pay for funeral services for the applicant must be turned over to DMAHS to reimburse the Division for Medicaid benefits provided to the now-deceased Medicaid beneficiary.[64] For this reason, it makes no sense to overfund an irrevocable prepaid funeral fund.

62. *R.S. v. Div. of Medical Assistance and Health Services*, 434 N.J. Super. 250 (App. Div. 2014).

63. N.J.A.C. 13:36-11.6.

64. N.J.A.C. 13:36-11.6(c).

### 9-11:2 Home Improvements

The home is a non-countable resource;[65] accordingly, improvements to the home convert countable resources—the cash used to make the improvements—to a non-countable resource. There is no limit on the amount of the home improvements an applicant can make.

As discussed in Chapter 8, in certain circumstances, there is an equity value limitation on the home.[66] If a spouse is going to reside in the home, then the home will remain non-countable. If the spouse will continue to reside in the home, there is no equity value limitation on the home and there is no limitation on the value of the improvements that can be made to the home.

Making home improvements when the community spouse will continue to reside in the home is an excellent method of spending down/converting countable resources into non-countable resources.

### 9-11:3 Purchase of Car

One automobile, irrespective of value, is a non-countable resource.[67] If the applicant or the community spouse needs an automobile, purchasing a new car can be an excellent method of converting countable resources into a non-countable resource.

It is important to bear in mind that a car is a highly depreciable asset; accordingly, this technique only makes sense if the community spouse or the applicant truly needs a new car. If the community spouse or applicant does not need a car, there are probably other methods that can be employed to preserve resources.

### 9-11:4 Purchase of Household Goods and Personal Effects

Household goods and personal effects (clothing, furniture, appliances, etc.) are non-countable resources.[68] If the applicant or his spouse needs any of these items, it is advisable for the client to spend down his countable resources purchasing such items.

---

65. 42 U.S.C. § 1382b.
66. 42 U.S.C. § 1396p(f), N.J.A.C. 10:71-41.(d)(1)(v).
67. N.J.A.C. 10:71-4.4(b)(2).
68. N.J.A.C. 10:71-4.4(b)(3).

As with an automobile, these items are highly depreciable and are often worth far less than their purchase price the moment after sale, so it is only advisable for an applicant or his spouse to purchase those household goods and personal effects that are truly needed.

## 9-12 PURCHASE OF AN ANNUITY

The purchase of a properly structured annuity can effectively convert countable resources (for instance, cash) into an income item. The conversion of a resource to income can be helpful in the context of planning for Medicaid eligibility.

There are two primary issues when using an annuity to attain eligibility for Medicaid. First, the purchase of the annuity must be structured in such a way as to avoid the transfer of asset rules.[69] The federal Medicaid Act contains provisions that address whether or not the purchase of an annuity is an uncompensated transfer. Secondly, the annuity must be structured in such a way that it will be considered an income item, not a resource.[70]

### 9-12:1 Annuities and the Asset Transfer Rules

When reviewing an annuity, an initial question that must be answered is whether or not the purchase of the annuity is a purchase for value. The Medicaid Act contains rules for determining whether or not the purchase of an annuity was a purchase for value.[71]

There are three separate exceptions to the transfer of assets rules as those rules relate to the purchase of an annuity. If an annuity satisfies any one of the three exceptions, then the purchase of the annuity is not an uncompensated transfer.

#### 9-12:1.1 Qualified Annuity Exception

If the annuity is purchased by the institutionalized individual inside her IRA or certain other qualified accounts, then the annuity is not an "asset" for purposes of the transfer of assets rules;[72] accordingly, the purchase of the annuity cannot result in

---

69. 42 U.S.C. §§ 1396p(c)(1)(F), (G).
70. 20 C.F.R. § 416.1121.
71. 42 U.S.C. §§ 1396p(c)(1)(F), (G).
72. 42 U.S.C. § 1396p(c)(1)(G)(i).

the imposition of a penalty period for purposes of the transfer of assets rules.

This exception to the transfer of assets rules only applies to an annuity that is purchased "by or on behalf of an annuitant who has applied for medical assistance,"[73] to wit, an institutionalized individual. This exception does not apply to an annuity that the community spouse purchases.

### 9-12:1.2 Irrevocable Annuity Exception

In order for a non-qualified annuity to not be an "asset" for purposes of the transfer of assets rules, the annuity must satisfy four criteria.[74] As with the Qualified Annuity Exception, this exception to the transfer of assets rules only applies to an annuity that is purchased "by or on behalf of an annuitant who has applied for medical assistance," to wit, an institutionalized individual. This exception does not apply to an annuity that the community spouse purchases.

#### 9-12:1.2.a Irrevocable

The annuity must be irrevocable, meaning that the terms of the annuity cannot be altered.[75]

#### 9-12:1.2.b Non-assignable

The annuity must be non-assignable, meaning that the owner cannot assign the payments of the annuity to another person or entity.[76]

#### 9-12:1.2.c Equal Payments/Actuarially Sound

The payments must be made over a period of time that is actuarially sound according to the life tables published by the United States Social Security Administration's Chief Actuary.[77] In addition, the payments must be made in equal installments.

---

73. 42 U.S.C. § 1396p(c)(1)(G).
74. 42 U.S.C. § 1396p(c)(1)(G)(ii).
75. 42 U.S.C. § 1396p(c)(1)(G)(ii)(I).
76. 42 U.S.C. § 1396p(c)(1)(G)(ii)(I).
77. 42 U.S.C. § 1396p(c)(1)(G)(ii)(II); http://www.ssa.gov/OACT/STATS/table4c6.html (Social Security actuarial tables).

So, if Mrs. Smith purchases an annuity and her life expectancy is 5 years or 60 months, the annuity must pay her back in 60 equal monthly installments or over a period of time shorter than 60 months.

The payments cannot exceed 60 months, since that is Mrs. Smith's actuarial life expectancy.[78] To the extent the payments exceed 60 months, the payments would not be actuarially sound and would result in the imposition of a penalty period for Medicaid eligibility. If the payments are made over a period of time that is less than 60 months, then the payment schedule is actuarially sound.

### 9-12:1.2.d No Deferral or Balloon Payments

The annuity cannot permit deferred payments or a balloon payment.[79] So, the annuity cannot begin paying six months after it is purchased. Or, the annuity cannot pay small amounts for the first four years with larger payment(s) in the fifth year.

### 9-12:1.2.e Named Beneficiary Exception

The federal Medicaid Act requires an annuity to name the state as first remainder beneficiary for the total amount of medical assistance provided to the institutionalized individual in order for the purchase of the annuity to be a purchase for value.[80] An exception is made if the purchaser of the annuity has a spouse or minor or disabled child.[81] If the purchaser of the annuity has a spouse or a minor or disabled child, then the purchaser can name her spouse or minor or disabled child in the first position and the state in the second position without the purchase of the annuity being treated as an uncompensated transfer.

The section of the federal Medicaid Act that addresses the naming of a beneficiary applies to annuities purchased by the community spouse, the institutionalized spouse or an unmarried individual. As discussed above, the same is not true of the other two exceptions: the Qualified Annuity Exception and the Irrevocable

---

78. SMM § 3258.9.B.
79. 42 U.S.C. § 1396p(c)(1)(G)(ii)(III).
80. 42 U.S.C. § 1396p(c)(1)(F)(i).
81. 42 U.S.C. § 1396p(c)(1)(F)(ii).

Annuity Exception; these exceptions only apply to annuities that the institutionalized individual purchases.

But a Qualified Annuity and an Irrevocable Annuity are not "assets" for purposes of the transfer of assets rules. Based upon this fact, an annuity satisfying either the Qualified Annuity Exception or the Irrevocable Annuity Exception does not have to satisfy the Named-Beneficiary Exception. If an annuity is not an "asset" for purposes of the transfer of assets rules, the failure of such an annuity to name a beneficiary cannot result in a transfer of assets penalty period being imposed because the annuity is not even an asset for purposes of the transfer of assets rules.

From a practical standpoint, though, the fact that an institutionalized individual purchasing an annuity that satisfies the Qualified Annuity or Irrevocable Annuity exceptions does not have to satisfy the Named-Beneficiary Exception is of no value. As discussed more fully below, the only annuity that an institutionalized individual would purchase in order to assist with Medicaid planning would pay out in full before that institutionalized individual ever begins receiving Medicaid benefits, so the fact that such an annuity does not have to name the state as remainder beneficiary is of no consequence.

## 9-12:2 Annuity as Resource or Income

Whether the purchase of an annuity is a transfer of an asset or not is a different issue than whether the purchase of the annuity effectively converted a countable resource into a stream of income, though the issues have a significant amount of overlap. Because of the overlap between the two issues, even experienced elder law practitioners confuse these issues.

Sections of the federal Medicaid Act, discussed immediately above, address whether or not the purchase of an annuity is an uncompensated transfer of an asset or, to state it another way, whether or not the purchase of an annuity is a purchase for value.[82] The federal Medicaid Act does not directly address whether or not an annuity is a resource or an income item.

---

82. 42 U.S.C. §§ 1396p(c)(1)(F), (G).

Instead, the analysis of resource versus income can be found in the Code of Federal Regulations and the POMS.[83] In essence, an annuity is treated as a stream of income if the annuity is irrevocable and non-assignable.

If the annuity cannot be sold, then it will not be treated as a resource.[84] If the annuity were a revocable annuity, for instance, then the annuity can be sold and it is a resource.[85]

Obviously, annuities that satisfy the Irrevocable Annuity Exception to the transfer of asset rules are irrevocable and non-assignable. In addition, an annuity that satisfies the Qualified Annuity Exception is non-assignable by definition of the section of the Internal Revenue Code that creates such annuities.[86]

So, even though the Irrevocable Annuity Exception and the Qualified Annuity Exception only apply to annuities that the institutionalized individual purchases, not the community spouse, from a practical standpoint, the requirements of those sections affect an annuity that a community spouse purchases, as well.

The main difference is that an institutionalized spouse's annuity would not be an "asset" for purposes of the transfer of assets rules if it complied with one of those sections whereas a community spouse's annuity would remain an asset for transfer of assets purposes even if it satisfied one of those exceptions.[87] This means that when a community spouse purchases an annuity, he must name the state as a remainder beneficiary in order for the purchase to not be considered a transfer of an asset,[88] even if his annuity is irrevocable/non-assignable or a qualified annuity.[89]

---

83. 20 C.F.R. § 416.1121, POMS SI § 00830.160.

84. *James v. Richmond*, 547 F. 3d 214, 218-219 (3d Cir. 2008), *compare with N.M. v. Div. of Medical Assistance and Health Services*, 405 N.J. Super. 353 (App. Div. 2009) (holding that if an annuity can be sold it is a countable resource).

85. *N.M. v. Div. of Medical Assistance and Health Services*, 405 N.J. Super. 353 (App. Div. 2009).

86. 26 U.S.C. § 408(b).

87. SMM § 3258.9.B. (outlining procedure for whether or not a community spouse's annuity is a transfer of assets).

88. 42 U.S.C. § 1396p(c)(1)(F).

89. 42 U.S.C. § 1396p(c)(1)(G).

## 9-13 COMMUNITY SPOUSE ANNUITY

Given the ability of a properly structured annuity to convert a countable resource into an income stream, planning opportunities for your client arise. These opportunities differ depending on whether your client is a married couple or a single individual.

As discussed in Chapter 8, all the resources of a married couple, with the exception of the CSRA, count against the institutionalized spouse's eligibility for Medicaid benefits.[90] Whatever resources either member of the couple owns, the institutionalized spouse owns for purposes of determining his eligibility for Medicaid benefits. So, it is irrelevant in which spouse's name a resource is owned.

On the other hand, income follows the "name on the check rule." The income of the community spouse does not count against the institutionalized spouse and vice-versa.[91] If the community spouse's name is on the check, then that income is the community spouse's income. If the institutionalized spouse's name is on the check, then that income is the institutionalized spouse's income.

Unlike resources, the income of each spouse is not combined. The income of the institutionalized spouse belongs to the institutionalized spouse, and the income of the community spouse belongs to the community spouse.

A properly structured annuity can effectively convert a resource (for instance, cash) into an income item. A couple can expedite the institutionalized spouse's eligibility for Medicaid benefits by converting resources in excess of the CSRA into income that belongs to the community spouse. By doing this, the couple converts a resource that weighs against the institutionalized spouse's eligibility for Medicaid benefits into an income item that belongs to the community spouse and does not count against the institutionalized spouse's eligibility for Medicaid benefits.

The annuity must be irrevocable and non-assignable and the annuity must name the state in the proper remainder beneficiary position.[92] The annuity must distribute principal and income to the community spouse in a manner that is actuarially sound based

---

90. 42 U.S.C. § 1396r-5(c).
91. 42 U.S.C. § 1396r-5(b).
92. 42 U.S.C. §§ 1396p(c)(1)(F), (G).

upon the life expectancy of the community spouse in order for the purchase of the annuity to be considered a purchase for value. The actuarially sound requirement for a community spouse's annuity comes not from the federal Medicaid Act but from the SMM.[93]

Since the Qualified Annuity Exception and the Irrevocable Annuity Exception apply only to annuities that the institutionalized individual purchases,[94] not the community spouse, it would appear that a community spouse's qualified annuity must pay out in a manner that is actuarially sound in order for the purchase of such an annuity to be considered a purchase for value.

In the absence of the provisions of the federal Medicaid Act that address annuities and the transfer of assets rules (the Qualified Annuity Exception and the Irrevocable Annuity Exception), the SMM provides the only guidance as to when the purchase of an annuity is a purchase for value. The SMM requires an annuity to be actuarially sound in order for the purchase to be considered a purchase for value; accordingly, any annuity that a community spouse purchases must be actuarially sound in order to be a purchase for value, including qualified annuities.

If the community spouse's annuity meets these requirements (irrevocable, non-assignable, actuarially-sound and names the state as remainder beneficiary in the proper position),[95] then the purchase of the annuity will be considered a purchase for value and the annuity will effectively convert a countable resource into a stream of income.

Here is an example of how a community spouse can purchase a Medicaid-compliant annuity (irrevocable, non-assignable, actuarially-sound and names the state as remainder beneficiary in the proper position) and achieve Medicaid eligibility for the institutionalized spouse: Mr. and Mrs. Smith own their home, a car and $200,000 in a checking account. Mrs. Smith is in a nursing home. Mr. Smith is residing at home.

The standard provisions of the Medicaid Act would permit Mr. Smith to retain the home, the car and $100,000 in cash. The county board would expect the Smiths to spend $100,000 on

---

93. SMM § 3258.9.B.

94. 42 U.S.C. § 1396p(c)(1)(G).

95. 42 U.S.C. § 1396p(c)(1)(F), 20 C.F.R. § 416.1121, SMM § 3258.9.B.

Mrs. Smith's nursing home bills and other expenses they may have; however, if Mr. Smith were to spend down a portion of the $100,000 and purchase a Medicaid-complaint annuity with the remainder of the $100,000, then Mrs. Smith will qualify for Medicaid benefit almost immediately.

Mr. Smith could purchase an irrevocable, prepaid funeral for Mrs. Smith (assume $10,000), make some home improvements (assume $5,000) and purchase some household goods (assume $2,000). If Mr. Smith purchases these items after Mrs. Smith entered the nursing home, which is the snapshot date for purposes of calculating Mr. Smith's CSRA,[96] then these spend down items will effectively reduce the excess $100,000 that the Smiths own from $100,000 to $83,000 [$100,000 – ($10,000 + $5,000 + $2,000) = $83,000].

Mr. Smith can now purchase a Medicaid-compliant annuity for $85,000 (a bit more than is required to reduce Mr. Smith's CSRA to an appropriate level for safety's sake), and Mrs. Smith will be eligible for Medicaid benefits as of the first day of the next month. Mr. Smith has effectively converted $85,000 in countable resources (money from his checking account) into a stream of income that belongs to him and does not count against Mrs. Smith's eligibility for Medicaid benefits.

A word of caution: A Medicaid-compliant annuity can effectively convert any amount of excess resources into a stream of income; however, converting large dollar amounts of resources (e.g., $1,000,000 or more) into a stream of income in order to achieve Medicaid eligibility for the institutionalized spouse only invites criticism and attack from the state. There is this myth that millionaires achieve Medicaid eligibility with the assistance of scheming elder law attorneys. This is a myth, but myths become reality if people repeat the myth enough times.

The reality is there wealthy individuals do not seek the assistance of Medicaid benefits. The typical Medicaid planning client has assets between $20,000 and $700,000. Those on the high end of the asset spectrum are typically couples and a large portion of the $700,000 is typically the equity value of the marital home. Wealthy

96. 42 U.S.C. § 1396r-5(c)(1).

individuals can self-insure against the costs of long term care and are frequently unwilling to give up control of their assets.

## 9-14 ANNUITY GIFT PLANNING

An unmarried individual can also plan for Medicaid eligibility using an annuity. In these instances, the annuity is used to remove resources from the applicant's name without gifting the assets and to provide a source of income to the applicant that the applicant can use to pay for his care.

As discussed in Chapter 8, a penalty period will not be imposed against an institutionalized individual who has made an uncompensated asset transfer within the lookback period until such time as the individual would otherwise be receiving institutional level care services but for the imposition of the penalty period.[97] In other words, the applicant must be eligible for Medicaid but for the fact that she made an uncompensated asset transfer during the lookback period.

This means that the applicant must be income-eligible, resource-eligible and health-eligible for institutional level Medicaid services before the county board will begin a penalty period for any asset transfer the applicant made within the lookback period. The applicant must have less than $2,000 in countable resource and her income must be insufficient to pay for her care. (If the applicant were applying for home- and community-based waiver services, she would have to have income below the income cap, which is a gross monthly income of $2,163 in the year 2014. For reasons that will become apparent, using an annuity to achieve eligibility for an HCBS waiver program is unworkable given the income cap.) The applicant must also require hands-on assistance with three activities of daily living, which is the health criteria for Medicaid eligibility.[98]

With an annuity/gift plan, the applicant gifts a portion of her countable resources and purchases an annuity with the remainder of her countable resources. The gift removes a portion of the resources from her name and the purchase of the annuity converts the remainder of the countable resources in excess of the

---

97. 42 U.S.C. § 1396p(c)(1)(D).

98. N.J.A.C. 8:85-1.2.

$2,000 resource limit into a stream of income.[99] After making the gift and purchasing the annuity, the applicant now has countable resources below the $2,000 countable resource limit, making the applicant otherwise eligible for institutional level care services but for the imposition of the penalty period.

This statement assumes that the applicant satisfies the health criteria (i.e., she requires hands-on assistance with three or more activities of daily living) and has income insufficient to pay for her care. Currently, since New Jersey's HCBS waiver programs have an income cap of $2,163, using an annuity that will convert resources into income will typically throw the applicant's income over the income cap. For this reason, annuity/gift planning for HCBS waiver services currently is impracticable.

But when an applicant is applying for institutional level care services in a nursing home, the income cap is not an issue. The Medically Needy Medicaid program,[100] which will pay for the cost of nursing home services, does not have an income cap. As long as the applicant's income is insufficient to pay for her care, she is income-eligible for nursing home care.

Because the applicant's income must remain insufficient to pay for her care after the purchase of the annuity, it is important to leave a deficit between the cost of the applicant's nursing home care and her income from the annuity and other sources. The workings of the annuity/gift planning technique are best explained through an example.

Assume that Mrs. Smith enters a nursing home costing $10,500 per month, or $350 per day. Her income is $1,000 per month from Social Security. Mrs. Smith has $100,000 in a checking account. The checking account is her only resource. Mrs. Smith requires hands-on assistance with at least three activities of daily living.[101]

At this point in time, Mrs. Smith is income eligible for institutional level Medicaid care services in the nursing home, because her income ($1,000 per month) is insufficient to pay for her care ($10,500 per month). She is also health eligible for institutional level Medicaid

---

99. 20 C.F.R. § 416.1121.

100. N.J.A.C. 10:70-1.1 et seq.

101. N.J.A.C. 8:85-1.2.

care services because she requires hands-on assistance with at least three activities of daily living.

It is important that Mrs. Smith obtain a PAS, or PreAdmission Screen, from OCCO because only OCCO can make the assessment that Mrs. Smith satisfies the health criteria for Medicaid eligibility. So, before purchasing an annuity, Mrs. Smith should obtain a PAS.

If Mrs. Smith were simply to gift her remaining countable resources ($100,000) she would be ineligible for Medicaid benefits for 10.5 months ($100,000/$9,500 = 10.5). That number of months would cost Mrs. Smith $100,700 [($10,500 – $1,000 income = $9,500) x 10.5 = $100,700]. Since $100,700 is more than $100,000, gifting $100,000 makes no sense.

On the other hand, if Mrs. Smith were to gift $47,025, she would be ineligible for institutional level care Medicaid services for 5 months ($47,025/$9,500 = 5). If Mrs. Smith uses most of the remaining $52,975 ($100,000 – $47,025 = $52,975) to purchase a Medicaid-compliant annuity that pays her $8,800 per month for six months ($8,800 x 6 = $52,800), Mrs. Smith will now be resource eligible for Medicaid after five months.

Mrs. Smith also will have $8,800 in monthly income ($8,800 + $1,000 = $9,800) to pay for her nursing home care for the next six months. This amount of income is insufficient to pay for her care, so she remains income eligible for Medicaid services, yet her income leaves only a $700 monthly deficit in the cost of her care ($10,500 – $9,800 = $700).

Over the five months that Mrs. Smith is ineligible for Medicaid nursing home services, she will have a deficit of $3,500 ($700 x 5 = $3,500). If the person to whom she transferred the $47,025 returns $3,500 to pay the deficit, Mrs. Smith will have successfully preserved $43,525 ($47,025 – $3,500 = $43,525) of her $100,000.

Of course, the recipient of the gift has no legal obligation to return the $3,500, but a typical gift recipient would be a family member, and in all likelihood, that family member would feel a moral obligation to return the needed assets.

When employing this technique, it is of paramount importance to bear in mind that the applicant must otherwise be receiving institutional level care services but for the imposition of the penalty period. The applicant must be resource eligible, income eligible and health eligible. The making of the gift and purchase of the annuity is what get the applicant below the $2,000 resource limit.

The applicant should obtain a PAS from the OCCO before making the gift and purchasing the annuity, and the applicant must ensure that her income is insufficient to pay for her care after she begins receiving the income from the annuity. As a general guide, it is best to leave a two-day monthly deficit based upon the cost of the nursing home. For instance, if the nursing home costs $350 per day, then the deficit should be at least $700 taking into consideration the income from the annuity and the applicant's other income.

Though technically permissible[102] it is probably ill-advised to take into consideration the client's other medical expenses (such as her health insurance premium) when calculating the amount of her income post-annuity purchase and the cost of her care; only take into consideration the cost of the nursing home.

Finally, the applicant must file an application for institutional level care services with the county board before a penalty period will begin. All of these factors must come together before a penalty period will begin. Even experienced practitioners miss some of these points; it is important that you pay attention to detail when employing the gift/annuity technique.

## 9-15 PROMISSORY NOTE GIFT PLANNING

Theoretically, a promissory note should be able to be used in a manner similar to an annuity. However, unlike an annuity that converts resources to income, a promissory note should convert an available, countable resource into a countable resource with no value on an open market. The effect on the institutionalized individual's eligibility for Medicaid would be the same.

The federal Medicaid Act addresses whether or not the purchase of a promissory note is an uncompensated asset transfer.[103] In order for the purchase to be a purchase for value, the note must have a payment term that is actuarially sound based upon the life expectancy of the lender. The note must pay out in equal monthly installments. Finally, the note must prohibit cancellation upon the

102. Medicaid Communication 95-11.

103. 42 U.S.C. § 1396p(c)(1)(I).

death of the lender. If the note satisfies these three criteria, then the purchase of the note is a purchase for value, not an uncompensated asset transfer.[104]

As with annuities, though, the federal Medicaid Act only addresses whether or not the purchase of the promissory note is a purchase for value. The Medicaid Act does not address whether the promissory note is an income item or a resource item.

In order to determine the resource-income nature of a promissory note, you need to examine the Code of Federal Regulations and the POMS.[105] The promissory note that would be used for Medicaid planning would be an unsecured note; stated otherwise, the note would not have any collateral securing its repayment. As such, the ability of the lender to sell the note on the open market is greatly diminished. For instance, if Mrs. Smith loans her son money pursuant to an unsecured promissory note, few individuals would want to buy this unsecured debt from Mrs. Smith if she ever wanted to sell the note.

Pursuant to the POMS, if the promissory note is negotiable, then the promissory note is a resource;[106] however, because the promissory note is unsecured, the note is a resource with no or little value on the open market. The fact that the note has no value does not impair the nature of the note as a resource.[107] A resource is still a resource even if the resource has no value.

If the note is a resource, then the note cannot, as a matter of law, be treated as a trust-like device, which is the state's main argument against promissory notes.[108] The state takes the position that the promissory note between Mrs. Smith and her son is merely a trust-like device through which her son is holding her money and returning the money to her pursuant to the terms of the promissory note. But a promissory note that is a resource, even a resource with no value, cannot be treated as a trust-like device.

Mrs. Smith has now successfully converted her available, countable resources (cash) into an unavailable, countable resource

---

104. 42 U.S.C. § 1396p(c)(1)(I).
105. 20 C.F.R. § 416.1201, POMS SI § 01120.220.
106. POMS SI § 01120.220.
107. POMS SI § 01110.100.B.
108. POMS SI § 01120.201.G.1.

(the promissory note) a resource with no cash value since there is little to no market for the unsecured debt, effectively removing the resources used to purchase the promissory note §from her name. While the promissory note is still a resource, the fact that it is a resource with no value means that it does not count against the $2,000 resource eligibility criterion.

Once you have a promissory note that can accomplish the removal of resources from Mrs. Smith's name without gifting those resources, you have a device (the promissory note) that can work in a manner very similar to an annuity. A community spouse or an unmarried individual can use the promissory note in a manner that is similar to how an annuity would be used.

The bad news is that although promissory notes are widely used in some jurisdictions, such as New York, the federal court for the district of New Jersey has stood behind the state of New Jersey's argument that a promissory note can be treated as a trust-like device, even if that promissory note is negotiable.[109] For now, promissory notes cannot be used as a planning method in New Jersey.

## 9-16 CAREGIVER AGREEMENTS

Family members and friends often provide care to elderly individuals. The care that a family member provides may be part-time or full-time. Caring for an elderly person is no easy task. The work is difficult and draining, both physically and emotionally.

A client may ask if they can be compensated for the care that she provides to her family member. For instance, a daughter might have quit her job just to provide necessary care to her mother that enables the mother to reside at home as opposed to in a nursing home.

In order for the daughter to be compensated for the care that she provides to her mother, a written caregiver agreement must be in place regarding the daughter's compensation for services before the mother can compensate the daughter.[110] The daughter cannot be compensated for any services she provides to the mother

---

109. *Sable v. Velez*, 437 Fed. Appx. 73 (3d Cir. 2011).

110. N.J.A.C. 10:71-4.10(b)(6)(ii).

if those services pre-date the drafting and signing of a caregiver agreement.

The compensation called for under the agreement must be at prevailing rates for the location in which those services are provided. In other words, the rate of compensation must be based upon what others performing the same work in the same area are paid.

These standards are found in New Jersey's regulations governing its Medicaid program.[111] The unwritten policies of DMAHS are far more fraught with issues than DMAHS's written regulations.

The unwritten policy of DMAHS requires the caregiver to maintain detailed records of the time spent providing care to the family member and the nature of the care that was provided. The person receiving the care must issue an IRS form 1099 to the caregiver for the payments the caregiver received during any given year.

Most significantly, a family caregiver cannot receive the prevailing rate that others similarly situated in that area receive. Instead, a related caregiver can only receive compensation at unnaturally low rates, such as $9 or $10 an hour.

Even if the person receiving the care complies with all of these unwritten procedures, the county board of social services may still challenge compensation provided to a family member pursuant to a written caregiver agreement.

## 9-17 COMPENSATION OF POWER OF ATTORNEY AGENT

A financial power of attorney agent can be compensated for his services if the power of attorney document provides for compensation or if a court awards compensation for the services that the agent performs on behalf of the principal.[112] The power of attorney agent, often a family member of the principal, frequently performs a significant amount of work for his principal.

By having the principal compensate the agent for the services the agent performs on behalf of the principal, assets can be transferred to the agent for value received.

---

111. N.J.A.C. 10:71-4.10(b)(6)(ii).

112. N.J.S.A. 46:2B-8.12.

## 9-18 PLANNING FOR ELIGIBILITY UNDER THE GO PROGRAM

Individuals who are residing at home and in assisted living residences can qualify for Medicaid HCBS waiver services.[113] HCBS waiver programs provided institutional level care services at home or in an assisted living residence. New Jersey's primary HCBS waiver program is called Global Options or GO.[114]

The countable resource limit for the GO program is $2,000. The GO program also has an income cap, which is 300% of the SSI federal benefit rate. In 2014, the income cap is $2,163. An institutionalized individual seeking to qualify for GO benefits must have a gross monthly income no greater than $2,163.[115]

### 9-18:1 Calculating the Cost of Care

Let's assume that Mr. Smith is residing at home with a gross monthly income of $2,000. Let's further assume that his living expenses and long term care expenses (a home health aide he employs) are $6,000. Based upon these figures, Mr. Smith has a monthly deficit of $4,000 ($6,000 – $2,000 = $4,000).

Alternatively, assume that Mr. Smith resides in an assisted living residence costing $7,000. His monthly deficit in the assisted living residence would be $5,000 ($7,000 – $2,000 = $5,000).

Because the monthly deficit in either of these scenarios is less than the divisor figure that the State uses to calculate penalty periods for uncompensated transfers that occur within the loookback period ($9,535), assets can be preserved by making a wholesale asset transfer.

### 9-18:2 Calculating the Penalty Period

Assume Mr. Smith resides in the assisted living residence specified above. His monthly deficit is $5,000. Mr. Smith has $100,000 in resources.

If Mr. Smith were to transfer $99,000 of his resources, he would be resource-eligible for Medicaid. Mr. Smith is also income eligible for the GO program, because his income is below the $2,163 income

---

113. 42 U.S.C. § 1396n(d).

114. N.J.A.C. 10:71-1.1.

115. Medicaid Communication 14-01.

cap. Finally, assume that Mr. Smith requires hands-on assistance with three activities of daily living.

If Mr. Smith were to transfer the $99,000 and apply for the GO program, the county board would assess a 10.5 month penalty period ($99,000/$9,535 = 10.5). The cost of Mr. Smith's care and living expenses for the next 11 months will be $55,000 ($5,000 x 11 = $55,000).

By making this transfer, Mr. Smith preserves $44,000 ($99,000 – $55,000 = $44,000) in resources. In order to accomplish this, Mr. Smith must apply for the GO program twice—once just to be denied because he made an uncompensated asset transfer and would otherwise have been receiving institutional level care service but for the imposition of the penalty period and once again around the time that the penalty period is expiring.

## 9-19 WILL OF COMMUNITY SPOUSE

Whenever planning for the Medicaid eligibility of a married individual, the countable and non-countable resources of the couple get transferred into the name of the community spouse individually. The home, the car, the personal goods and household effects and the CSRA all get transferred into the name of the community spouse individually.

Although the institutionalized spouse is typically sicklier than the community spouse, there is always the chance that the community spouse may predecease the institutionalized spouse. For this reason, it is advisable to have the community spouse draft a Will that devises the smallest fraction of his estate to the institutionalized spouse necessary to fulfill her elective share claim.[116]

If the community spouse were to predecease the institutionalized spouse, the institutionalized spouse would receive one-third of the community spouse's estate. The remainder of the community spouse's estate would pass to the children. Having a Will such as this minimizes the financial impact of the community spouse's death on the institutionalized spouse's eligibility for Medicaid.

---

116. N.J.S.A. 3B:8-1 et seq.

# Chapter 10

# Estate Administration

## 10-1 THE COUNTY SURROGATE

The county surrogate is an elected position that has a five-year term.[1] There are 21 counties in the state of New Jersey and there are 21 county surrogates in the state of New Jersey.

The surrogate's office for a given county serves as the Clerk of the Superior Court of New Jersey, Probate Part;[2] accordingly, filings for the probate part are to be filed with the appropriate surrogate's office.

The surrogate's office is also known as the Surrogate's Court.[3] As the clerk of the probate part, the Surrogate's Court reviews and files actions involving adoption, declaration of death, appointment of a guardian for an incapacitated or minor person, trusteeship, conservatorship and fiduciary's accountings.[4]

The surrogate of a given county is also a judge of the Surrogate's Court.[5] In some counties, when you file an action involving one of the matters that the surrogate reviews and files with the Superior Court, the surrogate, not the judge of the probate part, will sign the order to show cause. Whether the surrogate signs the order to show cause or the probate judge signs the order is a matter of county preference, so you will need to check with the local surrogate to determine how the surrogate and the judge handle such matters.

---

1. N.J.S.A. 2B:14-1.
2. N.J. Const., Art. XI, Sec. VI(c), *R.* 1:34-2.
3. N.J.S.A. 2B:14-1.
4. N.J.S.A. 2B:14-6.
5. N.J.S.A. 2B:14-1.

Aside from his duties as a deputy clerk of the Superior Court, the surrogate is responsible for submitting the last will and testament of a decedent to probate, for appointing an executor or administrator of a decedent's estate, for appointing certain trustees, for overseeing the proper administration of estates and for overseeing the proper administration of a guardianship of minor or disabled individuals.[6]

## 10-2 WHAT IS PROBATE

Many clients will come to you and tell you that they want to avoid probate at all costs, but most of these clients are confusing the concept of submitting a Will to probate with the concept of estate administration. Submitting a Will to probate involves lodging the original last will and testament of the decedent with the surrogate, filling out a one-page estate questionnaire and paying a filing fee, which averages around $150.00 In short, the process of submitting a Will to probate in New Jersey is extremely simple, inexpensive and very quick, taking about thirty minutes to accomplish.

This is not the case in many other states. Many states, such as Florida and California, have probate processes that are far more involved than the probate process in New Jersey. After the executor submits a Will to probate in New Jersey, he may never have contact with the surrogate's office again.

Estate administration is the process of submitting the Will to probate, marshalling/gathering the assets of the estate, paying the creditors of the estate, filing the appropriate tax returns, preparing an executor's accounting and distributing the estate's assets to the beneficiaries. Submitting a Will to probate is only one part of estate administration. In fact, it is probably the easiest part of estate administration and the part that takes the least amount of time.

For this reason, when a client says they want to avoid probate, they typically do not understand the process of estate administration, so it is your job to educate the client about the process of estate administration.

The primary goal of having a Will admitted to probate is to have the surrogate formally appointed the individual who has been

---

[6] Each of the surrogates maintains his/her own website. Here is the Monmouth County Surrogate's website. http://www.visitmonmouth.com/page.aspx?ID=130.

nominated to be the executor in the last will and testament of the decedent as executor.[7] The surrogate does this by issuing Letters of Executorship and Executor Short Certificates to the executor.

An executor will receive one Letter of Executorship and can obtain as many Executor Short Certificates as he desires. The standard probate package comes with two Executor Short Certificates; additional short certificates can be obtained by paying a fee of $5.00 per short certificate requested.

A short certificate is a document that the surrogate signs and seals. The executor will provide an original short certificate to individuals or entities, such as banks, to prove he is the executor; accordingly, the executor may wish to obtain as many short certificates as there are financial institutions at which the decedent held accounts. The executor can always obtain additional short certificates if more are needed for the $5.00 fee per certificate.

### 10-2:1 The Original Will

An individual who dies having a last will and testament is said to have died testate. An individual dying without a Will is said to have died intestate. When an individual dies testate, his Will controls how his property devolves or passes. When an individual dies intestate, the intestate succession statute[8] governs how the property of the decedent devolves.

In order to admit the last will and testament of a decedent to probate, the executor nominated in the Will needs the original last will and testament. Only the original Will can be admitted to probate in common form.

Common form probate is when the surrogate admits the Will to probate without involving a judge of the Superior Court of New Jersey, Probate Part. A Will admitted to probate in common form is submitted on an application to the surrogate.

If the nominated executor cannot locate the original Will, then he will need to file an order to show cause in the Superior Court of New Jersey, Probate Part, in an attempt to admit a copy of the Will to probate. The surrogate will not admit a copy of the Will to

---

7. N.J.S.A. 3B:3-18.

8. N.J.S.A. 3B:5-1. et seq.

probate on application; only a superior court judge can admit a copy of a Will to probate.[9]

Whenever a nominated executor seeks to admit a copy of the Will to probate, there is doubt as to whether or not the judge will admit the Will. For instance, if an interested party objects to the admission of the copy of the Will to probate, perhaps because the copy of the Will disinherits a child, it is less likely that a judge will admit the copy to probate.

Each case must be judged on its own merit, though, and no universal statement can be made as to whether or not a copy of a Will can be admitted to probate. The only universal statements that can be made are that it is possible to admit a copy of a Will to probate and that admitting a copy of a Will to probate costs far more money and time than admitting the original Will to probate. For this reason, the client should be advised to maintain the original Will in a safe location.

## 10-2:2 The Original Death Certificate

In order to have the last will and testament admitted to probate, the executor nominated in the Will needs to present the original death certificate to the surrogate (along with the original Will).[10] Typically, the funeral director obtains multiple originals of the death certificate for the executor. Originals can also be obtained from the department of vital statistics for the town in which the decedent died or the state Office of Vital Statistics and Registry in Trenton.

## 10-2:3 The Estate Information Sheet

Most surrogates have the nominated executor complete an estate information sheet.[11] The information sheet asks the executor various questions about the decedent and the decedent's estate, such as the decedent's name, address, next of kin, marital status, etc. Most individuals who have been nominated to serve as the executor of an estate would know the answers to the surrogate's questions off the top of their heads.

---

9. N.J. Ct. R. 4:82.
10. N.J. Ct. R. 4:80-1(b).
11. N.J. Ct. R. 4:80-1(a).

### 10-2:4 Timeframe to Submit a Will to Probate

A Will cannot be admitted to probate until 10 days after the decedent has died.[12] The surrogate will accept the paperwork prior to the expiration of the ten-day period but will not admit the Will to probate until after the expiration of the ten-day period.

## 10-3 WHAT IF THERE IS NO WILL

When an individual dies without a last will and testament, he is said to have died intestate. When an individual dies intestate, the intestate succession statute governs how his property devolves.[13]

A person seeking to be nominated as the administrator of an intestate estate is requesting that the surrogate issue Letters of Administration and Administrator Short Certificates to him.

### 10-3:1 Who Can Be Administrator

If a decedent failed to execute a last will and testament, then in all likelihood, he also failed to nominate the executor of his estate. (Technically, an individual could execute a document simply nominating the executor of his estate, not devising any of his assets, and this document would be a Will, but this would be a very rare occurrence.[14]) Since the decedent failed to nominate an executor, the surrogate must appoint an administrator of his intestate estate.

An administrator performs all of the same functions as an executor with one exception, an administrator does not ask the surrogate to admit the decedent's Will to probate because no Will exists. Other than that one small exception, the administrator performs all of the same functions as an executor.[15]

The spouse or domestic partner of the decedent is given top priority to be appointed the administrator of the estate of an intestate decedent.[16] If there is no spouse or if the spouse will not accept letters of administration, then the heirs of the decedent are given priority. If no heirs exist or will accept the letters of administration,

---

12. N.J.S.A. 3B:3-22.

13. N.J.S.A. 3B:5-1. et seq.

14. N.J.S.A. 3B:1-2 (definition of "Will").

15. An executor and an administrator are both known as a "personal representative of the estate."

16. N.J.S.A. 3B:10-2.

then any fit person can be appointed as administrator of an intestate's estate.

As between two people with equal priority, New Jersey state residents are granted priority over non-residents as to the grant of letters of administration, though this rule can be disregarded for cause.[17]

## 10-3:2 The Estate Information Sheet

The person seeking to be appointed as administrator of the intestate's estate must complete an estate information sheet, the same as an executor.[18] The questions are the same as those that the executor must answer; however, one question takes on more importance when dealing with an intestate estate.

Most estate information sheets ask for a value of the estate's assets.[19] When a decedent dies testate, the value of the estate is irrelevant in the vast majority of cases because most every Will waives the requirement that the executor post a probate bond.[20] In fact, it would probably be malpractice for an attorney to draft a Will for an individual that failed to waive the requirement that the executor post a bond.

When an individual dies intestate, he failed to sign a Will and, therefore, failed to nominate an executor and failed to waive the requirement of the probate bond. For this reason, most administrator's have to post a bond to secure their faithful performance of the duties and obligations of the administrator.[21]

The value of the bond is typically proportionate to the value of the estate. For this reason, the questions on the information sheet that inquire as to the value of the estate bear far more importance when the decedent died intestate. Some surrogates require very specific information about the estate's value before they will set the probate bond and issue letters of administration.

---

17. N.J. Ct. R. 4:80-5.

18. N.J. Ct. R. 4:80-1(a).

19. This question is not a requirement of N.J. Ct. R. 4:80-1(a); however, most of the surrogates' estate information sheets ask this question.

20. N.J.S.A. 3B:15-1.

21. N.J.S.A. 3B:15-1(a).

### 10-3:3 The Original Death Certificate

As with an executor, an individual seeking to be appointed as administrator of an intestate's estate must present the original death certificate to the surrogate.[22] In most instances, the funeral director will obtain the death certificate for the administrator or for the decedent's family members.

### 10-3:4 Timeframe to Appoint an Administrator

The surrogate will not issues letters of administration until five days after the decedent's death.[23]

## 10-4 NOTICE OF PROBATE

After the surrogate has issued letters of executorship or letters of administration to an individual, the executor/administrator[24] must serve a notice of probate on the interested parties, which would include the next of kin of the decedent and the beneficiaries named in his Will.[25] The notice of probate is a simple document that lets the interested parties know that a certain individual has been appointed as the personal representative of the estate, as the case may be, and that a Will, if applicable, has been admitted to probate.

The notice of probate must also inform the interested parties that they can request the personal representative to provide them with a copy of the decedent's last will and testament, if an interested party requests the Will. Obviously, this only applies in instances in which the decedent died testate, as an intestate estate would have no Will to provide to the interested parties.

Because the interested parties can always request a copy of the Will and because most any interested party would be interested in the terms of the Will, it is advisable to simply provide a copy of the Will to the interested parties along with the notice of probate.

---

22. N.J. Ct. R. 4:80-1(b).

23. N.J.S.A. 3B:5-1 (stating that an individual who fails to survive the decedent by five days is deemed to have predeceased the decedent).

24. The term "personal representative" will be used to refer to either an executor or administrator.

25. N.J. Ct. R. 4:80-6.

## 10-5 MARSHALLING THE ASSETS

Once the surrogate has formally appointed a personal representative the executor or administrator of the estate must marshal the assets of the estate.[26] Marshalling the assets is simply a more formal way of saying that the personal representative must collect the assets of the estate.

The personal representative may decide to open one estate account and place all of the assets of the estate into that account or he may open multiple estate accounts. Because of the limits with the Federal Deposit Insurance Corporation,[27] it is advisable that a personal representative refrain from depositing too much of the estate's assets in one place.

A statute governing the distribution of an estate's assets favors distributions in-kind.[28] In other words, if the decedent died owning stock in Exxon, a statute governing the distribution of estates requires the personal representative to distribute the Exxon stock to the beneficiaries where practicable.

With many estates, the beneficiaries want cash, not in-kind distributions. In these cases, the personal representative can marshal and liquidate the assets of the estate. Having cash, as opposed to various non-liquid assets, can be helpful to the personal representative who must pay various debts of the estate.

## 10-6 OBTAINING AN EIN

In order to open an estate account, a personal representative will need a tax identification number for the estate. A tax identification number (TIN) is also called an employer identification number (EIN).[29]

Since the decedent has died, his Social Security number can no longer be used for income his assets receive after the date of his death, for instance, dividends and interest. The estate must have its own tax number to use to report income the estate receives, such as dividend income or interest income.

---

26. N.J.S.A. 3B:10-29.

27. Current limit is $250,000 per account ownership category. http://www.fdic.gov/deposit/deposits/insured/basics.html.

28. N.J.S.A. 3B:23-1.

29. http://www.irs.gov/Businesses/Small-Businesses-%26-Self-Employed/Employer-ID-Numbers-EINs.

The personal representative would use the estate's EIN when opening an account in the name of the estate.

## 10-7 OPENING AN ESTATE ACCOUNT

Once the personal representative has admitted the Will to probate and once the personal representative has obtained an EIN for the estate, he can open an account or multiple accounts in the name of the estate.

## 10-8 PROVIDING AN INVENTORY OF ASSETS

A personal representative may, but is not required to, file an inventory of the assets of the estate.[30] The court can compel a personal representative to file an inventory, but with limited exception, the court cannot compel an inventory from the personal representative until three months have passed since the surrogate has appointed the personal representative.

An inventory is a rather simple document that merely provides a brief description and a value for the assets of the estate that have come into the hands of the personal representative or of which the personal representative is aware.

## 10-9 NOTICE TO CREDITORS

A personal representative is obligated to pay the legitimate debts of the estate.[31] Because a personal representative needs to administer the estate with reasonable promptness,[32] the Probate Code gives creditors nine months following the death of the decedent to present a claim to the personal representative.[33]

If the personal representative waits the statutory nine month period of time before making distributions to the beneficiaries, he cannot be held liable for the non-payment of the debt based upon his distributing the assets to the beneficiaries in a premature manner. For instance, if the personal representative waits nine-months without a certain creditor presenting a claim, then the personal representative distributes all the assets of the estate to

---

30. N.J.S.A. 3B:16-2.
31. N.J.S.A. 3B:22-10 et seq.
32. N.J.S.A. 3B:10-23.
33. N.J.S.A. 3B:22-4.

the beneficiaries, the creditor could not file an action against the personal representative claiming the personal representative failed to pay the creditor on his claim.

Prior to a revision to the Probate Code that took effect in 2005, a personal representative was responsible for publishing a notice to creditors in a local paper giving creditors notice that they were required to present their claims to the personal representative.[34] Now, no notice is required, but the creditor is still required to present his claim to the personal representative within the statutory nine-month period of time.

A creditor must provide his claim to the personal representative under oath.[35] If a creditor fails to notify the personal representative, the personal representative cannot be held personally liable for making a distribution to a beneficiary of the estate, thereby depriving the estate of sufficient assets to pay the debt. However, just because the nine-month period of time has lapsed does not mean that the creditor's debt is void.

The creditor can still sue on his claim; the creditor simply cannot hold the personal representative liable for distributing the assets of the estate in a premature manner. Most claims against an estate are contractual claims that have a six-year statute of limitations associated with the claim.[36] The creditor will now have to sue the beneficiary for a return of the assets, asserting a right to a return of the distribution pursuant to the release and refunding bond that the beneficiary signed, which is discussed below.

## 10-10 PAYING THE DEBTS OF THE ESTATE

There is a specific order in which the debts of the estate must be paid.[37] In most instances, the estate is solvent, meaning it has sufficient assets with which to pay all of its debts, so the order in which the debts are paid is not relevant (except, of course, if you are a creditor who would want his debt paid with the utmost priority).

With an insolvent estate, the order in which the debts are paid is highly relevant because an insolvent estate has insufficient assets

34. N.J. Ct. R. 4:80-8 [deleted].
35. N.J.S.A. 3B:22-4.
36. N.J.S.A. 2A:14-1.
37. N.J.S.A. 3B:22-2.

with which to pay all of its debts. The order in which the personal representative chooses to pay the debts may be the difference between a creditor receiving payment of his debt or partial payment of his debts and no payment at all.

The Probate Code contains a priority in which debts must be paid if the estate is insolvent. That order is specified below. When the estate is insolvent, the personal representative should file an order to show cause and verified complaint to have the estate declared to be insolvent and to approve his proposed creditor payment plan.[38] Notice of the action should be provided to all of the interested parties, which would include the creditors.

### 10-10:1 Funeral Expenses

The debt with the highest priority is reasonable funeral expenses.[39] This creditor is tempered by the word "reasonable," but few people spend extravagantly on a funeral. In most cases, the entirety of the funeral bill is paid before all other debts.

### 10-10:2 Administration Expenses

Costs and expenses of administration are paid next.[40] This would include the personal representative's commission, all expenses the personal representative incurs (such as the cost of submitting the Will to probate), legal fees and accounting fees.

### 10-10:3 Office of the Public Guardian

In those cases in which the decedent had the Office of the Public Guardian for Elderly Adults serving as his guardian during his life, the Public Guardian's fees get paid in the next order of priority.[41]

### 10-10:4 Debts with Preference Under Federal and State Law; Medicaid Lien

The next priority of debts are those with preference under federal and state law.[42] Examples of these debts would income federal or

---

38. N.J. Ct. R. 4:91-1 et seq.
39. N.J.S.A. 3B:22-2(a).
40. N.J.S.A. 3B:22-2(b).
41. N.J.S.A. 3B:22-2(c).
42. N.J.S.A. 3B:22-2(d).

state income tax and the Medicaid lien for those decedents who received Medicaid benefits during their life. From a practical standpoint, even if the Internal Revenue Service is put on notice of the action to declare the estate insolvent, the IRS probably will continue to attempt to collect any debt owed to it.

### 10-10:5 Debts Associated with the Last Illness

Debts associated with the last illness including the fees of persons attending to the decedent are paid next.[43] This would include a home health aide if the aide's services were associated with the last illness of the decedent.

### 10-10:6 Judgments

The next order of priority is reserved for judgments that were entered against the decedent in the order in which the judgments were entered.[44]

### 10-10:7 All Other Debts

The last order of priority is reserved for all other debts. Any debts not covered above are lumped into this catch-all category.[45]

### 10-10:8 Action to Declare the Estate Insolvent

If the estate is insolvent, the personal representative can file an action to have the estate declared insolvent any time after nine months following the date of the decedent's death. The personal representative should file an order to show cause supported by a verified complaint.[46] The complaint and supporting documents are filed with the appropriate surrogate as the deputy clerk of the Superior Court, Probate Part.

The complaint should outline the assets and income of the estate and the known debts of the estate. The complaint should also contain a proposed payment plan.

---

43. N.J.S.A. 3B:22-2(e).
44. N.J.S.A. 3B:22-2(f).
45. N.J.S.A. 3B:22-2(g).
46. *R.* 4:91-1 et seq.

The payment plan would adhere to the order of priority specified above. Debts within the same category are paid proportionately if the estate's assets are insufficient to pay all debts within a given category.[47]

Notice of the action should be provided to all interested parties, which would include the creditors. Notice also should be published in order to provide notice to unknown creditors, if any.

## 10-11 FEDERAL ESTATE TAX

The federal estate tax is a tax imposed upon a decedent's estate based upon the gross value of the estate.[48] The gross estate includes most assets that the decedent died owning plus adjusted taxable gifts.

"Adjusted taxable gifts" are gifts that the decedent made during his lifetime that exceeded the annual exclusion amount in a given year;[49] for instance, in 2014, the annual gift exclusion is $14,000 per person, so if the decedent made a $20,000 gift to one person, then $6,000 of that gift would be brought back into his gross estate for purposes of calculating the federal estate tax.[50]

If the gross estate exceeds $5,340,000 in value (2014 figure),[51] then the estate must file a federal estate tax return. The appropriate Internal Revenue Service form for filing a federal estate tax return is a Form 706.[52] The $5,340,000 figure is known as the "exemption equivalent" because the amount each estate receives as a credit against the federal estate tax is equivalent to $5,340,000.

New Jersey is a state that is frequently one of the top five states for the number of residents who are millionaires, so there certainly are more people in New Jersey who have federal estate tax issues than in most of the other states. With that said, for most elder law practitioners, a client with a gross estate that exceeds $5,340,000 is still a rare client.

---

47. N.J.S.A. 3B:22-2.

48. 26 U.S.C. §§ 2001 et seq.

49. 26 U.S.C. § 2503(b).

50. 26 U.S.C. § 2511.

51. 26 U.S.C. § 2010, http://www.irs.gov/uac/Newsroom/In-2014,-Various-Tax-Benefits-Increase-Due-to-Inflation-Adjustments.

52. http://www.irs.gov/pub/irs-pdf/f706.pdf.

### 10-11:1 What Is Included in the Gross Estate

The "gross estate" includes all property in which the decedent had an interest at the time of his death.[53] The gross proceeds from a life insurance policy that the decedent owned and that insured his life would be included in his estate.

Many clients, even clients who are quite well off, tend to believe that the gross estate does not include non-probate assets, such as assets passing by beneficiary designation. This is incorrect. Non-probate assets are included in the gross estate.

Property that is held jointly with an individual other than the decedent's spouse is included entirely in the decedent's estate unless the surviving joint owner can prove that she contributed to the asset and the amount of her contribution.[54] For instance, a joint brokerage accounts that a brother and sister own would be wholly included in the brother's estate unless the sister could prove that she made contributions to the account and the amount of those contributions.

When a husband and wife own an account and one of them dies, one-half the value of the account is included in the estate of the first-to-die spouse.[55] The surviving spouse does not have to prove contribution or the amount of the contribution.

### 10-11:2 Deductions

Without going into great detail, certain deductions from the gross estate are permitted before the calculation of the federal estate tax.[56] Examples of common deductions would be the following: funeral expenses, unpaid medical bills, reasonable accountant's fees, reasonable lawyer's fees, accrued and unpaid real estate taxes, accrued and unpaid utility bills and the personal representative's commission.

If the gross estate exceeds $5,340,000, then a federal estate tax return must be filed; however, a federal estate tax is owed only

---

53. 26 U.S.C. § 2031 et seq.
54. 26 U.S.C. § 2040.
55. 26 U.S.C. § 2040(b).
56. 26 U.S.C. §§ 2053, 2054.

if the taxable estate[57] (gross estate less deductions) exceeds the $5,340,000 threshold.[58]

### 10-11:3 Rate of Tax

The tax rate on the amount of the net estate that exceeds the federal exemption equivalent is 40%.

### 10-11:4 When to Pay and File a Federal Estate Tax Return

If the gross estate exceeds the exemption equivalent ($5,340,000 in 2014), then the personal representative must file a federal estate tax return within nine months of the date of the decedent's death.[59] Payment of the federal estate tax is due within nine months of the decedent's death.

## 10-12 NEW JERSEY ESTATE TAX

The state of New Jersey imposes an estate tax on estates that exceed $675,000 in value.[60] The New Jersey estate tax is based upon the federal estate tax law as that law existed on December 31, 2001.[61]

On December 31, 2001, the federal exemption equivalent against federal estate tax was $675,000; accordingly, the New Jersey exemption equivalent against the New Jersey estate tax is $675,000.

If the gross estate exceeds $675,000, then a New Jersey estate tax return must be filed. As with the federal estate tax, the "gross estate" includes all property in which the decedent had an interest at the time of death plus adjusted taxable gifts.

### 10-12:1 What Is Included in the Gross Estate?

The "gross estate" includes all property in which the decedent had an interest at the time of his death.[62] The gross proceeds from

---

57. 26 U.S.C. § 2106.

58. http://www.irs.gov/uac/Newsroom/In-2014,-Various-Tax-Benefits-Increase-Due-to-Inflation-Adjustments.

59. http://www.irs.gov/pub/irs-pdf/i709.pdf.

60. N.J.S.A. 54:38-1 et seq.; N.J.A.C. 18:26-3A.1 et seq.

61. N.J.A.C. 18:26-3A.1., 18:26-3A.2.

62. 26 U.S.C. §§ 2031 et seq.

a life insurance policy that the decedent owned and that insured his life would be included in his estate.

Many clients, even clients who are quite well off, tend to believe that the gross estate does not include non-probate assets, such as assets passing by beneficiary designation. This is incorrect. Non-probate assets are included in the gross estate.

Property that is held jointly with an individual other than the decedent's spouse is included entirely in the decedent's estate unless the surviving joint owner can prove that she contributed to the asset and the amount of her contribution.[63] For instance, a joint brokerage accounts that a brother and sister own would be wholly included in the brother's estate unless the sister could prove that she made contributions to the account and the amount of those contributions.

When a husband and wife own an account and one of them dies, one-half the value of the account is included in the estate of the first-to-die spouse.[64] The surviving spouse does not have to prove contribution or the amount of the contribution.

### 10-12:2 Deductions

As with the federal estate tax, certain deductions from the gross estate are permitted before the calculation of the New Jersey estate tax.[65] Examples of common deductions would be the following: funeral expenses, unpaid medical bills, reasonable accountant's fees, reasonable lawyer's fees, accrued and unpaid real estate taxes, accrued and unpaid utility bills and the personal representative's commission.

If the gross estate exceeds $675,000, then a New Jersey estate tax return must be filed; however, a New Jersey estate tax is owed only if the taxable estate[66] (gross estate less deductions) exceeds the $675,000 threshold.

---

63. 26 U.S.C. § 2040.
64. 26 U.S.C. § 2040(b).
65. 26 U.S.C. §§ 2053, 2054.
66. 26 U.S.C. § 2106.

## 10-12:3 How to File the Return

There are two methods for filing the New Jersey estate tax return: the 706 Method and the Simplified Method.[67] The 706 Method must be used in those instances where the estate was required to file a federal estate tax return.[68] For those estates that are not required to file a federal estate tax return, the personal representative can file using either the 706 Method or the Simplified Method.[69]

### 10-12:3.1 The 706 Method

The 706 Method requires the filing of a New Jersey form IT-Estate and a 2001 federal IRS form 706, completed in accordance with the federal estate tax law as it existed on December 31, 2001.[70] If the estate filed a federal estate tax return, the personal representative must include a copy of the federal estate tax return with the New Jersey filing.

If the estate filed a federal estate tax return, any elections that the personal representative made on the federal estate tax return must also be made on the New Jersey estate tax return. The personal representative cannot make different elections on the federal and state estate tax returns. For instance, if the personal representative made a marital deduction election on the federal estate tax return—a marital deduction election would exempt the property passing to the surviving spouse from the federal estate tax—then the personal representative must make that election on the New Jersey estate tax return.

### 10-12:3.2 The Simplified Method

The Simplified Method can be used only for those estates that are not required to file a federal estate tax return.[71] The estate must file a New Jersey form IT-Estate and a New Jersey Inheritance Tax Return, Form IT-R. The IT-R form must be completed in accordance with the laws governing the New Jersey Inheritance Tax as it existed on December 31, 2001.

---

67. N.J.A.C. 18:26-3A.2.
68. N.J.A.C. 18:26-3A.2(a)(2).
69. http://www.state.nj.us/treasury/taxation/revesttax.shtml.
70. N.J.A.C. 18:26-3A.2(a)(1).
71. N.J.A.C. 18:26-3A.2(a)(2).

According to the New Jersey Division of Taxation, the New Jersey estate tax is calculated as follows when using the Simplified Method:[72]

- The taxable value of the estate using the Simplified Tax System method is the net estate as determined and reflected on line 7 of the New Jersey inheritance tax return (Form IT-R) adjusted to reflect:
    - Real and tangible personal property located outside of New Jersey; plus
    - The proceeds of life insurance on the decedent's life owned by the decedent (or transferred within three (3) years of his/her death) paid to any beneficiary other than the estate, executor or administrator; plus
    - All transfers made by the decedent within three years of death not included in the inheritance tax net estate; plus
    - In the event that the decedent was a surviving spouse or a civil union partner and received qualified terminable interest property (QTIP) from the predeceased spouse or civil union partner for which a marital deduction was elected for Federal and/or New Jersey purposes, the full value of the QTIP property; plus
    - Any other property includable in the Federal gross estate under the provisions of the Federal Internal Revenue Code in effect on December 31, 2001; less
    - Property passing outright to the decedent's surviving spouse or civil union partner who died on or after February 19, 2007 provided he/she was a U.S. citizen on the decedent's date of death. This deduction does not include QTIP (Qualified Terminable Interest Property)

72. N.J.A.C. 18:26-3A.3.

or similar property. QTIP property is property that passes from the decedent and in which the surviving spouse or civil union partner has a qualifying income interest for life. The surviving spouse or civil union partner has a qualifying income interest for life if he/she is entitled to all or a specific portion of the income from the property payable annually or at more frequent intervals, or has a usufruct interest in the property (right to enjoy the property) for life, and during the surviving spouse's or civil union partner's lifetime no person has a power to appoint any part of the property to any person other than the surviving spouse or civil union partner. Additionally, the surviving spouse or civil union partner must be a citizen of the United States on the decedent's date of death. If QTIP property or the surviving spouse's or civil union partner's citizenship is a significant factor, consideration should be given to the use of the Form 706 method of filing; less

- Property passing for charitable purposes.

## 10-12:4 When to File a New Jersey Estate Tax Return

If the 706 Method is used, the estate must file the tax return within nine months plus 30 days of the decedent's death; however, in all cases, the New Jersey estate tax is due within nine months of the decedent's death.[73]

If the simplified method is used, the estate must file the tax return within nine months of the decedent's death. As stated above, in all cases, the tax is due within nine months of the decedent's death.

## 10-12:5 Rate of Tax

A very rough estimate of the average New Jersey estate tax rate is 10%. For instance, the New Jersey estate tax on an estate worth $1,000,000 is approximately $32,500; a $1,000,000 estate has a

---

73. N.J.A.C. 18:26-3A.10.

value $325,000 greater than the $675,000 exemption equivalent against the tax.

The actual rates range from approximately 5% to approximately 16% based upon the value of the estate.[74]

The New Jersey estate tax is reduced by the value of real property located outside New Jersey. The Division has developed a formula for reducing the tax owed by the value of foreign real estate.

### 10-12:6 Tax as a Lien

The New Jersey estate tax is a lien on the assets of the estate until such time as the tax is paid. Unpaid tax bears interest at the rate of 10% per annum, which begins to accrue nine months after the death of the decedent.[75]

Until the tax is paid, the personal representative is personally liable for the payment of the tax.[76]

## 10-13 NEW JERSEY INHERITANCE TAX RETURN

New Jersey is one of the few states that has an estate tax and an inheritance tax.[77] As discussed above, the New Jersey estate tax is based upon the gross value of the estate. If the gross estate exceeds $675,000, then a New Jersey estate tax return must be filed and an estate tax may be owned, depending upon deductions and exclusions.

The New Jersey inheritance tax is based, primarily, upon the individual who or entity that is the beneficiary of the estate.[78] While a more valuable inheritance can change the tax rate, it is the relationship between the decedent and the beneficiary that is the driver of the New Jersey inheritance tax.[79]

Individuals with a very close relationship to the decedent, whether by consanguinity or affinity, cause no inheritance tax to

---

74. N.J.A.C. 18:26-3A.3(b).
75. N.J.A.C. 18:26-3A.6.
76. N.J.A.C. 18:26-9.11.
77. N.J.S.A. 54:33-1 et seq., N.J.A.C. 18:26-2.1 et seq.
78. N.J.S.A. 54:34-1.
79. N.J.S.A. 54:34-2.

the estate,[80] while those who bear a more distant relation to the decedent cause inheritance tax to the decedent's estate.[81]

## 10-13:1 Beneficiary Classes

There are four classes of beneficiaries: A, C, D and E. Depending upon the class that the beneficiary is in, various rates of tax are imposed upon the estate.[82]

### 10-13:1.1 Class A Beneficiaries

Class A beneficiaries bear the following relationship to the decedent: mother, father, spouse, civil union partner, domestic partner, child, grandchild, great-grandchild, mutually acknowledged child and stepchild.[83] Step-grandchildren are not class A beneficiaries; they are class D beneficiaries.

Class A beneficiaries do not cause inheritance tax to the estate.

### 10-13:1.2 Class C Beneficiaries

Class C beneficiaries bear the following relationship to the decedent: brother, sister, daughter-in-law and son-in-law.[84] In-laws could be the traditional spouse or an in-law by way of civil union partnership or domestic partnership.[85]

Class C beneficiaries receive a $25,000 exempt from the inheritance tax. If the decedent devises more than $25,000 to a class C beneficiary, the devise to the beneficiary causes tax to the estate at the following rates:

> A devise up to $1,075,000 in excess of the $25,000 exemption is taxed at 11%;
>
> The next $300,000 is taxed at 13%;
>
> The next $300,000 is taxed at 14%;
>
> Finally, a devise in excess of $1,700,000 is taxed at 16%.

---

80. N.J.S.A. 54:34-2(a), N.J.A.C. 18:26-2.5.
81. N.J.S.A. 54:34-2(c), (d); N.J.A.C. 18:27-2.7, -2.8
82. N.J.S.A. 54:32-2.
83. N.J.S.A. 54:34-2, N.J.S.A. 54:34-2.1.
84. N.J.S.A. 54:34-2(c), N.J.A.C. 18:26-2.7.
85. N.J.A.C. 18:26-2.6.

### 10-13:1.3 Class D Beneficiaries

Class D beneficiaries are all individuals and entities that are not a class A, C or E beneficiary.[86] Class D beneficiaries cause tax to the estate at the following rates:

The first $700,00 devised is taxed at 15%;

A devise in excess of $700,000 is taxed at 16%.

### 10-13:1.4 Class E Beneficiaries

A devise to a class E beneficiary would be a devise to the State of New Jersey or any of the state's political subdivisions for public or charitable purposes, an educational institution, church, hospital, orphanage, public library and certain non-profit organizations.[87]

A devise to a class E beneficiary causes no tax to the estate.[88]

### 10-13:1.5 What About Class B?

If you are a student of the alphabet, you know that A is followed by B, so why is there no class B group of beneficiaries? Class B was deleted in 1963.[89]

## 10-13:2 When to File an Inheritance Tax Return

The inheritance tax return is due within eight months of the decedent's death if any of the decedent's property is passing to a beneficiary other than a class A beneficiary.[90] If the entire estate is passing to class A beneficiaries, then no inheritance tax return need be filed.

## 10-13:3 What Is Included in the Estate?

The taxable estate of a resident decedent for purposes of the New Jersey inheritance tax includes all property (real, tangible personal property and intangible personal property) that a resident decedent owned at the time of death[91] with certain additions[92] and

---

86. N.J.S.A. 54:34-2(d), N.J.A.C. 18:26-2.8.
87. N.J.S.A. 26:18-1.1.
88. N.J.A.C. 26:18-6.12.
89. N.J.S.A. 54:34-2(b).
90. N.J.A.C. 18:26-9.1.
91. N.J.S.A. 54:34-1, N.J.A.C. 18:26-2.1.
92. N.J.A.C. 18:26-5.7.

exemptions[93] applying to the property the decedent owned at time of death.

The taxable estate of a non-resident decedent for purposes of the New Jersey inheritance tax includes real and tangible personal property located within the state of New Jersey.[94] Intangible personal property of a non-resident decedent is not subject to the inheritance tax.

The most common addition, or add-back, to the estate of a resident decedent is for transfers that the decedent made within three years of death, which is deemed to be a transfer made in contemplation of death.[95] If the decedent made a gift in excess of $500 within three years of death, then that transfer must be brought back into the estate on the New Jersey inheritance tax return. So, for instance, if the decedent gifted $10,000 to a friend two years before he died, then that $10,000 transfer to a class D beneficiary (the friend) must be reflected on the inheritance tax return.

Any transfer less than $500, no matter the class of the beneficiary is exempt from the inheritance tax. So, for instance, if Mr. Smith devises $499 to his friend, no inheritance tax will be imposed upon that devise, but an inheritance tax return must be filed because the entire estate did not pass to a class A beneficiary.

Common exemptions from the inheritance tax include life insurance proceeds payable to a named beneficiary.[96] No matter the class of the beneficiary, if the life insurance policy named the beneficiary, then that transfer is exempt from inheritance tax.

Out-of-state real estate is excluded from the inheritance tax calculation.[97] Contrariwise, the estate of a non-resident who owned real property in New Jersey passing to a beneficiary other than a class A beneficiary must pay inheritance tax.[98]

Gifts and devises to charities are exempt from the inheritance tax.[99]

---

93. N.J.S.A. 54:34-4
94. N.J.S.A. 54:34-1, N.J.A.C. 18:26-2.1(a)(2).
95. N.J.A.C. 18:26-5.7.
96. N.J.A.C. 18:26-6.8.
97. N.J.A.C. 18:26-2.1(a)(1).
98. N.J.A.C. 18:26-2.1(a)(2).
99. N.J.A.C. 18:26-6.12.

### 10-13:4 Tax as a Lien

The inheritance tax is a lien against the estate. The lien will remain on the estate until the tax is paid or until 15 years after the death of the decedent, whichever occurs first. Unpaid inheritance tax bears interest at the rate of 10% per annum, beginning eight months after the death of the decedent.[100]

Until the tax is paid, the personal representative is personally liable for the payment of the tax.[101]

## 10-14 PERSONAL INCOME TAX RETURN OF DECEDENT

The decedent's death does not negate the requirement that the decedent file personal income tax returns for federal and state tax. The executor, as the personal representative of the decedent's estate, is responsible for filing the appropriate forms—IRS Form 1040 and New Jersey Division of Taxation Form NJ-1040.

The tax year for the decedent ends as of the date of his death. In other words, if the individual dies on June 2nd, then June 2nd is the last day of that individual's tax year for purposes of his personal income tax returns, not December 31st. In all other respects, the tax forms are completed in the same manner, based upon the truncated year.

The decedent's final tax return is due three and half months after the taxable year, that is, April 15th.

## 10-15 ESTATE INCOME TAX RETURN

In addition to a personal income tax return for the decedent, the estate, which is an entity separate and apart from the decedent, may need to file income tax returns for each of its taxable years. As discussed above, an estate must obtain a tax identification number, commonly known as an EIN or TIN. The estate uses its EIN to report any income it receives with the federal government and the state of New Jersey.

An estate uses IRS Form 1041 and New Jersey Division of Taxation Form NJ-1041 to report its gross income. The personal representative must file IRS Form 1041 if the estate receives more

---

100. N.J.A.C. 18:26-10.2.
101. N.J.A.C. 18:26-9.11.

than $600 of gross income in any taxable year.[102] The personal representative must file NJ-1041 if the estate receives more than $10,000 in gross income in any taxable year.[103]

An estate can report income on a fiscal year basis or a calendar year basis. The estate must prorate the return for any filing that covers only a partial year. As with personal income tax returns, estate income tax returns that are filed on a calendar year basis are due by April 15th of the year following the end of the taxable year.

While practitioners may disagree, a personal representative may find it easier to use a calendar year for reporting purposes. Financial institutions issue tax reporting forms (for instance, Form 1099) on a calendar year basis. While 1099's can be requested from the institutions on a fiscal year basis, the time (and expense) of obtaining fiscal year 1099's could outweigh the time (and expense) of filing on a calendar year basis, then prorating the final calendar year if the estate winds down during a calendar year.

The personal representative can always retain a portion of the estate's assets after the initial distribution to the beneficiaries of the estate in order to cover any expenses (such as calendar-year income taxes that will not be due for many months after the initial distribution to beneficiaries) that may accrue after the initial distribution. For instance, the personal representative might want initially to distribute 90% of the estate's assets to the beneficiaries and withhold 10% of the estate's assets to cover any liabilities that are not due at that time, such as estate income tax that will not be due for several months following the initial distribution.

## 10-16 ACCOUNTING TO BENEFICIARIES

Unless an interested party, such as a beneficiary or creditor, files an action to compel an accounting, the personal representative of the estate is not required to file an accounting.[104] With that said, it is often to the personal representative's benefit to file an accounting.

An accounting that the Superior Court of New Jersey, Probate Part, has approved is res adjudicata as to all exceptions that any

---

102. http://www.irs.gov/pub/irs-pdf/i1041.pdf.

103. http://www.state.nj.us/treasury/taxation/pdf/current/1041i.pdf.

104. N.J.S.A. 3B:17-1.

person could have filed against the accounting.[105] An approved accounting is also an adjudication as to the correctness and propriety of the investments that the personal representative made, the correctness and propriety of the changes in assets that the personal representative made and the legality and propriety of all other matters covered by the accounting.[106]

In short, an approved accounting is something the personal representative can hold up as a final adjudication of the correctness of his actions during the time period covered by the accounting. For a fiduciary, such as a personal representative or administrator, being able to say that a court has approved once and for all the actions he took during the accounting time period is very valuable.

Without the approval of a formal accounting, an interested party, such as a beneficiary or a creditor, can institute an action against a personal representative for his actions during the time period that could have been covered by the accounting, unless the beneficiary has waived the accounting[107] and signed a release and refunding bond.[108]

Unless special cause is shown, a personal representative cannot be compelled to file an accounting until one year has passed following the surrogate appointing him as the personal representative of the estate.[109] A personal representative may voluntarily file an accounting any time he wishes.

From a practical standpoint, with most estates, the personal representative files one accounting immediately before he intends to distribute the remaining assets of the estate to the beneficiaries; this accounting would be called a First and Final Accounting.

If a personal representative files more than one accounting, the first accounting would be an intermediate accounting. For instance, the personal representative would file a First Intermediate Accounting, a Second Intermediate Accounting and so on. The final accounting would be a Third and Final Accounting, for example.

---

105. N.J.S.A. 3B:17-8.
106. N.J.S.A. 3B:17-8.
107. N.J. Ct. R. 4:87-9.
108. N.J.S.A. 3B:23-24.
109. N.J.S.A. 3B:17-2, *R.* 4:87-1(b).

### 10-16:1 Formal Accounting

A formal accounting is an accounting of a personal representative that is filed with the Superior Court of New Jersey, Probate Part, for approval on notice to the interested parties.[110] The filing and formatting of a formal accounting is governed by the provisions of New Jersey Court Rule 4:87.

As discussed above, the filing of a formal accounting can be a great benefit to a personal representative as the approval of the accounting serves as court approval as to the correctness of the personal representative's actions during the time period covered in the accounting. Without the approval of a formal accounting, an interested party, such as a beneficiary or a creditor, can institute an action against a personal representative for his actions during the time period that could have been covered in the accounting. With an approved accounting, a beneficiary or creditor cannot file such an action.

#### 10-16:1.1 Pleadings

An action to settle the account of a personal representative is governed by N.J. Ct. R. 4:87-1 et seq. The personal representative commences the action by filing an order to show cause in the Superior Court, Probate Part. The order to show cause must state any attorneys fees and commissions sought to be paid from the estate.

The order to show cause should be accompanied by a complaint. The complaint should include a list of the interested parties, including the beneficiaries and the surety on the probate bond, if the personal representative was required to obtain a bond. The complaint should note if any of the interested parties is a minor or is incapacitated, and if so, the guardian of said person.

If an interested party is a minor or a mentally incapacitated person, the court can appoint a guardian ad litem to express what is in the best interest of that party to the court with respect to the accounting.[111]

The complaint should specify the time period that the accounting covers, and it should contain a summary of the accounting. The summary must provide the following information: (1) for a first

---

110. N.J. Ct. R. 4:87-1 et seq.

111. N.J. Ct. R. 4:87-7

accounting, the amount of assets for which the personal representative became chargeable when the obligation devolved upon him; for subsequent accountings, the amount remaining in the personal representative's hands as shown in the previous accounting; (2) the amount, if any, for which the personal representative became chargeable in addition to the amount specified in (1) during the accounting time period; (3) the total of the first two items; (4) the amount of allowances claimed in the accounting; and (5) the balance in the accountant's hands.

The complaint should have the accounting annexed to it. The complaint should ask for an allowance of the accounting and any fees or commissions that the personal representative is seeking to be paid from the estate.

### 10-16:1.2 Schedules/Statements

The accounting itself must contain several statements or schedules. A full statement as to the assets composing the balance of the estate in the hands of the personal representative, setting for the value when the personal representative acquired the assets and the value as of the date of the accounting. A statement as to all changes that have been made in the assets of the estate since the personal representative acquired the assets. A statement showing items apportioned between income and principal. A statement showing apportionments made with respect to transfer inheritance tax and estate tax. A statement of allocation if counsel fees or commissions were paid out of corpus but the benefits of the deductions from corpus have been allocated to the income beneficiaries. Finally, a statement showing how the commissions requested with respect to corpus are calculated.

Many of the statements or schedules that are required to be filed with the court as part of an accounting have to do with the allocation of charges and expenses between income and principal. These schedules derive from the requirements of the Uniform Principal and Income Act of 2001 (Act).[112]

In short, the Act requires certain charges and expenses to be allocated to the income of the estate and certain charges and expenses to be allocated to the principal of the estate.

---

112. N.J.S.A. 3B:19B-1 et seq.

In the vast majority of estates, income is not devised to one beneficiary and corpus or principal to another. Most Wills provide something such as the following: "I devise my entire estate to my four children equally" or "I devise 50% of my estate to Joe, 20% to Mary, and 30% to Jane."

Given this reality, in the vast majority of estates, the allocation of charges and expenses between principal and income is wholly unnecessary and inappropriate. If income were devised to one beneficiary and corpus to another, then the requirements of the Act would have far more meaning for the estate and the accounting. As stated, though, this rarely is the case with a decedent's estate.

#### 10-16:1.3 Commission Schedule

One of the schedules that should comprise the accounting is a schedule showing how the commission of the personal representative was calculated. A personal representative (an administrator or an executor) is entitled to a commission for the work he performs and the liability he assumes as the personal representative of the estate.[113]

In short, a personal representative is entitled to a corpus commission of 5% on the first $200,000 the he received, 3.5% on the excess over $200,000 up to $1,000,000 and 2% on the excess over $1,000,000.[114] The personal representative is also entitled to an income commission of 6% of all income that he received.[115] The personal representative can take these commissions without court allowance.

In valuing items of corpus for purposes of the commission, personal representatives typically use the "presumptive value." The presumptive value is the value of the item when the personal representative received the item of corpus.[116] If the personal representative prefers, he can use the value of the item of corpus at the end of the accounting period for calculating his commissions;[117] a personal representative may choose to use this

---

113. N.J.S.A. 3B:1-1 (defining "Fiduciary"); N.J.S.A. 3B:10-26.
114. N.J.S.A. 3B:18-14.
115. N.J.S.A. 3B:18-13.
116. N.J.S.A. 3B:18-18.
117. N.J.S.A. 3B:18-18.

value if, for example, the estate consisted of a stock and the stock greatly appreciated in value during his administration of the estate.

### 10-16:1.4 Distribution Plan

The accounting should contain a distribution schedule,[118] showing the surrogate and the beneficiaries of the estate the distributions to the beneficiaries that the personal representative intends to make if the accounting is approved. If expenses have not been paid, such as legal fees or the personal representative's commission, then the personal representative should back these proposed expenses out of the amount to be distributed to the beneficiaries and reflect this fact as a footnote on the distribution plan schedule.

## 10-16:2 Informal Accounting

There are no rules governing informal accounting. An informal accounting is, by definition, informal and does not have to conform to the rules governing accountings.

On the other hand, it is advisable that an informal accounting follow the rules governing the formatting of a formal accounting. Personal representatives in the vast majority of cases use informal accountings to account to the beneficiaries of the estate, if the personal representative prepares an accounting at all.

It is far less expensive to account informally to the beneficiaries. The estate does not have to pay surrogate audit fees, discussed below. The personal representative does not have to pay an attorney to prepare a verified complaint, order to show cause and proposed judgment. There is no court filing fee.

But because an informal accounting may need to be filed as a formal accounting with the Superior Court of New Jersey, Probate Part, it is advisable for the personal representative to prepare his accounting following the rules governing the formatting of a formal accounting. If the personal representative prepares the accounting using the formal accounting formatting rules, his attorney will simply need to prepare the complaint, order to show cause and proposed judgment, then file his "informal" accounting with the Superior Court as a formal accounting, for instance, if a beneficiary objects to something in the informal accounting.

---

118. N.J.S.A. 3B:23-4.

### 10-16:3 Exceptions

An interested party can file exceptions to the personal representative's accounting with the Superior Court of New Jersey, Probate Part.[119] Since the county surrogate serves as the deputy clerk of the Superior Court for the probate part, those exceptions would be filed with the county surrogate.

An "exception" is an interested party taking exception to some portion of the accounting. For instance, the interested party may disagree with the amount for which the personal representative sold the decedent's home, claiming that the home was worth far more than the amount for which the personal representative sold the house. An interested party may take exception to a debt the personal representative paid, claiming that the debt did not represent an enforceable claim against the estate. An interested party may take exception to the calculation of the personal representative's commission. There are a multitude of reasons why an interested party could file an exception to an accounting, and those reasons must be handled on a case-by-case basis.

### 10-16:4 Surrogate Audit and Audit Fees

When an accounting is filed formally, the surrogate audits the accounting.[120] The surrogate ensures that the accounting conforms to the formatting requirements of New Jersey Court Rule 4:87 and that all the appropriate documentation is available to support the accounting. The surrogate also asks substantive questions about the accounting in order to assist the judge of the probate part who will review the accounting and approve or reject the accounting. The surrogate files a report with the Superior Court, Probate Part, as to any derelictions it may have found in the accounting.

For its service, the surrogate is entitled to an audit fee.[121] The amount of the fee is based upon the value of the estate. The fee schedule is as follows:

- In estates up to and including $2,000.00: no fee other than filing fee.

---

119. N.J. Ct. R. 4:87-8.
120. N.J. Ct. R. 4:87-6
121. N.J.S.A. 22A:2-15.

- In estates from $2,001.00 to and including $10,000.00: $100.00
- In estates from $10,001.00 to and including $30,000.00: $125.00
- In estates from $30,001.00 to and including $65,000.00: $150.00
- In estates from $65,001.00 to and including $200,000.00: 3/10 of 1% but not less than $300.00
- In estates exceeding $200,000.00: 4/10 of 1%, but not less than $400.00
- For each page of accounting in excess of one: $5.00
- In computing the amount of an estate for the purpose of fixing the fees of a surrogate for auditing and reporting the account, the balance from the prior account shall be excluded.

The estate pays the audit fee. The audit fee is one reason why proceeding with an informal accounting is less expensive than filing an accounting formally. Most accountings are filed on an informal basis, if the personal representative prepares an accounting at all.

### 10-16:5 Waiving the Accounting

The interested parties to the accounting can waive the requirement that the personal representative file an accounting.[122] If the personal representative has paid all the debts of the estate, the remaining interested parties would be the beneficiaries of the estate. If all the beneficiaries waive the requirement that the personal representative account and sign a release and refunding bond,[123] discussed below, then the personal representative can wind down the estate without fear of being sued in his capacity as a fiduciary.

## 10-17 DISTRIBUTIONS TO BENEFICIARIES

Eventually, the personal representative will need to make distributions of the estate's assets to the beneficiaries of the estate,

---

122. N.J. Ct. R. 4:87-9.

123. N.J.S.A. 3B:23-24.

assuming there are sufficient assets to pay all the debts of the estate, that is, assuming the estate is solvent.[124] Most beneficiaries have the same interests in an estate, receiving their distribution from the estate as soon as possible and ensuring that their distribution is as large as possible.

On the other hand, the personal representative wants to ensure that he has sufficient assets to pay any debt of the estate that may be presented to him. Because creditors have 9 months following the date of the decedent's death to present claims to the personal representative during which time a personal representative could be held personally liable if he were to make distributions from the estate without retaining sufficient assets to pay the debts of the estate,[125] every personal representative should retain the assets of the estate until 9 months have elapsed from the date of the decedent's death.

The nine-month period of time is a minimum. Many estates may remain open well passed the statutory nine-month time period.

The most conservative approach is for a personal representative to refrain from making any distributions until the estate is ready to be finalized and until at least 9 months have elapsed since the date of the decedent. When an estate remains open for a considerable period of time, it is often difficult for a personal representative to refrain from making any distributions.

A personal representative is free to make partial distributions before making the final distribution; however, if a partial distribution is made, the personal representative should obtain a release and refunding bond, discussed below, for the partial distribution.

## 10-18 RELEASE AND REFUNDING BOND

When a personal representative makes a distribution from the estate to a beneficiary of the estate, he should obtain a release and refunding bond from the beneficiary who is receiving the distribution.[126] A release and refunding bond is a two-part document—it is part release and part refunding bond.

---

124. N.J.S.A. 3B:23-1 et seq.

125. N.J.S.A. 3B:22-4.

126. N.J.S.A. 3B:23-24.

A personal representative is a fiduciary.[127] A personal representative owes each beneficiary of the estate the utmost duty of care. As such, a beneficiary of the estate may have various claims against the personal representative for his actions in handling the estate.

Because a personal representative owes such a high level of care to the beneficiaries, it is advisable for the personal representative to obtain a release from each beneficiary of the estate before making distributions to the beneficiaries. In this way, no beneficiary can later make a claim against the personal representative.

A beneficiary wants his share of the estate, so the best time for the personal representative to obtain the release is before the assets of the estate are distributed to the beneficiary. It is at this time that the personal representative holds the most sway over the beneficiaries.

A refunding bond is an agreement from the beneficiary to return/refund a proportionate share of the distribution necessary to pay that beneficiary's pro rata share of a debt that may be presented at a date after the distribution. For instance, if there are four beneficiaries of the estate and each receives $50,000 and after the distribution a creditor presents a claim for $1,000, each beneficiary agrees to return one-fourth of the $1,000 debt, or $250, by signing a refunding bond.[128]

From a practical standpoint, a beneficiary may not return his pro rata share of a debt, but if the personal representative waited out the statutory nine-month notice to creditor time period and if the personal representative obtained a refunding bond from the beneficiary, then the personal representative can in no way be held liable for the debt or for the failure of the beneficiary to remit his pro rata share of the debt. The creditor will need to sue the beneficiary on his agreement to return a pro rata share of the debt as memorialized in the refunding bond.

### 10-18:1 Filing Release and Refunding Bonds with Surrogate

Once the personal representative obtains a release and refunding bond from the beneficiaries of the estate, he should file those executed release and refunding bonds with the appropriate

127. N.J.S.A. 3B:1-1 (defining "Fiduciary"), N.J.S.A. 3B:10-26.
128. N.J.S.A. 3B:23-41.

surrogate's office.[129] If a probate bond needed to be posted (which is a more likely scenario when an administrator has been appointed), the bonding company will want a copy of the filed release and refunding bonds from each of the beneficiaries of the estate before retiring the probate bond. Until the probate bond has been terminated, a premium will remain due and owing to the bonding company.

### 10-18:2 Holding an Escrow Amount

Even if the personal representative waits out the statutory nine-month notice to creditor time period and obtains release and refunding bonds, it may be advisable for the personal representative to withhold a portion of the distribution to the beneficiaries. For instance, a personal representative may wish to distribute 90% of the estate's assets one year following the death of the decedent and hold back 10% of the estate's assets to cover any debts that may be presented after the distribution is made.

The personal representative could hold the 10% of the estate in escrow for another year to see if any other debts are presented, then release the remainder after the year escrow period has elapsed.

## 10-19 ADVICE AND DIRECTION

A personal representative of an estate has the right to file a summary action in the Superior Court, Probate Part, for instruction from the court as to any of his statutory powers or for advice and direction in making distributions from the estate.[130] Essentially, if a personal representative has a question about the propriety of any of his proposed actions, he can file an action in the Superior Court and ask for the court to tell him whether his proposed action is appropriate or not. Once the personal representative has obtained court approval for his action, the personal representative could not be held liable for performing that action.

For instance, if the personal representative wants to sell the decedent's house and he believes that a beneficiary may challenge the amount for which he is selling the house, the personal representative can request that the court approve the sales price.

---

129. N.J.S.A. 3B:23-24.

130. *R.* 4:95-2.

After he obtains this approval, no beneficiary could sue the personal representative for selling the decedent's house too cheaply.

## 10-20 CLOSING OUT THE EIN

When all the creditors of the estate have been paid and when all the distributions from the estate have been made to the beneficiaries, the personal representative will close the estate by closing the EIN with the IRS. IRS Form 56 is used to close the EIN with the taxing authority.

# Chapter 11

# Avoiding Estate Litigation

## 11-1 WHO IS THE CLIENT?

Whenever you represent a client, you should understand who the client is. This sounds like a silly statement, but unlike Family Law, which is often about a family breaking apart through divorce, the practice of elder law is truly family law. Clients frequently come to the consultation and follow up meetings with one or more non-client family members. When representing a client for purposes of emergent Medicaid planning, you may never meet with the actual client, instead dealing with the client's power of attorney agent. The power of attorney agent is often a child of the client, but the client may have four children all of whom believe they have an equal say in the management of the client's affairs.

Because the practice of elder and disability law involves so much interaction with non-client family members, it is of paramount importance that you specifically define who your client is and with whom you can share information.[1] Have the client sign a retainer agreement.[2] In the retainer agreement, specifically identify the client and specifically identify those individuals with whom you can share information about the representation. If you represent the power of attorney agent, not the principal, make sure your retainer agreement identifies the fact that you are representing the power of attorney agent, not the principal.

After the consultation or after follow up meetings or years after your representation of the client ends, you will get calls from

---

1. R.P.C. 1.6.
2. R.P.C. 1.5(b).

non-client family members asking questions about the work you performed for "mom" or for "dad." Identifying who the client is and with whom you can share information[3] provides you with the assurances that you have properly identified your client and that you have obtained consent from your client to share information with certain non-clients.

## 11-2 MENTAL CAPACITY

When you practice elder and disability law, the competency of your client may be challenged, particularly if an interested party (such as a child) is negatively impacted by some action your client took. For instance, if your 85 year old estate planning client asks you to draft a last will and testament disinheriting one of her four children, there is a high probability that the disinherited child will challenge the client's Will after the client dies and may claim that you drafted a Will for a person who lacked the capacity to make the Will.[4]

Now, this may be wholly unfounded. Just because a client is elderly or disabled does not mean that the client lacks mental capacity, but to many laypersons, the fact that the client was elderly or disabled creates just cause to challenge the client's, and your, actions. When a client is requesting that you assist them with taking some action that you believe is likely to be challenged, it is important to remember what level of mental capacity a client must have to take certain actions; not all legal actions require the same level of mental capacity.

### 11-2:1 Testamentary Capacity

The level of mental capacity required to make a last will and testament is often described as the lowest level of mental capacity. In order to have sufficient mental capacity, a client who is executing a Will must (1) be able to comprehend the property he is disposing of through the Will, (2) understand who the natural objects of his bounty are, (3) understand that he is executing a Will (4) understand the relation of all of these factors to the others and (5) understand

---

3. R.P.C. 1.6(a).

4. *Matter of Will of Liebl*, 260 N.J. Super. 519, 524 (App. Div.), *certif. den.*, 133 N.J. 432 (1993) (defining testamentary mental capacity).

the distribution that he is making through his Will.[5] In simple terms, for a client to have testamentary mental capacity, he must know what he owns, know who his relatives are, know he is signing a Will and come up with a plan for distributing his estate. Fairly basic.

A fundamental fact that you should bear in mind when drafting a Will is that when a challenge occurs, your client will not be around to defend the Will because he will have died. So, no matter how high the client's level of mental capacity may have been, when a challenge occurs, there will be allegations made that the client cannot defend for himself.

Document your file when you believe a challenge is likely. Note the fact that the client provided all of the information to you contained in your questionnaire. Your questionnaire should ask the client his personal information and the names and addresses of his close family members—his spouse and his children. The questionnaire should ask the client about his assets and about his health.

You should ask the client some basic orientation questions—day of the week, month, year, name of the President of the United States. You should ask the client about any medications he is currently taking and about his health generally.

### 11-2:2 Contractual Capacity

Contractual mental capacity is a higher level of mental capacity than the capacity needed to execute a last will and testament. A client enters a contract when the client executes a financial power of attorney, an advance healthcare directive or the retainer agreement with you as his attorney, so it is important that the client have a sufficient level of contractual mental capacity.

The person entering the contract must possess sufficient mental capacity to understand all of the following: (1) the *nature* of the transaction in which he is engaged; (2) the *extent* of the transaction in which he is engaged; (3) the *character* of the transaction in which he is engaged; and (4) the *effect* of the transaction in which he is engaged.[6] With testamentary mental capacity, the client basically has to know what he owns, who is relatives are and what

---

5. *Matter of Will of Liebl*, 260 N.J. Super. 519, 524 (App. Div.), *certif. den.*, 133 N.J. 432 (1993) (defining testamentary mental capacity).

6. *Matter of William Schiller*, 148 N.J. Super. 168, 180 (Ch. Div. 1977), citing 17 C.J.S. Contracts, § 133(1).

he is doing through his Will. With contractual mental capacity, the client must understand the transaction and its effects. A new transaction a person is entering is obviously more foreign to the person than the person's current circumstances (his family, his assets), so contractual mental capacity is a higher level of capacity than testamentary mental capacity.

### 11-2:3 Donative Capacity

In order to have the mental capacity necessary to make a gift, the donor must have a level of mental capacity sufficient to understand the nature of the transaction into which he is entering and the effect of that transaction.[7] In short, the donor must understand that he is making a gift of an item and that by making the gift he is relinquishing custody of and control over the item for all time.

## 11-3 PHYSICIAN CERTIFICATION OF CAPACITY

Whether you question the competency of a client to enter a transaction or whether you believe that the client's actions are such that those actions are likely to be challenged by others, you may wish to have a physician sign a certification attesting to his or her opinion regarding the mental capacity of the client. When the lawyer questions his own potential client's mental capacity to enter a transaction, the first thought the lawyer should have is, *Should I simply decline this representation*?

Of course, there are those marginal instances in which the lawyer believes the client has mental capacity but the client does or says something that makes the lawyer question his own assessment of the client. In those marginal cases, a physician's certification can be helpful, giving a third-party, professional opinion as to mental capacity. But the ultimate decision rests with the lawyer, and if you do not feel comfortable representing a client because you are uncomfortable with the client's level of mental capacity, then you should decline representation.

---

7. *Conners v. Murphy*, 100 N.J. Eq. 280, 282 (E&A 1926) ("The test of mental capacity to make a gift is that the donor shall have ability to understand the nature and effect of the transaction.").

The more likely scenario in which you will want a physician's certification is a case in which you believe the client has mental capacity, but the client is asking you to assist them with some transaction (for instance, disinheriting a child whom the client describes as litigious) that you believe will be challenged later. In cases such as these, it is helpful to have sought the opinion of a third-party professional.

Finally, you should be aware of the fact that your seeking the opinion of a third-party professional will likely serve as the basis of a challenge to the client's mental capacity in and of itself. An attorney for the disgruntled interested party will ask, "Why did you ask for a doctor's certification if you believed the client was competent to sign a Will?" The ready answer to that question is, "Because I thought I might be sitting here in court someday and my client, who was competent, wouldn't be here to defend himself, so I wanted to have my opinion and a doctor's opinion on this issue."

### 11-3:1 Treating Physician

A treating physician will know the client the best. The physician may have treated the client for decades and can draw on his experiences over that period of time to express a true, knowledge-based opinion of your client, his patient.

On the other hand, a treating physician may not be used to writing well-drafted competency opinion letters. The treating physician may not be used to testifying in court if the client or his estate are later embroiled in litigation over some transaction with which you assisted the client. A well-intentioned treating physician could come off poorly as a witness sometimes.

### 11-3:2 Examining Physician

An examining physician is a physician whom you retain specifically to examine the client for purposes of the competency report. In many instances, this physician may never have met the client/patient before his examination for purposes of the competency exam.

The downside to using an examining physician is that he has no prior experience with the patient. Also, he is a hired expert, a fact that may provide fodder to a lawyer for a disgruntled interested party.

On the other hand, an examining physician is probably used to writing well-drafted competency reports and to testifying in court. An examining physician will have experience with people challenging his reports and will have developed techniques for handling those challenges.

## 11-4 UNDUE INFLUENCE

A Will that you draft for a client or a gifting planning that you advise your client to employ may be challenged on the grounds that the client was being unduly influenced to make the Will or the gift.[8] Undue influence is influence that prevents the client from following his own free will and that compels the client to accept the will of another individual.

We are all influenced by other people. Undue influence occurs when another individual's intentions overcome the client's intentions.

As with mental capacity, a doctor can express his opinion as to whether or not an individual is susceptible to undue influence.

## 11-5 MEETING WITH THE CLIENT

When a client comes to your office with non-client family members, those family members will inevitably want to sit with the client and you during the meeting. If the client is coming to you to draft a Will that leaves everything equally to her four children and the four children get along, then there probably is no harm with other family members sitting in on the meeting. But if the client is disinheriting a child or engaging in a transaction that will cause hard feelings among family members, then it is best to meet with the client alone.

You should politely excuse the non-client family members from the room and meet with the client alone. Note the fact that you excused the non-client family members from the room during your interview with the client. You need to ensure that what the client

---

8. *Haynes v. First Nat'l State Bank*, 87 N.J. 163, 176 (1981) (defining testamentary undue influence as influence that has destroyed the free agency of the testator through mental, moral or physical exertion preventing the testator from following his own free will); *In re Catelli's Will*, 361 N.J. Super. 478, 486 (App. Div. 2003); *Bronson v. Bronson*, 218 N.J. Super. 389, 394 (App. Div. 1987) (defining undue influence with respect to a gift differently than with respect to a testamentary devise because with a gift, the presence of suspicious circumstances does not need to be proven).

is telling you is what the client wants, not what a non-client family member who brought the client to your office wants. You also need to ensure that the client has the capacity to express her intentions.

## 11-6 RECEIVING PAYMENT FROM THE CLIENT

Your client should pay for your services. If a non-client family member pays for your services, then there is always the assumption that the non-client family member was paying you to get something they wanted, not what the client wanted, or that the client was too incapacitated to handle her finances and pay you. The check for your services should come from your client.

This is particularly the case if the client is engaging in some transaction that will cause hard feelings amongst family members. If a non-client family member pays for your services and that family member benefits from the planning with which you are assisting the client to the exclusion of other family members, this creates an easy point of attack for those disgruntled family members.

## 11-7 STORING THE WILL

Who stores the original last will and testament can become an important issue in a Will contest case. For instance, if a daughter brings mom to your office and the daughter becomes mom's sole beneficiary to the exclusion of mom's other three children, there very well may be a Will contest after mom's death. In addition, if mom takes her original Will with her and, in turn, gives that Will to her daughter who is the sole beneficiary, there could be a claim that the daughter was hiding the Will from mom and from other family members so that no one could talk sense into mom.

One of the disinherited children might claim that mom lacked testamentary capacity and did not even remember she drafted a Will disinheriting her other children. Or, one of the disinherited children might argue that mom thought she had to get the original Will from the daughter before she could revoke that Will.

If the lawyer retains the Will and informs the client/mother, in writing, that she can always revoke or modify the Will at any time by contacting the lawyer, then these arguments are somewhat mitigated. Furthermore, because a lost Will that was in the possession of the client is presumed to be revoked, as a lawyer, you are doing the client a service by storing and safeguarding their Will.

Finally, since you are storing the client's Will, the family members will come to you to retrieve the Will after the client's passing, which can be a good opportunity to offer your services to the family for purposes of estate administration.

### 11-7:1 Receipt for Will

Whether you store the client's Will and other legal documents or not, you should obtain a signed receipt from the client that either acknowledges the fact that the client took the documents or that you retained the documents. If you retain the documents, your receipt should explain the terms and conditions under which the client or their representative can retrieve the documents.

Having a receipt can be helpful if a client claims that you retained the documents. A receipt can prove that you informed the client he had the documents and was responsible for safekeeping the documents, not you.

## 11-8 PRIOR REPRESENTATIONS

You should be mindful of how prior representations of other clients may impact your ability to represent a current client.[9] For instance, if a daughter has been your client for some time and she brings her mother into your office for purposes of estate planning, you should decline the representation if the mother wants to disinherit her other three children to the benefit of the daughter who has been your client.[10] If mom simply wants to draft Will that leaves her estate equally among her four children, your representation of mom is probably fine.

The point is to beaware of the people you have represented in the past and feel free to decline representation if you believe that your ability to advocate for your client is impaired in any way by a prior representation.

## 11-9 THE QUESTIONNAIRE

You should design a questionnaire for each of your major practice areas. Typical practice areas for an elder law attorney

---

9. R.P.C. 1.7(a)(2).

10. *Haynes v. First Nat'l State Bank*, 87 N.J. 163, 176 (1981).

include estate planning, Medicaid planning, estate administration and guardianships. See Appendix A for sample questionnaires

You should maintain notes on your meeting with the client. If you believe the representation of the client may result in eventual litigation, you should meet with the client alone and have the client provide the information requested on the questionnaire. In this way, there is support for the fact that the client understood the key elements necessary for you to represent the client.

## 11-10 NOTES FROM THE CLIENT

In certain instances, it may be beneficial to obtain a note from the client, in his handwriting, explaining why he is doing what he is doing. Sometimes clients come in with notes in their own handwriting. The notes might include their children's names and addresses or their assets. The notes may contain their thoughts on a dispositive plan.

It is advisable to retain these notes because the notes show that the client knew a vital piece of information that forms the basis of testamentary mental capacity[11] and that the client contemplated his meeting with you and took the time to put his own thoughts in writing.

In some instances, it may be advisable to have the client write out the reasons why he is taking a certain action. "I am disinheriting my daughter because we have been estranged for eight years." In this way, you have something in the client's own hand that shows why he took a certain action. The writing can be used to prove that the client was capable of writing (which requires a certain level of mental capacity) and in formulating a cogent thought.

## 11-11 COPIES OF PRIOR ESTATE PLANNING DOCUMENTS

You may find yourself drafting several revisions of estate planning documents through many years of representing the same client. The client may change his Will or other estate planning documents every few years for one reason or another.

---

11. *Matter of Will of Liebl*, 260 N.J. Super. 519, 524 (App. Div.), *certif. den.*, 133 N.J. 432 (1993) (defining testamentary mental capacity).

You should retain copies of the prior estate planning documents. Scan them to your database. In this way, you can prove the history of the client's actions. With your notes, the documents will paint a clear picture of why a client took a certain action.

The history will also support your knowledge of the client and his intentions. This will prove that you knew your client and understood his intentions and his mental state.

## 11-12 WITNESSES TO THE WILL

The statutes governing the execution of a Will permit a person who has an interest in the Will to be a witness.[12] In other words, assuming the person is otherwise competent to be a witness,[13] nothing prohibits an interested party from serving as the witness to the Will.

Having an interested person serve as a witness to a Will when a challenge to the Will is likely (for instance, if the testator is disinheriting a child) is ill-advised. If the Will is likely to be challenged, you should ensure that your witnesses will make good witnesses when called upon; at the very least, they should be impartial witnesses.

---

12. N.J.S.A. 3B:3-8.
13. N.J.S.A. 3B:3-7.

# Appendix—A Sample Questionnaires

## Table of Contents

## INTAKE CHECKLIST

In order to assist you in estate administration, this office needs the following documents. Please bring any that you have not already provided to the next scheduled meeting.

1. ORIGINAL WILL
2. DEATH CERTIFICATE
3. BANK STATEMENTS
4. CERTIFICATES OF DEPOSIT
5. GOVERNMENT BONDS
6. STOCK CERTIFICATES
7. MOTOR VEHICLE REGISTRATION
8. FUNERAL BILL
9. CERTIFICATE OF HONORABLE DISCHARGE (ONLY IF VA BENEFITS ARE BEING APPLIED FOR)
10. DEEDS TO REAL ESTATE
11. CORPORATE BONDS
12. LIST AND APPROXIMATE VALUE OF COLLECTIONS
13. LIST AND APPROXIMATE VALUE OF JEWELRY
14. LIST AND APPROXIMATE VALUE OF ART, ANTIQUES, SILVER
15. ALL LIFE INSURANCE POLICIES
16. LIST OF ALL KNOWN LIABILITIES, INCLUDING NAMES, ADDRESSES, TELEPHONE NUMBERS, AND ACCOUNT NUMBERS OF EACH CREDITOR.
17. DECEDENT'S PRIOR YEAR'S FEDERAL INCOME TAX RETURN

18. DECEDENT'S PRIOR YEAR'S STATE INCOME TAX RETURN

19. REAL ESTATE TAX BILL

Date:____________________

## 1.00 GENERAL INFORMATION RE: DECEDENT

1.01 NAME OF DECEDENT______________________________

1.02 ADDRESS OF DECEDENT__________________________

1.03 DATE OF DEATH__________________________________

1.04 DATE OF WILL ___________________________________

1.05 COUNTY OF PROBATE____________________________

1.06 DATE OF PROBATE ______________________________

1.07 ESTATE ID NO. __________________________________

1.07.a SOCIAL SECURITY NO.___________________

1.08 HEIRS AT LAW AND NEXT OF KIN:

NAME ADDRESS RELATIONSHIP AGE SOCIAL SECURITY #

(A) ______________________________________________________

(B) ______________________________________________________

(C) ______________________________________________________

(D) ______________________________________________________

(E) ______________________________________________________

1.09 PLACE OF DEATH________________________________

1.10 AGE AT DEATH/DATE OF DEATH________________

1.11 DATE OF BIRTH__________________________________

1.12 CITIZENSHIP_____________________________________

1.13 DOMICILE_______________________________________

1.14 SPOUSE'S DATE OF DEATH_____________________

## 2.00 PROBATE INFORMATION

2.01 WITNESS NAME____________________________________

A. ADDRESS ______________________________

B. TELEPHONE NO. ________________________

2.02 SHORT CERTIFICATES—NUMBER REQUIRED:____

2.03 RULE TO BAR CREDITORS—REQUIRED?

YES ☐ NO ☐

2.04 BENEFICIARIES:

NAME ADDRESS

(A) ________________________________________

(B) ________________________________________

(C) ________________________________________

(D) ________________________________________

(E) ________________________________________

## 3.00 PERSONAL REPRESENTATIVE

A. INDIVIDUAL

3.01 NAME________________________________

3.02 ADDRESS _____________________________

3.03 SOCIAL SECURITY NUMBER_______________

3.04 HOME TELEPHONE NO.___________________

3.05 WORK TELEPHONE NO.___________________

3.06 FAX NO.______________________________

## 4.00 SAFE DEPOSIT BOX

4.01 NAME OF BANK _________________________

4.02 ADDRESS OF BRANCH ____________________

4.03 TELEPHONE NO.________________________

4.04 CONTACT PERSON________________________________

4.05 NAME(S) IN WHICH BOX WAS HELD ______________

**5.00 SOCIAL SECURITY & VETERANS BENEFITS**

5.01 DECEDENT'S SOCIAL SECURITY NO.______________

5.02 HAS FUNERAL DIRECTOR APPLIED FOR LUMP-SUM DEATH BENEFIT?

YES ☐ NO ☐

5.03 HAS SURVIVING SPOUSE APPLIED FOR SURVIVORS BENEFIT?

YES ☐ NO ☐

5.04 HAS FUNERAL DIRECTOR APPLIED FOR VETERANS BENEFITS FOR HEADSTONE?

YES ☐ NO ☐

**6.00 BANK DEPOSITORIES**

6.01 (A) NAME ________________________________________

6.02 (A) ADDRESS______________________________________

6.03 (A) TELEPHONE NO. ______________________________

6.04 (A) CONTACT PERSON_____________________________

6.05 (A) ACCOUNT NO. _________________________________

6.06 (A) TYPE OF ACCOUNT____________________________

6.01 (B) NAME ________________________________________

6.02 (B) ADDRESS______________________________________

6.03 (B) TELEPHONE NO. ______________________________

6.04 (B) CONTACT PERSON_____________________________

6.05 (B) ACCOUNT NO. _________________________________

6.06 (B) TYPE OF ACCOUNT____________________________

6.01 (C) NAME ______________________________________

6.02 (C) ADDRESS____________________________________

6.03 (C) TELEPHONE NO.______________________________

6.04 (C) CONTACT PERSON_____________________________

6.05 (C) ACCOUNT NO. _______________________________

6.06 (C) TYPE OF ACCOUNT____________________________

6.01 (D) NAME ______________________________________

6.02 (D) ADDRESS____________________________________

6.03 (D) TELEPHONE NO.______________________________

6.04 (D) CONTACT PERSON_____________________________

6.05 (D) ACCOUNT NO. _______________________________

6.06 (D) TYPE OF ACCOUNT____________________________

6.01 (E) NAME ______________________________________

6.02 (E) ADDRESS____________________________________

6.03 (E) TELEPHONE NO.______________________________

6.04 (E) CONTACT PERSON_____________________________

6.05 (E) ACCOUNT NO. _______________________________

6.06 (E) TYPE OF ACCOUNT____________________________

6.01 (F) NAME ______________________________________

6.02 (F) ADDRESS____________________________________

6.03 (F) TELEPHONE NO.______________________________

6.04 (F) CONTACT PERSON_____________________________

6.05 (F) ACCOUNT NO. _______________________________

6.06 (F) TYPE OF ACCOUNT____________________________

6.01 (G) NAME ______________________________________

6.02 (G) ADDRESS____________________________________

6.03 (G) TELEPHONE NO. ______________________

6.04 (G) CONTACT PERSON______________________

6.05 (G) ACCOUNT NO. ______________________

6.06 (G) TYPE OF ACCOUNT______________________

6.01 (H) NAME ______________________

6.02 (H) ADDRESS______________________

6.03 (H) TELEPHONE NO. ______________________

6.04 (H) CONTACT PERSON______________________

6.05 (H) ACCOUNT NO. ______________________

6.06 (H) TYPE OF ACCOUNT______________________

6.01 (I) NAME ______________________

6.02 (I) ADDRESS______________________

6.03 (I) TELEPHONE NO. ______________________

6.04 (I) CONTACT PERSON______________________

6.05 (I) ACCOUNT NO. ______________________

6.06 (I) TYPE OF ACCOUNT______________________

## 7.00 BROKERAGE FIRM

7.01 (A) NAME OF FIRM______________________

7.02 (A) ADDRESS______________________

7.03 (A) TELEPHONE NO. ______________________

7.04 (A) FAX NO. ______________________

7.05 (A) CONTACT PERSON______________________

7.06 (A) ATTACH BROKERAGE STATEMENT__________

7.01 (B) NAME OF FIRM______________________

7.02 (B) ADDRESS ______________________________

7.03 (B) TELEPHONE NO. ______________________________

7.04 (B) FAX NO. ______________________________

7.05 (B) CONTACT PERSON ______________________________

7.06 (B) ATTACH BROKERAGE STATEMENT __________

7.01 (C) NAME OF FIRM ______________________________

7.02 (C) ADDRESS ______________________________

7.03 (C) TELEPHONE NO. ______________________________

7.04 (C) FAX NO. ______________________________

7.05 (C) CONTACT PERSON ______________________________

7.06 (C) ATTACH BROKERAGE STATEMENT __________

**8.00 <u>LIFE INSURANCE</u>**

8.01 (A) NAME OF COMPANY ______________________________

8.02 (A) ADDRESS AT WHICH TO FILE CLAIM __________

______________________________

8.03 (A) TELEPHONE NO. ______________________________

8.04 (A) FAX NO. ______________________________

8.05 (A) CONTACT PERSON ______________________________

8.06 (A) HAVE CLAIMS BEEN FILED ON ALL LIFE INSURANCE POLICIES?

YES ☐ NO ☐

8.01 (B) NAME OF COMPANY ______________________________

8.02 (B) ADDRESS AT WHICH TO FILE CLAIM __________

8.03 (B) TELEPHONE NO. ______________________________

8.04 (B) FAX NO. ______________________________

8.05 (B) CONTACT PERSON ____________________

8.06 (B) HAVE CLAIMS BEEN FILED ON ALL LIFE INSURANCE POLICIES?

YES ☐ NO ☐

8.01 (C) NAME OF COMPANY ____________________

8.02 (C) ADDRESS AT WHICH TO FILE CLAIM ________

8.03 (C) TELEPHONE NO. ____________________

8.04 (C) FAX NO. ____________________

8.05 (C) CONTACT PERSON ____________________

8.06 (C) HAVE CLAIMS BEEN FILED ON ALL LIFE INSURANCE POLICIES?

YES ☐ NO ☐

8.01 (D) NAME OF COMPANY ____________________

8.02 (D) ADDRESS AT WHICH TO FILE CLAIM ________

______________________________________________

8.03 (D) TELEPHONE NO. ____________________

8.04 (D) FAX NO. ____________________

8.05 (D) CONTACT PERSON ____________________

8.06 (D) HAVE CLAIMS BEEN FILED ON ALL LIFE INSURANCE POLICIES? ____________________

YES ☐ NO ☐

## 9.00 AUTOMOBILE DEALER

9.01 NAME ____________________

9.02 ADDRESS ____________________

9.03 TELEPHONE NO. ____________________

9.04 FAX NO. ____________________

9.05 CONTACT PERSON________________________

9.06 DESCRIPTION OF VEHICLES

<u>YEAR</u> <u>MAKE</u> <u>MODEL</u> <u>EQUIPMENT</u> <u>MILEAGE</u>

(A) ________________________________________

(B) ________________________________________

(C) ________________________________________

**10.00 <u>TRANSFER AGENT</u>**

10.01 (A) NAME OF TRANSFER AGENT______________

10.02 (A) ADDRESS OF TRANSFER AGENT ___________

10.03 (A) NAME OF STOCK TRANSFERRED __________

10.04 (A) NUMBER OF SHARES____________________

10.01 (B) NAME OF TRANSFER AGENT______________

10.02 (B) ADDRESS OF TRANSFER AGENT ___________

10.03 (B) NAME OF STOCK TRANSFERRED __________

10.04 (B) NUMBER OF SHARES____________________

10.01 (C) NAME OF TRANSFER AGENT______________

10.02 (C) ADDRESS OF TRANSFER AGENT ___________

10.03 (C) NAME OF STOCK TRANSFERRED __________

10.04 (C) NUMBER OF SHARES____________________

10.01 (D) NAME OF TRANSFER AGENT______________

10.02 (D) ADDRESS OF TRANSFER AGENT ___________

10.03 (D) NAME OF STOCK TRANSFERRED __________

10.04 (D) NUMBER OF SHARES____________________

10.01 (E) NAME OF TRANSFER AGENT______________

10.02 (E) ADDRESS OF TRANSFER AGENT ___________

10.03 (E) NAME OF STOCK TRANSFERRED __________

10.04 (E) NUMBER OF SHARES____________________

10.01 (F) NAME OF TRANSFER AGENT______________

10.02 (F) ADDRESS OF TRANSFER AGENT ___________

10.03 (F) NAME OF STOCK TRANSFERRED __________

10.04 (F) NUMBER OF SHARES____________________

10.01 (G) NAME OF TRANSFER AGENT______________

10.02 (G) ADDRESS OF TRANSFER AGENT ___________

10.03 (G) NAME OF STOCK TRANSFERRED __________

10.04 (G) NUMBER OF SHARES____________________

10.01 (H) NAME OF TRANSFER AGENT______________

10.02 (H) ADDRESS OF TRANSFER AGENT ___________

10.03 (H) NAME OF STOCK TRANSFERRED __________

10.04 (H) NUMBER OF SHARES____________________

10.01 (I) NAME OF TRANSFER AGENT______________

10.02 (I) ADDRESS OF TRANSFER AGENT ___________

10.03 (I) NAME OF STOCK TRANSFERRED __________

10.04 (I) NUMBER OF SHARES____________________

**11.00 <u>REAL ESTATE</u>**

11.01 (A) STREET ADDRESS OF REAL ESTATE________

11.02 (A) MUNICIPALITY __________________________

11.03 (A) TAX BLOCK_____________________________

11.04 (A) TAX LOT _______________________________

11.05 (A) DEED BOOK_____________________________

11.06 (A) PAGE__________________________________

11.07 (A) TAX ASSESSMENT ____________________

11.08 (A) NAME OF MORTGAGE LENDER ____________

11.09 (A) ADDRESS OF MORTGAGE LENDER ________

11.10 (A) TELEPHONE NO. ____________________

11.11 (A) FAX NO. ____________________________

11.12 (A) DID PROPERTY PASS BY RIGHT OF SURVIVORSHIP?

YES ☐ NO ☐

11.01 (B) STREET ADDRESS OF REAL ESTATE ________

11.02 (B) MUNICIPALITY ______________________

11.03 (B) TAX BLOCK _________________________

11.04 (A) TAX LOT ___________________________

11.05 (B) DEED BOOK_________________________

11.06 (A) PAGE______________________________

11.07 (B) TAX ASSESSMENT ____________________

11.08 (B) NAME OF MORTGAGE LENDER ____________

11.09 (B) ADDRESS OF MORTGAGE LENDER ________

11.10 (B) TELEPHONE NO. ____________________

11.11 (A) FAX NO. ____________________________

11.12 (B) DID PROPERTY PASS BY RIGHT OF SURVIVORSHIP?

YES ☐ NO ☐

11.01 (C) STREET ADDRESS OF REAL ESTATE ________

11.02 (C) MUNICIPALITY ______________________

11.03 (C) TAX BLOCK _________________________

11.04 (A) TAX LOT ___________________________

11.05 (C) DEED BOOK_________________________

11.06 (A) PAGE ______________________

11.07 (C) TAX ASSESSMENT ______________________

11.08 (C) NAME OF MORTGAGE LENDER ______________________

11.09 (C) ADDRESS OF MORTGAGE LENDER ______________________

11.10 (C) TELEPHONE NO. ______________________

11.11 (A) FAX NO. ______________________

11.12 (C) DID PROPERTY PASS BY RIGHT OF SURVIVORSHIP?

YES ☐ NO ☐

11.13 NAME OF APPRAISER ______________________

11.14 ADDRESS OF APPRAISE ______________________

11.15 TELEPHONE NO. ______________________

11.16 FAX NO. ______________________

11.17 CONTACT PERSON ______________________

## 12.00 PERSONAL PROPERTY

12.01 IS AN APPRAISAL REQUIRED OF PERSONAL PROPERTY?

YES ☐ NO ☐

12.02 IF REQUIRED, NAME OF APPRAISER ______________________

12.03 ADDRESS ______________________

12.04 TELEPHONE NO. ______________________

12.05 FAX NO. ______________________

12.06 CONTACT PERSON ______________________

**13.00** **DEBTS** List all debts owe by decedent or decedent's estate:

| | NAME OF CREDITOR | AMOUNT OF DEBT |
|---|---|---|
| 13.01 | | |
| 13.02 | | |
| 13.03 | | |
| 13.04 | | |
| 13.05 | | |
| 13.06 | | |
| 13.07 | | |

## ESTATE PLANNING QUESTIONAIRE

Office: Total______ Deposit_________

Date___________ Home Phone No.______________

Business Phone No._______________

### A. PERSONAL DATA

Full Name_____________________________________________

(print name as shown on your checks)

Address ______________________________________________

City_________________________ State________ Zip______

Birth Date________________ Social Security No.__________

U.S. Citizen? Yes • No • Annual Income______________

If widowed, date of death of spouse____________________; Domestic Partner? Yes [ ]; No [ ]

### B. REFERRAL. By whom were you referred to this office?

Name_________________________________________________

Address_______________________________________________

City_________________________ State______ Zip___________

Add to mailing list: Yes_____

WHO WILL RETAIN WILL? Client______ Attorney______

SIGNING CEREMONY SET FOR:

DATE: ____________________ TIME: ____________

DISPOSITIVE INTENTIONS

1. CHILDREN. If you have children, do you wish to treat all your children equally?

   Yes • No •

If not, why not?____________________________________

After your death, at what age do you want distribution to your children?____________________________________

____________________________________________

(e.g., a plan might provide "immediate" or "1/3 at age 25, 1/3 at age 30, 1/3 at age 35")

2. GRANDCHILDREN. If you have grandchildren, do you wish to leave a specific amount of money or a percentage of your estate to your grandchildren?

   Yes • No •

Do you wish to treat all your grandchildren equally?

   Yes • No •

If you do not wish to treat all your grandchildren equally, why not?

____________________________________________

____________________________________________

How much do you want to leave to your grandchildren?________

________________________________________

At what age do you want distributions to your grandchildren?___

________________________________________

(e.g., a plan might provide "immediate" or "1/3 at age 25, 1/3 at age 30, 1/3 at age 35")

3. CHARITIES. Do you want to leave a specific amount of money or other assets to any charity?

   Yes • No •

   (1) Name of Charity________________________

   Address____________________________

   City________________ State______ Zip______

   Amount: $__________________________

   (2) Name of Charity________________________

   Address ____________________________

   City________________ State______ Zip______

   Amount: $__________________________

4. OTHER BENEFICIARIES. Do you want your Will to benefit anyone other than children, grandchildren, or a charity?

   Yes • No •

If so, please list the name of beneficiary and relationship:

(1) Name__________________ Relationship__________

Address______________________________________

City__________________ State______ Zip______

Amount: $____________________________________

(2) Name__________________ Relationship________

Address _____________________________________

City__________________ State______ Zip______

Amount: $____________________________________

(3) Name__________________ Relationship__________

Address______________________________________

City__________________ State______ Zip______

Amount: $____________________________________

TAX CLAUSE: ____________ allocation clause or ____________ residuary clause

D. EXECUTOR. Whom do you wish to serve as your Executor?

First Choice__________________________________________

Second Choice________________________________________

COMPENSATION CLAUSE:_____________with compensation or without compensation

E. TRUSTEE. Whom do you wish to serve as your Trustee?

First Choice__________________________________________

Second Choice______________________________________

F. GUARDIAN. If you have a minor or disabled child or children, whom do you wish to act as Guardian?

First Choice_______________________________________

Second Choice______________________________________

G. LIVING WILL. Do you want your Living Will to provide for withdrawal of artificial food and fluid?

Yes • No •

Do you want to donate your eyes or organs?

Yes • No •

Do you want your Health Care Agent to consult with any other person prior to acting?

Yes • No •

If yes, with whom?__________________________________

How do you want your Living Will drafted:? [ ] Treat Aggressively; [ ] Do Not Treat

Name of Proposed Health Care Agent__________________
(usually family member or friend)

Address___________________________________________
(if other than child)

City________________________ State________ Zip______

Name of Proposed Alternate Health Care Agent___________

Address___________________________________________
(if other than child)

City______________________ State________ Zip_______

Who is your primary care physician?

Name of Physician____________________________________

Address____________________________________________

City______________________ State________ Zip_______

H. POWER OF ATTORNEY

Name of Proposed Financial Agent______________________
(usually family member or friend)

Address____________________________________________
(if other than child)

City______________________ State________ Zip_______

Name of Proposed Alternate Financial

Agent______________________________________________

Address____________________________________________
(if other than child)

City______________________ State________ Zip_______

Effective: [ ] Immediately; [ ] Springing

I. MISCELLANEOUS. Do you have any other legal issues of which I should be aware?

Yes • No •

If yes, please explain _________________________________

Where are your important papers?_______________________

Do you have a Safe Deposit Box?

Yes • No •

If yes, please indicate its location

___________________________________________________________

Have you ever made gifts to any one person in excess of $10,000 in any one calendar year?

Yes • No •

Have you ever filed a Federal Gift Tax Return?

Yes • No •

CHILDREN (if applicable) (PROVIDE NAME, D.O.B., AND ADDRESS)

1. Name________________________________________ Date of Birth___________

   Address _______________________________________________

   City_________________________ State______ Zip______

2. Name________________________________________ Date of Birth___________

   Address _______________________________________________

   City_________________________ State______ Zip______

3. Name________________________________________ Date of Birth___________

Address ______________________________________________

City________________________ State______ Zip______

4. Name______________________________________ Date of Birth___________

Address ______________________________________________

City________________________ State______ Zip______

5. Name______________________________________ Date of Birth___________

Address ______________________________________________

City________________________ State______ Zip______

Do you have any stepchildren? Yes ☐ No ☐

Are all your children in good health? Yes • No •

Are any of your children blind? Yes • No •

Are any of your children disabled? Yes • No •

Are any of your children receiving SSI or other form of government entitlement? Yes • No •

Do any of your family members have problems with:

Aids? Yes • No •

Drug Addiction? Yes • No •

Alcoholism? Yes • No •

Spendthrift? Yes • No •

GRANDCHILDREN (if applicable) (PROVIDE NAME, D.O.B., AND ADDRESS)

1. Name____________________________________ Date of

   Birth__________

   Address ________________________________________

   City______________________ State_____ Zip_____

2. Name____________________________________ Date of

   Birth__________

   Address ________________________________________

   City______________________ State_____ Zip_____

3. Name____________________________________ Date of

   Birth__________

   Address ________________________________________

   City______________________ State_____ Zip_____

4. Name____________________________________ Date of

   Birth__________

   Address ________________________________________

   City______________________ State_____ Zip_____

5. Name__________________________________________ Date of
Birth___________

Address ________________________________________________

City__________________________ State______ Zip______

6. Name__________________________________________ Date of

Birth___________

Address ________________________________________________

City__________________________ State______ Zip______

L. FINANCIAL SUMMARY

| | ASSETS | LIABILITIES |
|---|---|---|
| Bank Accounts [attach copies of statements] | $___________ | $___________ |
| Real Estate (residence) [attach copy of deed] | $___________ | $___________ |
| Real Estate (other) [attach copies of all deeds] | $___________ | $___________ |
| Certificates of Deposit (CDs) [attach copies of statements] | $___________ | $___________ |
| Stocks—Nonmutual Funds (Not Held by Broker) [attach copies of all certificates] | $___________ | $___________ |

| | | |
|---|---|---|
| Stocks—Nonmutual Funds (Held by Broker) [attach copies of brokerage statements] | $__________ | $__________ |
| Bonds—Nonmutual Funds (Not Held by Broker) [attach copies of all bonds] | $__________ | $__________ |
| Bonds—Nonmutual Funds (Held by Broker) [attach copies of brokerage statements] | $__________ | $__________ |
| Mutual Funds [attach copies of statements] | $__________ | $__________ |
| Note and Mortgage Receivables [attach copies of Notes & Mortgages] | $__________ | $__________ |
| Business Interests | $__________ | $__________ |
| [attach copies of stock certificates, partnership agreements and/or other documentation] | | |
| Inheritance, etc. | $__________ | $__________ |
| Automobiles | $__________ | $__________ |
| Jewelry and Collection | $__________ | $__________ |
| Non-IRA Tax-Qualified Retirement Plans [attach copies of statements] | $__________ | $__________ |

| | | |
|---|---|---|
| IRAs [attach copies of statements] | $__________ | $__________ |
| Life Insurance [attach copies of all policies] | $__________ | $__________ |
| Annuities [attach copies of all policies] | $__________ | $__________ |
| Other Assets [attach copies of documentation pertaining to such assets] | $__________ | $__________ |
| TOTALS | $__________ | $__________ |

M. HEALTH

General Description of Client's Health:

______________________________________________

______________________________________________

Would you prefer that the documents I draft for you be streamlined and easily understood by a person unfamiliar with elder law issues, i.e., a layperson?

[ ] Simple documents

Or, would you prefer the documents to be comprehensive and drafted in such a way that although not entirely clear to a layperson, clearly carry-out your intentions and empower your executor/agent to carry-out those intentions even if those actions are challenged by others?

[ ] standard documents

## Estate Planning Personal Data Sheet

Office: Total______ Deposit_______

Date____________ Home Phone No.____________

Business Phone No.__________

A. **PERSONAL DATA**

| **Husband** | **Wife** |
|---|---|
| Name______________________ (print name as shown on your checks) | Name________________ (print name as shown on your checks) |

Address_____________________________________________

City________________________ State________ Zip______

| **Husband** | **Wife** |
|---|---|
| Birth Date___________________ | Birth Date_____________ |
| Social Security No____________ | Social Security No.______ |
| U.S. Citizen? Yes ☐ No ☐ | U.S. Citizen? Yes ☐ No ☐ |
| Annual Income_______________ | Annual Income_________ |

Added to mailing list: Yes___

**WHO WILL RETAIN WILL?** Client_____ Attorney_____

B. **REFERRAL**. By whom were you referred to this office?

Name_______________________________________________

Address_____________________________________________

City________________________ State________ Zip_______

**SIGNING CEREMONY SET FOR:**

**DATE:** ________________________ **TIME:**________________

C. **DISPOSITIVE INTENTIONS**

1. SPOUSE AND CHILDREN. Do you wish to provide primarily for your spouse and secondarily for your children?

Yes ☐ No ☐

Do you wish to treat all your children equally?

Yes ☐ No ☐

If not, why not?________________________________________

____________________________________________________

After your spouse's death, at what age do you want distribution to your children?_____________________________________

____________________________________________________

(e.g., a plan might provide "immediate" or "1/3 at age 25, 1/3 at age 30, 1/3 at age 35")

2. GRANDCHILDREN. Do you want to leave a specific amount of money or a percentage of your estate to your grandchildren?

Yes ☐ No ☐

Do you wish to treat all your grandchildren equally?

Yes ☐ No ☐

If you do not want to treat all your grandchildren equally, why not?

____________________________________________________

How much do you want to leave your grandchildren?___________

At what age do you want distribution to your grandchildren?_____

___________________________________________________

(e.g., a plan might provide "immediate" or "1/3 at age 25, 1/3 at age 30, and 1/3 at age 35")

3. CHARITIES. Do you want to leave a specific amount of money or other assets to any charity?

Yes ☐ No ☐

(1) Name of Charity_________________________________

Address_______________________________________

City_________________________ State________ Zip______

Amount: $__________________

(2) Name of Charity_________________________________

Address_______________________________________

City_________________________ State________ Zip______

Amount: $__________________

4. OTHER BENEFICIARIES. Do you want your Will to benefit anyone other than children, grandchildren, or a charity?

Yes ☐ No ☐

If so, please list the name of beneficiary and relationship:

(1) Name________________ Relationship_________________

Address____________________________________________

City________________________ State________ Zip_______

Amount: $___________________

(2) Name________________ Relationship__________________

Address____________________________________________

City________________________ State________ Zip_______

Amount: $___________________

(3) Name________________ Relationship__________________

Address____________________________________________

City________________________ State________ Zip_______

Amount: $___________________

**TAX CLAUSE:** ___________Allocation Clause or___________
Residuary Clause

D. **<u>EXECUTOR</u>**. Whom do you wish to serve as your Executor?

**Husband**

First Choice_________________________________________

Address____________________________________________

City________________________ State________ Zip_______

Second Choice________________________________________

Address________________________________________________

City_________________________ State________ Zip_______

**Wife**

First Choice_____________________________________________

Address________________________________________________

City_________________________ State________ Zip_______

Second Choice___________________________________________

Address________________________________________________

City_________________________ State________ Zip_______

**COMPENSATION:** __________with compensation or__________ without compensation

E. **<u>TRUSTEE</u>**. Whom do you wish to serve as your Trustee?

**Husband**

First Choice_____________________________________________

Address________________________________________________

City_________________________ State________ Zip_______

Second Choice___________________________________________

Address________________________________________________

City_________________________ State________ Zip_______

**Wife**

First Choice_____________________________________________

Address________________________________________________

City_________________________ State________ Zip_______

Second Choice__________________________________________

Address________________________________________________

City_________________________ State________ Zip_______

F. **GUARDIAN**. If you have a minor or disabled child or children, whom do you wish to act as Guardian?

**Husband**

First Choice___________________________________________

Address________________________________________________

City_________________________ State________ Zip_______

Second Choice__________________________________________

Address________________________________________________

City_________________________ State________ Zip_______

**Wife**

First Choice___________________________________________

Address________________________________________________

City_________________________ State________ Zip_______

Second Choice__________________________________________

Address_______________________________________________

City_____________________________ State_________ Zip_______

G. <u>LIVING WILL</u>

**Husband**

Do you want your Living Will to provide for withdrawal of artificial food and fluid? Yes ☐ No ☐

Do you want to donate your eyes or organs? Yes ☐ No ☐

Do you want your Health Care Agent to consult with any other person prior to acting? Yes ☐ No ☐

If yes, with whom?_______________________________________

How do you want your Living Will drafted:? [ ] **Treat Aggressively;** [ ] **Do Not Treat**

Name of Proposed Health Care Agent__________________________
(usually family member or friend)

Address_______________________________________________
(if other than child)

City_____________________________ State_________ Zip_______

Name of Proposed Alternate Health Care

Agent_________________________________________________

Address_______________________________________________
(if other than child)

City_____________________________ State_________ Zip_______

Who is your primary care physician?

Name of Physician________________________________________

Address__________________________________________________

City__________________________ State________ Zip_______

**Wife**

Do you want your Living Will to provide for withdrawal of artificial food and fluid? Yes ☐ No ☐

Do you want to donate your eyes or organs? Yes ☐ No ☐

Do you want your Health Care Agent to consult with any other person prior to acting? Yes ☐ No ☐

If yes, with whom?_______________________________________

How do you want your Living Will drafted:? [ ] **Treat Aggressively;** [ ] **Do Not Treat**

Name of Proposed Health Care Agent______________________
(usually family member or friend)

Address__________________________________________________
(if other than child)

City_________________ State________ Zip_______________

Name of Proposed Alternate Health Care

Agent____________________________________________________

Address__________________________________________________
(if other than child)

City__________________________ State________ Zip_______

Who is your primary care physician?
Name of Physician______________________________

Address______________________________________

City_____________________ State________ Zip______

## H. <u>POWER OF ATTORNEY</u>

**Husband**

Name of Proposed Financial Agent____________________
(usually family member or friend)

Address______________________________________
(if other than child)

City_____________________ State________ Zip______

Name of Proposed Alternate Financial Agent____________

Address______________________________________
(if other than child)

City_____________________ State________ Zip______

Effective: [ ] **Immediately; [ ] Springing**

**Wife**

Name of Proposed Financial Agent____________________

Address______________________________________
(if other than child)

City_____________________ State________ Zip______

Name of Proposed Alternate Financial Agent_______________

Address_______________________________________________
(if other than child)

City________________________ State_______ Zip______

**Effective: [ ] Immediately; [ ] Springing**

## I. MISCELLANEOUS

Do you have any other legal issues of which I should be aware?

Yes ☐ No ☐

If yes, please explain__________________________________

________________________________________________________

Where are your important papers? ______________________

Do you have a Safe Deposit Box? Yes ☐ No ☐

If yes, please indicate its location___________________

________________________________________________________

## J. CHILDREN (if applicable) (provide full name, date of birth, address with zip code)

1. Name____________________________________ Date of Birth__________

Address_______________________________________________

City________________________ State_______ Zip______

2. Name_______________________________ Date of Birth__________

Address_______________________________________________

City________________________ State________ Zip______

3. Name_______________________________ Date of Birth__________

Address_______________________________________________

City________________________ State________ Zip______

4. Name_______________________________ Date of Birth__________

Address_______________________________________________

City________________________ State________ Zip______

5. Name_______________________________ Date of Birth__________

Address_______________________________________________

City________________________ State________ Zip______

6. Name_______________________________ Date of Birth__________

Address________________________________________________

City_________________________ State________ Zip_______

Does the Husband have any children by a previous marriage?

Yes ☐ No ☐

Does the Wife have any children by a previous marriage?

Yes ☐ No ☐

Are all your children in good health? Yes ☐ No ☐

Are any of your children blind? Yes ☐ No ☐

Are any of your children disabled? Yes ☐ No ☐

Have all your children completed their education?

Yes ☐ No ☐

Are any of your children receiving SSI or other form of government entitlement? Yes ☐ No ☐

Do any of your family members have any problems with:

Aids? Yes ☐ No ☐

Drug Addiction? Yes ☐ No ☐

Alcoholism? Yes ☐ No ☐

Spendthrift? Yes ☐ No ☐

**<u>GRANDCHILDREN</u>** (if applicable) (provide full name, date of birth, and address with zip code)

1. Name_______________________________________ Date of Birth__________

Address_______________________________________________

City___________________________ State________ Zip______

2. Name_______________________________________ Date of Birth__________

Address_______________________________________________

City___________________________ State________ Zip______

3. Name_______________________________________ Date of Birth__________

Address_______________________________________________

City___________________________ State________ Zip______

4. Name_______________________________________ Date of Birth__________

Address_______________________________________________

City___________________________ State________ Zip______

5. Name_________________________________ Date of Birth__________

Address______________________________________________

City____________________________ State________ Zip_______

6. Name_________________________________ Date of Birth__________

Address______________________________________________

City____________________________ State________ Zip_______

7. Name_________________________________ Date of Birth__________

Address______________________________________________

City____________________________ State________ Zip_______

8. Name_________________________________ Date of Birth__________

Address______________________________________________

City____________________________ State________ Zip_______

## L. FINANCIAL SUMMARY

| | ASSETS | | | LIABILITIES |
|---|---|---|---|---|
| | Husband | Wife | Joint | |
| Bank Accounts [attach copies of statements] | $______ | $____ | $____ | $____ |
| Real Estate (residence) [attach copy of deed] | $______ | $____ | $____ | $____ |
| Real Estate (other) [attach copies of all deeds] | $______ | $____ | $____ | $____ |
| Savings Certificates (CDs) [attach copies of statements] | $______ | $____ | $____ | $____ |
| Stocks—Nonmutual Funds (Not Held by Broker) [attach copies of all certificates] | $______ | $____ | $____ | $____ |
| Stocks—Nonmutual Funds (Held by Broker) [attach copies of brokerage statements] | $______ | $____ | $____ | $____ |
| Bonds—Nonmutual Funds (Not Held by Broker) [attach copies of all bonds] | $______ | $____ | $____ | $____ |
| Bonds—Nonmutual Funds (Held by Broker) [attach copies of brokerage statements] | $______ | $____ | $____ | $____ |
| Mutual Funds [attach copies of statements] | $____ | $____ | $____ | $____ |

| | | | | |
|---|---|---|---|---|
| Note and Mortgages Receivables [attach copies of Notes and Mortgages] | $______ | $____ | $____ | $____ |
| Business Interests [attach copies of stock certificates, partnership agreements, and/or other documentation] | $______ | $____ | $____ | $____ |
| Inheritance, etc. | $______ | $____ | $____ | $____ |
| Automobiles | $______ | $____ | $____ | $____ |
| Jewelry and Collections | $______ | $____ | $____ | $____ |
| Non-IRA Tax-Qualified Retirement Plans [attach copies of statements] | $______ | $____ | $____ | $____ |
| IRAs [attach copies of statements] | $______ | $____ | $____ | $____ |
| Life Insurance [attach copies of all policies] | $______ | $____ | $____ | $____ |
| Annuities [attach copies of all policies] | $______ | $____ | $____ | $____ |
| Other Assets [attach copies of documentation pertaining to such assets] | $______ | $____ | $____ | $____ |
| **TOTALS** | $______ | $____ | $____ | $____ |

## M. HEALTH

**General Description of Wife's Health:**

______________________________________________________________

______________________________________________________________

**General Description of Husband's Health:**

______________________________________________________________

______________________________________________________________

**Would you prefer that the documents I draft for you be streamlined and easily understood by a person unfamiliar with elder law issues, i.e., a layperson?**

**[ ] Simple documents**

**Or, would you prefer the documents to be comprehensive and drafted in such a way that although not entirely clear to a layperson, clearly carry-out your intentions and empower your executor/agent to carry-out those intentions even if those actions are challenged by others?**

**[ ] standard documents**

# MEDICAID PLANNING QUESTIONAIRE

Office: Total______ Deposit________

## A. CONTACT PERSON

Name ________________________ Date ________________

Address ____________________________________________

City________________________ State________ Zip_______

Home Phone No.____________ Business Phone No. _________

E-Mail Address _______________ Fax No. ________________

Add Contact Person to Mailing List: ____ yes; _____ no

## B. PERSONAL INFORMATION—CLIENT

Full Name __________________________________________

(print name as shown on your checks)

Address ____________________________________________

City________________________ State________ Zip_______

Telephone No.______________ Fax No. __________________

How long have you resided at this address:___________________

If less than five years, location of prior residence:______________

____________________________________________________

Birth Date___________ Social Security No. ____________________

Add Client to Mailing List: ____ yes; ____ no

**SIGNING CEREMONY SET FOR:**

**DATE:** ________________________ **TIME:** _________________

U.S. Citizen? Yes ☐ No ☐

Veteran? Yes ☐ No ☐ War Veteran? Yes ☐ No ☐

If widowed, your spouse's date of death _______________________

Was your former spouse a Veteran? Yes ☐ No ☐

War Veteran? Yes ☐ No ☐

**C.** **<u>CHILDREN</u>** (if applicable) (provide name, telephone number, date of birth, social security number)

1.

2.

3.

4.

5. (CIRCLE ONE)

Are all your children in good health? Yes No

Are any of your children blind? Yes No

Are any of your children disabled? Yes No

Are any of your children receiving SSI or another form of government entitlement? Yes No

Do any of your family members have problem with Aids?

Yes No

Drug Addiction? Yes No

Alcoholism? Yes No

Spendthrift? Yes No

Do any of your children live with you? Yes No

Does a sibling live with you? Yes No

**D. <u>GRANDCHILDREN</u>** (if applicable)

| GRANDCHILD'S NAME | ADDRESS (WITH ZIP CODE) |
|---|---|
| ____________________ | ________________________ |
| ____________________ | ________________________ |
| ____________________ | ________________________ |
| ____________________ | ________________________ |

**E. <u>MEDICAL INFORMATION—CLIENT</u>**

**1.** <u>HEALTH</u>

Diagnosis______________________________________________

_______________________________________________________

Do you live in a nursing home or an assisted-living facility?

Yes No

If yes, name of facility ______________________________

Do you have any unpaid medical bills, which have been incurred in the last three months?—Yes No;
If so, please bring bills with you.

2. PHYSICIAN

Name of Primary Physician ______________________________

Address ______________________________

City______________________ State________ Zip________

Do you have a policy of private health insurance? Yes No;

If yes, what is the name of the company and your member #_____

______________________________

3. STATE PHARMACEUTICAL PLAN

Are you currently receiving benefits from a state pharmaceutical plan? Yes ☐ No ☐

**F. MONTHLY INCOME**

Social Security Benefits $____________

Medicare Part B Deduction $____________

Retirement Benefits (Gross)* $____________

Veterans Disability Income $____________________

Annuity Income $____________________

Rental Income $____________________

TOTAL MONTHLY INCOME $____________________

*If there is a pension, please list the gross pension amount under Retirement Benefits, including any monies taken out for federal income taxes, health insurance, or any other reason.

Could the Retirement Benefits amount increase in the future?

Yes ☐ No ☐

Note: Do not include investment income on this form.

## G. MONTHLY COSTS OF NURSING HOME

Monthly Nursing Home Cost $____________________

Monthly Prescription Cost $____________________

Monthly Incontinent Cost $____________________

Monthly Other Cost $____________________

TOTAL MONTHLY COST $____________________

The nursing home is paid through the month of ______________

## H. GIFTS

List all gifts greater than $1,000 made in the past five years:

Recipient __________________ Date ________ Amount _______

Recipient ____________________ Date ________ Amount __________

Recipient ____________________ Date ________ Amount __________

Recipient ____________________ Date ________ Amount __________

Recipient ____________________ Date ________ Amount __________

Recipient ____________________ Date ________ Amount __________

Recipient ____________________ Date ________ Amount __________

Recipient ____________________ Date ________ Amount __________

Recipient ____________________ Date ________ Amount __________

## I. ASSETS/LIABILITIES

Please insert the value of each asset/liability in the appropriate space.

| Asset/Liability | Asset Total | Liability Total |
|---|---|---|
| PERSONAL EFFECTS | ____________ | ____________ |
| CHECKING ACCOUNT | ____________ | ____________ |
| SAVINGS ACCOUNT | ____________ | ____________ |
| MONEY MARKET ACCOUNT | ____________ | ____________ |
| CERTIFICATES OF DEPOSIT | ____________ | ____________ |
| RESIDENCE (ASSESSED VALUE) | ____________ | ____________ |

| | | |
|---|---|---|
| OTHER REAL ESTATE | ________ | ________ |
| AUTOMOBILE(S) | ________ | ________ |
| BROKERAGE ACCOUNTS | ________ | ________ |
| MUTUAL FUNDS NOT HELD BY BROKER | ________ | ________ |
| STOCKS NOT HELD BY BROKER | ________ | ________ |
| BONDS NOT HELD BY BROKER | ________ | ________ |
| ANNUITIES | ________ | ________ |
| CASH VALUE OF LIFE INSURANCE | ________ | ________ |
| IRA | ________ | ________ |
| NURSING HOME DEPOSIT | ________ | ________ |
| OTHER | ________ | ________ |
| OTHER | ________ | ________ |
| TOTAL | ________ | ________ |

What did you pay for your current home including any improvements?

$________________________________________

## J. REFERRAL

By whom were you referred to this office?

Name ______________________________________________

Address ____________________________________________

City_________________________ State________ Zip_______

## MEDICAID PLANNING QUESTIONNAIRE

**Office:** **Total**______ **Deposit**_________

### A. CONTACT PERSON (your information)

Name ____________________________________ Date ________

Address ________________________________________________

City_________________________ State________ Zip_______

Home Phone No. ______________ Business Phone No. _________

E-Mail Address ______________________ Fax No. ___________

Add Contact Person to Mailing List: ____ yes; _____ no

### B. PERSONAL INFORMATION

Husband Wife

Full Name____________________ ______________________

(print names as they appear on your checks)

Address_________________________________________________

City_________________________ State________ Zip_______

Telephone No.____________________ Fax No. ______________

How long have you resided at this address:____________________

If less than five years, location of prior residence:______________

_______________________________________________________

Add Client to Mailing List: _____ yes; _____ no

**SIGNING CEREMONY SET FOR:**

**DATE:** __________________________ **TIME:** ____________________

Husband | Wife

Birth Date ______________________ ___________________________

Social Security No. ______________ ___________________________

U.S. Citizen? Yes ☐ No ☐ U.S. Citizen? Yes ☐ No ☐

Veteran? Yes ☐ No ☐ War Veteran? Yes ☐ No ☐

Veteran? Yes ☐ No ☐

**C.** **CHILDREN** (if applicable) (provide full name, address, date of birth, phone number, and social security number of each)

**1.** Name ___________________________ Date __________________

Address ______________________________________________________

City_____________________________ State_________ Zip_______

Home Phone No. __________________ Date of Birth _____________

Social Security Number: __________________________________

**2.** Name ___________________________ Date __________________

Address ______________________________________________________

City_____________________________ State_________ Zip_______

Home Phone No. ____________________ Date of Birth ____________

Social Security Number: ________________________________

**3.** Name ___________________________ Date __________________

Address ______________________________________________

City_____________________________ State_________ Zip_______

Home Phone No. ________________ Date of Birth _______________

Social Security Number: ________________________________

**4.** Name ___________________________Date __________________

Address ______________________________________________

City_____________________________ State_________ Zip_______

Home Phone No. ________________ Date of Birth _______________

Social Security Number: ________________________________

**5.** Name ___________________________Date __________________

Address ______________________________________________

City_____________________________ State_________ Zip_______

Home Phone No. ________________ Date of Birth _______________

Social Security Number: ________________________________

Does the Husband have any children by a previous marriage?

Yes ☐ No ☐

Does the Wife have any children by a previous marriage?

Yes ☐ No ☐

Are all your children in good health?

Yes ☐ No ☐

Are any of your children blind?

Yes ☐ No ☐

Are any of your children disabled?

Yes ☐ No ☐

Have all your children completed their education?

Yes ☐ No ☐

Are any of your children receiving SSI or other form of government entitlement?

Yes ☐ No ☐

Do any of your family members have any problems with:

| | |
|---|---|
| Aids? | Yes ☐ No ☐ |
| Drug Addiction? | Yes ☐ No ☐ |
| Alcoholism? | Yes ☐ No ☐ |
| Spendthrift? | Yes ☐ No ☐ |

Do any of your children live with you?

Yes ☐ No ☐

**D. GRANDCHILDREN** (if applicable)

| GRANDCHILD'S NAME | ADDRESS (WITH ZIP CODE) |
|---|---|
| ______________________ | ____________________________ |
| ______________________ | ____________________________ |
| ______________________ | ____________________________ |
| ______________________ | ____________________________ |

**E. MEDICAL INFORMATION**

**1. HEALTH**

Name of Ill Spouse ________________________________________

Diagnosis________________________________________________

Prognosis________________________________________________

Course of Treatment ______________________________________

Where Ill Spouse Currently Resides_________________________

__________________________________________________________

Is this a nursing home? Yes No

If yes, date entered _______________________________________

Name of Well Spouse ______________________________________

Health of Well Spouse _____________________________________

Where Well Spouse Currently Resides ______________________

______________________________________________________

Is this a nursing home? Yes No

If yes, date entered ____________________________________

## 2. PHYSICIAN

Husband

Name of Primary Physician ______________________________

Address_________________________________________________

City_________________________ State_________ Zip_______

Wife

Name of Primary Physician ______________________________

Address_________________________________________________

City_________________________ State_________ Zip_______

Do you or your spouse have a policy of private health insurance? Yes No; If yes, what is the name of the company and your member id number(s)

## 3. STATE PHARMACEUTICAL PLAN

Are you currently on the Pharmaceutical Assistance to the Aged and Disabled (PAAD) program or any other state pharmaceutical plan? Yes ☐ No ☐

## F. MONTHLY INCOME

| Husband's Monthly Income | Wife's Monthly Income |
|---|---|
| Social Security Benefits | |
| $______________________ | $______________________ |
| Medicare Part B Deduction | |
| $______________________ | $______________________ |
| Retirement Benefits (Gross)* | |
| $______________________ | $______________________ |
| VA Disability Benefit | |
| $______________________ | $______________________ |
| Annuity Income | |
| $______________________ | $______________________ |
| Rental Income | |
| $______________________ | $______________________ |
| TOTAL MONTHLY INCOME | |
| $______________________ | $______________________ |

*If there is a pension, list the gross pension amount under Retirement Benefits, including any monies taken out for federal income taxes, health insurance, or any other reason.

Could the Retirement Benefits amount increase in the future?

Yes ☐ No ☐

Note: Do not include investment income on this form.

## G. MONTHLY COSTS OF NURSING HOME

Monthly Nursing Home Cost $____________________

Monthly Prescription Cost $____________________

Monthly Incontinent Cost $____________________

Monthly Other Cost $____________________

Total Monthly Costs $____________________

The nursing home is paid through the month of_______________

## H. MONTHLY SHELTER EXPENSES

(Please divide annual expenses by 12 and quarterly expenses by 3)

Rent/Mortgage $____________________

Real Estate Taxes $____________________

Water $____________________

Sewer $____________________

Utilities $____________________

(Heat, Electricity, Phone)

(1/12th of last 12 months)

Homeowner's insurance premium $____________________
Condominium fees $____________________

Total Monthly Housing Expenses $____________________

## I. MONTHLY NON-SHELTER LIVING EXPENSES

Food $____________________

Medical $____________________

Clothing $____________________

Transportation
(including auto insurance) $____________________

Home Maintenance $____________________

Life Insurance Premiums $____________________

Health Insurance Premiums $____________________

Cable TV $____________________

Federal and State Income Taxes $____________________

Other $____________________

Total Monthly Non-Shelter

Living Expenses $____________________

## J. GIFTS

List all gifts greater than $1,000 made in the past five years:

Recipient __________________ Date ________ Amount _______

Recipient __________________ Date ________ Amount _______

Recipient __________________ Date ________ Amount _______

Recipient __________________ Date ________ Amount _______

Recipient __________________ Date ________ Amount _______

Recipient __________________ Date ________ Amount _______

Recipient __________________ Date ________ Amount _______

Recipient __________________ Date ________ Amount _______

## K. ASSETS/LIABILITIES

Please insert the value (in dollars) of each asset/liability in the appropriate space.

| | Assets | | | |
|---|---|---|---|---|
| | Husband | Wife | Joint | Liabilities |
| PERSONAL EFFECTS | $_____ | $_____ | $_____ | $_____ |
| AUTOMOBILE | $_____ | $_____ | $_____ | $_____ |
| ADDITIONAL AUTOMOBILES | $_____ | $_____ | $_____ | $_____ |
| CHECKING ACCOUNT | $_____ | $_____ | $_____ | $_____ |
| SAVINGS ACCOUNT | $_____ | $_____ | $_____ | $_____ |

| | | | | |
|---|---|---|---|---|
| MONEY MARKET ACCOUNT | $_____ | $_____ | $_____ | $_____ |
| CERTIFICATES OF DEPOSIT | $_____ | $_____ | $_____ | $_____ |
| RESIDENCE (ASSESSED VALUE) | $_____ | $_____ | $_____ | $_____ |
| OTHER REAL ESTATE | $_____ | $_____ | $_____ | $_____ |
| BROKERAGE ACCOUNT | $_____ | $_____ | $_____ | $_____ |
| MUTUAL FUNDS NOT HELD BY BROKER | $_____ | $_____ | $_____ | $_____ |
| STOCKS NOT HELD BY BROKER | $_____ | $_____ | $_____ | $_____ |
| BONDS NOT HELD BY BROKER | $_____ | $_____ | $_____ | $_____ |
| ANNUITIES | $_____ | $_____ | $_____ | $_____ |
| CASH VALUE OF LIFE INSURANCE | $_____ | $_____ | $_____ | $_____ |
| IRA | $_____ | $_____ | $_____ | $_____ |
| NURSING HOME DEPOSIT | $_____ | $_____ | $_____ | $_____ |
| OTHER | $_____ | $_____ | $_____ | $_____ |
| TOTALS | $_____ | $_____ | $_____ | $_____ |

What did you pay for your current home? $________________

Improvement costs? $________________

Address of any real property other than personal residence:

(1) Address____________________________________________

City ____________________________ State ______ Zip_______

Tax Block #________ Lot # __________ (Can be obtained from Tax Bill)

What did you pay for this property, including any improvements?

$_______________________________________________________

(2) Address____________________________________________

City ____________________________ State ______ Zip_______

Tax Block #________ Lot # __________ (Can be obtained from Tax Bill

What did you pay for this property? $______________

Improvement costs? $______________

Name of Homeowner's Insurance Company________________

Address_______________________________________________

City ____________________________ State ______ Zip_______

Phone No.______________________ Policy No.______________

**L.** **LIFE INSURANCE** (provide company name, address, face amount, cash surrender value, if any)

Name of Life Insurance Company____________________________

Address__________________________________________________

City ______________________________ State _______ Zip________

Phone No.________________________ Policy No.________________

**M.** **REFERRAL**

By whom were you referred to this office?

Name____________________________________________________

Address__________________________________________________

City ______________________________ State _______ Zip________

## Guardianship Questionnaire

Office: Total_____ Deposit_________

Date__________________ Home Phone No.____________

Business Phone No.____________________

I. <u>GENERAL</u>

Full Name of Proposed Ward______________________________
(print name as Proposed Ward signed checks)

Address ________________________________________________

City_________________________ State________ Zip______

Date Domicile Established__________________________________

Place of Confinement or Hospitalization (if different from address above):

Name of Institution________________________________________

Address__________________________________________________

City_________________________ State________ Zip______

Date of Confinement or Hospitalization____________________

Birth Date___________ Age____ Social Security No._______

## II. PROPOSED GUARDIAN(S)

### A. PROPOSED GUARDIAN

Full Name of Proposed Guardian______________________________

Address____________________________________________________

City____________________________ State_________ Zip_______

Home Phone No.______________Business Phone No.____________

Birth Date____________________Social Security No.____________

Added to mailing list: Yes___

Relationship to Proposed Ward or Interest in Proceedings:

____________________________________________________________

Educational Background and occupation

____________________________________________________________

### B. PROPOSED CO-GUARDIAN

Full Name of Proposed Co-Guardian (if applicable)

____________________________________________________________

Address____________________________________________________

City____________________________ State_________ Zip_______

Home Phone No.______________Business Phone No.____________

Birth Date____________________Social Security No.____________

Relationship to Proposed Ward or Interest in Proceedings:

______________________________________________

Educational background and occupation:

______________________________________________

C. POTENTIAL CONFLICTS

1. Is the Proposed Guardian receiving any compensation from the Proposed Ward for services rendered? Yes ☐ No ☐

If yes, how much is the compensation? $______________

2. Does the Proposed Guardian owe any funds to the Proposed Ward? Yes ☐ No ☐

If yes, how much? $______________

3. Does the Proposed Ward owe any funds to the Proposed Guardian? Yes ☐ No ☐

If yes, how much? $______________

4. Has the Proposed Guardian encountered any of the following problems?

a. Conviction of a crime? Yes ☐ No ☐

(other than a misdemeanor)

b. Bankruptcy? Yes ☐ No ☐

c. Revocation of a professional or occupational license? Yes ☐ No ☐

III. NAMES, ADDRESSES, AND RELATIONSHIPS OF PERSONS ENTITLED TO NOTICE OF HEARING

A. PROPOSED WARD. Is it anticipated that the Proposed Ward will remain at the above address for the next six (6) weeks? Yes ☐ No ☐

B. PROPOSED WARD'S SPOUSE

Married ☐ Separated ☐ Divorced ☐ Deceased ☐

Name of Proposed Ward's Spouse__________________________

Address______________________________________________

City_________________________ State________ Zip_______

Home Phone No._____________Business Phone No.____________

Birth Date___________ Age____ Social Security No._______

B. PROPOSED WARD'S FATHER

Name of Proposed Ward's Father (if living)____________________

Address______________________________________________

City_________________________ State________ Zip_______

Home Phone No._____________Business Phone No.____________

C. PROPOSED WARD'S MOTHER

Name of Proposed Ward's Mother (if living)___________________

Address______________________________________________

City_________________________ State________ Zip______

Home Phone No.____________Business Phone No.__________

## D. PROPOSED WARD'S CHILDREN

1. Name of Child________________________________________

Address___________________________________________________

City_________________________ State________ Zip______

Home Phone No.____________ Business Phone No.__________

Birth Date__________________ Age______________________

2. Name of Child________________________________________

Address___________________________________________________

City_________________________ State________ Zip______

Home Phone No.____________ Business Phone No.__________

Birth Date__________________ Age______________________

3. Name of Child________________________________________

Address___________________________________________________

City_________________________ State________ Zip______

Home Phone No.____________ Business Phone No.__________

Birth Date__________________ Age______________________

4. Name of Child______________________________

Address______________________________

City__________________ State________ Zip________

Home Phone No.____________ Business Phone No.__________

Birth Date______________ Age______________

5. Name of Child______________________________

Address______________________________

City__________________ State________ Zip________

Home Phone No.____________ Business Phone No.__________

Birth Date______________ Age______________

6. Name of Child______________________________

Address______________________________

City__________________ State________ Zip________

Home Phone No.____________ Business Phone No.__________

Birth Date______________ Age______________

E. <u>CLOSEST RELATIVE(S) OF PROPOSED WARD (IF NO PARENTS, SPOUSE, OR CHILDREN)</u>

1. Name of Relative______________________________

Address______________________________

City________________________ State________ Zip______

Home Phone No.____________ Business Phone No.__________

Birth Date__________________ Age______________________

2. Name of Relative________________________________

Address________________________________________________

City________________________ State________ Zip______

Home Phone No.____________ Business Phone No.__________

Birth Date__________________ Age______________________

3. Name of Relative________________________________

Address________________________________________________

City________________________ State________ Zip______

Home Phone No.____________ Business Phone No.__________

Birth Date__________________ Age______________________

F. INDIVIDUAL LIVING WITH PROPOSED WARD.
Full Name of Individual Living With Proposed Ward

________________________________________________

G. ADMINISTRATOR OF FACILITY IN WHICH PROPOSED WARD IS LIVING (IF APPLICABLE)

Name of Administrator____________________________

Address________________________________________

City______________________ State_______ Zip____

Business Phone No._______________________________

H. <u>BUSINESS PARTNER(S) OR ASSOCIATE(S) OF PROPOSED WARD</u>

1. Name of Partner or Associate_______________________

Address________________________________________

City___________________ State_______ Zip______

Home Phone No._______ Business Phone No._________

2. Name of Partner or Associate_______________________

Address________________________________________

City___________________ State_______ Zip______

Home Phone No._______ Business Phone No._________

I. <u>POTENTIAL WITNESSES (INDEPENDENT OF FAMILY MEMBERS)</u>

1. Name of Potential Witness_________________________

Address________________________________________

City___________________ State_______ Zip______

Home Phone No._______ Business Phone No._________

2. Name of Potential Witness ______________________

Address ______________________

City ____________ State ________ Zip ______

Home Phone No. ________ Business Phone No. __________

3. Name of Potential Witness ______________________

Address ______________________

City ____________ State ________ Zip ______

Home Phone No. ________ Business Phone No. __________

IV. WHY DOES PROPOSED WARD NEED A GUARDIAN?

A. Name(s) of medical condition(s):

______________________

______________________

B. Examples of mental incapacity:

______________________

______________________

C. If an emergency temporary guardianship is necessary, what immediate harm will be prevented by such guardianship?

______________________

V. MEDICAL

A. PHYSICIAN OF PROPOSED WARD

1. Name of Physician/Psychiatrist (if any)

______________________________________________

Address________________________________________

City__________________ State________ Zip_______

Business Phone No.______________________________

Attending ☐ or Examining ☐

2. Name of Physician/Psychiatrist (if any)

______________________________________________

Address________________________________________

City__________________ State________ Zip_______

Business Phone No.______________________________

Attending ☐ or Examining ☐

B. INSURANCE

1. Medicare: Medicare Part A ☐ Medicare Part B ☐

2. Private Insurance (Please provide copy of policy)

Name of Private Medical Insurance Company

______________________________________________

Address________________________________________

City______________________________ State_________ Zip_______

Business Phone No.______________________________________________

Policy No.______________________________________________________

3. Long-Term Health Care Insurance (Please provide copy of policy)

Name of Long-Term Health Insurance Company

________________________________________________________________

Address_________________________________________________________

City______________________________ State_________ Zip_______

Business Phone No.______________________________________________

Policy No.______________________________________________________

Home Care ☐ or Custodial Care ☐

VI. SUMMARY OF INCOME AND EXPENSES. Please list Proposed Ward's estimated income and expenses for this year from the following sources:

| | Monthly Amounts | |
|---|---|---|
| Income | Proposed Ward | Proposed Ward's Spouse |
| Social Security | ______________ | ______________ |
| Interest | ______________ | ______________ |
| Dividends | ______________ | ______________ |
| Pension Benefits | ______________ | ______________ |

| | | |
|---|---|---|
| IRA Benefits | ________ | ________ |
| Rental Income | ________ | ________ |
| Capital Gains (Losses) | ________ | ________ |
| Other Taxable Income | ________ | ________ |
| Other Nontaxable Income | ________ | ________ |

(Please provide copies of statements.)

VII. ASSETS AND LIABILITIES

A. ASSETS

1. Real Estate (Please provide copies of all deeds or leases.)

| | Location and Basis | | |
|---|---|---|---|
| Owner(s) | (Purchase Price Plus Estimated Improvements) | Mortgage Value | Balance |
| ________ | ________ | $________ | $______ |
| ________ | ________ | $________ | $______ |
| ________ | ________ | $________ | $______ |
| ________ | ________ | $________ | $______ |

| Owner(s) | Leases | Annual Rent |
|---|---|---|
| ________ | ________ | ________ |
| ________ | ________ | ________ |
| ________ | ________ | ________ |

2. Stocks and Bonds (Please provide copies of statement or certificates.)

   a. Held by Ward

   ______________________________ $____________

   ______________________________ $____________

   ______________________________ $____________

   b. Held by Spouse

   ______________________________ $____________

   ______________________________ $____________

   ______________________________ $____________

   c. Held in Joint Names

   ______________________________ $____________

   ______________________________ $____________

   ______________________________ $____________

3. Partnership or Closely Held Corporate Interests (Please provide partnership agreement, shareholder's agreements, and copies of stock certificates.)

| Owner(s) | Business | Percentage of Interest | Value of Interest |
|---|---|---|---|
| ____________ | ____________ | ____________ | _______ |
| ____________ | ____________ | ____________ | _______ |
| ____________ | ____________ | ____________ | _______ |

4. Cash, Mortgage, and Notes (Please provide copies of bank statements, mortgages, and notes receivable.)

   a. Cash

   ________________________________ $________

   b. Checking Accounts [Name(s) on Account(s) and Name(s) of Bank(s)]

Owner(s) Bank

________________ ______________________ $________

________________ ______________________ $________

________________ ______________________ $________

   c. Savings Accounts [Name(s) on Account(s) and Name(s) of Bank(s)]

Owner(s) Bank

________________ ______________________ $________

________________ ______________________ $________

________________ ______________________ $________

   d. Mortgages Receivable

Owner(s) Mortgage(s)

________________ ______________________ $________

________________ ______________________ $________

________________ ______________________ $________

e. Notes Receivable [Name(s) of Holder(s)]

| Owner(s) | Debtor(s) | |
|---|---|---|
| ________________ | ____________________ | $________ |
| ________________ | ____________________ | $________ |
| ________________ | ____________________ | $________ |

5. Life Insurance (Please provide copies of all policies.)

| Owner(s) | Company | Amount | Loan | Beneficiary |
|---|---|---|---|---|
| _________ | _________ | $____ | $______ | __________ |
| _________ | _________ | $____ | $______ | __________ |
| _________ | _________ | $____ | $______ | __________ |

6. Tangible Personal Property $______________

7. Household Furnishing, Jewelry, Collections

a. Ward $______________

b. Ward's Spouse $______________

c. Other Tangible Personal Property (e.g., Boats)

| Owner(s) | Property | |
|---|---|---|
| ________________ | ____________________ | $______ |
| ________________ | ____________________ | $______ |
| ________________ | ____________________ | $______ |

d. Automobiles (Please provide a copy of each registration.)

| Owner(s) | Automobile | Current Value |
|---|---|---|
| ______________ | __________________ | $_________ |
| ______________ | __________________ | $_________ |
| ______________ | __________________ | $_________ |

e. Safe Deposit Boxes Yes ☐ No ☐

| Name and Location of Box | Contents | Estimated Value |
|---|---|---|
| ______________________ | _________ | $____________ |
| ______________________ | _________ | $____________ |
| ______________________ | _________ | $____________ |

f. Collections included in any category above (e.g., jewelry, antiques, art)

| Location and Owner(s) | Estimated Value |
|---|---|
| __________________________________ | $______________ |
| __________________________________ | $______________ |
| __________________________________ | $______________ |

8. Retirement Benefits—Proposed Ward (Please provide copies of statements.)

a. Pension

| | Beneficiary | |
|---|---|---|
| _______________ | _____________ | $________ |
| _______________ | _____________ | $________ |
| _______________ | _____________ | $________ |

b. Profit Sharing

| | | |
|---|---|---|
| ________________ | ______________ | $________ |
| ________________ | ______________ | $________ |
| ________________ | ______________ | $________ |

c. IRA Accounts

| | | |
|---|---|---|
| ________________ | ______________ | $________ |
| ________________ | ______________ | $________ |
| ________________ | ______________ | $________ |

## VIII. CURRENT ESTATE PLANNING

A. Has the Proposed Ward executed any of the following estate planning documents:

1. Will Yes ☐ No ☐
2. Living Trust Yes ☐ No ☐
3. Living Will or Health Care Power of Attorney
   Yes ☐ No ☐
4. Power of Attorney Yes ☐ No ☐
5. Other:_________________ Yes ☐ No ☐

# Table of Cases

# Index

## Q



## R



## S